BY DAVID MCCULLOUGH

John Adams
Brave Companions
Truman
Mornings on Horseback
The Path Between the Seas
The Great Bridge
The Johnstown Flood

Mornings
on Horseback

————————

David McCullough

Simon & Schuster Paperbacks
New York   London   Toronto   Sydney

Simon & Schuster Paperbacks
Rockefeller Center
1230 Avenue of the Americas
New York, New York 10020

First Simon & Schuster paperback edition 2003
SIMON & SCHUSTER PAPERBACKS and colophon are registered
trademarks of Simon & Schuster, Inc.

For information about special discounts for bulk purchases,
please contact Simon & Schuster Special Sales:
1-800-456-6798 or business@simonandschuster.com

Designed by Edith Fowler

Manufactured in the United States of America

40   39

The Library of Congress has cataloged the hardcover edition as follows:
McCullough, David G.
    Mornings on horseback: the story of an extraordinary family,
a vanished way of life, and the unique child who became
Theodore Roosevelt / David McCullough.
        p. cm.
    Includes bibliographical references and index.
    1. Roosevelt, Theodore, 1858–1919—Childhood and youth.
2. Presidents—United States—Biography. I. Title.
E757.M45 2001   973.91'1'092—dcB21   2001027005
ISBN-13: 978-0-671-22711-1
ISBN-10:   0-671-22711-4
ISBN-13: 978-0-671-44754-0 (Pbk.)
ISBN-10:   0-671-44754-8 (Pbk.)

For Melissa

Contents

Picture sections follow pages 128 and 224

Author's Note

My first encounter with Theodore Roosevelt was in Pittsburgh about 1943. He was busy stealing the show in a Peabody High School production of *Arsenic and Old Lace* and I, at age ten or so, thought him sensational, and especially since in real life he was my oldest brother, Hax.

I have no idea how much or how little I knew of the historical TR before that night, but the impression that lasted was of a wondrously high-powered, comical, slightly loony, tremendously alive and appealing figure, all teeth, glasses, and mustache, who said "Bully!" at every chance and blew on a bugle and yelled "C-H-A-R-G-E!" at just the moment when it would bring the house down. I came away, in other words, with pretty much the impression of our twenty-sixth President that so many of us have grown up with, except that for me he happened also to be one of my very own family.

Years later, doing background reading on the Panama Canal, I encountered another Theodore Roosevelt—still the showman, still in command of the stage, but also shrewd, complex, a man of many gifts and masks—and it was what I read of his early life in particular that led to this book. My intention was not to write a biography of him. What intrigued me was how he came to be. Having written about the creation of two of the most conspicuous inanimate wonders of his era, the Brooklyn Bridge and the Panama Canal, and having acquired as a result great appreciation for the simple idea that such things don't just happen, I was interested in knowing what was involved in the metamorphosis of this most conspicuous

9

animate wonder. There were pieces of the puzzle that fascinated
me—his childhood battle with asthma, for example, his beautiful
southern mother, the adoration he had for his father. What, who,
were involved in the forming of all that energy and persistence?
How much of him was playacting or a composite of borrowings
from others who were important to him?

The underlying theme would be the same as that of my earlier
work—the creative effort, the testing and struggle, the elements of
chance and inspiration involved in any great human achievement.
The book would end when I thought he was formed as a person, at
whatever age that happened, when I felt I could say, when the
reader could say, there he is. San Juan Hill, the White House, the
Canal, the trust-busting and Big Stick wielding, the Bull Moose
with his "hat in the ring," would all be after the fact, another story,
so far as my interests.

But it was when I discovered the range and richness of surviving Roosevelt family correspondence—the many thousands of letters written not just by TR but by his mother, father, sisters,
brother, grandmother, aunts, uncles, the private diaries and journals in the great Theodore Roosevelt Collection at Harvard's
Houghton Library—that I realized what a truly marvelous and very
large subject I had. The letters, only a small fraction of which have
been published, offered the chance to get inside the life of a well-
to-do Victorian American family—a very particular and vanished
way of life—to go below the surface of their world, in a way that is
seldom possible for a writer, except in fiction. It became the most
engrossing work imaginable. The point that one of their number
was to "make history" one day seemed almost immaterial. It was a
story I would have wanted to tell had their names been something
other than Roosevelt or had none of them done anything special
later in life.

"During all this period New York was very much in the condition described in Edith Wharton's novel *The Age of Innocence*,"
writes Anna Roosevelt, Theodore's older sister, in a private reminiscence that is part of the collection; "though naturally I did not
realize it at the time," she adds. Nor, importantly, did any of the
family realize then that they were to be figures in history. The
name Roosevelt was not yet a household word. National fame had
not as yet touched any of the family and there was no reason to
expect it might. And so there is an absence of affectation in almost
everything they wrote to one another then, a wonderful candidness
not always present in surviving correspondence from later stages.

Few of the Roosevelts could spell very well and punctuation for them, as for so many Victorians, was largely a matter of personal preference. Theodore, who graduated Phi Beta Kappa from Harvard, had the poorest spelling of all. He could handle "hippopotamus" or come close with "antediluvian," even as a small boy, but words like "Chicago" or "forest" could prove too much for him. His brother, Elliott, had to write him at one point, "As you don't know how to spell my name, I have entirely forgotten how to spell 'yourn.' Elliot does not spell Elliott, my dear Teedore."

So for the benefit of the reader, the spelling in the writings quoted here has been corrected and punctuation made to conform to present standards, except in a few instances where the idiosyncrasy adds to the spirit of what is being said.

The volume of published work one must become familiar with when dealing with even part of such a life as Theodore led is almost overwhelming. It is not just that so much has been written about him and about other Roosevelts, but that he wrote and published so much himself *and* read so much that had a direct bearing on his life. Though a bibliography and source notes are included at the back of the book, I would like to express my particular indebtedness to two published works from the 1950s: the monumental *The Letters of Theodore Roosevelt* (in eight volumes), edited by Elting E. Morison, John M. Blum, and John J. Buckley; and Carleton Putnam's masterful *Theodore Roosevelt: The Formative Years, 1858–1886*. Numbers of other books were helpful and a pleasure— Henry F. Pringle's biased and lively *Theodore Roosevelt*, William H. Harbaugh's *The Life and Times of Theodore Roosevelt*, which is much the best one-volume biography of TR, John Morton Blum's superb *The Republican Roosevelt*, Hermann Hagedorn's *Roosevelt in the Bad Lands*, Nicholas Roosevelt's *Theodore Roosevelt: The Man as I Knew Him*—but the *Letters* and the Putnam biography have been indispensable.

For his advice on research, his valuable comments on the manuscript, his friendship over the past four years, I thank especially Dr. John Allen Gable, Executive Director of the Theodore Roosevelt Association and author of the definitive *The Bull Moose Years*. I am also greatly indebted to Wallace F. Dailey, Curator of the Theodore Roosevelt Collection at Harvard, which in total comprises some seventeen thousand manuscript papers (mostly letters) and ten thousand photographs housed in the Houghton Library plus approximately twelve thousand volumes housed in the Widener Library. I thank Rodney G. Dennis, Curator of Manuscripts at the Houghton Library, and Martha Eliza Shaw and the others of the Houghton Reading Room staff who were so helpful. I salute, too, the resourceful John D. Knowlton of the Manuscript Division of the Library of Congress for his efforts in determining what was concealed beneath an ink blot in one of TR's diaries; I thank Timothy Beard of the New York Public Library's genealogy division for sharing some of his latest findings on the remarkable private life of Robert B. Roosevelt. For the very thorough tour he gave me through TR's home at Oyster Bay, his quick and helpful answers to my written queries over the years, I thank Gary Roth, Curator of the Sagamore Hill National Historic Site.

In Mr. and Mrs. W. Sheffield Cowles, Jr., of Farmington, Connecticut, who were so generous with their time and memories, I found invaluable living links with several key figures in the story. Mr. Cowles, who is the son of TR's sister Anna, not only talked with me at length about his mother, his Uncle Theodore, his Aunt Corinne, but provided rare documentary material to be found nowhere else and was good enough to go over the manuscript and give me his views.

Other present-day descendants of the family who have been helpful include two of TR's granddaughters, Sarah Alden Gannett and Edith Roosevelt Williams (Mrs. Gannett also read and commented on the manuscript); Mrs. Philip J. Roosevelt of Oyster Bay, who is the granddaughter of Robert B. Roosevelt; and her son, P. James Roosevelt, who made a remark at lunch one day four years ago that did as much as anything to set the course of my work. Was there, I asked him, any important missing ingredient in the existing biographies of TR? "Yes," he said. "No writer seems to have understood the degree to which he was part of a clan."

In no part of the work have I been assisted by others quite so much as in my effort to get to the bottom of Theodore's asthma, and most helpful in this respect has been Dr. Peter H. Knapp of the Boston University Medical Center, who is a leading authority on the psychosomatic aspects of the disease. My indebtedness to Dr. Knapp is very great. He took hours of his time to discuss the Roosevelt "case" with me, to guide me in my reading, and to go over my work as it progressed, telling me what to watch for in the family record, which were often quite different things from what I would have been watching for normally.

In addition to Dr. Knapp, the following physicians contributed ideas and/or shared with me their experiences in dealing with asthmatic children, for which I am most grateful: Tully Benaron, William H. Dietz, Richard Galdston, Milton Mazer, Shirley Murphy, and George Simson. And for their illuminating comments on the manuscript, I thank Dr. Robert Eisendrath and Dianthe Eisendrath.

Among the first things a layman discovers when trying to learn about asthma is that there is practically nothing in the literature on what the victim of an attack actually feels. (The best, most vivid account I could find was in a professional treatise published in 1864.) So for their willingness to talk openly and subjectively about the disease—something asthmatics commonly refuse to do because even talking about it can be painful for them—I am particularly grateful to Jeanne Crosby, Edward T. Hall, Jack D. Enns, and Cort Sutton. For sharing their experiences and insights as the parents of an asthmatic child, I am also grateful to Mr. and Mrs. John Curtiss. (Most of these interviews were conducted during an extended stay in New Mexico, where I was also fortunate to have access to the Medical Library of the University of New Mexico.)

During my time in North Dakota, I was offered help and hospitality at almost every turn, but wish to thank especially Liess Vantine and Frank E. Vyzralek of the State Historical Society at Bismarck; and in Medora and vicinity, Tom Adams, Mr. and Mrs. William Connell, William Herr, who is the wildlife specialist at the Theodore Roosevelt National Park, Joe L. Hild, who owns and runs TR's old Chimney Butte Ranch, John O. Lancaster, Superintendent of the Theodore Roosevelt National Park, Harold and Sheila Schafer, Al Tescher, and Mayor Rod Tjaden; also, Harry Roberts of Dickinson and Mrs. Janet Buldhaupt of Beach.

My thanks to those who have assisted me at the Albuquerque Public Library, the American Museum of Natural History, the Boston Athenaeum, the Boston Public Library, the Franklin D. Roosevelt Library at Hyde Park, the Georgia State Historical Society in Savannah, the Massachusetts Historical Society, the Oral History Collection at Columbia University, the Theodore Roosevelt Birthplace, the University of New Mexico Library, and the West Tisbury Public Library.

And to all of the following I am grateful for favors large and small, for advice, encouragement, and ideas: Thomas A. Ashley, Clarence A. Barnes, Jr., William Bentinck-Smith, Edith Blake, the late Bruce Catton, J. Felton Covington, Jr., Robert Ferguson, John and Ruth Galvin, John Hawkins, Woody Jackson, David Kahn, Jessica Kraft, George McCullough, Elinor and George Montgomery, Tony de Mores, Elting Morison, Royall D. O'Brien, Audre Proctor,

Paul R. Reynolds, Robbin Reynolds, Philippa Roosevelt, Elizabeth Saltonstall, and Margot Street.

I thank my literary agent, Morton L. Janklow, and those at Simon and Schuster who have been such a pleasure to work with and who have contributed greatly: my editor, Peter Schwed; Kim Honig, Edith Fowler, Pat Miller, and Frank Metz.

Above all there is my family: Melissa and John McDonald, David, William, Geoffrey, and Dorie McCullough, who have played a larger part, helped more than they know; and my wife, Rosalee, who with her understanding of people, her editorial judgment, her good spirits, patience, and devotion, has been an unfailing inspiration.

And lastly, thanks to brother Hax for getting up there on the stage in the first place.

DAVID MCCULLOUGH

West Tisbury, Massachusetts
December 5, 1980

Black care rarely sits behind a rider
whose pace is fast enough.

—THEODORE ROOSEVELT

Part One

CHAPTER ONE

Greatheart's Circle

· 1 ·

IN THE YEAR 1869, when the population of New York City had reached nearly a million, the occupants of 28 East 20th Street, a five-story brownstone, numbered six, exclusive of the servants.

The head of the household was Theodore Roosevelt (no middle name or initial), who was thirty-seven years of age, an importer and philanthropist, and the son of old Cornelius Van Schaack Roosevelt, one of the richest men in the city. Mrs. Theodore Roosevelt —Martha Bulloch Roosevelt, or Mittie, as she was called—was thirty-three, a southerner and a beauty. The children, two girls and two boys, all conceived by the same father and mother, and born in the same front bedroom, over the parlor, ranged in age from fourteen to seven. The oldest, Anna, was known as Bamie (from *bambina*, and pronounced to rhyme with Sammy). Next came ten-year-old Theodore, Jr., who was called Teedie (pronounced to rhyme with T.D.). Elliott, aged nine, was Ellie or Nell, and the youngest, Corinne, was called Conie.

Of the servants little is known, except for Dora Watkins, an Irish nursemaid who had been employed since before the Civil War. Another Irish girl named Mary Ann was also much in evidence, beloved by the children and well regarded by the parents —it was she they picked to go with the family on the Grand Tour that May—but in family papers dating from the time, nobody bothered to give Mary Ann a last name. Concerning the others, the various cooks, valets, coachmen, and housemaids who seem to have come and gone with regularity, the record is no help. But to judge by the size of the house and the accepted standards for families of comparable means and station, there were probably never less than four or five "below stairs" at any given time, and the degree to which they figured in the overall atmosphere was considerable.

The house stood in the block between Broadway and Fourth Avenue, on the south side of the street, and it looked like any other New York brownstone, a narrow-fronted, sober building wholly devoid of those architectural niceties (marble sills, fanlights) that enlivened the red-brick houses of an earlier era downtown. The standard high stoop with cast-iron railings approached a tall front door at the second-floor level, the ground floor being the standard English basement, with its servants' entrance. A formal parlor (cut-glass chandelier, round-arched marble fireplace, piano) opened onto a long, narrow hall, as did a parlor or "library," this a windowless room remembered for its stale air and look of "gloomy respectability." The dining room was at the rear, again according to the standard floor plan. Upstairs were the master bedroom and nursery, then three more bedrooms on the floor above, with the servants' quarters on the top floor.

Only one thing about the house was thought to be out of the ordinary, a deep porch, or piazza, at the rear on the third-floor level. Enclosed with a nine-foot wooden railing, it had been a bedroom before the Roosevelts tore out the back wall and converted it to an open-air playroom. It overlooked not only their own and neighboring yards, but the garden of the Goelet mansion on 19th Street, one of the largest private gardens in the city, within which roamed numbers of exotic birds with their wings clipped. Daily, in their "piazza clothes," the children were put out to play or, in Bamie's case, in early childhood, to lie on a sofa.

The house had been a wedding present from Cornelius Van Schaack Roosevelt—CVS to the family—whose own red-brick mansion on Union Square, six blocks south, was the figurative center of the Roosevelt tribal circle. The father of five sons, CVS had presented them all with houses as they married and the one given Theodore, youngest of his five, adjoined that of Robert B. Roosevelt, the fourth son, who was a lawyer.

With their full beards and eyeglasses, these two neighboring brothers bore a certain physical resemblance. The difference in age was only two years. Beyond appearances, however, they were not the least alike. Robert was the conspicuous, unconventional

Roosevelt, the one for whom the family had often to do some explaining. Robert wrote books; Robert was bursting with ideas. He was a gifted raconteur, a sportsman, yachtsman, New York's pioneer conservationist (fish were his pet concern), an enthusiastic cook, an authority on family origins. He was loud and witty and cherished the limelight, seeking it inexplicably in the tumult of Tammany politics. Until the Civil War, the Roosevelts had all been Democrats. As late as 1863, Theodore had still been an avowed War Democrat—one who supported the war and thus the Republican Administration—but when he and the rest of CVS's line at last turned Republican, Robert alone remained in the Democratic fold and was never to be anything but proud of the fact. ("Our party is the party of the people!")

Robert's middle name was his mother's maiden name, Barnhill, but in anticipation of what his political foes might make of this ("manure pile" or variations to that effect), he had changed it to Barnwell and it was as Uncle Barnwell that he was sometimes known to the small nieces and nephews in the house beside his.

Robert's wife, Elizabeth Ellis Roosevelt, was called Aunt Lizzie Ellis to distinguish her from still another Aunt Lizzie in the family, and she too was considered "unorthodox." At the back of her third floor—the floor corresponding to the piazza next door—she maintained a marvelous and odorous menagerie of guinea pigs, chickens, pigeons, a parrot, a monkey, "everything under the sun that ought not be kept in a house." The monkey, her favorite, was a violent little creature that bit. She dressed it like a fashionable child, complete with ruffled shirts and gold studs. Once Aunt Lizzie Ellis aroused the neighborhood with the purchase of a cow that had to be led from East 20th Street into her back yard by the only available route, through the house, an event that, for excitement, was surpassed only by the removal of the cow, once Aunt Lizzie Ellis was threatened with legal action. On the return trip through the house the animal became so terrified it had to be dragged bodily, its legs tied, its eyes blindfolded.

To the children next door such occasions naturally figured very large, as did Uncle Barnwell with his talk of fishing and hunting, his yacht, and his flashy political friends. So it is somewhat puzzling that so little was to be said of him in later years. His immediate proximity would be passed over rather quickly, his influence barely touched on. He is the Roosevelt everybody chose to forget about. Politics undoubtedly had much to do with this, but more important, it would appear, was his private life. For in addition to all else, brother Rob was a bit lax in his morals. He was what polite society referred to as a Bohemian, the kind of man who kept company with "actresses and such." An admiring later-day kinsman would describe him as an Elizabethan in the Victorian era and a story has come down the generations of the ladies' gloves Robert purchased in bulk at A. T. Stewart's department store, these in a violent shade of green. The gloves had been on sale, according to the story, and he distributed them liberally among his "lady friends," with the result that for years those who knew him well knew also to watch for the gloves while strolling Fifth Avenue or driving in the park.

Ordinarily, such stories might prompt some question as to whether Robert only *seemed* scandalous—so very straitlaced was the family, so quick was "the best society" to leap on the least deviation from the prescribed code and call it, if not immoral, then indecent. But in truth Robert was something more than a mere rake or charming boulevardier. He was a man living a remarkable double life, keeping another woman and ultimately an entire second family in a house only a block or so distant on the same street, an arrangement that would come to light only long afterward as a result of genealogical research sponsored by some of his descendants. Her name was Minnie O'Shea, or Mrs. Robert F. Fortescue, as he had decided she should be called, and in 1869 she was already pregnant with their first child.

How much of this Theodore knew, how strenuously he disapproved, if at all, is impossible to say. But the contrast between the two could hardly have been more striking.

Theodore was invariably upright, conservative, the very model of self-control. He cared nothing for public acclaim, "never put himself forward," as friends would remember. Theodore was the model duty-bound husband and father, a junior partner at Roosevelt and Son. He was a faithful communicant at the Madison Square Presbyterian Church, who often attended two services on the same Sunday. He belonged to the Union League Club and the Century Association. He served on charitable boards, raised money for museums. Not in seven generations on the island of Manhattan had the Roosevelts produced so sturdy or so winsome an example of upper-class probity, or so fine a figure of a man—physically imposing, athletic, with china-blue eyes, chestnut hair and beard, and a good, square Dutch jaw. In his formal photographs, the eyeglasses removed, he is someone who will do what he has to, direct, sure of himself. Only the eyes raise questions, with their unmistakable hint of severity, which seems odd in a man remembered mainly for the "sunshine of his affection."

Clothes concerned him. The choice of a suit, the right hat for the occasion, were issues of consequence. His suits were of the best quality and beautifully tailored. Appearances mattered. Indeed, it may be said that appearances figured quite as much in the life at 28 East 20th Street as everywhere else within the circumscribed world of New York's "good old families." "Did I tell you that he took the other end of the table at the dinner I gave to Captain Cook and behaved admirably?" Theodore writes of brother Rob to Mittie. "He was dressed perfectly, except for a colored cravat with his dress suit."

Together at dinners and balls, he and the exquisite Mittie made a picture people did not forget. It was in the Roosevelt tradition to be solicitous to women. While their mother was alive, the five brothers stopped regularly every morning en route to work to pay her their respects. But Theodore seems to have genuinely preferred the company of women—he had an eye for feminine beauty, his children all remembered—and the attention he showered on Mittie was exceptional even for that day and those circles. An employee at one of his charities remarked that he had never understood the meaning of the word "gentleman" until the evening he watched Theodore Roosevelt escort his wife about the premises.

In all Theodore was a seemingly uncomplicated person. He had no particular gifts. He was not musical as Mittie was. He shared little of her love of art. He was not creative; he did not write or charm after-dinner audiences as Robert could. He dabbled in nothing. He was perfectly intelligent, to be sure; he enjoyed books, enjoyed the talk of lawyers, editors, and others who traded in words and abstract ideas, but he was unintellectual. In matters of taste he habitually deferred to his wife, refusing even to buy a bottle of wine unless she had passed on it. If he regarded himself as an authority on anything, it was horses.

But greatest of all was his interest in and feeling for children. He responded immediately to them, and they to him. "My personal impression," a nephew would recall, ". . . is that he was a large, broad, bright, cheerful man with an intense sympathy with everything you brought to him. He loved children especially."

From childhood he had been called Thee and as the youngest son, the Benjamin of the family, he had been doted on. He was Mama's darling and did nothing but shine in her eyes until her dying day. In turn, he adored her and would credit any good qual-

ities he had to her and her "settled notions." She had been an
event in the Roosevelt line, the first non-Dutch entry on the family
tree. She was Margaret Barnhill of Philadelphia. Her background
was English-Irish-Quaker. She was gentle but dominating and the
first of the Roosevelts to espouse the spirit of *noblesse oblige.* Great
wealth imposed obligations, she preached; the opportunities bestowed by private fortunes must be put to "some good purpose."
Bamie, as the oldest of her father's children, could remember going
as a very small child to call on her at the house on Union Square.
There was a cavernous front hall with a floor of polished black-and-
white marble and great mahogany doors with silver knobs and
hinges that opened to the dining room. "In the dining room, where
a bright soft-coal fire was always burning in the fireplace, between
two south windows, we invariably found my grandmother sitting
in her corner with her work basket on a table near her, and some
books, always apparently delighted to see us, and with a most
lovely smile."

Through Theodore's youth, dinner conversation in that same
room, at his father's end of the table, had been in Dutch. Short,
homely, pink-faced, invariably punctual, CVS Roosevelt regarded
his brood with rather quizzical large, round eyes that were made to
look even larger by his small, square gold-framed spectacles. He
was the essence of old-fashioned New York. "Economy is my doctrine at all times," he had once informed Margaret Barnhill in the
midst of their courtship, "at all events till I become, if it is to be so,
a man of fortune." And though Roosevelt and Son had been
founded by his own father and grandfather, it was he, CVS, who
had become the family's initial man of fortune, the first Roosevelt
millionaire. It was he who switched the family business from hard-
ware to importing plate glass. And still more fortuitously, in the
Panic of 1837, when Theodore was a child of six, he bought up
building lots, "hither and yon," on the island of Manhattan, all at a
good price.

Theodore's formal education had been limited and erratic, as
his spelling gave evidence. There had been a private tutor through
boyhood and never a lack of books at hand, but college was ruled
out because CVS thought it would ruin him. (Weir Roosevelt, the
oldest brother, had gone to Columbia College, but to study law,
which apparently made it tolerable in the father's eyes; Robert, in
his turn, had become a lawyer without going to college, as was still
possible then.)

In 1851, however, at age nineteen, Theodore was sent off on a

Grand Tour, something his brothers had been denied and that Robert for one greatly envied. It was the year of the London Exhibition and the opening of the Crystal Palace, an event of obvious importance to a family in the glass business. He saw the Exhibition, traveled the Continent, even went on to Russia, which was unheard of. He improved his French, acquired a little German and Italian, and sent home dutiful, descriptive letters that were his mother's joy and to Robert a large annoyance.

"I'm afraid, Theodore, you have mistaken the object of traveling," Robert lectured. "It is not to see scenery, you can see finer at home. It is not to see places where great people lived and died, that is a stupidity. But it is to see men. To enlarge your mind, which will never be enlarged by looking at a large hill, but by conversing with, and seeing the bent of the minds of other people."

A month later, after still more from Theodore on the churches and monuments he was seeing, Robert could barely contain himself.

I have it in mind to go to all the big stores in Broadway and write you an account. So look out as sure as you describe to me any more big buildings, you may know what to expect. Now answer seriously, have you been anywhere but to monuments, etc.? Have you been to a masked ball, a theater, an opera, or even into a French store where little girls tend the counters? Have you seen a Dutchman, a Frenchman, an Irishman; besides the porters who carried your trunks? If so, what did you say to them and what did they say to you? Have you seen anything odd or original? Where have you been, where are you going?

But six months later, Robert felt obliged to rescind.

Firstly, Advice. Don't write any more experience in the lower walks of life, or moralize upon its wickedness. . . . Mother gets into a pigeon fit and thinks her "darling innocent" is going straight to destruction. And the old gentleman ruminates on the disappearance of the £1,000 and looks blank when it is suggested to him that he is supporting Theodore's "French teacher." The old lady takes it hard and no matter what you do perhaps you had better not write about it. You had better keep to towers and castles.

Russia—the overwhelming splendors of St. Petersburg, the squalor of Moscow—affected Theodore profoundly. "I scarce know

terms strong enough to express my feelings. . . . Everything is in
the extremes." Conceivably it had taken Robert's admonitions to
bring him to see the human element; still, the kind of sensitivity
that began to emerge in his letters and in his journal was very much
his own. He toured a Moscow foundling hospital where every year
some six thousand infants were received. On the edge of the city
early one Sunday he watched a thousand prisoners start the long
march to Siberia. A dignified, elderly figure he identifies in the
journal only as Dr. Haase had come to bid the prisoners farewell.
Nothing or no one that Theodore encountered in his travels seems
to have impressed him as this man did.

> He was dressed in the old style with silk stockings and slip-
> pers, his breast decked with honor. . . . He is one of the finest-
> looking old gentlemen I ever saw and his actions carry out his
> appearance. He went around among the prisoners asking them
> if they were well and content . . . when they were departing
> he distributed among those whom he thought deserving. It
> was more the universal feeling of kindness which prompted
> every movement than any particular action which I can adduce
> which evinced his character.

The prisoners must be fairly treated, the old man insisted, for
at Judgment Day their word would count as much as that of anyone.
Though a few of the sick had been put in wagons, the rest had
started off on foot with the prospect of six months of continual
walking before them.

To the great relief of his father, Theodore came home with no
new revolutionary ideas or worldly airs. Nor, apparently, was it
with the least misgiving that he entered directly into the family
firm, downtown at 94 Maiden Lane. The Russian journal would be
taken up and reread from time to time and one "treasure" among
the few he had brought back, a small square of malachite supporting a small gilt Russian peasant pulling a gilt sledge, was to occupy
a prominent position in the 20th Street parlor. Only after they were
grown would the children become aware that it was anything other
than a priceless work of art.

The impression is that the family business more or less ran
itself. CVS had announced his retirement soon after Theodore
joined the firm, and another brother, James Alfred Roosevelt, was
made senior partner. James Alfred, as nobody disputed, had the
best head for business. He was shrewd and tough, and he had
married an Emlen from Philadelphia, a move which, in the words

of one descendant, "did the family's fortune no harm." James, too, like his father, was made a director of the Chemical Bank, and the Chemical Bank, with real estate, was of greatest importance to the Roosevelts and their standing in the financial community. CVS had been a founding father of the Chemical Bank, the only bank in New York that had never failed to meet its obligations in gold, even during the Civil War.

The family's real-estate holdings were lumped under what was called the Broadway Improvement Association, of which James Alfred was also head and chief spokesman.

So it was James Alfred, ultimately, who had the final say on all questions pertaining to money, a subject about which all Roosevelts cared deeply, but which they preferred also to keep altogether private. When, in 1868, a publication called *Gallaxy* presented the names of New York's ten bona fide millionaires, with CVS listed among them, Weir Roosevelt responded angrily in a letter to *The New York Times* that no man's privacy was safe any longer. "I ask you whether it is the present opinion of the respectable newspapers that a rich man has no rights, or, in other words, whether the mere accumulation of property by a private citizen is of itself a sufficient offense against society to call for a public exposure and justify the interference of the press?"

One of Theodore's rare observations on the atmosphere at Roosevelt and Son is contained in a love letter to Mittie written hastily at his desk in 1853, shortly before they were married. So wonderful was the mere thought of her, he said, it could even brighten a day at 94 Maiden Lane, "where such a thing as sentiment would be laughed at as a humbug worthy of Mr. Barnum's collection." The bookkeeper, he cheerfully informed her, had warned him never to marry a southern girl.

As a businessman Theodore appears to have been miscast. He had no apparent aversion to trade, or any philosophical conflict with moneymaking as such. (For a time he even thought seriously of leaving the family firm in order to make more in some other line, though what that might be he had no idea.) Rather he appears to have found little or no satisfaction in the work. His letters rarely touch on it. The one picture we get of him having any fun on the job, evincing any of his usual enthusiasm, is an account of a winter day in Washington when he scaled the snow-covered roof of the new Treasury Building to measure for skylights. He felt like a mountaineer, sometimes sliding thirty or forty feet down the roof.

All he needed was his alpenstock, he said. Otherwise, the impression is of years at a desk going through the motions, performing dutifully as the proper Victorian breadwinner, a prudent, attractive figure, quite in the Roosevelt mold, but uninspired, unaggressive, and, probably, not very good at what he did.

The power rested in the older brother's hands. Theodore was free to do Europe at will, while James Alfred stayed on and ran things, and Theodore seems to have gone off to Europe—or to the country or to his eager philanthropy—at every chance.

As time went on, his crusades among the needy, his hospital and museum projects, became his true vocation. It was thus that he became one of the prominent men of the city, as truly good a good citizen as New York had ever known. "Whatever he had to do, he did all out," remembered Charles Loring Brace, the pioneer social worker. To some, he seemed strangely driven. John Hay, another friend, spoke of his "maniacal benevolence," and in letters to his wife Theodore himself infers occasionally that "with so much to do" he has no choice. "I feel that as much as I enjoy loafing, there is something higher for which to live."

Together with Brace and a friend named Howard Potter, he had helped establish the Children's Aid Society, to do something for the city's homeless children—"street rats" as the police chose to call them—whose numbers by 1869 probably exceeded twenty thousand. Largely through Theodore's initiative a permanent Newsboys' Lodging House had been established on West 18th Street, where nightly several hundred stray boys, most of them newsboys, were given a clean bed in a warm room for five cents, a fraction of what was charged by the lowest kind of commercial flophouse. It was Brace's contention—the theme by which he appealed for funds and enlisted the efforts of men like Theodore—that decent society had no greater threat than the existence of a "class of vagabond, ignorant, ungoverned children." The time would come, Brace warned, when these children would have the vote, "the same rights as ourselves"—a very different justification for Christian mercy from that espoused by Theodore's old gentleman in Moscow, but one that carried Brace and his projects far.

The mission of the Children's Aid Society was to bring "moral disinfectants" to the festering "crime nests" of New York. A kind-hearted agent or "visitor" was first dispatched to the "infected quarter," someone who could naturally befriend the homeless waifs, this being work that Theodore, for one, did extremely well. Then an informal religious meeting, or mission class, was established; then a reading room, then an industrial school or workshop. Presently came the Lodging House. But the long-range objective was to return as many of the children as possible to their own families, if such existed, or, more often, to ship them off to farms in the Middle West or beyond, to get them out of the city entirely. By 1869 some 4,500 children had been thus dispatched to Ohio, Illinois, and points beyond. In time more than 100,000 would be sent.

When Brace first asked Theodore if he might spend every other Sunday evening at the Lodging House, talking with the boys, Theodore declined, saying his "troublesome conscience" would not permit it. He would be there *every* Sunday.

He "threw himself" into the work, Brace remembered: "He knew them by name, he knew their histories . . . they would gather round him, and he would question each one as to what he was doing, and give him advice and sympathy and direction. You felt the moment Mr. Roosevelt was in the room that he was a help to those poor fellows."

As generous with his money as his time, he gave regularly to this and other causes, and raised still more among his well-to-do friends, some of whom eventually learned to take out their checkbooks the moment he came into their offices. One man, on hearing that Theodore was going abroad, estimated it would save him at least a thousand dollars.

Importantly, Theodore's influence was felt just at that stage in the city's growth when it could have the greatest effect, a point he never lost sight of. He believed in New York, he said, not so much for what it was as for what it might become, the example it could set. No city offered more opportunity for those wishing to do something for the good of mankind; his joy, he said, was being connected with new work, worthy institutions in their infancy, the influence of which would be felt throughout the country. The year following the war he helped start the New York Orthopedic Dispensary and Hospital, for the treatment of children deformed by spinal disease. With Joseph Choate, Pierpont Morgan, Howard Potter, and others he had founded the Metropolitan Museum of Art and the American Museum of Natural History. It was in the front parlor at 28 East 20th Street that the original charter for the Museum of Natural History was approved the evening of April 8, 1869.

No one seems ever to have spoken ill of him. A man who knew him in business for more than twenty years said he never heard him utter an angry word, never saw him out of sorts. When Albert S. Bickmore, the brilliant young naturalist, first came to the city with his idea for a natural history museum, it was to Theodore that he went, because he had been told that Theodore Roosevelt was "just the man" to make such a project a success. Thirty years later Bickmore could still quote Theodore's response: "Professor, New York wants a museum of natural history and it shall have one, and if you will stay here and cooperate with us, you shall be its first head."

Most memorable was what Brace called his "rich power of enjoyment of everything human." Pious as he was, as solemn sounding as his religious speculations might become, he adored parties and would dance all night. Like the new President of the United States, Ulysses S. Grant, he had a passion for fine horses and to see him astride one of his own in Central Park was, as one friend remarked, to see the model of Christian manhood.

He would make the most of any situation, of every moment, often replenishing his energies with occupations or chance conversations that others would have found irksome or boring. "I amused myself by drawing the little there was in him out," he would say of someone he met on a train.

Best were the pleasures of a morning walk or his books or a good cigar or what he called the quiet luxury of home life. He loved flowers, yellow roses especially, and the Palisades along the Hudson River. Separated from home and the beloved "home faces," he could slip rapidly into abject homesickness and sound, on paper at least, most uncharacteristically plaintive. He felt bereft of real friends, he wrote to Mittie one such summer evening. "The city is deserted by all my acquaintances and I scarce meet anyone now in the Park that I know."

> I wonder in so large a city, living here all my life, how it comes that I have so few intimate friends; it seems strange, especially when I know that you consider me so very sociable. But I have no more time to moralize. Those who I love love me and I would not give up their affection for the lukewarm article called by that name by thousands.

To his own children he was at once the ultimate voice of authority and, when time allowed, their most exuberant companion. He never fired their imaginations or made them laugh as their mother could, but he was unfailingly interested in them, sympathetic, confiding, entering into their lives in ways few fathers ever do. It was as though he was in league with them. As Ellie once told

him, he was one of those rare grown men who seem never to forget
that they were once children themselves—"just my ideal," Ellie
said, "made to govern and doing it so lightly and affectionately."
Sweetest of all was his undivided attention, the "sunshine of his
affection."

Day began with the three youngest poised at the foot of the
long stairway waiting for his descent and their morning prayers
together, this ritual being held on the library sofa, two of them
seated to one side of him, the third wedged into what they regarded
as the prime position between him and the arm of the sofa. Evenings, in the library, they would wait for the sound of his key at the
door, then rush to greet him and troop after him up the stairs to his
room to watch him dress for dinner. (He always dressed for dinner
and with what seemed to them the most amazing speed.)

He taught them to ride and to climb trees. Conie remembered
"the careful way in which he would show us dead limbs and warn
us about watching out for them, and then, having taught us and
having warned us, he gave us full liberty to try our wings . . ." As
they grew older he tried to include them in his own outside activities, taking along one or more, for example, on his Sunday-night
visits to the Newsboys' Lodging House. Those evenings when he
brought some friend of special interest to the house—John Hay,
Matthew Arnold, Albert Bickmore—he saw that the children sat
and listened to what was being said.

His own preachments were fundamental and heartfelt, and it
would be hard to overemphasize the extent to which they charged
the atmosphere. Cultivate a hopeful disposition, he told them. Accept the love of others and you will be loved.

"I always believe in showing affection by doing what will
please the one we love, not by talking." (To show their love for
him, they could improve their handwriting or learn to swim or
memorize a passage from the Bible.)

"I have often thought that unselfishness combined in one word
more of the teachings of the Bible than any other in the language."

He hated idleness. Every hour must be accounted for and one
must also enjoy everything one did. Get action, he said. Seize the
moment. "Man was never intended to become an oyster."

Deceit or cowardice was not to be tolerated. Courage he rewarded openly and sometimes with dramatic effect. At a rented
country house in New Jersey one summer, he surprised the three
youngest children with a new pony. When he asked who would
jump on, Conie, then four, was the only one not to hang back, and

so he declared the pony was hers, to the humiliation of her older brothers. "I think I did it," she would write long afterward, "to see the light in Father's eyes."

That a great, bearded figure of a man was also one so readily touched by the sufferings of others, so tender-hearted with children, so sensitive to the pulls of conscience, seemed strangely incongruous to some who knew him. But to those closest to him this androgynous quality was the essence of his personality. Howard Potter, the friend who probably knew him best, saw him as a "singular compound of feminine and masculine qualities, lovable as a woman, and as strong as a man."

To Teedie, the little namesake, he was at once the most magnificent creature on earth and quite frightening, but then Teedie was full of fears of all kinds, as he would acknowledge in time. Anna Bulloch Gracie, the elder Theodore's pious and adoring sister-in-law, called him Greatheart. It had come to her on a Sunday morning as she watched him go off to church with his children—the warrior Puritan, Greatheart, from *The Pilgrim's Progress*, stout Greatheart, guide and protector of wayfaring innocents, fearless leader in life's purposeful journey. *"Come now, and follow me, and no hurt shall happen to you from the lions. . . ."*

"There never was anyone so wonderful as my father," Bamie remembered. And the fact that he swept in and out of the house, in and out of their lives, the fact that he was not always around as their mother was, made him seem all the more special and "wonderful."

· 2 ·

OF THE FOUR CHILDREN it was Bamie who most closely resembled him; Bamie, who, to use her own words, never let herself be young, and who, as would be said, probably had the best mind in the family.

Bamie was the mainstay, then and for as long as she lived. For a girl born into New York society she was also severely handicapped. She was not in the least pretty, for one thing. Her dark-blue eyes were deep-set, the lids heavy, which made her look tired and years older than she was. In repose she could look painfully sad.

More seriously, she was also somewhat physically deformed. The standard family explanation for this has been that as an infant she had been dropped by a careless nurse. However, no mention of such an incident is to be found in family records dating from the time it supposedly occurred, or afterward. The one specific early reference to the problem is in a letter written by Grandmamma Bulloch, an observant member of the household in that earlier day. Writing of the infant Bamie, she said, "I am quite uneasy about her back. There is something wrong there. She cannot stand more than a second on her feet, then her countenance expresses pain, and she crumbles down."

The problem, in fact, was Pott's disease, the form of tuberculosis which softens and destroys the bones and which, when localized in the spine, causes hunchback. Known to have been a child crippler since the time of the Pharaohs, it was first identified in the eighteenth century by a British physician, Percivall Pott. Still, by the late nineteenth century, it remained a mystery and was thought to be incurable.

In Bamie's case the effect was severe curvature of the spine and intense suffering. At age three, at the time of Teedie's birth, she was fitted with her "terrible instrument," a heavy steel-and-leather apparatus that left her immobile and rubbed a hideous sore on her back. The doctor came regularly each morning to wash and dress the sore and to strap her in again, and through the rest of the day she had to be picked up and carried from room to room or out to her sofa on the piazza. She could lie face down only. In the evening it was her father who removed the apparatus and at bedtime Grandmamma Bulloch would rub her legs until she fell asleep.

Her father's devotion became the most important thing in her life. A summer when she had to be left behind at 20th Street while her mother, grandmother, the new baby, and Dora Watkins went off to the country was a summer of untold happiness because he was there with her so much of the time, because at the end of his business day he would come directly to her on the piazza, bringing her ice cream or fresh peaches or some small gift, because he would sit with her while she had her supper, then carry her to bed "with his very strong arms."

She was also released from the "terrible instrument" that same summer, the summer of 1850, when she was four. He had found another doctor for her, Charles Fayette Taylor, an orthopedic surgeon who in some professional quarters was thought to be a quack. Pott's disease was Taylor's specialty. He treated it with what he called the "movement cure," a form of physical therapy based on

Swedish techniques that he had learned in Europe. Bamie was among his first patients and he not only transformed her daily regimen, giving her virtually a new life, but interjected into the family circle his conviction that physical well-being and mental outlook are directly correlated.

She was fitted with a radically different kind of back brace, a custom-made "spinal assistant" that was light in weight and designed so that she could be up and moving about, which, Taylor stressed, was the whole point. He wanted her moving about, both for her back and for what it would do to her spirits. Improvement was slow but unmistakable, and it was seeing this, seeing what Taylor had done for his own child, that led Theodore to establish the Orthopedic Dispensary and Hospital with Taylor at its head.

A full cure was never to come, however. Through most of childhood she was required to lie down part of every day and, by Roosevelt standards, her physical activity was limited. The rest of her life she wore a piece of ram's wool on her back beneath her clothes in order to sit comfortably in a chair. She was not, by the time she attained her full growth, exactly a hunchback, but she did have an odd hunched stance. The small figure she presented to the world, or that she confronted in the hall mirror, was plainly "curious," thick through the shoulders.

"Poor little thing," her father wrote when she was seven. "I never think of Bamie without pain. It seems such a dreary life that is in store for her."

He wanted her with him whenever possible. At some point during the war, on one of his periodic trips to Washington—the exact date is not known—he took her along and she sat on Abraham Lincoln's lap. She would remember nothing of the event, only that she had been with her father.

In a family notable for its intense attachments, theirs was perhaps the most intense of all. She was emphatically "Papa's pet." He kept her photograph in a leather case and carried it with him wherever he traveled. His letters to "My own Darling Bamie" were overflowing with tenderness, with concern for her every move, with advice, warnings, and not a little baring of his own soul. "Try to cultivate a quiet sober style," he would write, "and bottle up your spirits a little until I have possession of you. Then you may let them out again as much as you please."

The one and only time he ever physically punished Teedie— possibly the only time he ever physically punished any of his children—was when, at age four, Teedie bit Bamie on the arm.

Bright, conscientious, she picked things up quickly (French, the piano) and her energy was very nearly the match of Theodore's. "Dear busy Bamie," Grandmamma Bulloch called her. But it was her odd, almost quaint maturity that set her off. She was "competent beyond her years," even when very small. She had no interest in games or toys. She wished only to be "useful," to look after her own needs, to look after the younger three, to whom she never seemed like anything but another grownup. Teedie, by way of introduction to his diary of the European tour, was to explain, "When I put 'We 3' I mean Ellie, Conie, and I. When I put 'big people' I mean Papa, Mama, and Bamie." That she was plain and deformed seems never to have figured in their picture of her. Not once in all that Mittie wrote about her children is there even a trace of pity or worry over Bamie. Bamie was strength. Bamie was good sense, the one to lean on, to turn to for help. She was, as Teedie would tell her fondly, "a kind of little feminine Atlas with a small world on her shoulders."

Of the youngest three, Ellie was the best-looking and the most convivial, and in many ways the most endearing. As a baby he had been "decidedly pretty." At two he could speak more clearly than his older brother and in no time became larger, better coordinated, the natural athlete of the two. Little brother was big brother. He was also distinguished by a sweet, even temper and what seemed an inordinate fund of kindness for someone so young. Once, at about the age of seven, he had gone off for a walk wearing a new overcoat and returned without it. He had given it away, he explained, to a ragged child who had none and looked cold.

Unlike Bamie, whose hair was dark brown, he, Teedie, and Conie were all fair-haired and Conie was known for her "ardent" blue eyes.

Teedie, in Bamie's expression, was the "great little home-boy" of the family. He was extremely frail and undersized for ten, a nervous, timid, often solitary child with bad color and what his mother described as a "quiet patrician air . . . his large blue eyes not looking at anything present." His joy was in stories of high adventure, in birds and animals, almost anything to do with nature. "My mouth opened wide with astonish[ment] when I heard how many flowers were sent in to you," he had written to his mother the spring before, in April 1868, when she was in Savannah. "I could revel in the buggie ones. I jumped with delight when I found you heard the mockingbird, get some of its feathers if you can." He kept pet mice in a bureau drawer, and, in partnership with a cousin, West Roosevelt, had founded his own "Roosevelt Museum of Natural History" in the back hall on the fourth floor, a collection already comprising some several hundred specimens.

Teedie was an asthmatic. His attacks had started at about the age of three and more even than Bamie's affliction they had had a profound effect on the life of the family—summer plans, sudden cancellations of dinner engagements, changes in plans of all kinds being determined time and again by the status of his health. During the first few days at any summer house or hotel, his mother would keep her bags packed, knowing from experience that some unknown something might trigger an attack and off she would have to go with him, back to the city or to try still another, different locale.

Conie, too, had "the asthma," but very infrequently and never so seriously. Teedie, moreover, was beset by chronic stomach trouble, by headaches, by colds, fevers, and a recurring nightmare that a werewolf was coming at him from the bottom of his bed. Earlier in the year, in January 1869, he had fallen into such a low state that Mittie had taken him off to Philadelphia for a stay with her half sister, Susan, whose husband, Hilborne West, was a physician. Teedie, as Mittie said, kept everyone "on the stretch." Rarely could he sleep without being propped up in bed or in a big chair, so difficult was it for him to breathe. For a time, his father had thought possibly the trouble had something to do with the furnace at East 20th Street.

The attacks were a dreadful experience for everyone. They happened nearly always at night and there was little anybody could do. Theodore would gather the child up in his arms and walk the floor with him for hours. Some nights, in desperation, he would bundle him up against the cold, servants would be roused to fetch the carriage to the door, and father and child would drive off in the dark in the hope that the sudden change of air might bring relief —which sometimes it did.

Like other parents of their social position, the Roosevelts did not wish to see their children "coarsened" by public schools. But mainly it was from worry over their health that all four were kept from school of any kind, public or private. They were tutored within the home walls and from within the home ranks by their own Aunt Anna, who, until her marriage to James K. Gracie in 1866, was, like Grandmamma Bulloch, a vital part of the household. At one point Teedie and Ellie were sent down the street to private classes only a stone's throw from the house, these conducted by

Theodore's own boyhood tutor, but even so cautious a departure had proved unsatisfactory. The boys were withdrawn after only a month or two and not made to go again.

Since school played no part in their lives, they were cut off from their contemporaries. The only accessible—the only permissible—playmates were those within the family circle, namely cousins and the approved offspring of a few old family friends of comparable station and antecedents. Bamie seems to have had no childhood friends, while the youngest three had but one who had figured significantly thus far—little Edith Carow, who was Conie's age and the daughter of Charles Carow, a lifelong friend of Theodore's.

But then neither did any of them suffer from a lack of affection or stimulation. If anything, there was a surplus of both. Aunt Anna, who had no children, was as devoted as though they were her own. Grandmamma in her lace cap was famous for her "melts," overwhelming outbursts of maternal, southern affection; and nurse Dora Watkins was considered so overly indulgent to the children as to be a possible hindrance to their health and/or moral character. Years after her death, the mere mention of Grandmamma's name was enough to make the youngest three burst into tears.

The charming, erudite Dr. Hilborne West, the Philadelphia uncle, spent part of each summer with them, read and acted Shakespeare with all four children under the trees, and allegedly no one had more to do with their "early stirring of intellectual desires." "The very fact that he was not achieving a thousand worthwhile things, as was my father," wrote Conie years afterward, "the very fact that he was not busied with the practical care and thought for us, as were my mother and aunt, brought about between us that delightful relationship when the older person leads rather than drives the younger into paths of literature and learning."

It was, plainly, a family of paradoxes: privileged and cushioned beyond most people's imagining, yet little like the stereotype of the vapid, insular rich; uneducated in any usual, formal fashion but also uninhibited by education—ardent readers, insatiable askers of questions; chronically troubled, cursed it would often seem, by one illness or mysterious disorder after another, yet refusing to subject others to their troubles or to give in to despair.

Of the tawdriness and drudgery of the workaday world they knew almost nothing. They had never experienced drought or hunger or steerage or any of a dozen other ordeals common to so many Americans of the day. They were never without money or servants.

They scarcely knew what it was to clean out a stall or put their hands in dishwater. When a cook got drunk one evening at the Union Square house and CVS went to see what the fuss was about, it marked the first time he had set foot in his own kitchen.

They knew themselves to be aristocrats, though it is unlikely they used that word: "people of good family" was preferred. They had little patience with bad manners, no use for social climbers, little knack for the kind of easy familiarity that businessmen and politicians traded on and that Europeans thought so very American. "Be careful always in chance acquaintances" was another of father Theodore's admonitions to the children.

"Family" and "stocks" or "antecedents" were favorite topics. Their own position relative to that of the common herd was an accepted fact of life. Theodore was no more averse to using an expression like "our class" than was anyone else of comparable background. But if conscious of their position, they were also conscious of their duty. They had standards, standards which they never questioned. They were Roosevelts, but, being Roosevelts, that in itself could never be thought of as enough. Duty and the family name demanded more.

And then, in addition, there was Mittie, in some regards the most fascinating of them all, "darling little Mittie," a Roosevelt by marriage only.

CHAPTER TWO

Lady from the South

––––––––––––––

· 1 ·

THE BULLOCHS OF GEORGIA were nothing like the Roosevelts of New York. For several hundred years the good, solid Roosevelts had kept to their mercantile pursuits, content with the same horizons. Seldom had any of them ventured beyond the confines of Manhattan Island for reasons other than business, and never longer than necessary. They had lived and applied their renowned family acumen, met and married their Dutch wives, bred, prospered, and died, generation after generation, all within a radius of about three miles. "The Roosevelt stock," observed the New York *World*, "has always been noted for a tendency . . . to cling to the fixed and the venerable." A move from one Manhattan address to another was as serious a disruption of the pattern as a true Roosevelt cared to suffer in a lifetime. CVS had been born in Maiden Lane; the family business had been located in Maiden Lane since 1797. When, in the 1830s, CVS at last succumbed to the tide of fashion and built the house on Union Square, at 14th Street and Broadway, he did so with the consoling thought that by going that far uptown he had at least relieved his progeny for several generations from ever having to move again.

One searches the Roosevelt family history nearly in vain for a sign of daring or spontaneity or a sense of humor. The family reputation for probity in business and personal conduct demanded certain restraints, of course, and so such uniform absence of color may have been partly disguise, another bow to appearances. There

39

were also exceptions. One Nicholas Roosevelt, an uncle of CVS, had an interest in steamboats early in the century and made the first descent by steam down the Mississippi from Pittsburgh to New Orleans. But he and a figure like Robert stand out against the rest of the line as conspicuous as mutations. It is said of James Alfred Roosevelt, for example, that if he ever had an unconventional thought in his life he kept it to himself. Of his private, domestic enthusiasms, it is recorded that he was inordinately fond of waffles.

About the only break Theodore had made from the established pattern was to leave the Dutch Reformed Church to join the Presbyterians; unless, of course, one considers his bringing Mittie Bulloch into the family.

The Bullochs, by contrast, were not only southern in background and outlook—antebellum slaveholding Georgia patricians—they were an entirely different breed, of Scottish blood mostly and "spirited," as Theodore said of Mittie.

The first to reach the New World was James Bulloch of Glasgow, a scholar versed in Latin and Greek, who landed at Charleston, South Carolina, about 1729, which, as the Roosevelts measured such things, was rather late in the game, their own Claes Martenszen van Rosenvelt having arrived in New Amsterdam in 1649. (All that is known of Claes Martenszen is that he was a farmer with a wife named Jannetje, and that he was called Kleytjen, which in the idiom of the day meant Shorty.) James Bulloch became a planter, married, and attained some standing in South Carolina politics before removing to coastal Georgia, where he received a grant of several thousand acres in the Sea Island district. His wife was Jean Stobo, also of Glasgow, who, with her mother and her father, Archibald Stobo, a noted Presbyterian divine, had set forth in 1699 as part of the ill-fated effort to found a utopian Scottish colony in the jungles of Darién, on the Isthmus of Panama. The situation at Darién being hopeless, the expedition, a flotilla of three ships, turned back, and on the voyage home to Scotland the Stobos' ship, *Rising Sun*, stopped at Charleston to take on water and supplies. The ship anchored outside the harbor, passengers remaining aboard, but the people of Charleston, hearing Stobo was so close at hand, requested that he come preach. So consequently he, his wife, and daughter, Jean, were safely ashore the following day when a hurricane struck, sinking the ship and taking the lives of nearly all aboard. Stobo was at once offered a pulpit—the congregation being "obedient to the finger of Providence"—and in time he became a

Charleston institution, his customary sermon running to such length that it was possible to leave in the middle, go home for a large midday meal, and return to find him still going strong.

Thus began the Bulloch line in America, the annals of which, by Mittie's time, included one noted "radical," several valorous soldiers, frontiersmen, politicians, young men who went off to sea, at least one scandal, a dozen or more handsome women, "even a French strain of blood." Archibald Bulloch, a son born to James Bulloch and Jean Stobo, was the radical and a man of consequence in Georgia history. He was elected the first president of the Provincial Congress of Georgia and a delegate to the Continental Congress. In 1776 he became the first president and commander in chief of Georgia, only to die suddenly and mysteriously, and the Savannah burial vault in which he was placed long remained a subject of gossip and speculation since it had no inscription, no identifying mark whatsoever except a snake carved in the shape of a circle.

Archibald's wife, Mary de Veaux, was the daughter of James de Veaux, judge of the King's Court of Georgia before the Revolution and a colonel in the Continental Army. Archibald's son, another James and a captain in the Continental Army, married Anne Irvine, the daughter of Dr. John Irvine, head of the Georgia Medical Society; and they, in turn, produced still another James—James Stephens as he was called—who was Mittie's father and who managed to complicate the Bulloch family tree in such a way as to leave many people wondering how it could possibly be respectable.

The situation was as follows:

As a young man James Stephens Bulloch married Hester Elliott, who was the oldest daughter of John Elliott, a United States senator from Georgia and a widower. That was in 1817. A year later, Senator John Elliott was himself married to Martha Stewart of Savannah, who was young enough to be his daughter and who at some point prior to 1817 had turned down a proposal from James Stephens Bulloch. It is said the marriage was arranged by her father, a legendary figure named Daniel Stewart, General Daniel Stewart, a Revolutionary War hero who had decided to push on to the Florida frontier and thought his beautiful daughter would be better off staying behind as the wife of his friend John Elliott. But whatever the reason for the marriage, it made Martha the stepmother-in-law of her former suitor.

One child, James Dunwody, was born to James Stephens and Hester Bulloch before Hester died; and with the death of Senator

John Elliott, Martha Stewart was left a widow with three children
of her own, Susan, Georgia, and Daniel. By the standards of the
day, she and James Stephens were middle-aged when they at last
married: she was thirty-three; he, thirty-nine. Among her Elliott
stepchildren, some of whom were older than she, it was also
thought scandalous that "Mother" should be marrying "Brother"
James Stephens.

From this union came Anna, Mittie, and, finally, Irvine, who
arrived twenty-two years after Martha Stewart's firstborn, Susan. In
the course of this extended life as wife and mother, Martha Stewart
Elliott Bulloch—she who became the Roosevelt children's beloved Grandmamma—had to cope altogether with four categories
of children: her Elliott stepchildren, her own Elliott children, her
Bulloch stepson (who was also her stepgrandson), and her own
Bulloch children. The total came to fourteen.

Like his forebears, James Stephens was a low-country planter
(cotton and rice), but also a banker, Deputy Collector of the Port of
Savannah, and a director of the company that built the *Savannah*,
the first steamship to cross the Atlantic. Savannah was his home
and Anna and Mittie spent their first years there. Then about 1839,
when Mittie was four, James Stephens moved his large, composite
household about 250 miles inland, to Cobb County in northwest
Georgia, to what a few years earlier had been Cherokee country.
There, in a settlement called Roswell, among rolling green hills
twenty miles north of Atlanta, Mittie did most of her growing up,
never considering her family as anything other than perfectly normal, though apparently the infinite number of Stewart, Elliott, and
Bulloch aunts, uncles, cousins close and distant—the whole geometric progression of the Savannah kinships—was something only
her mother could make heads or tails of. "The relationships in
Savannah are more bewildering than ever," sister Anna wrote Mittie during a visit to the coastal city after they were both grown
women. "I would not be at all surprised to find out that Miss Har-
riet Campbell was my sister."

Roswell, forever "home" to Mittie, was a mere dozen or so
buildings, some exceedingly impressive, strung along a hilltop
close by the Chattahoochee River. A coastal Georgian named Roswell King—once manager of the Pierce Butler plantation on Sea
Island—had found the site while exploring for gold, and with his
son Barrington laid out a future community with wide streets and
a park. The idea was to make it a summer colony for a few wealthy
friends, a refuge from the deadly fevers that plagued Savannah and

the coastal lowlands during the hottest months. The elevation was exactly one thousand feet. "Exposure to cold and rain is hardly ever attended by serious consequences," declared one observer. "No case of consumption has ever occurred in the country. The summer diseases are bowel complaints, etc."

With the water power available, the Roswell Manufacturing Company, a small cotton mill, was also established by Barrington King, this in the valley below town.

Six or seven prominent Savannah families joined in the venture, built houses and, as time passed, spent more of each year there, living quite handsomely on incomes derived from holdings on the coast, where by the mid-1840s the slave population had advanced to some twenty thousand. There was a Roswell general store, a small "academy" for boys, another for girls, a white frame Presbyterian church, and a graveyard. The Barrington King family (nine children and a tutor) occupied Barrington Hall, a columned Greek Revival mansion with the incongruous New England touch of a widow's walk. (The architect-builder of the house, and much else in town, including Bulloch Hall, was a Connecticut man named Willis Ball.) Phoenix Hall was the home of the Dunwody family. Great Oakes, Roswell's red-brick manse, housed the Reverend Nathaniel Pratt, whose wife was a King. Holly Hill belonged to a Savannah family named Lewis.

Bulloch Hall stood a few hundred yards west of the King place, on the gentle knoll that formed the highest point in town. Bulloch Hall faced east, its deep veranda supported by four massive Doric columns: a white clapboard Greek temple set among giant oaks and Virginia cedars, magnolias, mimosa—the quintessence of the Old Plantation, classic Greece by way of Thomas Jefferson as interpreted by the Connecticut Yankee Willis Ball.

For the Roosevelt children, stories of the life in this house, the parties, the games of *tableaux vivants*, the constant stream of friends, family, neighbors, servants, all the people, white and black, recounted by the hour by their mother, aunt, and grandmother, were as magical, as different from what they knew, as anything in books. Mittie herself, with her liquid southern-gentry voice, her everlasting interest in people, her gift for mimicry, her overflowing romanticism, could not have been more unlike the Roosevelts her children encountered if she had been reared in some distant foreign land. She adored to tell stories and, as Conie said, no one told them better. Also, she had very southern ideas about the meaning of manhood. Inherent to her stories was a great love of the heroic. It was "Little Mama," so exquisite and fragile, who could fire the spirit of adventure—impart to a child a sense of bloodline kinship with real-life men of action. The ancestral feats of daring, the family heroes the children were raised on, were all on her side; they were not Roosevelts, they were "Mama's people." James Dunwody Bulloch, the older half brother, had gone to sea as a midshipman in the Navy, become a captain of a packet ship, later a Confederate admiral assigned to secret missions in England. It was James Bulloch who built the famous Confederate raider *Alabama*, and Irvine Bulloch, Mittie's younger full brother who served on the *Alabama*, was said to have fired the last shot in the fight with the *Kearsarge* off Cherbourg.

There were stories of old Senator Elliott's daughter Corinne, for whom Conie was named, who with her two children was lost at sea when the steamer *Pulaski* sank in 1838, while her rich husband escaped on a raft; of Grandfather Stewart, the Revolutionary War general who left Georgia to fight Indians in Florida, marching off with his six sons, all of whom were more than six feet tall; of Georgia bear hunts and a black slave named Bear Bob, so named because a bear once tore away part of his scalp. The stories were at once bizarre, scary, always long ago and far away, always exciting. At night, with the onset of stomach cramps or an attack of asthma, they could soothe and distract as could almost nothing else, as we know from Teedie's diaries. "It was all so picturesque, so different from northern life, that it made an indelible impression," Bamie would remember.

In 1849, when Mittie was fourteen, James Stephens dropped dead of a heart attack while teaching Sunday school, and from that point on, to make ends meet, family sojourns in Savannah were dispensed with and Roswell became the permanent home. In the census of the following year, the widowed Martha, aged fifty, listed herself as a farmer. Her new son-in-law, Susan's husband, Hilborne West, came on from Philadelphia to help manage things temporarily, but for all practicalities it was Martha herself who was in charge of household, children, crops, and those referred to always as "the servants." As an agricultural enterprise it was nothing much. To rank as a true planter, one was supposed to have land and twenty slaves. Her slaves numbered nineteen, eight of whom were children. Still, it was no small task for a woman and she faced it gallantly.

That her Grandmamma Bulloch had owned slaves, "and all that implied," seemed incredible, Bamie said, but also, somehow, very special. Daddy Luke had been the coachman; Mom Charlotte, the head housekeeper and cook. Mittie and Anna had been served hand and foot by a nurse called Mom Grace, but each also had her own slave child, her little black shadow, as was the expression. Mittie's was called Toy, Anna's, Bess; and Toy and Bess slept on straw mats on the floor of the girls' bedroom. Another black child slept beneath Grandmamma's big four-poster, "to run errands for her in the night," it was explained, which probably meant to empty her slop jar.

Half brother Daniel Stuart Elliott once had to be sent abroad for a year of travel, so full of remorse was he. In a fit of rage he had shot and killed his "little shadow," who by then, like Daniel Elliott himself, was no longer very little.

Guns, violence, savage death, episodes that seemed more like the stuff of fable or fantasy, were all part of the world Mittie spun. Ellie spoke for all her offspring when he called her his "sweet little Dresden china" mother; she seemed so delicate, like an exquisite work of art, as Conie said. Yet she could portray in marvelous detail how a pack of bloodhounds pulled a cougar to pieces or describe the midnight death struggle between a cougar and a half-naked black man, one of great-grandfather Daniel Stewart's slaves, a story the impressionable little Teedie would remember all his life. The black man, "a man of colossal strength," had been cutting through a Florida swamp in the dark of night, taking a shortcut to "see his sweetheart." His torn body was found the next day with that of the cougar lying beside him.

How much the Roosevelt children were told of the duel fought by Daniel Elliott we can only surmise. But in 1857, the year before Teedie was born, Daniel Elliott shot and killed the son of a prominent Savannah family, Tom Daniell, in a duel fought with rifles on a mud embankment beside the Savannah River. There had been an argument at the Chatham Club, where Savannah's "young bloods" met for billiards and cards and a good deal of heavy drinking. Daniell had thrown a glass of wine in Daniel Elliott's face, which by the *code duello* meant but one thing. Daniel Elliott, who was an expert shot, had been willing to accept a reasonable apology and forget that anything had happened, but Daniell refused. Seconds were named, the whole grim, stilted ritual was acted out at a chosen spot on the opposite shore of the river, in South Carolina, where dueling had yet to be outlawed. At the signal both men fired and Daniell dropped, a bullet through the heart. The news caused a sensation in Savannah society—Daniell's father, William Coffee

Daniell, was a leading physician and a former mayor of the city—
and Daniel Elliott was in disgrace. When it became known a year
later that he would wed Lucy Sorrel of Savannah, one eminent
chronicler noted privately, "Were I a lady, I would certainly be
very loath to marry one who had the guilt of homicide upon his
skirts."

The Roosevelt children never knew their Uncle Dan—he died
of tuberculosis during the Civil War—but his widow, Aunt Lucy
Sorrel Elliott, and her two children, cousins Maud and Johnny
Elliott, had come on from Savannah several times to spend summers with them in New Jersey. Another vivid southerner, another
effusively affectionate female presence, Aunt Lucy was the sister
of Gilbert Moxley Sorrel, who had been a brigadier general in the
Army of Northern Virginia at the age of twenty-six and credited as
"the best staff officer in the Confederate service."

Everything recalled of the life at Roswell was utterly fascinating, we are told in Conie's recollections. "In the roomy old home
with its simple white columns there was led an ideal life," she
thought. Her mother described picnics and riding parties, a life
spent almost constantly in the out of doors, in all seasons, in unspoiled open country, with sweet-smelling trees and flowers in
bloom. A particular variety of blue violet grew beside the house
and the view of the valley to the west was especially lovely in the
late-afternoon light. And there was the looping Chattahoochee,
which ran the color of heavily creamed coffee.

Uncle Dan, whatever his tragic failings, was "brilliant," with
a particular love of art and music. He played the flute and James
Dunwody—Uncle Jimmie—played the violin. Mittie and Anna
sang together, Mittie alto, Anna soprano. "They apparently none of
them had any particular education," Bamie said, "but all of them
had the most delightful gifts. They were all good-looking, and all
had entrancingly stormy love affairs, rarely marrying the people
whose lives we adored hearing about." Anna had been engaged for
a time to Henry Stiles of Savannah, who rode a Morgan horse no
one could handle; Mittie had a running flirtation with one of the
Kings, Tom, who thought the world of her.

For her children to picture Mittie as she was when their father
first arrived on the scene required no effort of imagination, for in
appearance and manner she had aged hardly at all. At thirty-three
she looked to be in her early twenties. She was really quite extraordinary. Small, scarcely over five feet tall, very slender, she had
tiny, perfect hands, and extremely fine features, the eyes a soft,

clear blue. Hers was a flawless, delicate little face, the complexion "more moonlight-white than cream-white," and framed by a head of lustrous black hair that she and her French hairdresser could fuss over interminably. With company she was ever chattering, "bright and full of life," "sweet and winning," to quote some of her New York friends. She was "like some vision of exquisite beauty," "so young, so beautiful and gentle, that she might almost have been a sister to her children."

Many years later, in the early 1920s, in an altogether different time and world, a reporter for the Atlanta *Journal* drove out to Roswell to interview Mrs. William Baker, who had been Evelyn King in her youth, another of the nine King children, and who was still living, with one grandchild, in Barrington Hall. Mrs. Baker had been Mittie Bulloch's closest friend and a bridesmaid in Mittie's wedding. At eighty-seven she was the lone survivor of that whole generation in Roswell.

The reporter was a young woman who was then signing herself Peggy Mitchell; she was Margaret Mitchell, whose re-creation of the Old Plantation South in her *Gone With the Wind* would one day supplant all others in the popular mind. To what extent her book was fiction, how much she had based on actual people and places, were questions she would face repeatedly, once the book became famous, and her insistence that there was no real-life Scarlett O'Hara, no actual Tara to be found in the Atlanta vicinity, was no doubt sincere. Still, the combination of the beautiful dark-haired Mittie Bulloch with her tiny waist and perfect complexion and the aura of Bulloch Hall is remarkably close to what she created, in general outline and spirit if not in specific detail, and there is no question about the impress on the young writer's mind of what she saw and heard at Roswell. She noted the "stately silence engendered by the century-old oaks," the "atmosphere of dignity, ease and courtesy that was the soul of the Old South." Walking through Bulloch Hall, she found the rooms "unbelievably" large and airy and tried to picture the bridal party that had once clustered on the main staircase.

"Weddings were great affairs then," Mrs. Baker told her. People came from miles around and stayed for days in the big houses in the village. "Weddings were different from what they are now. The bride and groom didn't rush off right after the ceremony. They stayed at home sometimes for a week or two, and everybody gave them parties. . . . Of course, Mittie Bulloch's wedding was a very fine affair."

The groom, however, had been an abolitionist from the North. "A very nice man he was, to be sure," said Mrs. Baker. "But he was firm against slavery."

· 2 ·

THEODORE ROOSEVELT went south to Georgia for the first time when he was nineteen, in 1850, prior to his Grand Tour. Mittie's sister's husband, Hilborne West, had a sister who was the wife of Theodore's brother Weir, and by this somewhat circuitous chain of communication, Theodore had picked up enough about the charms of Roswell and of the two beautiful Bulloch sisters to go see for himself. He sent a letter in advance, but somehow the letter did not arrive in time; so when he appeared at Roswell, arriving in the middle of the night, it was without advance warning and his knock at the door roused the whole house from a sound sleep. The first face he saw was Toy's, peering through a crack in the door. He presented his visiting card, which she speedily delivered to the startled group upstairs.

He wound up staying several weeks and apparently for Mittie, too, it was love at first sight. She was then fifteen. A man who knew her at about this time in her life, a contemporary who became a prominent figure in Savannah, described her as a splendid horse-woman, as "full of spirit and courage as she was beautiful."

She did not see Theodore again for nearly three years, not until the spring of 1853, when she came north to visit Susan and Hilborne West at their home in Philadelphia, and then to stay briefly with the Weir Roosevelts in New York, at which time she became tacitly betrothed. "Does it not seem strange," she wrote Theodore soon afterward, "to think we should have met and become engaged, after having only known each other time enough to create a passing interest, then to be separated for almost three years. Sometimes when I think of it all I feel as though it were ordered by some high power." Then, as an afterthought, she told him, "If I fail to please, and if ever you should fail, I might persuade Tom King to retire with me in the far West."

Her mother approved the match. She had been "impressed favorably" by Theodore during his visit to Roswell. "I have never interfered with the matrimonial designs of my children," she told him, "and never will when the object chosen is a worthy one."

By early summer he was with Mittie once more at Roswell,

promising as they sat alone one evening on the veranda to love her with all her faults, promising voluntarily, as she would enjoy reminding him. Once the engagement was formally declared and he had left for New York, she wrote:

Roswell, July 26, 1853

THEE, DEAREST THEE,

I promised to tell you if I cried when you left me. I had determined not to do so if possible, but when the dreadful feeling came over me that you were, indeed, gone, I could not help my tears from springing and had to rush away and be alone with myself. Everything now seems associated with you. Even when I run up the stairs going to my own room, I feel as if you were near, and turn involuntarily to kiss my hand to you. I feel, dear Thee—as though you were part of my existence, and that I only live in your being, for now I am confident of my own deep love. When I went in to lunch today I felt very sad, for there was no one now to whom to make the request to move "just a quarter of an inch farther away"—but how foolish I am—you will be tired of this "rhapsody" . . .

Tom King has just been here to persuade us to join the Brush Mountain picnic tomorrow. We had refused but we are reconsidering.

She did go off to Brush Mountain, picnicked on chicken wings, bread and cheese, and had a "most delightful time." Tom King built a bonfire as the sun went down and on the way home she rode with Henry Stiles.

I had promised to ride back with Henry Stiles, so I did so [she explained to Theodore], and you cannot imagine what a picturesque effect our riding party had—not having any habit, I fixed a bright-red shawl as a skirt and a long red scarf on my head, turban fashion with long ends streaming. Lizzie Smith and Anna dressed in the same way, and we were all perfectly wild with spirits and created quite an excitement in Roswell by our gay cavalcade— But all the same I was joked all day by everybody, who said that they could see that my eyes were swollen and that I had been crying.

At a big family gathering in September she danced past midnight, as she told him. Another evening she and Anna put on a "grand supper party." When one of her accounts of still another such occasion brought a piqued response from New York, she responded: "My dear Thee, I kiss a great many different people and always expect to. I cannot allow you a monopoly there. Why just think of what the world would be without kisses. I could not think of depriving my friends of that pleasure."

They had agreed to a small wedding in November, but she changed her mind. She preferred December and she wanted to have bridesmaids, a decision he found mystifying. In the South, she informed him, a wedding was always done according to the wishes of the bride and her family; for a gentleman to interfere with the arrangements was quite unheard of.

Thee, I grant they may be different entirely, your northern customs, but will I ever be able to impress upon you the *fact* that it is a southern young lady and in a southern village that the wedding is to occur; consequently I must observe the rules and customs prevalent in that village. I cannot imagine you for one moment supposing I would take the step decided upon unless I had thought well of what I was doing.

"Capricious Mittie" she called herself. "How will you please me ever?"

She was having palpitations of the heart, which she thought "entirely nervous." Under no circumstances was he to arrive any sooner than two days before the wedding. "It may be a southern idea, but remember it is a southern young lady," she insisted still one more time. Then in mid-November, with only a month to go and feeling extremely agitated, she asked:

Dear Thee, how are you going to behave when we meet? If I see you first before them all, mind seriously please, don't kiss me or anything of the kind. I would not let the brothers see you do so for worlds. I am in earnest. I would regard my affections as misplaced if you should take any liberties. Please read this carefully and act like a perfect gentleman.

She herself would be as dignified as possible in the presence of her bridesmaids, "so as to show them how to do *the thing*, particularly as I am much younger than any of them."

The wedding took place at Bulloch Hall three days before Christmas—Thursday, December 22, 1853—the Reverend Nathaniel Pratt officiating. It was all she wished. The bridesmaids were sister Anna, Evelyn King, Mary Cooper Stiles, and Julia Hand. They were all in white, the bridesmaids in white muslin dresses with full skirts, Mittie in white satin with a long veil. "We carried flowers, too, and came down the wide steps of Bulloch Hall with the trailing clusters in our arms," remembered Mrs. Baker. The ceremony was held in the dining room, the bridal party grouped at the folding doors. Fires burned in every fireplace; mahogany tables were crowded with hams, turkeys, "cakes of every conceivable kind." Ice cream had been made with ice brought all the way from Savannah, a touch that especially impressed Theodore's mother and father, who were the only Roosevelts present. "It was their first trip south," said Mrs. Baker, "and like most northern people of that time, they were very ignorant about the South. Goodness only knows what they expected us to be like . . ."

When it was time for dancing, brother Dan played the flute. ("That is the only music we can engage," Mittie had explained to Theodore, "but he plays in such perfect time that it will be delightful.") According to family tradition, brother Dan also fell head over heels in love with one of the bridesmaids who was already engaged to another and much older man, and who rode off leaving Dan broken-hearted. This romantic episode, it is further said, ended tragically in the girl's unwilling marriage to the older man, to a duel and "much else that was unfortunate." But since the only known duel in Dan's stormy life, that with Tom Daniell, took place three years later and since Tom Daniell was both unmarried and Dan's own age, the story is open to a good deal of question—unless, of course, an entirely different duel was fought earlier and did not prove fatal, in which case there would be no record of its ever having occurred.

The bride and groom stayed on at Roswell through Christmas and there were parties every night. Then they were on their way to New York. "Everybody packed up and went home," Mrs. Baker said, "for it was all over and we were very tired."

Mittie returned again to Roswell with Theodore a year and a half later, in the spring of 1855, bringing her new baby daughter. She had not been feeling right since the baby's birth in January. Theodore worried intensely over her; she herself did not like the way she looked. "I do not think she will get strong until she breathes fresh air," her mother had declared and Theodore emphatically concurred, as little as he happened to care for Roswell and the life there. His belief in the therapeutic powers of fresh air —country air, mountain air, sea breezes, almost any air other than that of the city—exceeded even that of his mother-in-law. He

stayed in Roswell only long enough to pay his respects and see
Mittie settled.

Mittie was in love as never before. "Darling, it would be impossible to tell you how I have missed you," she wrote five days
after he had gone. "I feel so a part of you I cannot do without you."

> . . . I do not know what I would not give to be in your arms,
> petted and loved. I love you inexpressibly . . . I want to talk to
> you. I want to see you. I cannot live without you. . . . Write me
> everything about yourself and how you love me.

A day later she filled four pages with her love and longing:
"You have proved that you love me, dear, in a thousand ways and
still I long to hear it again and again. . . . darling, you cannot imagine what a *wanting* feeling I have."

He was trying his best to feel at home, he wrote his first night
back at East 20th Street. "It is of no use; everything is in apple-pie
order but there is a kind of dreariness reigning everywhere, the
one pillow on the bed positively gave me a shiver. I even handled
the crib, which I used to regard as rather an encumbrance to our
room, with a kind of reverence."

Her brother Jimmie was in town and staying with him temporarily. They were greatly enjoying each other's company, he told
her, and "keeping late hours," for which he was grateful. "Indeed,
bed does not offer me the same inducements as of yore and I rather
regret when the time comes for me to retire alone."

He wrote nearly every day. May 13: "Everything begins to
look like spring. . . . We have little glimpses of country over Mr.
Goelet's wall and the sounds of his numerous birds. . . . It is just
such a day as would give you a pleasant impression of a New York
spring . . ." May 15: "I exerted all my taste to please you in the
selection of my summer cravats this afternoon." May 16: "You
know how I love you, darling, and what an intense pleasure it
would be now to carry you up to bed in my arms . . ." May 23: "I
will be very glad to have charge of you again . . ."

On May 24, in his last letter before leaving to bring her home,
he told her he had bought a new felt hat especially for the trip, but
that his mother had disapproved, saying felt would be out of place
at Roswell. "If it must it must," he told Mittie, "but I will first hear
your opinion of it."

As difficult for her as anything about her new life in the North
was the separation from her mother and sister. She and Anna had

been inseparable for as long as either could remember and the bond between them, they were both convinced, was of a kind others could never understand. If anything, Anna had suffered worse than Mittie in the time since the wedding. "If anyone mentions you rather suddenly I feel like screaming," she wrote to Mittie. "I do not try to feel so, darling, but we were so happy together and it is all passed away." She had thought they would never be "anything but Anna and Mittie, inseparable, always sewing, reading, walking, riding, talking incessantly together." She consoled herself with the thought that at least they would be together in heaven.

But as things worked out they were all together again in less than a year. Mrs. Bulloch and Anna packed up and came north, moving in at East 20th Street to stay in 1856. So by the time the second baby arrived, the Roswell circle, or what remained of it, was happily reinstated under the same roof. Brother Irvine as well was an occasional member of the household, on vacations from the University of Pennsylvania.

Bulloch Hall, meantime, was left in the care of Daddy Luke and his wife.

Bulloch family finances appear to have been the real reason for this new arrangement. Mrs. Bulloch and Anna came to live with Mittie not just to be of help and comfort, but because they were extremely hard-pressed. To pay for the wedding and trousseau, for example, had required that four slaves be sold, including Anna's own Bess. (According to one bill of sale, $800 was received from a John F. Martin for "one Negro woman named Bess, and her child John.") "I hope that you will make so good a wife that Thee will never have cause to regret his not having married a girl with a fortune," Mrs. Bulloch advised shortly before she and Anna moved in. Anna would be governess to Mittie's children in return for her keep, and Mrs. Bulloch, it is known, received spending money from Susan West, to whom, on occasion, she wrote on cheap, blue-lined school paper, saying it was all she could afford.

The second baby arrived October 27, 1858, a Wednesday. Mittie had been feeling fine. After a morning's shopping she had returned for lunch, then went to her room to rest, which is where her mother found her in great pain at about half past three. The house was at once in turmoil, servants flying off to find the family doctor, who, it turned out, was himself too sick to respond. Until another man was found, Mrs. Bulloch was "almost the whole time alone with Mittie," as she told Susan. "Anna had taken Bamie over to Lizzie Ellis'—I sent over for her, but she was too unwell to come

—I could not bear the idea of having no female friend with me, so sent for Mrs. Roosevelt and she came over."

Mittie got "worse and worse" until quarter to eight that evening when "at last" the birth took place. As labor went, hers was, in her mother's experienced eye, "a safe but severe time."

No chloroform or any such thing was used, no instruments, consequently the dear little thing has no cuts or bruises about it. . . . Mittie has behaved throughout the whole time like a sensible woman, has objected to nothing that was right.

A few days later mother and child were doing splendidly. Mittie had no trouble nursing; the baby was in perfect health. "All quite well," noted Mrs. Bulloch the morning of November 3, ". . . little Theodore is a week old . . . Mittie is quite motherly, likes to have him lying quite near her." But it was not until December that Mittie came downstairs, which suggests she was suffering from depression, and it was then that Bamie was going through the worst of her ordeal with the back harness.

Two more pregnancies followed with little delay—Elliott was born in February 1860, a year and four months after Theodore; Corinne, in September 1861, a year and seven months after Elliott —which for Mittie meant three children in less than three years. And by the time Corinne was born, the Civil War had begun.

· 3 ·

IT WAS the great demarcation line in her life, the point at which her southern past was forever delineated as past and irretrievable. It put strains on her household, her marriage, her physical strength, and her emotions unlike anything in her experience. For her two oldest children, and for Teedie particularly, the war was the first news from the world outside to penetrate the secure haven of home and family. "Are me a soldier laddie?" he asked his Aunt Anna, as she tried to fit him for a little Zouave shirt the first year of the war. "I immediately took his own suggestion and told him he was and that I was the Captain," she told Mittie, ". . . this kept him still for a moment or two!"

The story that on the occasion of a Southern victory Mittie hung a Confederate flag from the house on East 20th Street is a story with no foundation in fact; it never happened. A gesture so

flamboyant would have been out of character, furthermore, and
publicly disrespectful of her husband, which was simply not in
her. The story is appropriate, however, in that the staid Roosevelt
brownstone with its three passionately loyal Georgian ladies did
indeed remain a stronghold of Southern sympathy; the colors of
the Confederacy flew in spirit, if not in fact, undaunted, from the
start of the conflict until Appomattox. On the news that Port Royal
had fallen, early in November 1861, Grandmamma Bulloch cried
for three days. Like all true southerners, she said, she would rather
be buried in one common grave than ever live again under the
Yankee government.

As time went on, with Theodore away—*only* with Theodore
away—Mittie, she, and Anna made up packages of flannel shirts,
woolen socks, scarves, combs, toothbrushes, and boxes of soap to
be sent secretly (by way of Nassau in the Bahamas) to family and
friends in the South. One of Bamie's most vivid memories of life in
the 20th Street house was of "the days of hushed and thrilling
excitement" when these bundles were being put together, she and
Teedie, at first, understanding little of what it was all about, "except that it was a mystery and that the box was going to run the
blockade."

In contrast to the Roosevelts, not one of whom went to war,
Captain James Bulloch, young Irvine, and Daniel Elliott were all
three fighting for the Confederacy, each having joined the cause as
rapidly as possible. Captain James, who had been in command of a
merchant ship when the war began, first sailed back to New York
and turned the ship over to the owners before going south to be
assigned his secret duties in England. Daniel enlisted as a private
in the Georgia Volunteers, and Irvine, at age nineteen, left the
University of Pennsylvania to sign on as a midshipman in the Confederate Navy. Virtually every able-bodied man Mittie had known
in Roswell or Savannah was in uniform—including six of the Kings
and Henry Stiles. Both Tom King and his brother Barrington were
to die in the war, and another brother, Joseph Henry, would never
fully recover from his wounds.

The least scrap of news from someone dear on the other side
was an enormous event. Early in 1862, for example, through contacts in Washington, Theodore learned that Captain Bulloch had
successfully run the blockade, bringing a "cargo of contraband
goods" from Nassau to Savannah. (Actually, it was a shipload of
military supplies—munitions, some fourteen thousand Enfield rifles, perhaps the most valuable cargo to reach the Confederacy

during the entire war.) Any letter that got through to the house in
New York became a treasure of untold import. Its contents would
have to be immediately shared, read aloud, then copied down and
sent on to Susan. "The amount of it is that Providence is on the
side of the right," wrote young Irvine in one such letter; ". . . the
life [at sea] is as hard as it is exciting, as painful to be away from
home and family as it is pleasant to think I am doing my all for my
oppressed country."

Saturday dinners at Grandfather Roosevelt's house, one of the
ironbound rituals in her married life, became such a trial for Mittie,
the air so thick with the "fulminations" of her northern in-laws,
that she could no longer bear to go.

Reminiscing about her mother and the Roosevelts long afterward, Bamie would remark, "I should hate to have married into
them at that time unless I had been one of them in thought. They
think they are just, but they are hard in a way."

In Theodore's presence Mittie kept her sentiments to herself,
as did her mother and sister. The evenings he entertained Union
officers, Grandmamma retired early. "You know he does not feel as
we do," she explained to Susan, "and it is his own house. It jars
upon my feelings, but of course I keep my room. Mittie can't do
this, and it is to please him that Anna does not absent herself."

For Theodore the approach of the war had loomed as a tragedy
beyond compare. Joining with prominent New York business people, he appealed to Congress to do everything possible to prevent
it. He signed petitions, helped promote a huge anti-war rally.
When it came, the war presented him with the most difficult decision of his life. And though only twenty-nine at the time and in
magnificent health as always, he chose not to fight, a determination
dictated, it is said, by the "peculiar circumstances" of his marriage:
he did what he did out of deference to Mittie and her feelings, for
all that he himself felt about the Union and the evils of slavery.

Possibly the teachings of his Quaker mother also played a part.
Nor can it be overlooked that few he knew of comparable social or
financial position and none of his brothers or kinsmen fought in the
war. The gentry of the city gloried in the power of Mrs. Howe's
"Battle Hymn"; they founded their Union League Club and
equipped the first units of black soldiers; they cheered heartily the
regiments of Germans and Irish, the upstate farm boys who
marched down Broadway. But they themselves chose not to march.
It was simply not done—any more, say, than one would go into
politics—and though this may not necessarily have been a measure

of Theodore's convictions or innermost desires, it at least meant his decision, within his own social circles, carried no stigma whatever.

He avoided the war by hiring a substitute. He paid to have some other man go in his place, which was both legal and costly. The sum he paid is not known, but the going rate, once the draft was initiated in 1863, was about $1,000, a figure far beyond the reach of the ordinary wage earner (the dollar then having roughly ten to fifteen times its present value), and went appreciably higher as the war dragged on and casualty reports became more appalling.

The regulation in the Conscription Act that permitted such an arrangement was as blatant a piece of class legislation as could be imagined. In essence, as one angry senator charged, it exempted the rich entirely. By paying a $300 commutation fee a man could become exempt from a particular draft call, but was still subject to subsequent calls. Hiring a substitute, on the other hand, provided permanent exemption. Substitute brokers operated in every northern city and the substitutes they sent to the Army were a sorry lot, largely criminals and drifters, who would desert at the first opportunity. The ordinary soldier had only contempt for such men and so the onus of the system, while the fighting lasted, was on the substitute rather than on the civilian who hired him. And the fact that in less than a year more than $12 million poured into the Treasury in draft-exemption fees of one or the other kind gives some idea of how many were eager to take advantage of the arrangement. A list of those who thus stayed out of the war would include nearly all the financial and industrial tycoons of the postwar era, and a future President of the United States, Grover Cleveland, not to mention most of the masculine element of New York's "best society."

According to Bamie, in a private memoir written in her old age, her father regretted the decision to his dying day. He "always afterward felt that he had done a very wrong thing in not having put every other feeling aside and joined the absolute fighting forces." Conie, for her part, would further contend that the decision had a profound effect on his older son and namesake, for whom it became the glaring single flaw in the life of an idolized father and one he would feel forever compelled to compensate for. Neither Theodore nor his sons ever discussed the subject that we know of, but there was no doubt as to which side little Teedie was taking at the time. In their pretend games played on a bridge in Central Park, Bamie was always the Rebel blockade-runner, Tee-

die the government boat. Once, kneeling at his evening prayers
with Aunt Anna, he implored the Almighty "to grind the southern
troops to powder."

For Mittie the thought of Theodore fighting against her brothers was abhorrent in the extreme. Still, it must have been with
some inner conflict that she saw him spared—saw herself spared
so much that other women were going through—by a system that
was the antithesis of every standard of patriotism and gallantry by
which she had been raised. For her brothers, or for any of the men
she had known in the South, to pay somebody else to do their
fighting for them would have been inconceivable. Nor could anyone of conscience blink the injustice of the system. When the Draft
Riots exploded in New York in July 1863, largely in reaction to this
injustice, the Roosevelt family was safely ensconced at an ocean-
front hotel at Long Branch. It was hoped that order could be
quickly restored, observed Mrs. Bulloch in the quiet of her room
overlooking the sea, "but really I do not wonder that the poor
mechanics oppose conscription. It certainly favors the rich at the
expense of the poor."

But though he refused to bear arms in the great crusade, Theodore was also incapable of sitting idly by. As he told Mittie in a
letter from Washington: "I would never have felt satisfied with
myself . . . if I had done nothing and . . . I do feel now that I am
only doing my duty. I know you will not regret having me do what
is right and I don't believe you will love me any the less for it."

He and two other wealthy New Yorkers, William E. Dodge, Jr.,
and Theodore Bronson, had conceived a plan whereby soldiers
could send home part of their pay on a regular basis and at no
additional cost to them or their families. The three men drafted a
bill for an Allotment Commission and after months of lobbying in
Washington succeeded in getting both congressional sanction and
the backing of the President. Then followed still more months in
the field, since the idea—all quite novel—had to be sold to the
soldiers themselves, which proved a slow and arduous task. Theodore was away from home nearly two years all told and approximately half that time was spent going from regiment to regiment,
by train, boat, but mostly on horseback in all weather and seasons.

Like his Newsboys' Lodging House or the Orthopedic Hospital, the allotment plan represented another determined effort to
help the helpless, those innocent victims of the war for whom the
government had been doing nothing, thousands upon thousands of
women and children made destitute by the absence of husbands

and fathers serving in the Army. It was the family of the fighting man that concerned him, rather than the fighting man himself who was being asked to sacrifice that part of his pay which customarily fell into the hands of sutlers and other traditional camp followers.

For his own family the months of separation seemed endless and especially the first long stretch when he was in Washington.

"Teedie was afraid last night that there was a bear in your dressing room," Mittie wrote. "He is the most affectionate, endearing little creature in his ways, but begins to require his papa's discipline badly. He is brimming full of mischief and has to be watched all the time."

One by one the children took sick. "You must not either get sick yourself or let the children do so," he told her. Mittie had "her hands full with the fretful little sick things," her mother noted; ". . . Thee has not returned . . . does not say when he will return." Then Mittie was reporting Teedie "very unwell," and though the word "asthma" never appears, it may have been at this point that the disease took hold. "I was up with him six or seven times during the night," she wrote, saying little or nothing about her own health or what Conie was to call her "mental suffering." Only once does she allow herself even a momentary flash of self-pity. It is night as she writes, that being the "only time unoccupied with the dear, troublesome little children deserted by their papa."

She was constantly in his thoughts, she knew, from the letters that arrived, often several a week, which was more than she wrote to him.

Ever the man to take the direct approach, he had gone to the White House the morning he got off the train. "I obtained a room at Willard's," he told her, "dressed myself and called upon Hay [John Hay, who was then Lincoln's private secretary], explained my object in a few words and was immediately shown into the next room where the President sat." Lincoln had listened "attentively," read the few documents Theodore presented, "then at my request endorsed them." Ten-year-old Willie Lincoln had come into the room "and the President's expression of face then for the first time softened into a very pleasant smile."

Mittie was instructed to address her letters in care of John Hay at the White House, for Theodore and the whimsical, boyish secretary had struck up the friendship that was to last a lifetime. One Sunday, in Lincoln's absence, Hay invited him to share the presidential pew at St. John's Church across Lafayette Square, and as the two walked down the aisle, many in the expectant congregation, seeing Theodore with his height and abundant whiskers, mistook him for Lincoln. Or such at least had been Theodore's impression.

Mrs. Lincoln, who was of southern background, found him charming and included him in her circle, a somewhat ambiguous honor, given the variety of sycophants she chose to surround herself with. He was asked to accompany her on afternoon carriage rides and on one occasion she insisted that he go with her to shop for a hat. The night of her famous *soirée* in the newly redecorated White House, February 5, 1862, he was among the select five hundred on her guest list and thus very pleased with himself. "I find that but six men under fifty are invited," he told Mittie.

The party had come under severe attack in the press because of the expenses involved and the limited guest list, but for Mrs. Lincoln it had proved a social triumph—everybody who was invited came, "the largest collection of notables there ever gathered in this country," Theodore crowed. "No one in the army lower than a division general, not even a brigadier, was invited. . . . Some complained of the supper but I have rarely seen a better and often a worse one. Terrapin, birds, ducks, and everything else were in great profusion." It was called a ball and the Marine Band played in the vestibule, but at the President's wish, there was no dancing, out of respect for "the national tribulation" and because upstairs young Willie Lincoln lay seriously ill. Theodore's one criticism of the evening was of the number of police present.

He stayed the whole time at Willard's Hotel, where in the bar and public rooms, amid clouds of blue cigar smoke, the endless dickering and dealing of war went on. (In his suite upstairs the pomaded Jim Fisk is said to have remarked, "You can sell anything to the government at almost any price you've got the guts to ask.") Theodore was spending the better part of his time on Capitol Hill, "gaining experience daily in a political point of view." Only after a month or more did his impatience begin to show. The problem, as his friend Dodge said, was "the utter inability of congressmen to understand why anyone should urge a bill from which no one could selfishly secure an advantage."

Waiting for Congress to act, with little or nothing to do but bide his time, he himself took sick; but then, amazingly, a week of continuous exposure in the field, standing out in the cold and damp while talking to troops, cured him completely.

His first real success selling his plan was with a New York regiment which, at first glance, struck him as the "scum of our city." An adjutant assigned to help was so drunk he could barely speak and did nothing as he was supposed to.

The delays were so great that I stood out with one of these companies after seven o'clock at night with one soldier holding a candle while I took down the names of those who desired to send home money. The men looked as hard as I have often seen before in our Mission neighborhood, but after a little talk explaining my object and reminding them of those they had left behind them, one after another put down his name, and from this company alone they allotted, while I was there, $600. . . . I stood out there in the dark night surrounded by the men with one candle showing glimpses of their faces, the tents all around us in the woods. One man putting down $5.00 a month said, "My old woman has always been good to me and if you please change it to $10.00." In a minute half a dozen others followed his example and doubled theirs.

In one forty-eight-hour spate of activity in Virginia, in the vicinity of Newport News, he emerged unharmed and unshaken from a derailed train, rode twenty-five miles on horseback ("As I had broken my eyeglasses I had to trust entirely to my horse who jumped over the ditches in a most independent manner"), used both his French and his German to proselytize in front of one New York regiment, then rode another twenty-five miles to talk to an Irish regiment, after which he spent one of "the most thoroughly Irish" nights of his life drinking with the officers until nearly dawn. The ride to Fortress Monroe the next day was "delightful"—a favorite Roosevelt word—and following lunch there with the officers he was on his way by boat back to Washington. His co-worker Bronson, he told Mittie, was so "used up" by the experience that he was quitting and going home. "Of course this makes me doubly homesick but I must see it through."

Once, writing to say he was on his way home for a visit, he told her not to expect him until very late and to leave the front door unlocked. "I hope you will take a good long nap in the daytime," he added.

Early in 1862, Mrs. Bulloch decided she must get through to Georgia to be with her son Daniel, who, she had learned, was dying of tuberculosis. "I think I am required there," she said simply. A pass was needed and so this, too, Theodore undertook, pulling what strings he could, something he pointedly disliked. The problem, he explained to Mittie, was greatly compounded by the family connection with Captain Bulloch, whose success in running the blockade had made the name anathema in Washington. But then in a letter from Baltimore he suddenly announced the arrangements were set. Her mother and Anna could both go, on the condition that they would not return. He himself strongly advised against it, but if such remained their wish they were to meet him the Friday following at Barnum's Museum in Baltimore and he would go with them by boat from Baltimore to Fortress Monroe, where he would see them off under a flag of truce. "Write me what you think will be her determination even if she is doubtful." But Mrs. Bulloch had backed down at the last. The mere mention of her leaving, she explained to Susan West, was enough to make Mittie break down in tears. When word came that Daniel was dead, she expressed the one wish that she would never live so long as to know that Irvine too was dead or that Richmond had fallen.

With his work in Washington drawing to a close, Theodore regretted he had not kept a diary. "All those whom I have seen in social intercourse day by day will be characters in history," he surmised, "and it would be pleasant hereafter [to read] my own impressions of them and recall their utterly different views upon the policy which should be pursued by the government."

Interestingly, his letters contain little or nothing of his feelings about the war itself or the direction it was taking. There is no sorrow expressed over the butchery and waste of it, nor any excitement over its pageantry. "Tell Bamie that the streets are all lined with wagons," he writes, ". . . that I have a soldier who always rides behind me to show me the way . . . and that several times soldiers here have pointed their guns at me to make me stop when I was riding through their lines." But that is about as far as he ever goes to suggest there is even a war in progress. It was his way of sparing Mittie, no doubt. The one note of tragedy in the entire picture he gives of wartime Washington is the death of the Lincolns' son Willie.

On a Sunday in March 1862, with snow falling outside his hotel window, he seems to have been trying to boost both their spirits by telling her what several high-ranking officers had been telling him, namely, that the war would be over by May. Even so, he confessed to feeling very sad: "I wish we sympathized together on this question of so vital moment to our country, but I know you cannot understand my feelings, and of course I do not expect it." This is the one known mention of even the existence of an issue between them, and to judge by the remembrances of their children, it was as demonstrative on the matter as either ever became.

The war, of course, did not end in May, but ground on for another three years. The work for the Allotment Commission continued, principally in upstate New York, he, Dodge, and Bronson having been named by Lincoln as New York's three Allotment Commissioners. In one two-month stretch Theodore spent, by his own reckoning, thirty-one nights sleeping on trains. "Thee," remarked his mother-in-law, "is a good young man. I really think if anyone ever tried to do their duty he does."

He received no pay for his efforts and the consensus was that he, as much as anyone, was responsible for the program's success. The grand total of the money sent home to soldiers' dependents as a result ran to many millions of dollars.

His family's health remained a constant concern the whole while. Mittie's troubles are never spelled out very clearly in the surviving record, but the summer of their stay at Long Branch she was being subjected to treatments with ether, treatments that greatly alarmed her mother. ("I think it was really running the risk of losing her life, or her reason.") Teedie's asthma, now spoken of by name, grew steadily more alarming, the "sweet invigorating sea breeze" of Long Branch notwithstanding. No sooner had the family arrived at the hotel than he was hit by an attack and had to be rushed back to a doctor in New York; then returning from the city he was struck a second time and so Theodore and Mittie took him off to Saratoga, leaving the others in the charge of Grandmamma.

Elsewhere we read that Bamie suffered with eyestrain, that Mittie was again having "palpitations" and "much pain about the region of the heart."

Troubles or not, Mittie kept pace with her husband and in a style the long indestructible Grandmamma was beginning to find exhausting and a bit inappropriate. In November 1863, when the Russian fleet paid a ceremonial visit to New York, a grand ball was staged at the Academy of Music, the great Russian Ball as it was to be remembered. Theodore took a leading part, served as secretary, lent his name to the announcements. "Thee was anxious for Mittie to go for political reasons," Grandmamma told Susan, "and Mittie would not go without Anna. So they both went." Grandmamma was not pleased. Life was too precious to be squandered on "trifles."

So much activity "confuses me," she wrote again from East

20th Street at the close of the year. "I think it ought to be a calm time for reflection. . . . But alas, there is too much gaiety. . . . There is so 'much to do' as to leave little time to think. Mittie and Thee give a large party New Year's evening. All *day* they will receive visitors. Just imagine how tiresome it will be."

"The reception is going on downstairs," she continued the next day. "Mittie and Anna are dressed beautifully and I hear the carriages constantly coming to the door."

· 4 ·

GRANDMAMMA DIED the following autumn, October 1864, at age sixty-five, and was buried across the river in Brooklyn's Green-wood-Cemetery, that incomparable Valhalla of nineteenth-century New York wherein are to be found so many of the kind—unsavory political bosses, Plymouth Church abolitionists—that the proud old southern lady could not abide. The following spring, in the first week of April, Richmond fell and a week later came Appomattox. The war was over. On April 25, with the city's church bells tolling, Lincoln's funeral procession marched up Broadway, and a photograph taken as it passed the CVS Roosevelt house at Union Square shows the heads of two small children in an open window on the second floor. It is believed they are Teedie and Ellie.

Of Mittie's original thirteen brothers and sisters four were still alive. Captain James Bulloch and brother Irvine had survived the war but, because of their involvement with the *Alabama*, were excluded temporarily from pardon and so took up residence in Liverpool, England. Susan remained in Philadelphia and Anna, the year following, 1866, was married to James K. Gracie, a New York banker, and moved to a home of her own. The house at Roswell, like the whole town, had been miraculously spared in Sherman's sweep through Georgia, but the old way of life there was ended forever. House and property were sold off.

Yet for all this—or perhaps because of it—Mittie entered upon a new life, very much renewed in spirit. She became, in the years immediately following the war, a figure of real consequence, or at least within the limits imposed by gender and the social order. To her already stunning physical beauty was now added the luster of success. She became a personage, quite as much as her husband, one of the great ladies of New York and one to whom society could naturally turn for example and leadership. She, the southerner, the outsider, ranked with Mrs. Hamilton Fish, Mrs. Lewis Rutherfurd, Mrs. Belmont, and the two Mrs. Astors as one of those "gentlewomen of such birth, breeding and tact that people were always glad to be led by them . . . whose entertainments claimed most comment, whose fiat none were found to dispute," to quote a contemporary authority, Mrs. Burton Harrison.

The great failings of the era, Grandmamma Bulloch had lectured, were "excessive extravagance and fondness for show." One must always choose the best in the way of furniture and the like but "avoid ostentation." But now, with her mother dead, Mittie did over the house, brightened up the parlor with pale French wallpaper, reupholstered the furniture in sky-blue damask. Her teas were attended by decorous little maids in lilac print dresses, white caps and aprons, and she invariably held center stage. In the "graciousness of her manner and that inherent talent for winning and holding the sympathetic interest of those around her," wrote Mrs. Harrison, "I have seen none to surpass her."

The one great mystery to Mrs. Harrison, as to others apparently, was why such radiant beauty and charm had failed to reappear among her four offspring. "Why nature, having found such a combination, should not be content with repeating it!"

Other transplanted southerners were to attain positions of influence in the city's postwar era, including such notable fellow Georgians as Charles C. Jones and John Elliott Ward, both attorneys, and the fawning Ward McAllister, whose social edicts held sway for more than a generation (it was he who invented the "Four Hundred"). But no southern woman had quite the presence of Mittie Roosevelt, or would be remembered so fondly for her irrepressible southern ways.

On an evening when he was a guest at dinner, John Hay happened to mention spending some time with his sister and, as Bamie recalled, Mittie suddenly looked at him in astonishment. "You have a sister?" she said. "Yes, I have a sister," Hay responded happily, "and I had a mother and a father, though I have always realized that you thought of me as being like Melchizedek, without beginning or end."

"Mother was embarrassed," wrote Bamie, "because, with her little aristocratic, southern feeling she had always considered Mr. Hay's family connection as entirely negligible."

She remained immutably herself. "There is nothing more like a Roosevelt than a Roosevelt wife," it would be said within the tribe, but in her case this was patently not so and never would be.

Neither the sufferings of the poor nor the call of the Christian faith touched her in the way they did her husband. She played no part in his good works, and those speculations on life in the hereafter or the status of one's soul, speculations that appear in Theodore's correspondence (as in a large proportion of private correspondence from that high-Victorian day), are not to be found in what she wrote. She was not an agnostic exactly. It was just that for her religion never became the central, pervading part of life it was for Theodore, or that it had been for her mother. ("If she was only a Christian, I think I could feel more satisfied," Mrs. Bulloch had lamented near the close of her life.) When Mittie found exhilaration or beauty in a church service, it was nearly always from the music.

In time to come a good deal would be said and repeated in print about her inadequacies and eccentricities. In the reminiscences of Roosevelt descendants who never knew her, she would be compared to her husband, measured against his strength, his Christian spirit, and nearly always to her disadvantage. And thus in many published accounts she has been kindly but pointedly dismissed as decorative and inconsequential, lovable enough in her way, but without weight, a sort of chatty, indolent, cliché southern belle prone to sick headaches and silly about money. The picture is not only unfair and inaccurate, it is considerably less interesting than the truth. As her letters and the observations of innumerable contemporaries attest, including those of her children and husband, she was an exceptional person in her own right, and a large part of that aliveness, the feeling for words, the warmth of personality that were to characterize the most outstanding of her children came from her.

The stories of her eccentricities are nearly all based on a later time in her life and seldom take into account several important factors. She was, for example, enormously fond of the color white and dressed in white more than any other shade, even in winter. In later years, as a widow, she seldom wore anything but white, which, to be sure, set her off as something out of the ordinary. But then one also finds in Theodore's correspondence that he greatly preferred her in white and liked to picture her in white whenever they were apart.

She wanted things in her life to be clean—clean house, clean clothes, clean children. Feverish bursts of housekeeping would leave her so exhausted she had to take to her bed. She bathed daily and always twice—the first time to wash, the second to rinse. She also had a stubborn reluctance to do anything on time. But considering her background, such behavior is not especially bizarre or incomprehensible and may perhaps be seen as very human responses to the two aspects of northern city life that distressed her most—excessive dirt and excessive hurry. Beyond her walls, and not far beyond, was a world of squalor and disease of a kind she had probably never imagined before coming to New York—families living in rat-infested cellars, people by the thousands packed into foul tenements. Smallpox and scarlet fever were rampant; typhus was worst of all. In one miserable house on East 17th Street there were 135 cases of typhus in the single year of 1869. For someone raised in Roswell, Georgia, it was no easy thing living with such realities, any more than it was to accept as axiomatic the idea that life must be played out according to timetables and the dictates of the clock.

As for the lavish expenditures, they too came later, when, as it happens, there was a very large amount of Roosevelt money with which to be lavish. If she was extragavant in Theodore's eyes, he apparently never said so. Indeed, in another of his letters dating from this earlier day, he tells her that she, by nature, is more economical than he and better suited to look after the family finances.

That she was and remained chronically troubled by sick spells and mysterious upsets is indisputable. She would be hit by what she called "my horror," violent intestinal trouble of some kind, perhaps brought on by a nervous condition, and perhaps not. She was put on restricted diets; she did retire to her room on occasion, not to return for hours. But this, it must be stressed, was not uncommon among women of her day and for someone of such exquisite, fragile beauty it was almost expected. Theodore worried incessantly over her health, even when she appears to have been perfectly fine. It was his way of expressing his love for her. She was his to protect and care for. "I have always been accustomed to think of you as one of my little babies," he tells her at one point, and at another implores, "Do not become a strong-minded woman." "My loving tyrant," she called him.

Yet there is no evidence that her health ever kept Mittie from doing anything she wanted to do, and there was no complaining on her part. It was she, not Theodore, who liked to stay up late talking, writing letters, who could quite literally wear him out with her "gaiety." On the first trip to Europe, as will be seen, she could keep a pace—set a pace—that would have left most healthy women her age exhausted.

Her children adored her and found her no less remarkable in her way than their father. "I have just received your letter!" Teedie once wrote. "What an excitement. . . . What long letters you do write. I don't see how you can write them." She could quote Dickens, Shakespeare. She "rushed into conversation," made conversation come alive. She was the first to see the humor in a situation. Teedie sternly praying that the Rebel troops be ground to powder had struck her as wonderfully funny, whereas Theodore, on hearing the story, had told him never to do it again. It was she who first insisted that Bamie be taken to the theater and to galleries, before the age when most children were permitted such things. It was she who induced Theodore to take them all abroad that spring of 1869.

Her "devotion wrapped us round as with a mantle," wrote Conie; hers was "the most loving heart imaginable." Yet "in spite of this rare beauty and her wit and charm, she never seemed to know that she was unusual in any degree . . ."

CHAPTER THREE

Grand Tour

· 1 ·

THE ROOSEVELTS SAILED the afternoon of May 12 on the *Scotia*, finest of the Cunard Line's paddle steamers and still, in 1869, the fastest ship to Europe. With Mary Ann, the nursemaid, they made a party of seven and we may picture them coming aboard in the bright sunshine of a spring day in New York, the ship's deck crowded with trunks and porters and several hundred other passengers, everybody looking exceptionally well turned out (the *Scotia* offered only first-class accommodations), and many, like the Roosevelts, traveling with children and servants. Among the familiar faces were Mr. and Mrs. Leopold Seligman and their three children; Mrs. Jesse Seligman and her daughter; the actor Lester Wallock, who was traveling with his wife and two young sons; the Egerton Winthrops and their three children. (Egerton Winthrop, a cultivated, superior-looking figure, was literally right out of an Edith Wharton novel: he was to appear in *The Age of Innocence* rather thinly disguised as the arch snob Sillerton Jackson, who carried between his narrow temples "most of the scandals and mysteries that had smouldered under the unruffled surface of New York society.")

To be going abroad was not the rare thing it once had been. Americans were crisscrossing the Atlantic, resolutely "doing" Europe's galleries and monuments, hiking the Alps, taking the waters in a dozen different spas, filling the best hotels, in numbers that would have been unheard of before the war. So near and common-

place had Europe become, announced the popular travel writer
Bayard Taylor, that he would write no more on the subject. It was
the year of *The Innocents Abroad,* Mark Twain's often jeering declaration that a touch of Old World culture was neither beyond the
ken of the ordinary citizen nor anything to be afraid of. "I basked
in the happiness of being for once in my life drifting with the tide
of a great popular movement," Twain wrote of his sojourn abroad.

Those notable Americans discovering Europe as tourists that
same year included such disparate figures as Jefferson Davis, who
went for his health, and young Henry James, who was finding
every other American he met "vulgar, vulgar, vulgar." Numerous
wealthy Americans, moreover, had happily taken up residence
abroad as a more or less permanent thing, and among their offspring, contemporaries of the Roosevelt children, were little Edith
Jones (the future Edith Wharton), John Singer Sargent, and Jennie
Jerome (the future Mrs. Randolph Churchill).

Still, for the Roosevelts it was a momentous undertaking, a first
complete break from the established pattern of their lives, a first
adventure as a family. In part, of course, they were going because
it was the thing to do—for the "cultural enrichment" of the experience. The children would "benefit," young as they were. Mittie
had never been out of the country. She wanted to see her brothers
in Liverpool and to be shown some of what Theodore had seen in
his own earlier travels. But they were going also for Teedie's
health. Grandfather Roosevelt, who came to see them off, later
wrote the child a little rhyme:

> We all shall gladly see you back
> Again at your home,
> And hope that sickness may no more
> Compel your feet to roam.

They were to be gone a year, which to the children seemed
like forever. On the ride from the house to the pier, Teedie had
cried most of the way.

The first several days at sea were so calm and clear that even
Theodore, a lifelong sufferer from seasickness, fared quite well.
Not until the fourth day out, a Sunday, when the wind picked up,
did he and Teedie take to their berths. "As it was a little rough and
I a little sick and being down," Teedie wrote in his diary, "I could
not go to [church] service."

Mittie spent her days on deck, wrapped up happily in a chair, enjoying the view and the salt tang of the air, chatting, reading (a popular romance called *The Heir of Redclyffe*), writing long letters to Anna, and keeping a weather eye on Teedie, who alone of her four refused to have anything to do with the other children on board. Elliott, as she told Anna, had quickly become the leader of the children's sports and played with the Winthrop children nearly all day.

The ship suited her perfectly. The air on deck was a bit sharper than she wished and the grand salon was invariably overheated, but she had grown to feel quite at home.

Six days out, as they entered the Gulf Stream, the weather turned warmer and Teedie at last found a friend. "I made the acquaintance of Mr. St. John, a most interesting gentleman from the West Indies," he wrote that night. "We had a long talk in the cabin after supper."

Mr. St. John—Thomas B. St. John, according to the passenger list—was traveling alone for his health and appeared to know no one. His name was pronounced "Singen," Mittie explained to Anna. He was a "quaint little well of knowledge" who suffered from heart trouble and spoke barely above a whisper, but whose interest in the natural sciences "fills Teedie's heart with delight." Teedie had introduced him very formally. "Mama, have you conversed with Mr. St. John?" he asked, as she put down her book. "I feel so tenderly to Teedie," she told Anna.

The afternoon of Friday, May 21, they were steaming through the smooth bottle-green waters of the Irish Sea, the coast of Wales on the starboard. By turns with a telescope, they picked out windmills and farmhouses along shore, then, with much excitement, the suspension bridge at Holyhead. By nightfall, having crossed some three thousand miles of ocean in nine days, they entered the Mersey at Liverpool.

> It was one wild scene of commotion [said Mittie of their arrival]. Passengers all ready, luggage heaped up, children fretting (not mine) . . . Custom House officers busy examining the trunks . . . all done by the aid of lamps . . . Finally a tender neared us on each side. . . . Thee suddenly said here they are, Irvine and brother Jimmie. Imagine our excitement! One gentleman would stay with the trunks thusly. Thee would find a trunk, Irvine sit on it until another was found. . . .

One person only seemed oblivious to what was happening. Teedie sat off to himself in the salon, reading a book. "Strange child!" his mother mused. She must wake him up to the world, "and *make him observe.*"

She herself seems to have missed nothing, her own considerable powers of observation plainly heightened by an unbound delight in being where she was and who she was.

The first several days with her brothers were filled with breathless talk and laughter. It had been eight years since she had seen Captain James Bulloch, and her one brief meeting with Irvine in that time had been under such strained circumstances that it seemed more like something they had imagined. A year or so after the war he had returned to New York illegally under an assumed name, working his way across on a sailing ship in order to see Mittie and Anna for all of an hour. They had been told nothing of the plan. An unsigned note in the morning mail said merely that at three on Thursday a young man "of interest" would be in the mall at Central Park, standing beneath the third tree on the left, a red handkerchief about his neck. They did as directed and when the hour was up he left for his ship and the return voyage to Liverpool.

Now, at twenty-seven, Irvine was a lanky, clean-shaven, altogether proper southern expatriate and Liverpool businessman who, Theodore observed, smoked his pipe as if it were the serious duty of his life. At the moment, he was also much in love with the daughter of an American couple living in Liverpool, Ella Sears.

Irvine, Ella, Mr. and Mrs. Sears, "brother Jimmie," his small children, and his wife, Hattie (Harriott Cross Foster, whom he had married before the war), converged on the hotel the first morning, Hattie hugging and kissing Mittie and crying profusely. After that there were drives in a varnished landau through Liverpool's Princess Park and a longer excursion to the suburbs down country roads with hawthorn hedges in bloom. Mittie picked her first primrose and cowslip. ("You have no idea of my enthusiasm," she told Anna. "You know every poet from Shakespeare mentions 'sweet cowslip and primrose.' ") Another day, May 24, they went to brother Jimmie's home at Waterloo, twenty minutes by train, where the children played on the beach and at dinner the "grown people" toasted the Queen's birthday (Victoria had turned fifty) and sang and danced until time to catch the last train back to Liverpool.

James and Irvine Bulloch had established themselves in the cotton business in Liverpool and managed to survive as well as they did largely through the contacts James had made during the war. Of the two, James was plainly the leader, a big, vital man with a military bearing and resplendent muttonchop whiskers. No English colonel looked more like an English colonel. As the young captain of a U.S. mail steamer before the war, he had impressed Richard Henry Dana as the model American officer—in his book *To Cuba and Back*, Dana told what a pleasure it was to stroll the deck with a man of such good cheer and obvious ability—and now in middle age he was said to be the personification of Thackeray's Colonel Newcome, the beloved ultimate gentleman of Victorian prose. He was kindly, reserved, rarely talked about himself or of his former exploits, which, as it happens, were again very much in the news. The Roosevelts had arrived—his little New York nieces and nephews were casting their eyes upon him for the first time—just as his former creation, the *Alabama*, had become a headline issue once again on both sides of the Atlantic.

The *Alabama* Claims, claims against Britain for damages done by the Confederate raider—*his* ship—had been made a thundering cause in Washington by the chairman of the Committee on Foreign Relations, Senator Charles Sumner of Massachusetts. Britain's involvement with the *Alabama* had doubled the length of the war, Sumner claimed, and the damages therefore might exceed $100 million. (In fact, in her two years at sea the *Alabama* had destroyed fifty-eight commercial vessels valued at $6,547,000.) "When civilization was fighting a last battle with slavery," Sumner declared in a famous speech, "England gave her name, her influence, her material resources to the wicked cause. . . ." Popular opinion in the United States was strongly behind him. The speech had roused a response in the Congress and the country of a kind that set the British back on their heels. Cartoons in the British press at the time the Roosevelts arrived portrayed an American brigand, his belt full of revolvers and knives, calculating how much he might make John Bull pay. Publications normally friendly to the United States—*The Spectator, The Pall Mall Gazette*, the London *Daily News*—denounced Sumner and his claims and said the whole nation "would go to war twenty times over" rather than accept such a national humiliation.

The crux of the issue was the degree to which the government had knowingly participated in the creation of the *Alabama* and under what circumstances the ship had escaped from Liverpool to begin her reign of destruction—in other words, to what extent had James D. Bulloch been aided and abetted in his efforts. If ever there was a central character to a drama it was he, he being the one man who knew all that happened and why, and had this been another, later day, he would have been made a newspaper and television sensation, an international somebody, overnight. As it was, the arrival of his sister and her family remained the sole disruption in the sedate life he had fashioned in exile, and his treasured privacy survived intact.

To the Roosevelt children, he and Irvine were almost mythical in stature. Here were two of the heroic figures from Mittie's stories, the real thing at last. Had some marvelous heroes from one of their books materialized before their eyes, the effect would not have been much greater. And most obviously stirred was Teedie, whose hunger for adventure in any printed or spoken form was insatiable and whose private musings on large matters of historic consequence were sometimes so out of proportion with his physical size and age as to be strangely amusing. ("Father," he would ask apropos of nothing a little later on in the trip, "did Texas wish to annex itself to the United States?")

"It was from the heroes of my favorite stories," he would explain as a grown man, "from hearing of the feats performed by my southern forefathers and kinsfolk, and from knowing my father [that] I felt great admiration for men who were fearless . . . and I had a great desire to be like them." To a crowd gathered in his honor at Roswell, he would one day tell in detail how his Uncle Irvine Bulloch had stuck to his post to the last as the guns of the United States corvette *Kearsarge* raked the *Alabama*. When the *Alabama* went down off Cherbourg, Irvine was among those survivors rescued by the British yacht *Deerhound,* and afterward he served on the raider *Shenandoah,* preying on whalers in the Bering Strait.

James Bulloch's story was larger, more important, more the stuff of fiction. His influence on the boy was to be considerable.

His original mission, as defined in orders from Jefferson Davis, had been to build "with the quickest possible dispatch" six steam vessels in England, for which the Confederate Congress appropriated a total of a million dollars. He had arrived in Liverpool in June 1861, and the first ship, *Florida,* was ready in less than a year. Then followed the *Alabama,* originally known as *No. 290,* because she was the two hundred ninetieth ship built at the Laird yards in Liverpool. Launching of the *Florida* had greatly alarmed the American minister to Britain, Charles Francis Adams, so everything concerning *No. 290* had to be done under secrecy and with unstinting sensitivity on Bulloch's part to the British laws that forbade the building of warships for belligerents. "I cannot exaggerate, sir, the caution and tact required to get a ship to sea with even the external appearance of a man-of-war," he wrote to James M. Mason, the Confederate diplomatic agent in London. *No. 290*, furthermore, was to be no ordinary ship and he expected to be given her command.

He had designed her specifically as a commerce raider, rather than for combat with other warships—900 tons, 230 feet in length, and drawing, when provisioned and coaled, all of 15 feet. Rigged as a barkentine, she carried large fore and aft sails and handled as well under sail as under steam—as most such vessels did not— because he had devised a means whereby, in a matter of minutes, the propeller could be detached and lifted high enough out of the water not to slow her down. Top speed was to be about thirteen knots. John Laird, the builder, thought her the finest cruiser of her class in the world.

The plan was for the ship to leave Liverpool as an innocent-looking merchantman, to be armed later in the Azores. He picked the island of Terceira as the rendezvous, secretly arranged for the purchase of armaments and stores, and had these sent by another ship, again devising detailed instructions for every necessary step. All in all it was a brilliant performance and things were falling together nicely, until Charles Francis Adams, supplied by his own agent in Liverpool, presented the British government with proof of what was afoot. The situation could have gone either way, but the Queen's Advocate went insane at this juncture; the documents supplied by Adams sat untouched for five crucial days, and Bulloch, determined to get the ship out of British waters, took her to sea himself, "very unexpectedly." Only by the narrowest margin did he bring it off. He arranged for a British crew, and on the morning of July 29, 1862, the still incomplete *No. 290* started down the Mersey draped in bright bunting and carrying a large party of fashionable ladies and gentlemen who had been invited for a short trial run and a picnic lunch. Several customs officials were also aboard to see that "no international wrong" was perpetrated. But about noon, a tug came alongside, the guests were put off, and *No. 290* sailed away—north through the Irish Sea—never to return. Bulloch had himself put ashore on the north coast of Ireland and made his way back to Liverpool. Three weeks later he was in the Azores seeing to final preparations before turning the ship over to Captain Raphael Semmes of the Confederate Navy, his superiors at home having decided his services on land were invaluable.

That he failed in a later attempt to build two ironclad rams at the Laird yards—ships which, in the long run, would have done far greater damage to the Union cause than did the *Alabama*—was due to the grim, unequivocal declaration by Charles Francis Adams to Foreign Secretary Lord John Russell that should the rams leave Liverpool, it would mean war.

Teedie's allegiance to the Union side—to his father's side—remained as passionate as always. Passing through Liverpool some months earlier, Jefferson Davis had enrolled his son in the same school at Waterloo attended by Teedie's cousin, and when Teedie and Ellie ran into the Davis boy during a visit to the school, "sharp words ensued," as Teedie reported proudly in his diary. But there could be no stigma surrounding James Bulloch, not ever. As an adult, Teedie would remember Uncle Jimmie as a "blessed" figure, "as valiant and simple and upright a soul as ever lived . . . one of the best men I have ever known." An important bond grew between them—important to each and to the writing of naval history—and this Liverpool visit of 1869 marked the beginning. It would be his very pro-Union nephew, ultimately, who persuaded James Bulloch to write the book only he could write, setting forth his part in the war and all he knew concerning the *Alabama*. (Called *The Secret Service of the Confederate States in Europe*, it appeared in two volumes in 1883.) And James Bulloch, in turn, would provide invaluable assistance to his nephew's own first effort as a historian, a study of the naval side of the War of 1812—all this taking place years after the *Alabama* Claims had been settled, the issue laid to rest.

The Roosevelts left Liverpool by train June 2, their party now increased to eight with the addition of a newly hired valet by name of Noel Paovitch. They were bound for the Lake Country and to Scotland, heading north, their first stop at Furness Abbey, the magnificent ruin of a monastery founded in the twelfth century in what had been the wilds of Icelandic-speaking Furness. It was a stop of only a night and a day and much that they were to see afterward was to be still grander in scale and more evocative in spirit, but the abbey was their maiden encounter with Europe's truly ancient past. They were on their own as tourists for the first time.

A tremendous complex covering some sixty-five acres, the abbey was set in a hidden valley named Bekangesgill in Icelandic, or the Vale of the Deadly Nightshade, "from the deadly herb," Mittie explained excitedly to Anna, "which with henbane grows here . . . two flourishing specimens of the former in one of the curved archways." Once a remote empire unto itself, the abbey and its way of life had survived unchallenged for centuries. The buildings were of red sandstone—a monumental church, cloisters, quarters for the lay brothers and novices, the abbot's private chapel, an infirmary, offices, school—and these with gardens and orchards and cemetery, as well as a modern hotel, were all contained within a great encircling wall. The end had come with Henry VIII and his break with Rome. The abbey was abandoned, roofs caved in, gates, windows, anything salvageable had been carted off long since. But the remaining shells of buildings were awesome. Among connoisseurs of ruins, of whom there were a great many in that Victorian day, they were considered among the choicest of all. What had been the floor of the abbey was now vivid green turf speckled with bluebells and buttercups and there were as yet no restrictions as to where one could walk or climb; everything was open to all comers and for children, a glorious playground.

The light of day was nearly gone when the Roosevelts arrived and a fine rain was falling, blotting out all but the barest outlines. It was only the next morning that the scale and power of the place burst upon them. The sun was shining, the day spectacular, with a few foamy clouds trailing overhead in a soft blue sky. The family was up and dressed by six and following breakfast set off with guidebooks in hand. The three small children, seeing the sweep of green turf, raced ahead, through archways, up broken staircases, then up a spiral stairway to the belfry, then to the top of what had been a water tower, where they "saw it all." "When we three were on the belfry," wrote Mittie, recounting for Anna the somewhat more sedate route she had taken with Theodore and Bamie, "on the opposite side were the three children peeping through one of the . . . lancet windows. . . . We beckoned to them and in a trice they all raced down, up the nave of the church and mounted the belfry steps. As I write . . . the children are climbing over the 'Porter's Lodge' (ruin). . . . It would be impossible to tell you all. . . ."

In the chancel, immediately in front of the high altar base, they stood before the stone effigy of a crusader, thought to be William de Lancaster, eighth Baron of Kendal, who died in 1246. By the way the moss had grown, the figure's stone limbs and sword were perfectly delineated. From the cracked stone helmet of another effigy Mittie picked a dandelion. Thrilled by the whole romantic spell of the place she found herself "gazing at the wide open windows and thinking how the glorious light must have streamed through . . . over the high altar [and] down upon the monks as they sang their solemn chants or the moonbeams when at their midnight devotions."

Her health was already improved, she told her sister. She had to watch what she ate, but could depict herself overall as "intensely interested and much freckled."

> We leave here at 5 PM for Windermere, where Noel and our baggage await us. . . . Thee and I wish for you incessantly. How you would appreciate it all. . . . I hurry to the close of this letter because I see Thee's coattails flitting around the ruined Abbey and he shall not know more than I do about it.

In the days that followed, as they cruised Lake Windermere and went on by train to Edinburgh, the weather held clear and fair. Mittie wished only that there were more time. Scotland was both a return to the ancestral home of the Bullochs and a literary pilgrimage to the world of Sir Walter Scott, who, with his love of the legendary and valorous, his open-air healthiness, his strong sense of the interlocking of human lives, appealed powerfully to the romantic Mittie. They saw Abbotsford, the sprawling stone mansion where Scott had lived like some feudal laird ("saw his clothes, . . . petrified things and armor and curiosities," wrote Teedie), traveled to Dryburgh to pay homage at Scott's tomb. In the Trossachs, the setting of Scott's epic poem *The Lady of the Lake,* Mittie felt "as though we were on magic ground." One fine morning they hiked beside Loch Katrine, as Theodore marched along reading the poem aloud. *"Hail to the Chief who in triumph advances!"*

"We had a charming drive on top of [the] coach, between Loch Katrine and Lomond," Mittie told Anna, "and steamed up the latter . . . which was beautiful all the time. I could not help thinking of the highland songs dear mother used to sing. . . ."

Then they turned south again, from Edinburgh to York, an exhausting, sooty eight hours "in the cars" relieved by some of the most appealing scenery of the whole trip: distant blue glances of the Firth of Forth, small white beaches, rolling surf, rolling country; then red-tiled Berwick-upon-Tweed and the Tweed emptying into the North Sea; then fields of sheep and cattle followed by Newcastle-upon-Tyne with its huddled houses and tall chimneys and thick yellow smoke. After this everything became more soft and green, more thoroughly English, Mittie thought, the hawthorn "perfectly lovely." She adored landscapes with "everything like the most perfect picture."

They were two days in York; then came Leamington (and Warwick Castle), Oxford, and, finally, London on June 21. Except for the time on trains, most every day was given to "hard sightseeing." And if not exploring a Roman wall (at York) or exclaiming over the heroic proportions of a Saxon giant's porridge bowl (at Warwick Castle) or seeing "some collages" (as Teedie wrote at Oxford), Mittie and the children were usually buried in their books, which, by the time they reached London, had been read and reread to such an extent that she had to go out and buy a "fresh lot." A few months later, in Venice, Teedie would reckon that since leaving New York they had read fifty books.

At times the strain would show. Bamie's feet had become so blistered in Scotland she could barely walk. Teedie's asthma kicked up once before reaching London and Ellie too suffered several days with a bad throat, then took offense when told to ease up and miss part of one day's touring. "I want to learn about things, too, like Teedie," he insisted.

Yet the pace only quickened. In three weeks' time there were repeated expeditions to the London Zoo and to the British Museum. They "did" Hampton Court, Kensington Gardens and Museum, the Tower of London, Westminster Abbey, Madame Tussaud's Wax Museum, and the "very wonderful" Crystal Palace, where the two boys were transfixed by a mechanical figure that played chess and they begged to go back again the next day. The zoo called for five visits.

She had seen *the real Rosetta Stone,* Mittie exclaimed in a letter to Anna following a day at the British Museum. She had seen the prayer book carried to the scaffold by Lady Jane Grey ("her own notes written in it!"), the original manuscripts of Pope's *Iliad*, Scott's *Kenilworth*, letters from Mary Queen of Scots, Elizabeth, Charles the First, Cromwell, George Washington. "Etc., etc." From the Ladies' Gallery at the House of Commons, she and Bamie watched the members nodding, laughing, doing "anything they pleased," their hats on, while one of their number droned on about cattle plague.

Shopping at Sears & Wells, she had the three youngest children fitted in matching sailor suits, with white braid and red silk ties, Conie's differing only in that it had a skirt. Time was made for riding lessons for the boys, Teedie's wheeze notwithstanding, and for innumerable "splendid romps" in Hyde Park under the surveillance of Mary Ann or Noel Paovitch, the latter, somewhere along the line, having acquired a red fez.

Most evenings about six, Mittie and Theodore took an hour's drive in the park and one Saturday, their last in London, they attended a party given by the Duke of Devonshire, a high point for Mittie and a chance to exercise her powers of observation (albeit with "furtive glances" only) for the benefit of sister Anna, whose interest in great houses, clothes, jewelry, and English gentry was apparently no less than her own. The following is only part of a letter written at top speed from the Netherlands several days later.

I wore my pale-green silk, lace cap arranged as a bertha and some lovely pale-pink real rosebuds in my hair which Bamie arranged prettily. We arrived at Devonshire House, Piccadilly W. . . . where we were met by policemen and servants in livery knee breeches, etc., now ushered into the first vestibule, more servants, into second vestibule, more liveried servants. Instead of being taken into dressing rooms, in this vestibule a servant behind a kind of counter covered with red cloth . . . took our cloaks, giving tickets in return. We ascended a beautiful wide winding staircase of pure white marble, *glass banisters;* about midway, a servant [who was] standing at [the] head of [the] stairs, then ushered us into the Saloon (I suppose), a beautiful very large room. Lord and Lady Frederick Cavendish [Lord Frederick was the son of the Duke of Devonshire] came up immediately, very cordially. She is a little like Mrs. Jimmie Dreer, taller, was dressed not very prettily but stylishly, deep-pink silk, trimmed with some lace, large diamond ornaments arranged on pink ribbon round [her] neck, which was tied behind in long streamers, wreath of pink roses and green leaves. Lord Frederick is [a] sweet, clean-looking person, very diffident, he is in the House of Commons. He introduced his father as "My father the Duke," who had the broad blue ribbon and star of the Order of Bath, blazing with diamonds. He received us very cordially. I forgot to say "Your Grace," but talked along quite pleasantly . . . [the] room was gold and white with beautiful pictures, soft carpet in-half the room (the other half apparently inlaid and waxed), furniture and curtains blue and gold . . . this opened into [a] beautiful salon, frescoed, high ceiling lighted from above, furniture light blue and vapor color; in one corner [at a] table in [the] shape of [a] crescent, served by servants (some maids in caps) . . . delicious reviving tea in lovely little cups, then slices of bread and butter, cakes, and other very light things. There were lovely flowers; two small anterooms and supper rooms were all that were thrown open. The supper seemed only to consist of ices, and

fruits, all in brilliant-looking glass and china. . . . All the people as they entered shook hands with their host and each other.
I had no idea the English did this, as Americans are generally
accused of doing so. Lady Frederick introduced several of her
friends to me, among them the Duchess of Manchester, very
brilliantly dressed in pink and lace; Lady Waterford, whom
she said had been a great beauty, walked most splendidly . . .
a tiara of diamonds, pearls wound in with her black hair. Lady
DeViser (I think this was the name) in deep blue and Venetian
point lace, red cherries in her hair; her daughter, Lady Bath,
[a] sweet delicate, refined-looking person, plain white silk, no
trimming except fine lace in [the] neck, [a] little white ostrich
tip in her hair. There was one fat Begum in blue satin and lace
who walked slowly about . . . leaning on or should I say leading about a deaf, dumb, blind, lame, very ill-looking stick covered with orders. There was an old gentleman with soft gray
curls, excessively refined-looking . . . with an immense diamond ring. . . . I asked Lord Frederick who he was, but he did
not know, said that he went very little out. I was disappointed
because I had seen and been interested in this same old
gentleman at the Conversazzione at the Kensington Museum.
. . . When we were leaving, the servants would call out "Lord
so and so's carriage stops," the way just as you read in Miss
Edgeworth's novels. I enjoyed everything very much but
would have liked to have *gazed* more, had to content myself
with furtive glances out of the sides of my eyes. . . .

Teedie provided the single disruption of the London stay. His
asthma returned and a doctor who was called to the hotel, finding
nothing wrong with the boy's lungs, recommended that he be taken
to the seashore. So off Teedie had gone with his father to Hastings,
by train, early Saturday, July 3. They registered at the Queen's
Hotel fronting on the sea and after a very man-sized midday dinner
set out for a walk on the beach. As the day wore on, Teedie was
treated to a ride in a goat cart and in the late-afternoon sunshine
the powerful-looking bearded father and the sallow, spindly little
son hiked the steep path up Castle Hill, to a castle ruin from Saxon
times. From the hilltop they could look back on the town and their
hotel with its turrets and flags flying. The sky and sea were beautiful. Everything was beautiful to the boy. The dinner that night was
"the best dinner I ever had."
    At the close of the following day, Sunday, he would say simply,
"This is the happiest day I have ever spent." After church they had
again hiked to the castle, where this time Theodore conducted a

private outdoor Sunday school. Then they walked on several more miles, atop high limestone cliffs, the beach and surf far below. On the return trek they cheered the Fourth of July together with all the lung power they could muster, a "feeble attempt," Teedie conceded, but "such fun." Putting himself to bed that night, finding he had too little breath even to blow out his candle, he doused the flame in a tumbler of water and dropped blissfully off to sleep.

Back in London they found Mittie and Bamie at the National Gallery, making their way slowly through Hogarth's *Marriage à la Mode*. "Both had enjoyed Hastings very much," Mittie wrote. Teedie was "decidedly better."

· 2 ·

THE GRAND TOUR of the Continent that got under way at Antwerp was an enormously ambitious undertaking, given the means of transportation available, the size of the party, the ages of the children, the staggering quantity and variety of baggage to be looked after in that day of large, elaborate wardrobes. Even to a seasoned present-day traveler the course of the Roosevelts' journey across the map of Europe looks slightly overwhelming.

They reached Antwerp July 14, 1869, and were scheduled to sail for home exactly ten months later on the *Russia*, departing Liverpool, May 14, 1870. Between times they would travel several thousand miles by countless different trains, by river steamer, lake steamer, and rowboat (across Lake Como), by carriage and stagecoach, on horseback, by mule, by donkey, and on foot (through much of Switzerland). They would stay at sixty-six different hotels in eight countries (including Monaco) and the numbers of porters required at each stop, the numbers of room clerks, ticket agents, and headwaiters who had to be dealt with—with or without the benefit of English—may be imagined.

After several days of sightseeing in Antwerp, The Hague, and Amsterdam, they started up the Rhine from Cologne, visiting Mainz, Frankfort, Heidelberg, Baden, and Strasbourg. They were in Basel by the end of July and from there made a long, looping path through Switzerland, south first, through the Jura Mountains to Bern, then on to Geneva. They cut southeast across part of France to Mont Blanc and Chamonix, then northeast up the valley of the Rhone to Visp. There was a stop at Zermatt. The children threw snowballs on top of the Eggishorn. They saw the Rhone

Glacier, crossed the Grimsel Pass to Grindelwald, steamed down Lake Brienz to Interlaken, filling their lungs with a lake breeze scented by freshly cut hay. At Lucerne they spent a week with Theodore's former colleague on the Allotment Commission, Theodore Bronson, and his family, after which came the requisite ascent to the Rigi-Kulm. In Zurich they stopped at the famous Hotel Baur au Lac, with its flower gardens and meticulously raked gravel walks. In all, they were six weeks in Switzerland, Theodore's favorite part of Europe and the place, it was hoped, that would do the most for Teedie. "A course of travel of this sort," an English physician had written, ". . . in a pure and bracing air, under a bright sky, amid some of the most attractive and most impressive scenes in nature, in cheerful company . . . will do all that the best medicines can do . . . and much that they never can accomplish." Henry James, trudging over the Swiss Alps that same summer, described his exertions as "a pledge, a token of some future potency."

After Switzerland came the Italian lakes, then Milan, followed by a week in Venice. From Venice, September 25, they went by night boat across the Adriatic to Trieste and from there to Vienna by train, one of the longest legs of the journey. They were another week in Vienna, after which they turned west to Salzburg and Munich before making the swing north to Berlin by way of Nuremberg and Dresden. From Berlin they doubled back to Cologne, arriving in time for Teedie's birthday, October 27.

The month of November was spent in Paris. Then followed a tour of southern France (Dijon, Marseilles, Nice) en route to Italy for the winter. With the return of spring they were back in Paris for a second and last stay of nearly two months, after which they left for London, Liverpool, and the ship home.

In time-honored tourist fashion they gathered up quantities of guidebooks and keepsakes—photographs, rare coins, stamps, crystals, bits of rock, souvenir spoons—and like countless other Americans abroad, then and since, they took huge pleasure in running into other Americans abroad. But never did they take Europe lightly, or in the smug or mocking way some did. There were times of disappointment and disillusion—"sunny Italy," their first week there, was "cold, dreary, smelly"—but far more often they were exhilarated or deeply moved by scenery, by art, architecture, the places of history. If few families could have afforded such a year, fewer still would have attempted anything so ambitious or kept to their schedule with such energy. They did everything that was expected. They saw Venice by moonlight; at the Volksgarten in Vienna they thrilled to the strains of "The Beautiful Blue Danube" as rendered by Professor Strauss himself. They climbed the Arc de Triomphe and saw Emperor Napoleon III ride by in the Tuileries; they climbed the Tower of Pisa; they climbed Vesuvius. They saw *The Last Supper,* Pompeii, St. Peter's and the Pope (Pius IX)—all that was obligatory and considerably more. There was hardly a church of note, a palace or ruin or gallery or garden en route that escaped their collective perusal, all six—"the whole of us," as Teedie said—generally going everywhere in a body.

Children took sick. Teeth had to be tended to (a morning in Berlin was lost at a dentist's office), birthdays and Christmas were celebrated (with Mittie and Theodore putting on full dress for each such occasion). Correspondence had to be kept up. Word came of the panic on Wall Street that began September 24, Black Friday, and, later, of the death of Theodore's brother Weir. Still, the pilgrimage went resolutely forward and the fact that there were no serious snags in the plan anywhere en route, no train tickets lost or timetables misread, no troubles with hotel reservations that we know of, speaks highly for Theodore, who, it appears, was responsible for all the advance arrangements.

On balance, probably Switzerland was the best time for everyone. Conie, recalling the trip in later years, would write fondly of "weeks in the great Swiss mountains" and "lovely times when we were not obliged to think of sculpture or painting." The distances covered on their family hikes through the Alps seem almost incredible. On August 11, for example, crossing the Tête-Noire, Theodore went twenty-two miles, Bamie eighteen miles, Ellie twelve, Conie three. Mittie, the supposed invalid, walked nine miles, while Teedie went very nearly as far as his father, nineteen miles. On August 21, crossing the Grimsel Pass, Teedie walked twenty miles to Theodore's twenty-two and this at an altitude of seven thousand feet! At Lucerne Ellie and Teedie were both sick, Teedie depressed and homesick, but then the trip to the heights of the Rigi rapidly restored all spirits.

Known as the "island mountain," the Rigi stands by itself above lakes Lucerne and Zug, and to many thousand "sensitive souls" of that day the spectacle of sunset and sunrise from its summit, the Rigi-Kulm, was the climax of a visit to Switzerland. The "incredible horizon," as Victor Hugo called it, takes in nearly three hundred miles, an utterly dazzling panorama of Alps on one side (to the southeast) and on the other, beyond the lakes, the lovely

Zurich countryside reaching to the Juras. Traditionally one went to the top in time for sunset, as the Roosevelts did, then stayed the night at the hotel to be awakened before dawn by an Alpine horn, which the morning of September 4 sounded at quarter to five.

> Rose immediately [Mittie wrote], but did not get out in time to see the first pink lights before the sun rising. All the panorama of high Alpine peaks visible . . . Litlis and its glaciers, Finisterahorn, Schreckhorn, Wetterhorn, Jungfrau, and Silverhorn and Blumis Alps. The Wetterhorn was beautifully peaked and covered with snow. A mass of thick clouds laid at the same level all around the Rigi in the early morning, looking something as a glacier, with its rifts of gray color, completely hiding the lower world.

"Down the mountain a different way," exclaimed Teedie. "Papa and I walked most. . . . I had a splendid day." Later, in Nice, writing in his diary of a descent from another mountain, this with a view of the sea, he would describe "little Mama and Bamie trying to follow as fast as they could, all of us laughing and talking about what a nice time we were having and that this was a second Switzerland."

Teedie was the diarist of the trip. Two or three other journals were begun and fragments of some have survived. Mittie, in hers, has an eye for nature—she names trees, flowers, birds—and for the "romantic" spell of places like Lake Como. Conie has exceptionally good handwriting for a child her age and frequently demonstrates her own sense of the romantic. ("We got up when it was pitch dark," she writes at San Remo, ". . . and Ellie and I went all over the garden and stood by the Mediterranean and heard the roaring waves as they came dashing in.") But Teedie alone kept methodically at his record, never missing a day during the entire year, however much else was going on and no matter how miserable he felt.

The diary has survived intact and it is an amazing document filled with innumerable revelations, not the least of them concerning the author himself. In physical form, it is actually several small, cheap stiff-backed notebooks. The entries are in pencil, the pages are nearly all badly smudged and blurred, and the handwriting is dreadful, sometimes nearly impossible to read. But his eye for detail is exceptional and he can be startlingly thorough. "He takes a great deal of interest now in everything he sees," Mittie reported to Anna. Some of his inventories of "sights" seen in a single day run to as many as thirty or even fifty items. He is tremendously fond of castles and of armor and armaments of all kinds, of fresh raspberries and dogs of any size or breed wherever he finds them. He loves all things Roman—Pompeii, Hadrian's Villa, Roman coins, Roman walls, the Colosseum. "I . . . was given by Papa what in my wildest dream I had never thought to have," he says at Naples, "a Roman vase and coin. Just think of it!!!"

There is an obvious interest in nature, but of the birds and animals that figure in the running chronicle, it is the bear that has the strongest fascination—a dancing bear at Lake Windermere, a game of "wild bears and hunting" with Conie and Ellie in the park at London and again in the Tuileries in Paris, a bear clock that he sees in a shop at Bern. At Florence he takes pad and pencil to the zoo to do a drawing of a bear.

Another entry made at Florence, a mention of a visit to "Mr. Elliot's where we saw a beautiful book of birds written by him," is of particular interest, since this was Daniel Giraud Elliot, the great American ornithologist whose collection of bird specimens, the finest collection then extant, was about to be acquired by the new American Museum of Natural History. Daniel Elliot was tall and bearded and enormously dignified. As a child he too had been "delicate in health."

The manner at times is wonderfully pompous. It is easy to imagine the response had he so expressed himself among other American boys his age. At the end of the day at Oxford he writes, "I had a headache and Conie and Ellie made a tremendous noise playing at my expense and rather laughed when I remonstrated. . . ." He declares of the route to Genoa, "this railroad is an abomination." The standard word of approval is "splendid" and once in Florence he is forced to excuse himself from play in order to "arrange my pantaloons."

That he was enjoying himself the large proportion of the time, and nearly always when his health was right, is apparent throughout. Page after page he is having "fine fun," "a great play," "great fun." There are touches of humor ("We are to write all our letters four pages, so much the worse for our friends!") and one surprising, pleasurable moment at Ellie's birthday party in Rome when he is kissed by a little girl named Elliese Van Schaack "as the boy she loved best in the room."

This memorable account of a battle that took place on the Pincian Hill in Rome is from the entry of January 15, 1870:

We had a splendid day today. Ellie went out to get a sword and gun and I went to Mrs. Dickey's for Charlie. Going back . . . we met Ellie with gun and sword. He lent the gun to Charlie and I picked up some stones. I was a little rebellious soldier. Ellie struck me with his sword. We then got for my weapons a club and two javelins. We then encamped and as I was sentinel, I revenged the blows of the sword by running away. I ran to a small hillock of dust and caves and took my stand. Up they came and Charlie made at me with the gun and cut my hand with it. I struck him in the chest and he fell on his back. But Ellie was on me with his sword and had me on my knees but I hurled him on Charlie. I saw, however, that I would be beaten in another battle and I rushed down a steep hill and when we fought again I defeated them and rushed up to another position and again encountered and beat them. They were now forced to receive me as an honored soldier.

But the same honored soldier plays dolls and "baby" with Conie, and he can be withered by the least sign of disapproval or ridicule. One entire evening at Nice is written off as "miserable" because "Papa called us children bothers. . . ."

At supper [another night] Mama laughed at me a great deal and made fun of me because I always say "Pretty Papa, Pretty Mama" and made me feel (and I feel now) very cut and ashamed of myself and I don't feel natural, though Mama and Papa both tried to make it up when they saw what she had done.

On being told that his Uncle Weir Roosevelt is dead, he turns to the diary and writes, "It is the third relation that has died in my short life. What will come?"

Best by far are the "fine sociable times" with Papa and Mama. "We went in the cars and had a tremendous play with Mama." "I and Mama and Papa had a sociable time by the fire with my stamp-book." "Papa and I had a jolly walk." "In the evening Mama told us incidents of her early life and adventures of my ancestors. . . ." "I had such nice real tea for supper and such a nice time we did have, especially Mama and I who petted each other up. . . . Did I say I had real tea."

Mama is all-comforting, never angry. Papa leads the way, Papa makes the rules; Papa gives out the spending money and requires an accounting of how it is used. Papa, dressed for the Vienna Opera, is "more handsome than I ever saw him." In a crowd at St.

Peter's, as the family waits for a glimpse of the Pope, a monk shoves Teedie out of the way and Papa springs forward to fling the man aside. Papa gives "a grand dinner" at the hotel in Rome and invites "22 persons!!!"

On a few occasions Papa appears not to have been at his best. He seems to step strangely out of character. In the entry for January 4, 1870, we are told how Papa tossed pennies to a crowd of beggar children outside Naples, but that when one child "transgressed" some rule Papa had made, Papa whipped him "till he cried." (It was immediately following this incident, interestingly, that he presented Teedie with the Roman vase and coin.) Another time, surrounded by a horde of half-starved Italian women and children, Papa bought baskets of cake. "We tossed the cakes to them," Teedie writes, ". . . fed them like chickens with small pieces, and like chickens they ate it. . . . We made them open their mouths and tossed cake into it." This was all great fun, according to Teedie. Papa was a marvel. "We made the crowds . . . give three cheers for the U.S.A. before we gave them cakes."

Bamie is "such a kind sister," but remains part of the adult world, more like a second mother. Ellie is "the chief" or "captain" in their games. Conie remains his favorite playmate.

Still, there runs a theme, a mounting refrain really, of the pleasure and pride in being the first to see or do something, an eagerness to set himself apart from the others, to distinguish himself, to get out ahead of them; or simply to be alone, absorbed in private thoughts. It begins as early as the shipboard friendship with Mr. St. John, which he had managed entirely on his own and in his own fashion. "I was the first one that got on the continent," he writes of the landing at Antwerp. "I walked with Papa before the rest most of the way," he says of their hike out of Switzerland over the Splügen Pass. On a September day beside Lake Como he sits in a shaded woodland "with no sound save the waterfall and the Italian breeze on my cheek. I all alone am writing my journal." "I began my ascent of the snow-covered Vesuvius," he writes the last day of 1869. "I soon passed the rest and left them far behind."

For Mittie, it may well have been the happiest year of her life. To judge by Teedie's account she was never once ill or even out of sorts. Ironically, she appears to have been the only one of the family who never took sick, who never missed a day.

Italy had thrilled her. She had led the children through one museum after another, often plunking one or the other of them before a favorite painting or piece of sculpture: "Now, darling, this is one of the greatest works of art in the world, and I am going to leave you here alone for five minutes, because I want you to sit very quietly and look at it . . ."

Arriving in Paris the second time, in early March 1870, she could still write glowingly of sights yet to be seen. "I have only been *once inside the Louvre*," she told Anna. "We are going to commence vigorously this week, it is so fascinating."

For reasons that remain obscure, it had also been decided that Bamie would stay on in Paris. She was to be put in the hands of Mlle. Marie Souvestre, headmistress of Les Ruches, a private school for girls in Fontainebleau, outside Paris. Then in her mid-thirties, with a long, distinguished career ahead of her, the remarkable Mlle. Souvestre was a woman of singular poise and great culture, but also an outspoken agnostic, and this, in view of Theodore's feelings on religion, makes the decision a little puzzling and suggests that Mittie may have had the final say. In any event, a first visit to Fontainebleau to see the school was made March 19, and as brief as Bamie's time there would be, Mlle. Souvestre's influence would carry far.

In one respect only had the year been a failure. Teedie's health, far from improving, had been conspicuously wretched throughout, as his amazing diary also reveals. From what he writes and from observations and clues to be found in family correspondence, the year can also be seen as a substantial medical profile of a very sick little boy whose case was by no means simple.

CHAPTER FOUR

A Disease
of the Direst Suffering

· 1 ·

BRONCHIAL ASTHMA is among the most serious of childhood afflictions—baffling, capricious, expensive, and, in its acute stages, terrifying. It is also a *family* affliction and a severe one, which is something seldom understood by those who have never lived with an asthmatic child, for rarely does anyone beyond the immediate family or the medical profession see an actual attack or have any idea of the suffering involved. The child known by the outside world is the child between attacks who appears to have little or nothing the matter with him, who can play and carry on like most any healthy youngster, even hike twenty miles in the Alps. It is only those closest to him who know how tenuous such intervals are. For the parents it is "living with a time bomb." The attacks, when they come, are a shattering, numbing experience—always, no matter how many times it has happened before. Nights are made a shambles, sleep is lost, nerves are frayed. Parents become intensely wary of anything that might bring on an attack. They grow increasingly protective, often engulfing in their good intentions. And if, as the years go by, the child shows no improvement, they begin feeling desperate and depleted; they see themselves caught in the grip of something altogether beyond comprehension and their ability to cope. Some mothers "just about go crazy" with worry.

On the third day of October 1869, her fifth day in Vienna, Mittie Roosevelt sat in the garden at the Schönbrunn Palace, writing still another long letter to her sister. Again that morning, as in London, it had been necessary for Theodore to rush Teedie out of the city for a "change of air." By this point in their married life, she and Theodore had been living with Teedie's asthma for about seven years.

> This morning Thee and Teedie left us immediately after breakfast to spend the day and sleep tonight at [Bad] Voslau, an hour by rail from Vienna. Teedie . . . seems hardly to have three or four days' complete exemption and keeps us constantly uneasy and on the stretch. For instance on Lake Como . . . it came to a point where he had to sit up in bed to breathe. After a strong cup of black coffee the spasmodic part of the attack ceased and he slept; consequently woke up partly restored. Had the coffee not taken effect, he would have gone on struggling through the night. . . . Thee had warded off one or two attacks with this coffee, but likes to keep it for our trump card. . . . On Saturday was exactly the fortnight since we reached Venice. *These entire two weeks* he has had nothing but diarrhea and threats of asthma . . . and this morning, as I said, they have gone out of the city for this little change of air. We had almost every day lovely weather in Venice and these few days in Vienna cloudless blue skies and soft breeze. So what it is that keeps up the attacks is a mystery.

How conversant she and Theodore were with the latest medical theories on asthma, what medical advice they were getting, we may only speculate; but their concern for health being what it was and given the frequent contact they had with physicians—Hilborne West, Charles Fayette Taylor, John Metcalfe, the family doctor—they probably knew as much as did any parents of that day. And while it is true that enormous strides have since been made in pulmonary medicine, the things then perceived were neither trivial nor tangential. Asthma had been recognized as a definitive clinical disease for more than a century. A hereditary tendency, the fact that there is a "genetic predisposition" to asthma, had been noted. A seasonal pattern was perceived by many physicians. Certain foods, certain odors, bed feathers, house dust, cat fur, as well as abrupt changes in temperature or humidity, were cited as specific irritants that could bring on an asthmatic "fit" and patients were advised accordingly.

Equally impressive was the mounting body of opinion that the key lay somewhere in the "neurotic character of the complaint."

The first experimental work on the psychological factors in asthma was not to come until the 1880s. Freud and his revelations concerning the unconscious world were further still in the future. But the idea that asthma might be somehow connected with the emotions was very old—allegedly Hippocrates had warned, "The asthmatic must guard against anger"—and from the early part of the nineteenth century increasing numbers of physicians had become convinced that states of grief, anger, joy, "nervous influences" or "passions of the mind" played a more important part than heretofore reckoned.

The fact that an asthmatic's lungs may be quite "perfect"—as the doctor in London found Teedie's lungs to be—had been determined as early as 1819 by the famous French physician René Laënnec, inventor of the stethoscope, who perceived no organic causes to which asthma could be attributed but listed "mental emotion" among the primary probable causes.

"A preternaturally nervous . . . temperament, if not the cause, wonderfully favors the attack of asthma," wrote an American doctor named Joshua Bicknell Chapin in 1843. "Extreme nervous irritability not only invites the attack, but aggravates the symptoms and prolongs continuance," he said, and elucidated on the frustrations of trying to pin down a specific dietary or environmental cause.

> What will almost universally relieve one case, will as assuredly induce a paroxysm in another. Ordinarily the air of low situations is more congenial than mountain breezes. . . . Some suffer in a certain room, but are immediately relieved if removed to an opposite room in the same house. One cannot sleep or rest in one street, or lane, but slumbers quietly if removed to another part of the same village or city. Another can breathe freely if he can only be allowed to sit in a room filled with smoke to suffocation, but pure air is almost intolerable. . . . While one is benefited by a journey in the country, another will find more relief in the contaminated atmosphere of the densest mart. . . . Most will avoid a crowded assembly as they would a pesthouse; but I have a friend who always resorts to such a place when practicable, for a moment of private breathing.

All such cases, he surmised, "owed their origin to certain mental impressions, or emotions."

In 1864, or two years after the infant Teedie's asthma had

begun, a highly important work was published in Philadelphia, a book of 256 pages titled *On Asthma*. The author was an English physician, Henry Hyde Salter, a very keen observer who as the father of an asthmatic child had "experienced the horrors" of the disease. Like Laënnec, Salter had found no abnormalities in the lungs of his asthmatic patients, no trace of the disease in either the respiratory or circulatory system, and hence concluded that the trouble lay in the nervous system. Asthma, a disease of "the direst suffering," a disease "about whose pathology more various and discrepant ideas prevail than any other," was "essentially a *nervous* disease."

Sudden "mental emotion," Salter said, could both bring on an attack and abruptly end one. He did not know why, only what he had observed. He reported on a patient whose attack ceased the moment he saw a fire outside the window and another who had his asthma stop when put on a fast horse. Still other patients found that as soon as they neared the doctor's office their asthma vanished, "suddenly and without any apparent cause except the mental perturbation at being within the precincts of the physician." The onset of an attack, he noted, was frequently preceded by a spell of depression or "heaviness" (what Teedie called feeling "doleful"), and twenty years in advance of what might be regarded as the first studies in the psychosomatic side of asthma he reported on a small boy who "found his disease a convenient immunity from correction."

"Don't scold me," he would say, if he had incurred his father's displeasure, "or I shall have the asthma." And so he would; his fears were as correct as they were convenient.

The nature of an actual attack was described by Salter in accurate, vivid detail and with considerable sympathy for anyone who had to try to deal with the situation. Specific kinds of treatment were described, including the "beneficial influence of sustained bodily exertion." It was the most comprehensive study on asthma that had as yet appeared, the definitive word, and either Hilborne West, Taylor, Metcalfe, or all three, must have known about it and so consequently would the Roosevelts, in part if not in whole. Much of what Salter wrote on the importance of exercise reads as if it might have been the very text for all Theodore was to preach to his small son and that the son himself would choose as his own lifelong creed. "Organs are made for action, not existence; they are made to *work*, not to *be*; and when they *work* well they can *be* well," insisted Dr. Salter.

The common methods then used to confront an attack varied greatly and to the present-day reader seem excessively harsh. Emetics and purges were standard. The common way to avert an attack was to make the patient violently ill, to dose him with ipecac or with incredibly nauseating potions made of garlic and mustard seed and "vinegar of squills," a dried plant also used for rat poison. Children were given enemas, plunged into cold baths. Whiskey and gin were used, laudanum (opium mixed with wine) and Indian hemp (marijuana). The patient was made to inhale chloroform or the fumes of burning nitrate paper or the smoke from dried jimson weed *(Datura stramonium)*, another poisonous plant, coarse and vile smelling, that had been used in treating asthma in India for centuries. Many children were made to smoke a ghastly medicinal cigarette concocted of jimson weed and chopped camphor.

Black coffee may have been the Roosevelts' "trump card," as Mittie said, but Teedie was also made to swallow ipecac and smoke cigars. The purpose of the cigar was to subject the child to what, in essence, was a dose of nicotine poisoning. "In those who have not established a tolerance to tobacco," explained Henry Hyde Salter, "its use is soon followed by a well-known condition of collapse, much resembling seasickness—vertigo, loss of power in the limbs, a sense of deadly faintness, cold sweat, inability to speak or think, nausea, vomiting."

The moment such a condition could be induced, he said, "the asthma ceases as if by a charm."

The picture of such loving parents as Mittie and Theodore inflicting punishment of this kind seems almost inconceivable. But they did, which, if nothing else, is a measure of the extremes to which a mother and a father will go to avoid a bad attack. Also, violent vomiting very often works, just as Salter said. It can in fact avert an attack and is still resorted to in certain situations. And black coffee, it happens, was also a sound choice; caffeine, a stimulant, is closely akin to theophylline, among those drugs used most frequently to treat present-day asthmatics.

The sensation of an acute asthmatic attack is that of being strangled or suffocated, only infinitely more complex. The whole body responds. When Victorians used the words "fit" or "seizure" they were close to the mark. The trouble is not just in the lungs. The central nervous system is involved, the endocrine system, both sides of the brain, possibly the stem of the brain as well. The agony is total, unlike that, say, of smashing a finger in a door, where the pain is concentrated at one point. And the largest part of the agony is psychological—inexpressible terror, panic.

"Witches in my chest" is an expression sometimes used by children, while most adult asthmatics find it impossible to give words to what they experience during an attack. A feeling like drowning is frequently mentioned—*slow* drowning—but not even that quite suits. In the words of one asthmatic, "If I were drowning I would know I was drowning and I was going to die and that wouldn't be so bad. Asthma is just plain terrifying. . . . You may die . . . but your fear is you won't."

Many asthmatics cannot bring themselves to talk about their illness, largely, it would seem, for fear that the mere thought of an attack might bring one on. Ten-year-old Teedie, for all that he was capable of including in his diary about the contents of museums or the events of a day, writes nothing of the feelings he experienced when "very sick" or having "a miserable night." In later years he would remain equally reticent—very uncharacteristically reticent —saying only that as a child he had been "wretched," "suffered much" from asthma and that "nobody seemed to think I would live."

For reasons that are still imperfectly understood, the attacks come nearly always at night, usually about three or four in the morning. Asthma is a disease of the night, which, for a small, impressionable child, can contribute greatly to its terrors. The onset may be sudden or gradual. The first stage is a tightening of the chest and a dry, hacking cough. Breathing becomes labored and shallow. The child starts to pant for air ("asthma" in Greek means panting). A high-pitched wheeze begins. The child has to sit up. If he tries to speak at all, it is in short, desperate bursts. Soon he is unable to speak or move, except with the utmost difficulty. He is battling for breath, tugging, straining, elbows planted on his knees, shoulders hunched high, his head thrown back, eyes popping. Fiercely as he pulls and gulps for air, what he gets is never enough. A distance runner near the point of collapse knows much the same agony, except he also knows he can quit running if he chooses. The asthmatic has no such choice, and there is no telling how long the agony will go on.

"I sat up for 4 successive hours and Papa made me smoke a cigar," reads the entry describing an attack the night of the crossing to Trieste.

"Poor little Teedie is sick again . . ." reads part of a letter written by Bamie from Munich, it was coming on all day yesterday, but in the evening he seemed a little better so Father went out—before his return, however, Teedie had a very bad attack. Mother and I were very much worried about the poor little fellow and at last Mother gave him a strong cup of coffee, which failed as he could not sleep but sat in the parlor to have stories of when Mother was a little girl told to him.

At another point in the diary, he writes that he was rubbed so hard on the chest "that the blood came out." By whom he does not say.

The cause of the horrendous difficulty in breathing is a swelling of the bronchial tubes which lead to the lungs, specifically the branchlike extensions of the bronchial tree. The normal involuntary muscular action of these airways is not functioning as it should. The bronchial tubes are filling with mucus. They are in spasm, no longer dilating (contracting and releasing) properly; they narrow and close down. Hyperventilation occurs, as less and less air is pulled into the lungs. The feeling, it has been said, is of taking in mere spoonfuls of air, these reaching only the top of the lungs, "and you know that no more is going to penetrate, that everything under that has turned to lead, and you're depending on that little tablespoon as fast as you can get it." Back and chest muscles are put to tremendous strain. The heart is pounding. The child coughs and perspires and turns deathly pale, a ring of compressed white around the mouth. He is being strangled to death. And the alarm of those with him does nothing to relieve his own terrible anxieties.

But though the sensation is of being unable to take air in, the problem is actually the reverse; the air already inside cannot be expired as in normal breathing. It is the used air trapped within the swollen lungs that is keeping the child from breathing in the fresh air so desperately wanted. The struggle is to get the used air out.

If the severity of the attack continues, if his strength begins to fail, the child will start to turn blue—the sign that he is in "status asthmaticus," very near death from asphyxiation. With modern drugs, with potent bronchodilators like epinephrine, ephedrine, or aminophylline, such a state can usually be avoided, the attack kept within bounds. Oxygen can also be given. But no such drugs, no nebulizers or oxygen tents, were available in the Roosevelts' day. How near Teedie came to dying during the worst of his attacks, whether, for example, he actually ever turned blue, is impossible to determine.

Once the attack is ended, the ordeal at last over, the child commonly experiences an upsurge of good feelings, an exuberance unlike any other. Nothing seems too big or too difficult to tackle. The fact that Teedie could get up and do all he did the day after a bad attack—that his best, most strenuous days during the European year were often those immediately following his worst nights—fits the pattern exactly. The attack the night of the crossing to Trieste was among the most severe, yet the day after, literally within hours, having had almost no sleep, he was out happily exploring the city on his own. The day following he hiked two hours "in the broiling sun," up and back, to a castle on a hilltop in what is now Postojna, Yugoslavia.

For the parents of the child, however, there is little such relief. As the attacks grow worse, their worry and frustration are compounded accordingly, as Mittie's letter from the garden of the Schönbrunn Palace amply illustrates. Still, such concerns, like asthma itself, remain largely private matters. It is not the severity of the child's condition or the anguish of the parents that the outside world sees. It is the special treatment the child gets, the costly, sometimes ostentatious things done in his behalf—special medicines, doctors, emergency travel to some distant, exotic change of scene. And if there happens to be money in the family, then such "signs" of the seriousness of the case are heavily accentuated, for while any family may be willing in theory to try almost anything to help the child, the family of wealth can in fact try almost anything. Money being no obstacle, the rich can respond to asthma in ways the poor or even the moderately well-to-do cannot, and this was particularly so in the days before public clinics and health insurance.

With asthma and wealth combined in the same family, it is as if the drama of the problem—and asthma is nothing if not dramatic—can be played out on a much larger, showier stage. And naturally the leading player, the small, ailing child, becomes even more special and out of the ordinary, his influence on the family destiny larger by far.

So it was not merely that Teedie was acutely asthmatic, but that he was acutely asthmatic in conjunction with virtually all the relief, diversion, every advantageous change of scene or consideration that money could buy. When he set things spinning, as every asthmatic does, the result was quite different from what it would have been for a child of lesser station. An attack comes at home and he is whisked into the night in a family carriage pulled by magnificent, matched horses, a carriage that may be summoned to the door at a moment's notice, whatever the hour. It is a very privileged kind of resolution to the crisis, not to mention an exciting one.

The ocean breezes at Long Branch do not suffice, so off he is taken to Saratoga. Visits to Philadelphia are arranged whenever need be. Or summers in the country. Or a year in Europe.

This is not to suggest that his suffering was any the less for such treatment—or that the burden he presented was any less heartrending for Mittie and Theodore—but to emphasize the special circumstances within which the problem was cast. For in the light of what has since become known about asthma, there is little question that the family milieu, the specific ways in which the family responds to the problem—as individuals and collectively— bear directly on the severity of the disorder, even the timing of attacks.

· 2 ·

THE EXACT ROLE of the emotions in asthma is still elusive, after nearly a century of study. Recent investigations strongly suggest that the disease is physiological in origin: something about the asthmatic makes him abnormally susceptible to an irritant of some kind—an airborne allergen in most instances—and so in the beginning stages, many physicians now contend, asthma can be properly described as allergic. But the interplay of emotions may also figure in the allergic process itself—nobody really knows—and once the asthmatic "mechanism" or "habit" is established, the part played by the emotions in "triggering" attacks is indisputable. It is as if the patient has somehow established a freak circuit and the emotions can trip it, setting him off. The attack is not deliberate (though it can be), rather it is provoked by certain painful feelings—buried anger, guilt, fear of abandonment, fears of all kinds—or of tensions that need not necessarily be unpleasant, the approach of a birthday or Christmas, for example. "It isn't that the emotions of the asthmatic patients are different from those of other people," stresses a specialist, "it is that with them the effects of an upset can be explosive." If the patient is a child, the causes are essentially "wrapped up in the fears which beset most children and which they find so hard to acknowledge or discuss." More important than the feeling itself is the fact that it remains bottled up inside. Dust, animal dander, the pollen season, damp night air, a hundred and one impersonal, external factors may play a part, but the psychological factors weigh heavy in the balance and it is in this sense that asthma is understood to be a psychosomatic disorder, like duodenal ulcers or hypertension. A view frequently heard among experts in pulmonary medicine is that there is no such thing as a totally nonpsychosomatic case of asthma—a view that, understandably, is often difficult for parents to accept.

The medical paper regarded as the first study of asthma's psychological side appeared in *The American Journal of the Medical Sciences* in 1886, too late to have any effect on Mittie or Theodore Roosevelt. A Baltimore physician, John Noland Mackenzie, reported on a severely asthmatic patient, a woman in her early thirties, whose attacks could be brought on by everything from thunderstorms to overeating to perfume, but who was particularly susceptible to the smell of roses. She was unable to be in a room where roses were present for more than a few minutes without having a violent attack. But then Mackenzie found that the sight of an artificial rose produced exactly the same result, a discovery, he said, that "opens our eyes to the fact that the association of ideas sometimes plays a more important role in awakening the paroxysm . . . than the alleged vital property of the pollen granule."

While the validity of Mackenzie's experiment was to be challenged, it nonetheless inspired countless studies along similar lines, the results of which were often astonishing. Asthmatic children said to be sensitive to house dust, for example, have been hospitalized in rooms generously supplied with dust from their own homes, and in nineteen out of twenty cases no asthma has resulted. Physicians have developed techniques whereby patients can be talked out of an oncoming attack. Important work has been done in the "family dynamics" of asthma—chronic unresolved conflicts within the "family constellation" are probed for—and a major facility, the Children's Asthma Research Institute and Hospital in Denver, Colorado, has been founded on the proposition that the best possible therapy for many acutely asthmatic children is to get them away from their families altogether.

Asthma is now commonly explained to parents as a form of behavior; the child is unconsciously "using" his affliction for purposes of his own. "We tend to use what is available to us to influence our environment or to solve our problems," writes a leading

authority. "Children with asthma have asthma available to them
. . . [and] behavior, not verbalization, is the language of children."

The likeliest source of the child's anxieties, it has long been
thought, is the mother. Asthma is repeatedly described as a "suppressed cry for the mother"—a cry of rage as well as a cry for help.
The child has an intense fear of being abandoned by the mother or
of any form of rivalry for her affection. If the advent of asthma
coincided with actual separation from the mother—from either parent—this too is considered an important piece to the puzzle. Thus
a present-day specialist analyzing Teedie's case would take very
seriously the fact that his troubles began during the Civil War,
years of great confusion and tension for the Roosevelts, when
Theodore was away months at a time and two new infants arrived
on the scene to vie for Mittie's attention. The whole "climate" of
ill health within the Roosevelt household—Mittie's palpitations
and headaches and intestinal grief, Bamie's troubles with her back,
Conie's asthma—would also be reckoned as much or more an environmental factor in Teedie's asthma than, say, the quality of the
air he happened to be breathing.

Oncoming attacks in his case were often signaled a day or so
in advance by moods of dark melancholy or homesickness. "I feel
very, very homesick tonight," he writes one Friday in Lucerne.
"Teedie threatened with asthma," Mittie notes in her journal the
same evening. The attack followed in less than forty-eight hours.

But in nothing the Roosevelts said or wrote during the year is
there even a suggestion that his condition was the result of an
allergy, or thought to be. There is no talk of the hay season, no
obvious avoidance of dogs or cats or specific foods.

Nor, we find, is there a seasonal pattern to the attacks. As the
diary shows, they came in every season, year around. They happen
in city and country, in damp, cold climates and the heat of summer,
at sea level and in Switzerland. No one time of year or environment
seems to be any more beneficial or harmful than another. The fact
that he was abroad—away from New York and anything at the 20th
Street house that might have been the cause—did him no apparent
good. If anything, the year abroad appears to have been his worst
yet.

Indeed, from looking at the diaries one might be inclined to
see the attacks as entirely random—that is if one were to note only
where they occurred or in what season, rather than which day of
the week. It is when the attacks are plotted day by day on a calen-

dar for the years 1869 and 1870 that a distinct pattern at once emerges.

His asthma strikes on weekends, usually Saturday night or what was actually early Sunday morning. There are exceptions, ordinary weekdays when he is "rather sick" or "still sick." Tuesday, October 26, the day before his birthday, his condition was serious enough to cause a hurried departure from Berlin, ahead of schedule, though in this instance apparently it was the sign of an oncoming attack, rather than an actual seizure, that set everyone in motion. ("I feel very doleful and sick and homesick and there is such a bustle my head aches. . . . Perhaps when I'm 14 I'll go to Minnesota, hip, hip hurrah!") But the number of times in which Sunday figures as his bad day is astonishing. The worst attacks, moreover, virtually all occur on Sunday.

His first illness of the trip, it will be recalled, the siege of seasickness, his one bad day aboard ship, occurred Sunday, May 16. In July he was rushed from London by train to spend the weekend of the fourth, a Sunday, at Hastings with his father. Sunday, August 29, at Lucerne, he writes, "I was very sick on the sofa and lay in bed all day. . . ." The bad night at Lake Como mentioned by Mittie in her Schönbrunn garden letter happened the weekend of September 11–12. The attack on the way to Trieste began at approximately three o'clock the morning of Sunday, September 26.

The following Sunday, October 3, was the morning Theodore took off with him from Vienna to Bad Voslau, the morning of Mittie's letter.

The attack at Munich described by Bamie took place the following Saturday night and Teedie's diary entry for that Sunday, October 10, reads: "I was very sick last night and Mama was so kind telling me stories and rubbing me with her delicate fingers. I was so sick in the morning that in the afternoon Father, Ellie, and I went to Starnberg."

This made the third such emergency exit to spend a Sunday out of town. In Paris it would happen twice again. On two consecutive weekends, because of his condition, the child was hurried from the city to the fresh air of Fontainebleau, these expeditions coming immediately after the initial trip to see Bamie's school.

The intriguing question, of course, is why this should have been so. Why the weekends? Why Sunday?

The pattern is too pronounced to be coincidental. How long it had been the pattern, what the timing of attacks may have been prior to that year abroad, is impossible to resolve, since there are no comparable records. References to his condition in earlier years rarely specify when the seizures came. Interestingly enough, however, the one bad time for which we do have a calendar date occurred on a weekend and reached its greatest severity on a Sunday. The letter in which Grandmamma Bulloch tells how Mittie and Theodore packed the child off from Long Branch to Saratoga—the first known mention of his asthma in family records—was written the day of their departure, Monday, June 22, 1863. The difficult time had been the day before.

Salter, in his book, had written on the strange "periodicity" of asthma among some patients, noting that a weekly cycle was not uncommon. His example was of a small boy whose attacks came every Monday morning, a pattern that appeared to be an effort to avoid school but that Salter attributed to the family routine of a large Sunday meal.

In Teedie's case the answer may lie in the nature of Sunday itself, which in the Victorian era was still the Lord's Day, the sanctified day of rest and the one day of the week when the head of the household was home from work and thus also available to his children. Among such properly devout families as the Roosevelts it was a day of rigidly prescribed dress and behavior, of formal family gatherings, of little or no play, of church, Bible readings, family prayers, evening hymn singing in the parlor. The Roosevelts "kept" the Sabbath. It was a day for letter writing, a quiet walk perhaps, and for Theodore, his weekly turn at the Newsboys' Lodging House (with other children outside the home). Teedie, in his mature years, would remember it as a day "we children did not enjoy—chiefly because we were all of us made to wear clean clothes and keep neat." The single redeeming feature was the chance to gather in the front parlor, a room of "splendor" with its cut-glass chandelier.

On the expedition across Europe, Sunday invariably meant church, wherever the Protestant variety could be found, and a day off from touring. The few Sundays when they did not attend church the children were required to remain quiet—to draw a church or memorize several verses from the Bible. It was permissible to *look* at things as the day went on, but not to *do* much. At Pisa one Sunday, the family went to see the tower, but not until the following day did they climb it.

As a very small child Teedie had also experienced a peculiar and memorable fear of church. It was a small incident that, in later years, made an amusing anecdote of the kind every Roosevelt loved to tell. But for him at the time it was no joke and should not be discounted.

Mittie had found he was so afraid of the Madison Square Church that he refused to set foot inside if alone and so she pressed him to tell her why. He was terrified, she discovered, of something called the "zeal." It was crouched in the dark corners of the church ready to jump at him, he said. When she asked what a zeal might be, he said he was not sure, but thought it was probably a large animal like an alligator or a dragon. He had heard the minister read about it from the Bible.

Using a concordance, she read him those passages containing the word "zeal" until suddenly, very excited, he told her to stop. The line was from the Book of John, chapter 2, verse 17: *And his disciples remembered that it was written, The zeal of thine house hath eaten me up.*

The Sundays he was sick in Europe he was seldom obliged to go to church. That certainly, the diaries show, was among the immediate, obvious consequences of a "bad night" or of merely being "a little sick," even those Sundays when he was not whisked off to the country. During the first stay in Paris, for instance, he missed church three consecutive Sundays. ("I was sick and did not go out at all except for my Russian bath.") In Rome, Saturday, January 8, 1870, he is "a little sick." Sunday, January 9, he "did not go to church at all." In Florence, Sunday, February 27: "As I was sick with a headache I and Ellie went out in the garden and made roads with stones. . . . No Sunday school."

But the outstanding examples, of course, are the Sundays afield, out of London, Vienna, Munich, Paris, immeasurably wonderful times in the blessed open air, the best being those spent alone with Papa. The Sunday at Hastings was "the happiest day I have ever spent." He did attend church in this instance, but Sunday school was conducted beside a castle wall, in view of the sea. The Sunday at Bad Voslau was again like Hastings, "viz, there were only the 2 of us," and "we had Sunday school out . . ." "Papa and I went a long way through the wood and had Sunday school in them." The Sunday away from Munich with Ellie also along was "splendid" and of the two escapades outside Paris he writes as follows:

Saturday, April 16, 1870

I had such a bad night that we went to Fontainebleau. We children went first. We played in the garden and woods. We had a nice time but in the night I was sick.

Easter Sunday, April 17, 1870

Today was the happiest Easter I ever spent. After breakfast and a walk in the woods alone, Mama, Papa, and all we children went out in the woods to hunt for violets. . . . We played . . . and then had Sunday school in the woods and picked cowslip and heard the cuckoo sing.

After dinner we all drove out through the woods to the rocks. We then walked all round the rocks and over crevasses. We saw a tree 1,400 years old and [an]other 300 years old. We saw a stream of pure and cold water. We had such a happy time.

Saturday, April 23, 1870

We went to Fontainebleau in the cars with Bamie. I had a bad time till two o'clock, when after dinner we went to the rocks and there we made such a scramble and went in dark caves and over big cracks, and up steep places and all over.

Sunday, April 24, 1870

We went in the park where on a sand bank we made tunnels 10 paces long. After dinner we went to the rocks where we jumped over crevasses and ran in them and had such fun. . . . In one of our rambles we saw very fresh traces of a deer.

All the stifling formality and constricted horizons of Sunday were at once transformed by the space and excitement of the natural world—by a tree 1,400 years old, streams of pure water, dark caves, and fresh deer traces. "If Raphael had only painted landscapes instead of church things," he laments in the diary after a visit to the Vatican. To be with Papa, to have Papa's undivided attention, to be off and away on an adventure together, was the ultimate joy. Any opportunity to be with Papa, then, later, made him feel better. ("Well, well, said Mr. Greatheart, let them that are most afraid, keep close to me.")

Their day at Bad Voslau was nearly ruined by a chance encounter with a few of "Papa's friends (or as I thought of them, enemies)." With their unexpected appearance, it became a "miserable time," he writes, adding quickly, "but it was not Papa's fault."

Neither Mittie nor Theodore, nor any of the family, appears to have been aware of the timing of the attacks. Nor, apparently, was Teedie. Twice, however, he reports testily that Conie tries to get attention by faking she is sick. She complained she was too weak to walk, "and then went bouncing down the stairs . . . until she saw Mama, when she suddenly became very sick again (sarcastic)." Another time, "Conie was sick but her sickness always decreased when Mama was out of the room and she could not be petted."

Both of these performances occurred on weekends, the first on a Saturday, the second on a Sunday, and at neither time did Teedie himself become ill. He was struck instead, in the first instance, by a siege of abject homesickness; in their hotel suite at Dresden he lay on the floor in the light of the fire pining away for "times at home in the country." Of the morning of Conie's own Sunday "sickness," he further reports, "Papa, Bamie, Ellie, and I went to church but I did not like it." Conie's condition required that Mama stay behind.

Mama's love and attention were magic. His physical need for her, the intense attachment he felt, are expressed with striking candor and frequency. In Paris they went together to the Russian baths six days in a row, to be subjected to clouds of steam and switches of fir boughs. She was with him through his headaches and stomach cramps. To pull him out of his doleful spells, she told him stories and looked at pictures with him. One evening in Paris she showed him a photograph of little Edith Carow and the effect was devastating. Her face, he noted in an air of grand tragedy, only "stirred up in me homesickness and longing for the past which will come again never, alack never."

Whereas Papa made him drink black coffee or smoke a cigar or swallow ipecac (with "dreadful effects"), Mama soothed, petted, "rubbed me with her delicate fingers." After a day of unremitting rain at Nice, when he was up late alone, "Mama came in and then she lay down and I stroked her head and she felt my hands and nearly cried because they were feverish. We had a fine sociable time. . . ." Papa took him to the doctor (in Vienna and Paris), and on the train from Berlin, it was Papa who made him get out for air at every station stop, despite the cold and the falling snow.

Why it was Papa nearly always who rushed him off to Hastings and the other places is an interesting point, since Mittie could have managed it as well, or she could have gone along with them to make a day of it. Or the whole thing could have been turned over to Bamie or a servant. Doubtless Theodore knew how large he loomed in the child's eyes, how desperately the boy needed him. Almost certainly he wanted to give Mittie some relief, to get him away from her, for *her* benefit.

Another likely possibility, of course, is that Theodore himself, for all his piety and adherence to convention, enjoyed being off and away; he wanted a day of freedom every bit as much as did his small companion. If so, then the asthma was serving both their needs—it was doubly "convenient," to use Dr. Salter's word—and Teedie, conceivably, would have sensed as much. In some way for which there were no words he could have understood perfectly what those days meant to his father and this too would have figured in whatever troubling, complex combination of feelings lay at the heart of his troubles.

· 3 ·

AS DIFFERENT—as very different—as is every case of asthma from another, much of the impact of the disease is commonly shared by severely asthmatic children. Many of the same feelings and fears are engendered, many of the same perceptions of the world, and there is no reason to believe Teedie was an exception. For a child as acutely sensitive and intelligent as he, the impact of asthma could not have been anything but profound, affecting personality, outlook, self-regard, the whole course of his young life, in marked fashion. The asthmatic child knows he is an oddity; that somehow, for some reason no one can explain, he is a defective, *different*. But he knows also that his particular abnormality lends a kind of power. He knows, in ways a normal child can scarcely imagine, what it is to be the absolute center of attention. His attacks, horrible as they are, dreaded as they may be, are riveting to all who are present, his hold on his audience is total. Nothing can go on as usual, no one can remain indifferent to him, in the presence of an attack, and it is for no mere fleeting moment that he commands center stage. "A beheading is over in seconds," observes one of the few chronic asthmatics who is willing to talk candidly. "A hanging —how long does that take? Three, four minutes, possibly five at the most. But an attack of asthma!"

The inclination, as time goes on, is to demand more and more attention—if not through asthma, then some other means.

Inevitably, as part of his way of coping with the world, the asthmatic also acquires a highly sensitized feeling for his surroundings. Of necessity he becomes acutely cognizant of the size and shape of rooms, the nearness of people and their comparative size, the whole look and feel and smell of spaces small and large, of fresh air, of skies and winds.

Ailments other than asthma, any of the inevitable knocks and scrapes of childhood, or of later life, are often taken with notable stoicism. It is as if having experienced asthma, he finds other pains and discomforts mild by comparison.

He has learned at an early age what a precarious, unpredictable thing life is—and how very vulnerable *he* is. He must be prepared always for the worst.

But the chief lesson is that life is quite literally a battle. And the test is how he responds, in essence whether he sees himself as a helpless victim or decides to fight back, whether he becomes, as Teedie was to say of a particular variety of desert bird, "extremely tenacious of life."

Oftentimes it is a question of which parent is chosen to identify with and emulate.

In the history of asthma, among the most celebrated cases is that of the French novelist Marcel Proust (1871-1922), who thought his asthma, like his homosexuality, was rooted in the unconscious and was part of a price he had to pay for his creative gifts. "We enjoy fine music, beautiful pictures, a thousand exquisite things," Proust wrote, "but we do not know what they cost those who wrought them in sleeplessness, tears, spasmodic laughter, rashes, asthma, epilepsy. . . . Neurosis has an absolute genius for malingering. There is no illness which it cannot counterfeit perfectly."

Some aspects of Proust's case have a familiar ring. His mother, like Mittie Roosevelt, was a cultivated, sensitive woman. Being a Jew set her off from her Catholic husband and his background much as Mittie's southern origins set her off from Theodore and the rest of the Roosevelts. Proust, like Teedie, had a younger brother, close in age, who was the stronger, more robust of the two. His father, however, unlike Theodore, was a distant and indifferent figure. As a child, Proust, also, had been considered too weak to live. His devotion to his mother was intense, overwhelming. Indeed, among those specialists who see asthma as a suppressed cry for the mother, Proust's case is the classic example. "You demolish everything until I am ill again," he once accused his mother, while on another occasion, he told her, "I'd rather have asthma and please you."

Proust never saw himself as anything but a victim. Proust,

sealed off in his cork-lined writing room, is the quintessential recluse. Following his mother's death, he remained a semi-invalid, dying ultimately of respiratory complications.

Just as no two cases of asthma are ever exactly alike, so the response to the disease varies infinitely. In the end, it seems to depend on the individual. Many children "grow out" of it. For others it is a life sentence. Henry Hyde Salter's prognosis was hardly encouraging. The asthmatic, he wrote, "knows that a certain percentage of his future life must be dedicated to suffering . . . and from many of the occupations of life he is cut off . . . his usefulness is crippled, his life marred. . . . The asthmatic is generally looked upon as an asthmatic for life."

For Teedie, in some powerful way, father and the out of doors meant salvation, and Theodore, in his efforts to bring the shy child out of himself—in all the ways he encouraged confidence, gave diversion, companionship, set an example of strength—was, consciously or not, taking the best possible approach, given the circumstances. The goal, according to a treatise written a century later, is to make the child "a participant, not a spectator in his own care." "I am to do everything for myself," Teedie wrote proudly at the close of one of those days alone with his father.

As interesting perhaps as any line in the journal, in what it foreshadows, is one written at Nice, in which he reflects on a joyous day's hiking. "It was," he writes, "the first time I had walked up a hill of decent size for a long time and I felt quite refreshed."

Walking—even a day of "severe walking"—was strongly recommended by Salter and other authorities, and horseback riding was considered the most beneficial exercise of all for asthmatics. Get action, Theodore had long preached. His beloved Bamie had been saved by the "movement cure" and by a doctor who believed in treating the patient as a whole being in mind and body.

"Organs are made for action . . ." Salter wrote; "they are made to *work*, not to *be*; and when they *work* well they can *be* well."

CHAPTER FIVE

Metamorphosis

· 1 ·

May 25, 1870

This morning we saw land of America and, swiftly coming on, passed Sandy Hook and went into the bay. New York!!! Hip! Hurrah! What a bustle we had getting off.

They were on home ground at last, back to aunts, uncles, cousins, servants ("all our friends"), and pink-faced, important Grandpa; back to the perpetual life and hubbub of the biggest, best city in the best country in the whole wide world; to traffic clogged to a standstill and the familiar New York smell of coal smoke and cooking and horses and hay and horse manure—with a damp, salt-air touch of the East River. The house on East 20th Street was found to be exactly as remembered. Life picked up with amazing ease, at about where it had left off—afternoon calls, teas, tutors, lessons, books, Father's morning paper, Father's office week, and those rectitudinous Roosevelt Sundays. There was talk of business, which was good, and of Grandfather's new summer house at Oyster Bay, Long Island. Over the back wall Mr. Goelet's garden was in its springtime glory.

One bright day, Red Cloud, chief of the Oglala Sioux, came riding down Fifth Avenue in an open carriage, a real-life warrior from the Dakota prairies wearing a stovepipe hat. There was a clamor in the papers for an eight-hour day and talk of "the engineering wonder of the age," the East River Bridge, which was finally under construction. One of its two colossal towers was to rise at the foot of Roosevelt Street.

A new experimental passenger tube, the first subway, had been opened downtown and the building boom uptown was thought to be "marvelous." Change was the order of the day, as always in New York, and a year was a long time to have been absent.

Some of what had transpired in the interval was not so marvelous, to be sure. The panic in September had sent shock waves among the established, old families. Bad enough that a couple of conniving parvenus like Fisk and Gould could have caused it all, but must they remain so outrageously vulgar, flaunting their money and political pull? What did it portend if such men could attain the pinnacles of financial power? The Gould-Fisk scheme to corner the gold market had nearly worked, and their crony Tweed, the new Grand Sachem of Tammany Hall, the most conspicuously corrupt politician in anyone's memory, was riding higher than ever. He owned the mayor, judges, editors, even some Republicans, as was noted sadly at the Union League. No decent man could enter public life any longer "without imminent danger of losing caste."

So surely it was with sinking hearts that Theodore, brothers Cornelius and James Alfred, and their father received word that brother Rob would shortly announce for Congress on the Tammany ticket.

But only with the onset of summer did life seem suddenly to bear down heavily on Theodore and Mittie. July brought a murderous heat wave, among the worst on record, and from France, where they had left Bamie, came news of the calamitous war with Prussia, which was declared July 15. No actual fighting took place for several weeks and Bamie herself happened to be hugely enjoying the excitement—she would tell in later years how French troops went marching past her school windows singing—but for her father especially it was a time of exceeding tension and worry, a condition felt by the entire household and one not greatly helped by his own father's insistence that he do something about the child's safety before it was too late.

Further, in combination with all this—or possibly as a consequence—Teedie, who had been "peculiarly well" since the return from Europe, went into a sharp decline. His attacks resumed, coming so often now that Theodore and Mittie had to take turns rushing him off to some country place or watering spot—to Saratoga or

Oyster Bay, a rented house at Spuyten Duyvil, a summer hotel at Richfield Springs. Theodore began to wear thin. "I am away with Teedie again much to my regret," he told Bamie in an undated letter written from his father's place on Long Island. "He had another attack, woke me up at night and last night, to make a break, I took him to Oyster Bay. It used me up entirely to have another attack come so soon after the last. I know and appreciate all the mercies for which I should be thankful but at the moment it seems hard to bear."

To drop everything and leave with the boy at any emergency was becoming very difficult for him, he told her in another letter. He had much too much to do.

On August 10 Mittie wrote to Bamie, "Teedie had an attack of asthma on last Sunday night and Papa took him to Oyster Bay where he passed Monday night and Tuesday night. Of course, Teedie was in ecstasies of delight . . ."

By the time the fighting broke out in France and the vaunted armies of Napoleon III began their spectacular collapse, Bamie was across the Channel safe in the care of Uncle Jimmie Bulloch, her exodus having been arranged by Theodore through American friends in Paris named Lamson. It had gone smoothly according to plan. "Do not let them spoil you in Liverpool," he chided her; he had troubles enough as it was. Her mother and Teedie were off to "take the waters" at Richfield Springs, for the second or third time, accompanied now by Uncle Hilborne.

"Your mother came back . . ." Theodore reported two weeks later, "Teedie still suffering . . . and they returned leaving me once more a bachelor."

Two days later at Richfield Springs, on a Sunday, Teedie had another attack. "The spasm yielded," Mittie reported, ". . . but [he] passed a wheezy miserable night and I have concluded to leave . . . for New York tomorrow, with the feeling that this last week Teedie has lost all he gained . . . and the sulfur baths and water proved no good."

"I have just received bad news from your mother," Theodore wrote to Bamie. "She returns with Teedie asthmatic again. His attacks have been more frequent. . . . All say that Denver City would be just the air for Teedie, but until he is older this seems impossible."

That was on September 6, when his patience was all but gone. How soon afterward he and Teedie had their talk is not known, but probably it was soon. As Mittie later recounted the scene, he called the boy to him and addressed him as Theodore.

"Theodore, you have the mind, but you have not the body, and without the help of the body the mind cannot go as far as it should." He must build himself up by his own effort. "You must *make* your body." It was a summons and the offer of a counterpoise, a way, the one way, to right his own balance.

"It is hard drudgery to make one's body," the father said, "but I know you will do it."

And with that, allegedly, the sorry little specimen threw back his head and declared he would do it.

Instead of Denver City he got Wood's Gymnasium, Mittie accompanying him—and Elliott as well—for daily workouts under the direction of Mr. John Wood, whose young protégés included Sloanes and Goelets and Vanderbilts and whose tutelage was claimed to be as beneficial to character as to physique. She never missed a session and a more unlikely presence in a gymnasium is hard to picture. She sat alone patiently on a large settee against one wall, intent on every part of the program. Standing in front of a weight machine, body forward, head and chest up, arms out, Teedie pulled and hauled, hoisted the weights up from the floor, then let them ride slowly back down again, time after time. He and Ellie hammered away at punching bags, swung dumbbells, spent hours straining at the horizontal bars. After about three months of this, Mittie had John Wood equip their own back piazza with all the required apparatus and it was thus, under her direction (as Wood later acknowledged), that the famous family gymnasium came into being.

As the weeks and months rolled by—as winter came and Bamie returned from Liverpool, as Uncle Rob went off to his newly won seat in Congress, as a besieged and starving Paris at last surrendered to the Germans—Teedie plugged away at his dreary regimen. His sisters would later write that among the most vivid of all childhood memories was the sight of him out on the piazza struggling between the horizontal bars, "widening his chest by regular, monotonous motion—drudgery indeed."

Long years afterward, reflecting on what had been on his mind at this critical juncture, he would tell a friend of certain lines from the Browning poem "The Flight of the Duchess" that had brought him up short. The passage described the overbred son of a noble line—"... *the pertest little ape / That ever affronted human shape.*"

So, all that the old Dukes had been, without knowing it,
This Duke would fain know he was, without being it; . . .
And chief in the chase his neck he perilled,
On a lathy horse, all legs and length,
With blood for bone, all speed, no strength; . . .

Suddenly, as he told the friend, he saw himself for what he was—can affront to human shape, boneless, all speed, no strength: a pretender. It was no good wishing to appear like the heroes he worshiped if he made no effort to *be* like them. Strength had to come first; one must be strong before everything else.

The sting of the poem was something quite different from and beyond a command to "make" a body. Now shame entered in. He felt "discovered."

Yet for all he put himself through as time passed, lifting and hauling on weights, his progress was pathetic. He remained embarrassingly undersized and underweight, a scrawny frame with stick arms and stick legs. If he dared venture beyond the family circle, he counted on Ellie to be his protector in case of trouble. Two years later, traveling to Maine for his asthma, but alone, he would be humiliated by a couple of boys of about his own age who, to pass the time during a ride in a stagecoach, decided to make life miserable for him. When at length he tried to fight back, he found either one could handle him with easy contempt, to use his own words, ". . . handle me so as not to hurt me much and yet . . . prevent my doing any damage whatever in return."

In overall health, he does appear to have improved somewhat, enough at least to lend encouragement. How much direct encouragement he was getting from Theodore, he never said. He did once remark later on, however, that his father "used now and then to say that he hesitated whether to tell me something favorable because he did not think a sugar diet was good for me."

The attention Theodore devoted to Bamie, meantime—now that she was back in his "possession"—was striking.

Saturday became their special day together. Nothing was allowed to interfere with "our Saturdays," she remembered. They would spend the morning on horseback in Central Park, usually dropping in at the Museum of Natural History, which was then temporarily located in the old arsenal just inside the park at 64th Street and Fifth Avenue. Or they might stop at one of his Children's Aid Society schools. "We would get home for lunch very late," she wrote, "and as a rule would find whoever was most interesting at the moment in New York lunching with us." In the afternoon they would go for a drive or visit a hospital. He was exhausting, she said proudly. At the day's end she was a "complete wreck—deeply attached to my father, but worn to a shred."

In Mittie's absences, Bamie ran the house for him. "Order it [dinner] at prompt quarter before seven," reads a note he left her. He was expecting guests.

Menu as usual—raw oysters if small, soup, oyster coquilles, saddle of venison if in the house, or turkey, croquettes, quail, lobster salad, cheese and crackers, candied fruit, ice cream of course. Give John [the new butler] the wines and tell him and Mary [Ann] that I wish everything nice.

Her life was increasingly determined by such directives, and to her very great satisfaction. Nothing pleased her—nothing pleased any of them—so much as pleasing him. And he appears to have resolved that if she was to have none of her mother's beauty, not a trace of that porcelain delicacy deemed so essential by fashion and that he himself prized so in Mittie, if she was to be homely and handicapped and still have any kind of life, then she must make up for it in other ways. She would know how to manage, to take charge, and be everlastingly useful.

The story among Roosevelts of later generations was that she actually took over from her mother and ran the household from the time she was about fifteen, but this simply was not so. It was only that she *seemed* to be running everything, she was so capable and eager to cope. Spinsterhood seemed her certain destiny, but one could also be a force in this world, like Theodore's fellow toiler in philanthropy, Louisa Schuyler, who, as was said, had the will power of a captain of industry.

· 2 ·

ALONE OF THE FAMILY the boy had his alternative world, his own dark continent to explore.

Once, as a very small child, he had seen the face of a fox in a book and declared it was the face of God. Father, he said, had the head of a lion. He drew endless numbers of mice and birds, filled notebooks with written descriptions of ants, spiders, beetles, dragonflies, all such entries being "gained by observation."

Nor was he ever anything but serious about his "career" in science, as he called it, the beginnings of which could be traced, he later said, to a dead seal he had seen laid out on a plank in a market on Broadway. He seems to have been about seven or eight at the time, which, interestingly, would correspond with his anguish over the "zeal" in the Madison Square Church.

"That seal," he later wrote, "filled me with every possible feeling of romance and adventure." He asked where it had been killed and was told in the harbor. He kept coming back to see it, day after day as long as it was there. He brought a pocket rule and measured it. He wanted to buy it for his "museum," but wound up getting the skull only—a memorable incident, since it was one of the few times in his life when he had not gotten what he wanted.

Dozens of books had passed through his hands, beginning with David Livingstone's mammoth *Missionary Travels and Researches in South Africa*, discovered when he was too young to read and barely big enough to lift it, but could gaze by the hour at the pictures. He liked the second part of *Robinson Crusoe* for its account of wolves, and then with the books of Captain Mayne Reid he was borne off spellbound to the Great West.

Captain Reid was among the most popular authors of the day and especially with boys. (Other contemporary devotees included young Robert Louis Stevenson and Arthur Conan Doyle.) An Irishman, Reid had exchanged the life of a tutor for that of trapper and trader on the American frontier and his books—*The Boy Hunters, Hunter's Feast, The Scalp Hunters*—were rollicking adventures, full of action, violence, and grand-scale visions of the out of doors. God was in nature—a force—and nowhere so plainly as beyond the Mississippi.

Unroll the world's map [begins *The Scalp Hunters*], and look upon the great northern continent of America. Away to the wild West—away towards the setting sun—away beyond many a far meridian. . . . You are looking upon a land . . . still bearing the marks of the Almighty mold, as upon the morning of creation. A region, whose every object wears the impress of God's magic. His ambient spirit lives in the silent grandeur of its mountains, and speaks in the roar of its mighty rivers. A region redolent of romance—rich in the reality of adventure.

Reid's world was all that the boy longed for, one of great manly quests and boundless inspiriting freedom. In such settings, with such a life, one could be reborn, made brave, made strong. He read

"enthralled," curled in a chair or standing on one leg, "like a pelican in the wilderness," the other leg raised and propped, foot on
thigh, to make a bookrest.

> What with the wild gallops by day, and the wilder tales by the
> night watch fires [says one hero] I became intoxicated with the
> romance of my new life. . . . My strength increased both phys-
> ically and intellectually. I experienced a buoyancy of spirits
> and vigor of body I had never known before. I felt a pleasure
> in action. My blood seemed to rush warmer and swifter
> through my veins; and I fancied my eyes reached to a more
> distant vision.

Along with his rollicking yarns Reid regularly provided descriptions of birds, animals, plant life, quantities of geology, geography—most of it quite accurate. A story suddenly stops so a
Darwinian "Chain of Destruction" may be dramatized. (A tarantula
is killed by a hummingbird, which is eaten by a chameleon, which
is done in by a scorpion lizard, which is swallowed by a snake,
which falls prey to a kite; then the kite is the victim of an eagle and
the eagle is shot by the boy-hero who is the "last link.") Even
proper zoological names may appear in the midst of a story, as
though the reader will of course wish to know such things.

> About noon, as they were riding through a thicket of the wild
> sage (*Artemisia tridentata*), a brace of those singular birds,
> sage cocks or prairie grouse (*Tetrao urophasi*), the largest of all
> the grouse family, whirred up before the heads of their horses.

On the heels of Reid's books came those of J. G. Wood, an
entertaining English writer who specialized in natural history, and
by age ten or so, even before the trip to Europe, he was led by
Uncle Hilborne, "my father in Science," to *On the Origin of Species*. Later, staying with the Wests in Philadelphia, he would report
to Theodore, "I go to the Academy every spare moment and am
allowed to have the run of all the 38,000 books in its library. They
have got quite a number of specimens, also." Mittie, writing from
a summer house at Dobbs Ferry, tells how Hilborne "talked science and natural history and medicine, etc., with Teedie, who
craves knowledge."

Summers now—those of '71 and '72, when Theodore rented a
succession of country houses in the hills along the Hudson—were

very near to paradise for the boy. No letup in lessons was permitted. ("I study English, French, German, and Latin now," he wrote to Aunt Annie.) It was also a rule that at the dinner table they speak only French. But the drudgery of weights and parallel bars could be replaced with riding, swimming, running barefoot; and nothing, not even French, could offset the ecstasy of open fields and living things. As a family they all adored the country. Summers, Conie wrote, were "the special delight of our lives." But Teedie led "a life apart," his love of nature becoming a passion and one which they all had to learn to live with. There were snapping turtles tied to laundry tubs, a litter of newborn squirrels, their eyes still closed, that needed feeding with a syringe three times daily. A tree frog positioned beside the lamp on the parlor table "proved a remarkable fly catcher," and when Mittie found he was storing dead mice in the icebox and ordered that they be thrown in the garbage, he despaired over "the loss to science."

His reading became steadily more ambitious. He moved on to the works of Audubon and those of Spencer Fullerton Baird, the foremost American naturalist of the day (*Catalogue of North American Birds, Review of American Birds, North American Reptiles, Catalogue of North American Mammals*).

The first encounter with actual wilderness came the summer of '71, in August, when Theodore initiated an expedition to the Adirondacks. Their destination was Paul Smith's, on Lake St. Regis, a favorite summer hostel among well-to-do sportsmen and their families.

They all went—in true Roosevelt fashion, in a swarm—Theodore, Mittie, and the four children, Uncle Cornelius and Aunt Laura, Uncle Hilborne, Aunt Susy, and Cousin West. Theodore packed a copy of *The Last of the Mohicans* to read by the campfire after dark and he, Teedie, Ellie, Uncle Hilborne, and Cousin West, separating from the others (who happily remained at Paul Smith's), spent three days roughing it "in the bush." So at long last Teedie could write from personal experience of "those grand and desolate wilds," write pages in his own journal that might have been penned by Captain Reid himself.

We wandered about and I picked up a salamander (*Diemictylus irridescens*). I saw a mouse here which from its looks I should judge to be a hamster mouse (*Hesperomys myoides*). We saw a bald-headed eagle (*Halietus leucocephalus*) sailing over the lake.

From the Adirondacks they went to the White Mountains, where the three boys climbed Mount Lafayette, and at no point in the journal for all the month of August is there even one mention of asthma.

That fall, at the American Museum of Natural History, it was officially recorded that the year's acquisitions (in addition to a human hand bestowed by Mr. P. T. Barnum) included one bat, twelve mice, a turtle, the skull of a red squirrel, and four birds' eggs presented by Mr. Theodore Roosevelt, Jr.

A year later he was receiving lessons in taxidermy from a striking old man who had been the great Audubon's own "stuffer." John G. Bell, who kept a musty little taxidermy shop on Broadway, had been to Dakota Territory with Audubon and to the upper reaches of the Yellowstone. It was for him that Audubon named the *Vireo belli*. Once on the Yellowstone he had actually saved Audubon's life by grabbing a rifle and shooting a wounded bull buffalo that was within feet of trampling Audubon to death. The boy would remember Bell for the rest of his life as a tall, white-haired figure in a black frock coat, "straight as an Indian," who had done "very valuable work for science."

Then, at a stroke, the summer of 1872, he was given a gun and a large pair of spectacles and nothing had prepared him for the shock, for the infinite difference in his entire perception of the world about him or his place in it.

The gun was a gift from Papa—a 12-gauge, double-barreled French-made (Lefaucheux) shotgun with a lot of kick and of such simple, rugged design that it could be hammered open with a brick if need be, the ideal gun for an awkward, frequently absent-minded thirteen-year-old. But blasting away with it in the woods near Dobbs Ferry he found he had trouble hitting anything. More puzzling, his friends were constantly shooting at things he never even saw. This and the fact that they could also read words on billboards that he could barely see, he reported to his father, and it was thus, at summer's end, that the spectacles were obtained.

They transformed everything. They "literally opened an entirely new world to me," he wrote years afterward, remembering the moment. His range of vision until then had been about thirty feet, perhaps less. Everything beyond was a blur. Yet neither he nor the family had sensed how handicapped he was. "I had no idea how beautiful the world was . . . I could not see, and yet was wholly ignorant that I was not seeing."

How such a condition could possibly have gone undetected for so long is something of a mystery, but once discovered it did much to explain his awkwardness and the characteristic detached look he had, those large blue eyes "not looking at anything present."

· 3 ·

IT WAS THE WORLD of birds—birds, above all—that burst upon him now, upstaging all else in his eyes, now that he could actually see them in colors and in numbers beyond anything he had ever imagined.

Normally, with summer ended and city life resumed, he would have had to wait until spring to return to the woods, but that same fall, in October 1872, the family set off for a second sojourn abroad, an even longer tour than the last, beginning with a winter on the Nile. So by mid-December, with gun and spectacles, he was tramping the shores of the "great and mysterious river," knocking birds from the sky as rapidly as he knew how, happy as he had ever been.

The birdlife of the Nile is extraordinary. The river is a flyway and a winter haven for thousands upon thousands of birds. The air is thick with them—larks, doves, herons, kingfishers, and tremendous flocks of snow-white cattle egrets, which are called ibises locally, or "the farmers' friends"; wild ducks of a dozen different varieties, geese and vultures and hawks, and magnificent black-and-yellow kites that sail like hawks against the sky, their wings golden in the sunshine. And he could see it all—"quite well through my spectacles." At sundown once, outside Cairo, he watched for nearly two hours as tens, then hundreds of "ibises" came in to roost in the treetops of a distant island in the river, until the trees were "whitened with immense multitudes." In an hour's time another day he counted fifteen different species of birds.

But seldom was he content merely to look. As a serious scientist, he must collect, and from the day the family expedition set forth, heading "up south" on the river, the collecting—the killing —commenced in earnest. He downed his first specimen, a warbler, the first bird he had ever killed, December 13, the first morning on the Nile, a few miles above Cairo. He next very proudly "blew a ohat to pieces" and in the days following, combing the riverbanks, wandering through groves of date palms, he fired away at just about anything in sight, killed a wagtail, a pelican, hawks, larks, doves, then an ibis. Christmas morning he was given another shotgun with which he found he could bring down five starlings with a single shot.

Theodore allowed he, too, had caught the spirit, so intense was the boy's pleasure. Theodore seems to have shown no prior enthusiasm for killing anything. He was the sort of father who, at breakfast, would rescue a yellow jacket from the honeypot, cup it in his hands and carry it out the door to freedom. But now it was "Father and I" who "sallied out with our guns," day after day, leaving the rest of the family on board the great Nile houseboat, or dahabeah, which Theodore had chartered for the trip. "Father and I went out shooting and procured eighteen birds," reads one entry. On another foray he "procured" a grosbeak, a sand lark, four chats, a crested lark, a ringed plover, and a dove. Writing to sister Anna, Mittie described how at Thebes Teedie came to her with "eyes sparkling with delight"—a dead crane in his arms. It was, he noted, the biggest thing he had as yet killed.

No one appears to have objected to any of this. To him it was all "splendid sport." Egypt was like another long summer of freedom, of brilliant skies and open space. Lessons in French and English taught by Bamie occupied only a few hours a day. Father was a steady companion.

Again his asthma vanished. He had never known such a winter, he wrote. To look over the desert gave one the same feeling as looking over the Great Prairies of America, said the boy who had never been west of Philadelphia but who knew his Cooper and Captain Mayne Reid. He was Natty Bumppo on the Nile. Or Rube Rawlings, Captain Reid's version of Natty. He was Humboldt on the Orinoco, seeing new worlds with the eyes of science. Or John James Audubon, who in his time may have killed more varieties of birds than any man who ever lived.

Sky and river and birds became his element. Work, his "serious work," was what gave the journey its "chief zest." Only on Sundays was he required to put up his gun and abstain from the assault.

And in all there was something faintly comic about him. He had, as would be said, a kind of headlong, harum-scarum quality that was more Don Quixote than Humboldt. Bamie, remembering the big spectacles and the great gun slung over one shoulder, described how he would charge off astride a small donkey, "ruthlessly" in chase of "whatever object he had in view." Appearing suddenly in the midst of other mounted tourists, his donkey out of control, he could be "distinctly dangerous," as he and his gun bounced every which way.

Theodore wrote of plunging after him through a bog (both were on foot in this instance), doing his all to keep up "at the risk of sinking hopelessly and helplessly, for hours . . . I felt I must keep up with Teedie."

The advent of gun and spectacles, moreover, had coincided with marked physical changes. He was rapidly growing out of his clothes. He was suddenly all wrists and anklebones, unkempt and shaggy, wearing his hair "à-la-mop," as he said. River mud clung to shoes and trousers. "The sporting is injurious to my trousers," he explained in mock annoyance.

The return to the dahabeah at the end of each day's hunt, game bag full, was his chance to shine. He performed right on deck, in the still, hot afternoons, his taxidermy kit—knives, scissors, arsenic, tweezers, needle, thread, cotton padding, an old toothbrush—spread before him. He worked in the shade of a long, sun-bleached canopy, skinning the day's kill, surrounded usually by odd members of the family, guests, or some of the boat's crew.

The procedure was the same for each bird, large or small. It was placed on its back on a clean towel or sheet of paper. He opened the beak, put in a bit of cotton padding, then bound the beak tight with thread. The anus also was packed with a bit of cotton, to keep it from excreting blood and excrement and soiling the feathers. Then he parted the feathers from the hollow of the breast to the anus and with his knife made an incision, being extremely careful not to bear down any more than necessary. With his fingers he then began slowly to peel the skin away from the body, again working with the greatest care, so as not to tear the skin. The legs had next to be cut away, at the first joint, then the end of the spine had to be severed, again very carefully, leaving all tail feathers intact. If he became too hurried, if he tore the skin or flooded the feathers with blood, the job would be ruined.

The wings were cut with scissors near the body. Then the skin from the skull had to be peeled back with utmost caution, and particularly around the eyes, the skin being pulled away up to the beak, at which point he would cut the neck at the base of the skull. This done he could clean out the brain, tongue, and palate, then pull the skin back over the skull. And once all that was accomplished he had only to skin the legs, wings, and tail, each in itself a ticklish process requiring equal care and patience.

It was, plainly, work neither for the squeamish nor for anyone accustomed to tossing things off in half-hearted fashion. Many adults might find it beyond them, even as spectators.

Once, dissecting a kestrel, he discovered in its crop (to his utter delight) the remains of a lark, a lizard, and several beetles.

Neither the game bag nor the taxidermy kit nor he himself smelled any too good apparently. It was, remembered Bamie, "to the discomfort of everyone connected with him" that he carried forth with this new passion.

· 4 ·

"THE TRAVELER is perfect king in his boat," explained Lloyd's guidebook to the Nile, and large, bearded Theodore Roosevelt might have served as the model. When not off with Teedie chasing after birds, he liked to sit on deck smoking his cigar or reading aloud to the assembled group from a heavy volume of Egyptian history. It was he who organized picnics ashore and planned their outings to the great monuments. Sundays he served as pastor to his fold, preaching on deck. Watching the shoreline slide by, he found that "everything carries me back to old Bible times." Like countless other travelers on the river, he seems to have been filled with a sense of the everlastingness of life. These were the people who had held the Jews in bondage, he said, and they looked no different, he imagined, from what they had then. "We have even seen the magicians with their snakes in the public streets," he wrote to Anna Gracie, "taking quietly scorpions and cobras out of their shirt bosoms, and the old bricks that gave the Jews so much worry are still made of mud and straw now lying on the bank as I look up."

Once, in Cairo, Teedie had noted how "a beautiful Circassian lady, inmate of a rich man's harem, was looking (with veil dropped) out of a window above us . . . and appeared to have no objection to being openly admired by Father."

Mittie, from what she and others wrote of the journey, may be pictured rising early each day to get the morning air, a slim, youthful woman in white, lovely as the morning, and tiny beneath the sweep of canopy. Temperatures by midday were in the high seventies, mornings and evenings were more like October, and though her dyspepsia caused her to feel "pretty bad" at times, her spirits were high. The heavenly air and sunshine, the slow, lulling rhythm of their progress on the river, stirred a sensual joy in the elements and in her own being. She relished the privacy and comfort of the boat, the "open air life with nothing to do," "the splendid sun." Theodore questioned how such advanced people as those of the ancient kingdoms could have worshiped birds and wolves. Mittie wrote, "In such a climate as this, I do not wonder that they became sun worshippers."

As a way to travel there was really nothing like it. Henry Adams, who was also "doing" the Nile that winter in a dahabeah, said he had never known until then what luxury was. To Mittie it was the ultimate departure from life as usual. She was the Roosevelt who knew how to relax; the hours of peace and quiet, the service on board, suited her exactly. "The children have gone to bed," she begins a letter about ten one evening. "I am seated in the little salon of our dahabeah. The door is open which leads to our deck, and by the lamp which is on the table there I can see Ibrahim, our waiter, ironing some of our linen. . . . Some of his front teeth are gone, but I love him still."

The boat, the *Aboul Irdan* (*Ibis* in English), had a crew of thirteen, not counting the captain and steersman, a "first-class cook" and his assistant, plus two servants. As specified in the contract, it was well supplied with "everything (excepting wines and liquors) necessary for the comfort of the passengers." Teedie described it as "the nicest, coziest, pleasantest little place you ever saw." Three meals daily were served in a paneled dining salon. There were staterooms for everyone, bath, divans on deck.

In total, in two months' time, they traveled nearly twelve hundred miles on the river, from Cairo to the First Cataract at Aswan and back again, and along with climate and scenery and monumental ruins, they enjoyed a very social time, since they were actually traveling in a small convoy with two other parties. Four young Harvard men—Nathaniel Thayer, Augustus Jay, Francis Merriam, and Harry Godey—were aboard the dahabeah *Rachel*. Mr. and Mrs. Smith Clift of New York, with their daughters Edith and Elizabeth, were on the *Gazelle*.

Because of Egypt's prevailing northerly winds, progress southbound, upriver on the Nile, was good most of the time. With sufficient wind they were under sail day and night. (It was also specified in the contract that day or night "one of the crew shall at all times of sailing hold the rope or sheet that is attached to each sail.") Those times when the wind suddenly dropped, the river would take hold. "Sometimes we sail head foremost," wrote Conie to her friend Edie Carow, "and sometimes the current turns us all

the way around . . ." On days when there was no wind at all, the
choices were to wait at anchor near shore, accept a tow from a
steam tug, or start "tracking," the immemorial system whereby the
crew went wading ashore to drag the boat forward.

Initially, it had been suggested that a steam tug be hired at
Cairo to tow the whole convoy of Americans to Aswan, but the
Roosevelts declined, "as we go for the entirely different life," Mit-
tie explained. On the return trip they could ride with the current.

To the children, for the rest of their lives it would always be
"that wonderful winter" on the Nile. "Our life on board I cannot
describe," wrote Ellie; "it is lazy I know and yet I have not a
minute to spare." Conie recalled "an absolute sense of well
being"; Bamie, the "golden sunshine with never a moment's rain."

They were all three years older than they had been the first
time abroad. It was not Teedie alone who was changing; they all
were. Bamie, who at Vienna in another few months would make
the first of her several debuts, turned eighteen at Aswan, an event
celebrated with a family expedition by moonlight to the island of
Philae. It had been discovered that she too was painfully near-
sighted and like Teedie she was fitted with spectacles, but so great
was her father's power over her that when he said—in jest presumably—that he had no wish to present a daughter to society who
wore such things, she put them away and refused ever to wear
them.

She sits with him in a studio portrait made at about this point
in her life, the only photograph we know for which he posed with
any one child. It is in the classic Victorian father-daughter mode.
There are yards of damask drapery, a tasseled bell cord, a pedestal,
a painted backdrop of a garden wall. She has a footstool and sits
hands in lap. Her feathered hat and tailored jacket, the large bow
at her neck, are the height of fashion, and her small figure, for all
that conceals it, is plainly that of a young woman. He studies her
from behind, one elbow on the pedestal, only his head and upper
torso revealed, which is what makes the picture so interesting.
Father is seen quite literally on a pedestal, his pensive, adoring
gaze fixed forever on the focal point of the arrangement, her plain,
pale, but somehow very determined little face.

She was interested, very interested, in the Harvard foursome
who came aboard to visit time after time, but then she realized all
at once that it was Mittie they came to see; it was her "darling little
mother" who so fascinated them, just as later in Europe Mittie
would be taken for her sister, her *younger* sister.

"Still, we all became devoted friends," she would recall by way of dismissing the incident, yet for her to have harbored no resentment, no jealousy toward her mother would have been nearly inhuman, and one day her own son would confirm that she was in fact quite jealous of Mittie through much of her youth.

Her duties as tutor to the younger three were assumed without complaint. It was an effort, she said, that "taught me more than I had ever learned before . . . it did make us work, and that was what Father wished. . . ."

Elliott, still the larger, more robust of the two brothers, was an ingratiating youngster, as naturally sociable, open-faced, and now as carefully combed and particular about his appearance as Teedie was the opposite. He seemed to have little of Teedie's hunger for attention. Conversation, friends, came easily. He loved to sing and to write nonsense verse and was good at both:

> There was an old fellow named Teedie,
> Whose clothes at best looked so seedy
> That his friends in dismay
> Hollered out, "Oh! I say!"
> At this dirty old fellow named Teedie.

His gift from Papa at Christmas was a rowboat, by which he put off from the dahabeah to wander alone over the river at will, disturbing neither man nor beast so far as we know.

Possibly the most changed of all the children was Corinne, who at eleven was an infant no more, but a pert, unmistakably female little presence, quick to learn, quick to laugh or cry over not very much, yet sufficiently mature to be moved both by the majesty of Karnak and the "mystic" face of Ralph Waldo Emerson.

Emerson too was on the Nile that same season, and when, at Rhoda, he and his daughter anchored close by the Roosevelts, Theodore at once took his four to meet him. Later Emerson and his daughter, Ellen, returned the visit and Ellen in a letter has left us one of the rare observations on the children written by somebody outside the family. "Enchanting children," she called them, "healthy, natural well-brought-up, and with beautiful manners."

New Year's Eve Theodore organized a party on deck that the children remembered as the high point of the trip. They were anchored at Minya, four dahabeahs tied up in the dark, another boat, *Waterlily*, with some people named Waitman, having joined the flotilla. With the newcomers, the Clift family, the Harvard men,

and the Roosevelts there were fifteen to twenty people by the time
everybody assembled. Theodore and Bamie made eggnog and
young Francis Merriam started off the singing with something
called "She's Naughty but So Nice." They did "Paddy, Come Over
the Hill" and "Clochette, Clochette, She Was a Sad Coquette" and
"Old Folks at Home":

> *All up and down the whole creation,*
> *Sadly I roam,*
> *Still longing for the old plantation,*
> *And for the old folks at home.*

Champagne was uncorked at midnight and space was cleared
for a Virginia reel. "Mamma joined," wrote Conie, "and Father
danced with Mr. Clift, he, 'Papa,' acting as a lady—'rather a large
one, was he not?' "

But nearing Cairo on the return voyage, Theodore became
downcast and sentimental. The boat must soon be turned over to
other travelers who would neither know nor care anything about
the times they had passed there. The boat was "not to be our home
but only one more step on our journey of life."

The picture is of a family strangely and most contentedly
adrift, riding the timeless river, as in some dreamy romantic nineteenth-century painting, an incongruous Stars and Stripes luffing
above a huge brown sail. It was a time of transition, as they all
appreciated. Their life as a family was about to change dramati-
cally; everything was to be different henceforth, something Theodore felt most acutely.

His own father was dead. Cornelius Van Schaack Roosevelt,
"merchant of the old school" (as said *The New York Times*), had
"passed from the scene" July 17, 1871. The loss to the family, their
grief, had been profound. The old man had seemed inviolable, an
institution unto himself, as a neighbor wrote. But with the estate
settled, Theodore had been made a very rich man. Though the total
left by his father has never been determined for certain, it appears
to have been somewhere between $3 million and $7 million, which
means Theodore's share could not have been less than $1 million
($10 million or more in present-day dollars).

A fortune had come into his hands at what was the height of
the postwar boom and this Egyptian winter was only among the
immediate, more obvious consequences. (Such travel was "horri-

bly expensive," as Henry Adams had discovered. In two months
Theodore spent something over $2,000, or about five times what
the average American family had to live on for a year.) Of far greater
consequence had been a decision to give up the house on East 20th
Street and build anew uptown. Theodore and his brother James
Alfred had bought adjoining lots on the south side of 57th Street,
just west of Fifth Avenue, which would put them two blocks from
Central Park, in the heart of what was becoming "the" section of
town. Theodore was brimming with enthusiasm for the project. He
and James Alfred had decided on adjoining houses. Their architect
was Russell Sturgis, whose Gothic country estates were all the
rage. Plans were drawn, approved, construction begun. It was to
be no mere brownstone this time. Indeed, little would be spared
in the way of expense. All the principal woodwork and furniture,
for example, were being custom made in Philadelphia, after designs by still another fashionable architect, Frank Furness.

To uproot everyone from East 20th Street after so many years
was no light decision, obviously, but probably a move somewhere
would have been forced upon them in any event—with or without
their new fortune—for the uptown tide was running strong.

Everything near 20th Street was turning commercial. Union
Square was being overrun by the needle trades. The stately old
Roosevelt house on Union Square had already been torn down to
make way for a sewing-machine factory. Lord & Taylor was moving
to new quarters at Broadway and 20th Street, less than a block from
Theodore's front door.

It was because the new house would not be ready until summer that Theodore had planned such an extended stay abroad.
After Egypt, the family would tour the Holy Land, then stop in
Vienna. By May they were to reach Dresden, where the youngest
three were to be placed in the care of a German family, to be
tutored in German for a few months. Mittie and Bamie would go
on to Paris and Carlsbad, meantime, and he would return to New
York to see to business and the final stages of the new house. Lucy
Sorrel Elliott and her children—cousins Johnny and Maud—were
living in Dresden temporarily, so such an arrangement seemed
eminently sensible.

"If one allowed himself to dwell upon the moral to be drawn
from all our surroundings here," Theodore wrote near the end of
their time on the Nile, "it would not be enlivening. Our gayest
parties are made up to visit tombs . . . of those who have passed

away centuries ago and whose names even are now unknown. . . .
It is more painful to reflect upon the people gone than even the
relics of their greatness."

His father had died at the age of seventy-seven. He was now
forty-one. His father's dream of a permanent tribal enclave in the
vicinity of Union Square and 20th Street had lasted all of twenty
years. *"One generation passeth away, and another generation
cometh: but the earth abideth for ever."*

But what chance he had for extended reverie seems open to
question, given the activities of his older son the nearer they drew
to Cairo and journey's end. The "collecting" reached a fever pitch
during their last weeks on the river—sixteen pigeons one day, a
peeweet, a zick-zack, two snipes, and eleven pigeons on another,
never a day but Sunday when the gun ceased blasting. It must have
seemed at times as if there were a war raging amid the palms, for
the boy was a poor shot, missing many more times than he hit.
Some days he hit nothing at all.

The grand total of birds killed during the two months came to
something between a hundred and two hundred. He really did not
know for certain. He had lost count.

Cornelius Van Schaack
Roosevelt.

Lincoln's funeral procession
approaches Union Square, April
1865. The Cornelius Van Schaack
Roosevelt house is on the left,
and the children watching from
the second-story window are
believed to be Theodore and
Elliott.

Martha Bulloch Roosevelt (Mittie), considered one of the most beautiful women in New York.

Theodore Roosevelt, Sr. (Greatheart), large, powerful, the idolized father and humanitarian.

Above left, Martha Stewart Elliott Bulloch (Grandmamma).

Above, Uncle Jimmie— Captain James Dunwody Bulloch.

Irvine Bulloch.

Two unidentified former
slaves of the Bulloch family
at Bulloch Hall, sometime
after the Civil War.

Bulloch Hall, Roswell,
Georgia, as it looks today.

Robert Barnwell Roosevelt.

Roosevelt & Son, 94 Maiden Lane, New York City.

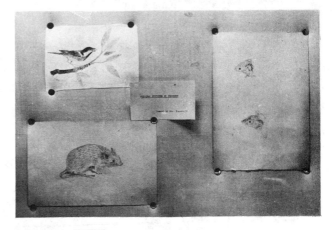

Early work by the student
naturalist, Theodore
Roosevelt, Jr.

"Teedie" at age ten.

Theodore, Sr., and his beloved Anna (Bamie).

Teedie, Elliott, Cousin Maud Elliott, Corinne, and Cousin John Elliott, Dresden, 1873.

Opposite top, a letter from Teedie to Edith Carow, written in 1869, during the family's first tour abroad.

Opposite bottom, Mittie, Dresden, 1873. (The necklace was a prized gift from Theodore, Sr., purchased in Egypt.)

Interior of a typical dahabieh of the type the Roosevelts used to "do" the Nile.

HOTEL ROYAL
à Baden-Baden
Propriétaire J. TH. KAUB

Baden Baden July 25th

My Dear Ellie

Papa and we 3 children
walked up to the old castle ye-sterday before breakfast. We first
went to the market and then
along a road untill we came to a
shed where there were donkeys for hire
and we got, in case we were tired
The hill where the castle was is about
600 feet high and by the path a mile
Ellie and Conie took turns in rid-ing the donkey and Papa and I walk-ed. Verry little of the castle is covered
but there is a fine view from the top.
We had breakfast there and I
got 2 photographs and mementos
of it. We had a swiming bath

Yours Truly

Theodore Roosevelt.

Senator Roscoe Conkling.

Chester A. Arthur.

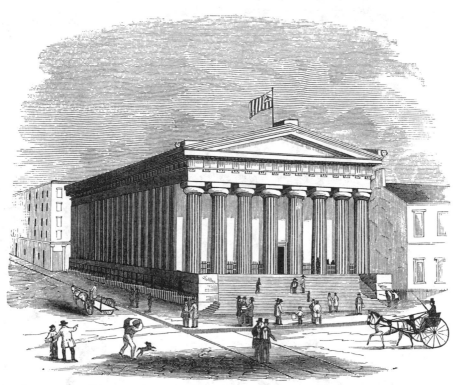

The New York Customhouse.

The American Museum of Natural History.

"Tranquillity," Oyster Bay, New York. Mittie and Theodore, Sr., are on the porch. Figures in the foreground are believed to be Corinne and Edith Carow. (The house no longer stands.)

Teedie, Elliott, Corinne, and Edith at Oyster Bay, probably the summer of 1876, before Teedie left for Harvard.

Part Two

———————————

CHAPTER SIX

Uptown

———————

· 1 ·

THE FOLLOWING SUMMER of 1873, alone in New York, Theodore kept steadily on the move. It was his way of fighting loneliness, he said, though the impression is of a man thoroughly enjoying himself. "You know I never approved of rusting out," he wrote Bamie, which sounds more like him.

The "perpetual rush" of his day began at six in the morning and seldom ended before midnight. The once leisurely pace at Roosevelt and Son was a thing of the past. Orders for plate glass were pouring in and particularly from Chicago, where a new city was being built in the aftermath of the Great Fire. But there were, besides, questions to be settled pertaining to Roosevelt investments and Roosevelt properties. People like Louisa Schuyler came to discuss further good works, others to talk of business schemes needing Roosevelt money. His museums, the Children's Aid Society, the Orthopedic Hospital, all suddenly required his attention, while work on the new house demanded that he look in there at least once a day, usually first thing in the morning.

He was staying at the Union League Club. Evenings he dined with friends; weekends, whenever possible, he went to the country. One letter mentions an "unexpectedly pleasant" visit with Secretary of State Hamilton Fish at his home in Garrison; in another he reports on a dinner across the river from Dobbs Ferry, "after which we took our cigars on the edge of the Palisades and enjoyed the last shadows of the setting sun." He went cruising on Long

Island Sound with the Aspinwalls on their yacht *Day Dream*. He bought an expensive new saddle horse named Fritz of which he was inordinately proud and a "very stylish" new T-cart for drives in the park. "Fritz goes beautifully," he reported, "and it is glorious to be able to go into the country at once from our door . . ."

Seeing the finished house for the first time, he had been astonished by its size and beauty, astonished and tremendously pleased. There was no better-built house in New York, he declared. When he noticed that the architect had included imitation oak beams— beams done with plaster—in the ceiling of the front hall, he ordered that the ceiling be torn down. It "seemed hard to destroy so much beautifully finished work," he explained to Mittie, but he knew how dissatisfied she would be with anything artificial. There would be real beams instead.

"I can see all who pass in Fifth Avenue nicely from your room," he told Bamie, "and just came in time to save a bathtub from going, as originally intended, into your closet."

Farther uptown, on the west side of Central Park at 77th Street, the new American Museum of Natural History was under construction. For the moment it was only a huge hole in the ground for one wing—this in the center of acres of mud and squatters' shacks— but the plan was for a great red-brick fortress, going on and on, nearly Egyptian in scale, to house one of the most valuable scientific collections in the world. The architect was Calvert Vaux, who, with Frederick Law Olmsted, had laid out Central Park. Theodore, as a member of the committee for plans, had become familiar with every detail. The final complex was to cover fifteen acres, fill a space three times larger than the British Museum. Plate glass for windows and showcases, as it happens, was also to be supplied by Roosevelt and Son.

No other project so appealed to his pride, he wrote Mittie the day he inspected the site. He liked to imagine the value of such a collection for all those who, "like Teedie," were in quest of scientific knowledge. If there was to be a monument to his own efforts on earth, to prove he had "done something" with his life, he wanted it to be this museum.

"I think without egotism this really would never have been carried through without my aid," he told her.

His financial contribution to the project that year was $2,250, double what it had been before. When a $10 annual membership was organized, he and five other Roosevelts (brothers, cousins) were among the charter subscribers.

Sunday was his day to write letters. This period was the long-est he and the family had been separated since the war and at times his concern for their well-being seems to have been no less than in those earlier years. (One letter is even mistakenly dated 1863.) Bamie was directed to "relieve your mother of every care pos-sible." Bamie must "bring her home able to undertake the cares of our large house." Mittie was told to rest, to obey her diet, to avoid "indulgences," to take every day at Carlsbad very seriously. Mittie must come home strong. "I am so anxious to see you home well, and so well that we will never be obliged to repeat this experi-ment."

Her stay at the famous spa had been his idea. ("The more I think of it, the better I am pleased with my own self-denial.") The regimen at Carlsbad, as he knew from her letters, was a far cry from their life on the Nile or at Vienna. She was living on zwieback and soft-boiled eggs and "nasty glasses" of mineral water, walking, reading, turning in no later than ten. His concern over "indul-gences" must have struck her as mildly amusing.

But the main worry, as for so long, was Teedie. His asthma had returned almost from the moment they left the Nile, the first attack coming the Saturday night they reached Port Said after touring the Suez Canal. More attacks followed in the Holy Land, including a "bad" one. He was "very sick" with colic at Constantinople, "had the asthma" again on a cruise up the Danube. At Vienna he turned listless and gloomy. They were staying in the Grand Hotel, enjoy-ing the best of everything. The city's parks and gardens were in spring bloom. But the "big three" were preoccupied with things in which he could take no part. Theodore had been suddenly pressed into service as a substitute American commissioner for the Vienna Exposition; Bamie and her mother had been taken up by Viennese society, and were busy buying clothes, going to receptions and balls. To Teedie it was all "the most dreary monotony."

In a letter to Theodore from Dresden, the boy asked forgive-ness for his handwriting, since "the asthma has made my hand tremble awfully." There were more attacks, violent headaches. Alarmed by what she heard, Mittie left Carlsbad for Dresden to find him wheezing badly and forced to sleep sitting up, as he had as a small child. What he needed, he told her, was a change of room. So a few weeks later came word from the Swiss Alps that all was well. They were enjoying the "bluest of blue skies," Mittie wrote. Teedie had "improved vastly," Teedie "goes to bed well."

• •

In September when the terrible Panic of 1873 burst upon the country, Theodore was as incredulous as everyone else. There had been warnings and most notably a run on the Vienna bourse in May, at the time the Roosevelts were there. Some newspapers and financial specialists kept insisting the country was sound, even as railroads began to fail, that this was only another "Wall Street panic," like that of 1869, and would soon pass. In fact, a great depression had begun, the worst of the century thus far, the causes of which were many and complex—the staggering costs of the Civil War and of the Franco-Prussian War, overspeculation in railroads, trade dislocations resulting from the opening of the Suez Canal, heavy borrowing to rebuild Chicago, too-easy credit, worldwide inflation. The heady postwar boom had ended with shattering finality. The suffering was to be widespread and of much longer duration than anyone as yet imagined.

It began in Philadelphia September 18 with the bankruptcy of Jay Cooke and Company. When the firm closed its doors shortly before eleven, it was as if the Bank of England had failed. In New York nearly forty banks and brokerage houses went under that same day. September 20 all trading was stopped, the Stock Exchange closed for ten days. "The failures continue in unheard-of numbers," Theodore wrote Mittie from the quiet of his club. Banks were being mobbed. Henry Clews and Company, a Wall Street bastion, had gone down that afternoon (September 23). He pitied especially "poor Mr. Clews, who has made his business his life. He told me a short time since that he had not for years taken a holiday. . . . Now all . . . is swept away in a day."

Mittie, again in Paris, wrote of feeling "very anxious" over the news from New York. "At supper last evening a note was handed [to me] telling of the suspension of three banks and [the] Union Trust Company." But then this seems to have ended such distasteful topics. Their correspondence returns at once to private matters. She is buying china soap dishes for the new house and bolts of claret-colored cloth for new livery for the servants. He is hiring servants (a much larger staff will be needed). A marble mantelpiece has arrived; the new furnace is in and going "full blast." A carpet she picked out earlier in Paris is in port. He has ordered gas fixtures that he hopes she will like and the old chandelier from the 20th Street library looks quite well, he thinks, in the room that is to be his study.

"I have left the billiard room without any chandelier at present," he tells Bamie, "only side lights, so if you do find it will answer for dancing it will [not] be in your way."

Everything on order from Philadelphia—furniture, woodwork, a huge hand-carved front staircase—was behind schedule. When the staircase arrived and was put in place, it missed its connection with the second floor by three feet. The architect had given the wrong measurements, with the result that the entire thing had to be taken out and remade.

The house was filled with ladders and workmen on October 5, the day Theodore moved in, and there was still considerable disorder and no front staircase when the family arrived on the *Russia* a month later to the day. But with Dora Watkins, Mary Ann, a footman named Frank, some four or five further additions to the "family below stairs," including a Sophie, a Mary, a George, and a black groom named Davis, they moved in bag and baggage—"all the way up on 57th Street." The new address was Number 6 West 57th Street.

A remark by Bamie years later that her mother's European buying spree for the house "proved rather fatal to the family fortunes" would seem to have no basis in fact. Nothing—not the house or its furnishings or the panic—appears to have put the slightest dent in the family fortune. The one inconvenience suffered was the postponement of Bamie's debut, which was to have taken place before Christmas. As it was, the party was given in January, and in the interim, to please her, Theodore arranged another dance in her honor in Philadelphia.

The house was a showplace, even by the extravagant standards being set in the vicinity along upper Fifth Avenue. There was no resemblance whatever to the house on East 20th Street. To move "uptown" was to move up in the world, but this was something more. The whole feeling was different, foreign. It was as if one had entered the domain of an altogether different family, another kind of people.

Rooms, hallways, mirrors, fireplaces, bookcases, furniture, everything was larger and infinitely more luxurious. There were tremendous mirrors everywhere, tasseled chandeliers, walls of glassed-in books, intricately carved sliding doors, paneled and tiled fireplaces, huge urns, inlaid woods, polished silver, Persian rugs on Persian rugs. East 20th Street had had a degree of restraint, even simplicity—or at least simplicity as understood by mid-Victorians. There the furniture had been largely the standard pieces for the standard domestic gentility. (Grandmamma Bulloch, it will be remembered, warned of "excessive extravagance and fondness for show.") But the sumptuous pieces conceived by Furness were all one of a kind, all of rich inlaid woods and mighty in scale— great hand-carved, leather-upholstered, brass-studded dining-room chairs, heavy as thrones and broad enough to accommodate even the very largest of that era's well-fed gentry; a bed for the master of the house and his lady that might have been commissioned for an Oriental potentate.

No one knows what such things cost. A generation later they would be considered in "horrid taste," "utterly ghastly," and, except for the bed and one or two other pieces, they would be happily sold off for little or nothing. A generation after that each would be a rare and magnificent period piece.

Windows were few and heavily curtained, closing off the world beyond. On the top floor was a fully equipped gymnasium. ("We are going to have boxing lessons . . ." wrote Ellie; "it will be jolly fun.") Space for Teedie's museum was provided in the attic, his collection now greatly expanded by the birds from the Nile, each of which was to be properly identified with its Latin name on a little card printed in pink.

For Bamie's "at home" debut, it is recorded, some five hundred invitations were sent, which gives an idea of how large a house it was.

How much of the interior look had been dictated by the architects, or to what degree it was expressive of Mittie or Theodore, is impossible to say. Nor is there any record of what the final bill came to. But it was the only time Theodore had everything built to order for him, and if, as he said, he expected to live out his days there, he obviously intended that no comforts be spared. Had his name not been Roosevelt, he might have been fairly accused of "ruinous display."

To keep the two boys and Conie on an upward path that winter, he hired a new tutor, a young Harvard graduate named Arthur Cutler, in whose care Cousin West, the son of Theodore's late brother Weir, was also placed. For several months, until Teedie began pulling ahead, the four youngsters worked at the same pace; but that summer—the summer of 1874—by which time Teedie was working six to eight hours a day at his studies, it was determined that he would be going on to college, whereas Ellie, most likely, would not. Teedie's efforts under Cutler were directed exclusively to passing the entrance examination at Harvard, this choice having possibly been influenced by the four young men on the Nile, or, more likely, by Harvard's preeminence in the field of natural science. Yale or Princeton would have been closer to home, Columbia closer still and there were family ties to Columbia. Harvard, however, produced men like Albert Bickmore, head of the Museum of Natural History. The whole approach to teaching the natural sciences had been transformed at Harvard by the late Louis Agassiz, whose son was curator of the new Harvard Museum of Comparative Zoology. Harvard had broken all precedent and made a man of science its president, Charles Eliot, and included on its faculty such figures as Nathaniel Southgate Shaler, the geologist, and William James, both of whom, like Bickmore, had been star pupils of the great Agassiz.

To his charitable efforts Theodore gave more and more of himself all the while, as the depression worsened and increasing misery was to be found everywhere. A decade earlier his money had enabled him to miss the war and now, like most of the very rich, he and his sailed high above the panic, quite untouched by it in any material way. But as in the earlier national tragedy, he was incapable of detachment or of withholding his compassion. "All that gives me most pleasure in the retrospect," he preached to his older son, "is connected with others, an evidence that we are not placed here to live exclusively for ourselves." He visited hospital wards, talked with the inmates of prisons, went into the slums to console and moralize. He urged the establishment of workhouses for vagrants. He toured the city's dreadful asylums for the insane on Ward's and Blackwell's islands and was so sickened by what he saw that he led a delegation of city officials back to both places. In an insane time the plight of the insane especially became uppermost for him. He lobbied for better conditions and humane care, for altogether different kinds of asylums, "where the patients could work out of doors, and gain strength and mental and physical health in useful occupations."

He gave money, wrote letters, often working at his desk until two in the morning. Friends remarked at his energy and "industry." Corinne, remembering all he managed to squeeze into a day, said he had the "power of being . . . focused."

"Without his power of concentration and great physical endurance such a life would have been impossible," said Louisa Schuyler. He made everything look easy, she said.

Together with Louisa Schuyler he tried to bring some system and order to the welter of charitable efforts going on in the city.

They launched a new Bureau of Charities, the first of its kind, with
Theodore as chairman, and enlisted the support of Charles Loring
Brace, Abram Hewitt, Frederick Law Olmsted, and others. They
decided to compile a list of all those on welfare in the city, something that had never been tried before, and in less than a month
had ten thousand names. He was particularly alarmed, Theodore
told reporters, by the hordes of begging children in the streets
whose numbers were increasing daily.

But if the plight of the homeless and downtrodden was tugging
him one way, the pleasures of his own extremely good fortune
were certainly not going awasting. He embraced his heightened
circumstances with open arms, living in style, living as never before, and apparently seeing nothing ambivalent or contradictory
about that.

In the spring of 1874, a cornerstone ceremony was being
planned for the Museum of Natural History. President Grant was
to come on from Washington to do the honors and it was suggested
that a silver trowel be specially made up by Tiffany. "My dear Mr.
Haines," wrote Theodore to a fellow member of the museum
board, "by all means order the trowel, one must certainly have it
and the President is entitled to a good one."

And he seems to have taken much the same view concerning
his own affairs—that he and his were also entitled to a good one, of
most anything they wished. It was in these years of dreadful want
that Theodore became a thoroughgoing sport, to borrow the word
used by his older son in a later-day reminiscence. He was "the first
American to drive four horses handsomely through New York—in
style, in the good English style, with everything that belonged."
He enjoyed himself to the full—fine clothes, "meals with courses"
—and a little more conspicuously every year. That "rich power of
enjoyment of everything human" remembered by Charles Loring
Brace now included his money as well.

One could be a moralist without being gloomy, one could work
for the welfare of others without being an ascetic, his behavior
seemed to say. He was "no ascetic," declared Louisa Schuyler
categorically and approvingly. To her, as to others, there was something wonderfully glamorous about him and this, in her eyes, made
him an even stronger force for good. She had been observing him
for years, from the time she first went to work as a teacher for the
Children's Aid Society, and of course she knew him socially (Miss
Schuyler was a descendant of both General Philip John Schuyler
and Alexander Hamilton). "I can see him now, in full evening

dress, serving a most generous supper to his newsboys in the Lodging House, and later dashing off to an evening party in Fifth
Avenue."

To build support for the Orthopedic Hospital, he and Mittie
gave a reception at 57th Street for their wealthiest friends, and with
the occasion in full swing he signaled for attention, then dramati-
cally threw back the doors to the dining room. On top of the great
round dining table, against a background of heavy paneled walls
with inlaid designs of lobsters, fish, and other such symbols of
plenty, he had placed several pathetically crippled children, some
sitting, some lying on their backs, all in various braces of the kind
only large donations could provide. Conie stood beside the children to help show how the braces were fitted and how they
worked. The effect was stunning. Mrs. John Jacob Astor III is said
to have announced at once that "of course" Theodore must have
help in his work.

He was, it was said, "neither spoiled by good fortune, nor
soured by zeal." He was interested in "every good thing," to quote
Louisa Schuyler one more time. To another friend, D. Willis James,
"He seemed to be able to control the strongest affections of the
heart, and to reach men who were not easily drawn into affection . . ."

Indeed, it is only in the private family correspondence and
reminiscences that one finds even an occasional hint that life with
such a person may not always have been easy. Mittie, in a letter
from Europe to her "dearest old Greatheart Darling," remarks out
of the blue, "I wish you were not *so good*, it makes me sad." And
later:

> I love you and wish to please you more than anyone else in the
> whole world and will do everything I can to please you . . . I
> think you have been perfectly lovely to me in your care of me
> always, and so good and indulgent and thoughtful, and I am so
> proud of you, and honor and respect you, so *don't be too hard
> upon me.*

Then she adds, "I have decided that your dear letters are just
a little plaintive and it rather comforts me to receive the 'Private'
letter to see that you have one little scrap of the devil in you yet."
(The "private letter" has not survived.)

Bamie, recalling her debut and the parties at which he was
her escort, writes of "mingled feelings of pleasure and disappoint-

ment." Knowing so few of her contemporaries had made that winter difficult; "and Father himself was so very young . . . and he was so popular that I felt like a wall flower."

Sunday mornings he led them two blocks south to the new Fifth Avenue Presbyterian Church, which opened its doors the spring of 1875. There they prayed among Auchinclosses and Blisses, Livingstons and Wolcotts, "the most influential congregation" in the city, and listened to the word as preached by John Hall, the Irishman of golden tongue, as Beecher called him.

Mittie organized a dancing class for the youngest three— rounding up some forty children altogether—and encouraged Bamie in a new friendship with tall, graceful Sara Delano, who came down from her family's estate on the Hudson to spend some of each winter season at 6 West 57th Street.

Mittie's portrait was painted, a first for any of the family, and it must have pleased Theodore greatly. The face that looks out from the canvas is radiant, poised, quite as beautiful as she is described in so many contemporary accounts. Dressed for one of those society occasions he so enjoyed, she must have been something to see. Bamie described later how she looked as she left for a wedding at the Jay estate.

> She had on an enormous crinoline and a perfectly exquisite white muslin dress over a pink silk lining, with all the little ruffles at the bottom edged with real lace, and the cloak, which was a very long sort of cape, matched the dress, and the bonnet tied under her chin with great pink ribbons and . . . on the brim of the bonnet was a great big pink rose with perfectly realistic little green dragonflies. She also had a parasol with a real ivory handle and the lining of pink covered with muslin and trimmed with real lace. She was considered one of the beauties at the wedding . . .

It was only at "the store" that things were not going so well any longer. The depression had produced not only business stagnation, but knife-edge competition of a kind that Theodore and James Alfred were unaccustomed to, and from domestic manufacturers of glass in particular. So rather than attempting to save their sagging import trade, the two brothers spent their time looking for new outlets for their money. They became financiers, James Alfred being the "guiding genius."

City real estate still comprised a large part of the family fortune, and no one, even in these worst of times, had lost faith in the

future of New York. The Chemical Bank, true to tradition, was also
surviving the depression with flying colors.

Yet rich as these Roosevelts had become, they might have become richer still. (All things are relative, including the disappointment of missed opportunities.) Some years earlier the brothers had
backed a copper-mining venture in Montana, the National Mining
and Exploring Company, of which James Alfred was president.
(Brother Rob, who had the least business sense supposedly, was
the only one who bothered to go out to see the site.) The copper
found did not amount to much. It was only with the discovery of
gold that the venture proved "not without profit" to the family. The
mines, however, were in the vicinity of Butte, in the heart, that is,
of what would become one of the richest copper regions of all. Had
deep mining been possible at the time, the Roosevelts might have
become some of the richest men of their day.

It is said also that among those who came looking for Roosevelt
backing was Alexander Graham Bell, who hooked up his newly
invented telephone so that Theodore could talk from his desk to a
room down the hall. While agreeing that it was an interesting de-
vice, with potential as a toy perhaps, Theodore thought it had no
real future and refused to put money into it.

He was made a Supervisor of the Census, a director of the
Bank of Commerce and of the North British and Mercantile Insurance Company. The glass import business was eventually sold to a
British firm in 1876, after which Roosevelt and Son switched over
entirely to private banking and investment. It was no longer to
Maiden Lane that Theodore went each morning, but to new offices
on Pine Street.

"What business I shall enter . . . I do not know," his older son
wrote, "for we have been forced to give up the glass business on
account of the 'panic.' " But were it not for this and one or two
other chance remarks, one might conclude that such workaday concerns as business, or so disturbing a word as "panic," never actually penetrated the charmed circle of family life, at the center of
which, like some elegant patron saint, stood Theodore.

· 2 ·

THE BEST OF TIMES for him—for all of them—were at Oyster Bay.
The years of random summer houses in New Jersey or along the
Hudson were also behind now. In conjunction with the move up-

town, he had decided to join the Roosevelt colony at the quiet little watering spot on Long Island's North Shore, beginning the summer of 1874. Oyster Bay itself was a mere hamlet of modest white clapboard houses built around the time of the Revolutionary War or earlier, many occupied by old local families with ties going back to the days of earliest settlement. The summer houses—the Beekmans', the Tiffanys', the Swan "place"—were of a different order and set on low wooded hills or bluffs beyond town and in view of the water.

The one Theodore "hired" was out Cove Road a short way from the village, a roomy, old white frame ark with long windows and a columned front porch reminiscent of Bulloch Hall. The requisite porch rockers faced the bay and the best air; the bathing beach was only a short walk across the road.

Now the customary family summer extended nearly four months, beginning as early in June as possible and lasting until late September or early October, the fashionable time to "return to town."

Theodore took the same house year after year. He longed for a country place of his own, he told Mittie, and anticipated the day when he might own one. The children always assumed the house was theirs, that naturally he owned it. To them it was "home," "dear home."

"I had a very delightful visit at Oyster Bay at the Roosevelts' and wish you could see their pleasant way of life there," Theodore's friend Joseph Choate wrote his wife. "They are only twenty-seven miles from New York, and in the midst of a country which doesn't correspond in the least to your ideas of Long Island. Instead of the dreary sandy wastes of the South Shore, it is pleasant and well-wooded rolling country and apparently filled with quiet good people."

The full complement of servants was in residence. As would be said, no Russians of the ruling class tucked away in a dacha were better tended or more safely removed from the unpleasantness of the world. The hard years of the depression, summers of breadlines and bloody labor violence, were times of "every special delight" at Oyster Bay, "the happiest summers of our lives."

There were lovely mornings on horseback, with Father leading the cavalcade, long sparkling afternoons on the water. Everyone had his own horse or pony. There were rowboats, a sailboat, other large Roosevelt houses for children to charge in and out of, miles of shoreline to explore, woods and fields to tramp and shoot in. To the noisy troop of Roosevelt cousins were added the Elliott cousins, who came as guests, and two other "regulars," Conie's friends Edie Carow and Fanny Smith, whose well-to-do fathers, both old friends of Theodore's, were experiencing "temporary reverses" due to the panic and could ill afford such vacations for their families.

Theodore had them put on theatrical productions and spent hours rehearsing them in their lines. ("But, Uncle, I am *not* a passionate man!" protested Johnny Elliott, upon being cast as the lover in something called *To Oblige Benson*.) At the dinner table, as the plates were being cleared, he would ask this child or that to get up and give an impromptu speech, an experience some of his young guests would remember until their dying day. "These Roosevelts were without inhibitions to an unusual degree," wrote Fanny Smith. She loved them for their vitality, their kindnesses, their "explosions of fun." To her they were "a family so rarely gifted as to seem . . . touched by the flame of the 'divine fire.' " Their gaiety was "unquenchable." They were lovers of books and poetry. They invested everything they did with their own "extraordinary vitality." Of Theodore Senior she remembered mainly the enthusiasm with which he entered into every activity, the inspiration he was. (It was she he picked for the female lead in *To Oblige Benson*—her first chance ever to put on make-up and play a part.) That he insisted on calling the house Tranquillity struck her as wonderfully inappropriate.

"How I will enjoy my holiday," he wrote at the start of the second summer at Oyster Bay. When he was absent everyone felt let down. Teedie, who had begun calling himself Thee or even Theodore on occasion, wrote of the tonic it was just to be in his presence.

> He will be with us now . . . enjoying his holiday with a vim. I wish he would not sit down on something black whenever he has on white trousers. At the close of the day he always has a curiously mottled aspect. Seriously, it is a perfect pleasure to see him, he is so happy and in such good health and spirits. We become quite stagnant when he is away.

· 3 ·

THERE WAS, however, one rather serious problem casting a shadow on all these perfect summers and the winters between, a peculiar turn of events about which as little as possible would ever be said outside the immediate family. Ellie had started having strange seizures—fainting spells, a rush of blood to the head as it was described, even fits of delirium.

The trouble had begun the very first summer at Oyster Bay, when the boy was fourteen, and it was for this reason that Theodore ruled out college for him. Almost overnight his hitherto robust, confident second son, "the strong one," the boy for whom there seemed to be no obstacles, had become the family's chief concern, a victim of spells, a child afraid of the dark, afraid to sleep alone.

The policy seems to have been the less said the better. Not even Fanny Smith appears to have known there was anything wrong with Elliott, close as she was; or, if she did, she also chose to delete that part of the story. In her account, as in others, he remains only the perennial family charmer. To judge by what she, Conie, and others said of those summers, there were no problems, no bad days, no bad nights. Teedie, in one letter, observes that Ellie has been at times "very ill," but then goes no further.

In later years, among later-day Roosevelts, it would be said Elliott suffered some form of epilepsy. There was no record of epilepsy in the family but then neither was there a record of asthma. The family physician attending him appears to have been baffled and diagnosed the trouble only as a nervous condition or "congestion of the brain." The word "epilepsy" does not appear in the multitude of family papers dating from the time.

Descriptions of what exactly went on during these seizures are also fragmentary and inconclusive. But the chance that the problem was in fact epilepsy seems remote. More likely the trouble stemmed from some intense inner turmoil. That the boy was chagrined by his failure to keep pace with Teedie academically, that he worried excessively over his future, his ability to live up to his father's expectations, are all quite evident and particularly in the confidences he shared with his father. Even before the return from Europe he had written of the extreme difficulty he was having with German, and a letter he mailed from Liverpool just before sailing for home could not have but touched Theodore deeply.

"What will I become when I am a man?" he had asked his father. "Are there not a very large number of partners in the store ... I think Teedie would be the boy to put in the store if you wanted to be sure of it, because he is much quicker and [a] more sure kind of boy, though I will try my best and try to be as good as you if [it] is in me, but it is hard. But I can tell you that better when I get home and it does not look nice to read."

In the fall of 1874, following the first summer at Oyster Bay, his condition was such that another sea voyage was arranged—still one more therapeutic "change of scene." Theodore took him back to England on a business trip. But Ellie had a relapse at Liverpool. When Theodore left him behind with the Bullochs while he went on to Paris, a serious attack followed and Theodore had to be summoned at once.

> The attack [Theodore wrote Mittie] has been decidedly the worst he has had and very difficult in character. It came from overexcitement but of so natural a kind that I foresee it will be very difficult to guard him from it. A pillow fight was perhaps the principal exciting cause; it was Harriott's children. It produced congestion of the brain with all its attendant horrors of delirium, etc. The doctor says that there is no cause for anxiety as it is only necessary to avoid all excitements for two or three years and he will entirely outgrow it. He is perfectly well again now, but of course weak and confined to his bed. . . . Ellie's sweetness entirely won the heart of the doctor as it has that of all the servants here. The doctor says . . . that the boy should lead a quiet life in the country and I have vainly puzzled my brain to think how this can be accomplished.

There were signs of improvement in another week. The one problem now, Theodore wrote, was nighttime. "He evidently still has a fear of being left alone at night (i.e., is nervous) although he stoutly denies it. He sleeps in my bed. I think it would be very wise for Theodore and himself to occupy the large bed in [the] back third-story room for a while together. I should be afraid to leave him alone."

A little later, in an affectionate letter to the son at home, Theodore said that, things being what they were, he, Teedie, would have to start acting more like the older brother. In some ways it may have been as important a directive as the one to make his body.

> It is a pleasure to receive your letters and gives Ellie so much enjoyment to hear them read. His first inquiry is if there is anything from Teedie when a bundle of letters is brought in. You will have to assume more of the responsibilities of elder

brother when we return. Ellie is anticipating all sorts of pleasures with you that he will not be able to realize, and it will require much tact on your part not to let him feel his deprivations too much. . . . His sickness at night, although worse, often reminds me of your old asthma, both of you showed so much patience and seemed more sorry on account of those about you than for yourselves. Aunt Ella is singing to him upstairs now; music often seems to soothe him when he is nervous.

"It is so funny, my illness," Ellie himself wrote to his brother, "it comes from the nerves and therefore is not at all serious, but my body is getting so thin I can get a handful of plain skin right off my stomach, and my arms as well as my legs look like I have the strength of a baby. I jump involuntarily at the smallest sound and have a perpetual headache (and: nearly always in low spirits) . . ."

The doctor came again and said the attacks were "hysteria." "I scarce know how I will come back to active life again," Theodore wrote Mittie.

Another trip was arranged for the boy that winter, almost from the time his father brought him home. He was sent south with the family physician, John Metcalfe, for several months of shooting and outdoor life and it did him wonders. "I have not had a respectable suit on since I left home, or a white shirt," he wrote proudly, "and as I have to clean all the guns on our return from shooting you may imagine the state of my hands. I am very well and happy." The one problem he acknowledged was homesickness, "sometimes."

Curiously, Theodore then wrote to say that in the future he must always stand by Teedie, who was a "noble boy," a charge Ellie took greatly to heart. Why Theodore did this, having so recently said almost the same thing to the other boy, is open to question. Possibly he felt that in Ellie's case the best medicine might be a feeling of importance, the assurance from his father that he qualified for so manly a mission no less than ever and had his father's confidence. Something of this same psychology may also, of course, have been behind what he wrote to Teedie from Liverpool, though in that instance, one senses that he did in truth need the boy's help and was counting on him.

Whatever his reasons, the directive evoked a heartrending response from his distant and obviously very heartsick second son.

Dear Old Governor—for I *will* call you that not in public but in private for it does seem to suit you, you splendid man, just my ideal . . . My darling Father you have made me a companion and a very happy one. I don't believe there is any boy that has had as happy and free of care life as I have had.

Oh, Father, will you ever think *me* a "noble boy"? You are right about Teedie, he is one and no mistake, a boy I would give a good deal to be like in many respects. If you ever see me not stand by Thee you may know I am entirely changed. No, Father, I am not likely to desert a fellow I love as I do my brother, even you don't know what a good noble boy he is and what a splendid man he is going to be as I do. No, I love him, love him very *very* dearly and will never desert him and if I know him he will *never* desert me.

Father, my own dear Father, God bless you and help me to be a good boy and worthy of you, goodbye.

YOUR SON.

[P.S.] This sounds foolish on looking over it, but you touched me when you said always to stand by Thee in your letter.

Elliott's closest friend by now was a cousin once removed, Archibald Gracie, and from the time Cousin Archie had been sent off to St. Paul's School in New Hampshire, Elliott had been begging that he be allowed to go also. The following summer (1875) Theodore consented. But only weeks after arriving, the boy was stricken, first by nearly paralyzing homesickness, then by the most severe attacks to date.

"Yesterday, during my Latin lesson, without the slightest warning, I had a bad rush of blood to my head," he wrote his father in a letter marked *Private;* "it hurt me so [much] that I can't remember what happened. I believe I screamed out . . .

"Don't forget *me* please and write *often*," he added.

By December he was in no condition to remain. "Poor Ellie Roosevelt has had to leave on account of his health," Archie Gracie wrote. "He has 'ever been subject to a rush of blood to his head' and while up here exerted himself too much both physically and mentally. He studied hard and late. One day he fainted just after leaving the table and fell down. . . . His brother came up to take him home."

That Theodore chose to respond as he did should come as no surprise. He had been warned to keep the boy from excitement, a quiet life in the country was what the doctor in England had advised, but he did exactly the opposite. Ellie was packed off to the wilds of central Texas, to "rough it" on an army post, Fort Mc-Kavett, where the officer staff included several friends of Theodore's from the war years. The decision was made at once and Ellie was on his way, accompanied yet again by Dr. Metcalfe, who appears to have gone more for the promise of sport and adventure than out of any great concern for his patient.

"Do you know, Father, it strikes me it's just a sell my being down here," the boy wrote during a stop at Houston; "it's a very pleasant one but a sell nevertheless, for I feel well enough to study and instead here am I spending all your money down here as if I was ill, I don't believe I will ever be 'weller' than I am; it's rather late to think of this but the Dr. evidently don't think I'm sick and I am not, and altogether I feel like a general fraud, who ought to be studying."

So it was Ellie, not his brother, who went first to try the great elixir of life in the West, who became the true-life Mayne Reid kind of boy-hunter on the prairie. The letters he wrote of his adventures were quite amazing—long, spirited, and wonderfully well written, disclosing his own full-hearted love of the hunt and the great outdoors (not to mention his own obvious appreciation for the Mayne Reid style). His brother was held spellbound. And it is hard to imagine Mittie and Theodore being anything but pleased and proud.

As time passed he wrote of "fearfully cold" nights about the campfire, of long days in the saddle and keeping company with "rough-looking chaps."

> I have not taken a drink or a smoke [he also reported to his father], but I do want to do the latter very much, I don't care how much you laugh and I can see you do it just as plainly as you did that night in the study. It seemed rather hard at first to say "I never drink" or "I never smoke," when asked about every five minutes of the day, for the young officers have unfortunately no way of spending their time but in one of the two of those employments, but it was a very difficult thing to do.

He was enjoying Texas "just as much as anyone ever enjoyed anything." He slept one night on the floor of a log hut, sharing a blanket with a real "cowboy from way out west" and using a dog for a pillow, "partly for warmth and partly to drown the smell of my bedfellow." It was all Teedie had ever dreamed of and the letters kept coming. Elliott's health was perfectly fine and Theodore, who so recently wondered how he would ever get back to active life again, had embarked already on a new adventure of his own in politics.

CHAPTER SEVEN

The Moral Effect

· 1 ·

POLITICAL REFORM and the Roosevelt name had already been joined in the public mind well before Theodore took up the cause in 1876. Brother Robert had in fact become one of New York's more celebrated champions of reform, albeit in a style quite his own and as one of "the other" party. Having happily accepted Tammany backing in his bid for Congress in 1870, Robert had turned on the notorious William Tweed in dramatic fashion less than a year later, in September 1871, the summer CVS died. He had denounced Tweed and Tammany electioneering tactics in a fiery speech at a mass meeting at Cooper Union, saying at one point that anyone caught tampering with a ballot box deserved to be shot on sight. Afterward, he served on the famous Committee of Seventy in its assault on Tweed, and once Tweed fell, Robert was looked upon as one of those distinguished few gentleman-Democrats, figures of wealth and position, of whom New Yorkers could be most proud. He was commonly mentioned in the same breath with such reform Democrats as Abram Hewitt and the present governor, Samuel Tilden. He held no office any longer, but with his writing and after-dinner speaking, he kept himself in the forefront. While Theodore went about his philanthropy in his quiet way, Robert called for government action to alleviate the sufferings of the poor. In angry letters to the New York papers, he warned of uprisings unless something was done. People were starving, he said. "Let us try some plan and convince the poor that we have the blood of civilized men in our veins." He called for the city to mount a program of public works, to give men jobs on the city payroll building docks and paving streets; and he was immediately denounced as a well-meaning fool. ("Absolutely the only protection which we can have against the dangerous tendency of laborers to crowd into large cities," answered the *Tribune*, "is the sure punishment which nature brings, in want of work, suffering or starvation. If a workman is wise he will quit a city whenever he finds no employment, as he would quit a house infested with fatal disease.")

Robert, too, of late, like Theodore, had been living in style, in a country house on Long Island, but at Sayville, on the South Shore, well separated from the other Roosevelts at Oyster Bay.

As it had taken Tweed to bestir the Democrat Robert into righteous wrath, so it took the scandalous Grant regime to inspire the Republican Theodore to join the great Republican reform crusade of 1876. The idea was to rescue the party from the hands of the professionals, which was no new idea in American politics certainly; nor did Theodore's part call for any particular courage or personal sacrifice. Still, it was an experience of a kind he had not had before, and as with everything else he ever did, he entered wholeheartedly, certain the crusade was just, and thoroughly innocent, by all appearances, as to where it might be taking him. Brother Robert, from what may be seen in some of his private political correspondence, was seldom if ever innocent about anything, but now there were two Roosevelts having their say in their different ways. Theodore knew and admired the people leading the Republican reform movement; he enjoyed their company, enjoyed their obvious high regard for him. Mittie, it appears, thought little of such doings, but things seemed to follow very naturally, and before he knew it, Theodore was off to Cincinnati to his first convention.

At the head of the crusade were Senator Carl Schurz and George William Curtis, editor of *Harper's Weekly*, two lifelong battlers for liberal reform—women's rights, civil service reform— and true Lincoln Republicans, which was what Theodore liked to call himself. Curtis was the one Theodore knew best, a tidy, erudite man much in the Emerson mold, silver-haired and priestly. In his youth he had helped build Thoreau's cabin on Walden Pond, and a novel he wrote in the 1850s, a satire on New York society called *The Potiphar Papers*, was high among Theodore's favorite books. Curtis, above all, was a moralist. He had made a career of preaching the public—political—duty of "the educated class."

("While good men sit at home, not knowing that there is anything to be done, not caring to know; cultivating a feeling that politics are tiresome and dirty, and politicians vulgar bullies and bravoes; half persuaded that a republic is the contemptible rule of a mob, and secretly longing for a splendid and vigorous despotism—then remember it is not a government mastered by ignorance, it is a government betrayed by intelligence.") He was totally sincere, highly influential, and not without political ambition of his own; he saw in Theodore, as he later said, the living example of what he preached. Theodore Roosevelt "walked these streets the image and figure of the citizen which every American should hope to be," he would say. They were never close friends. They knew each other at the Union League and the Century, saw each other socially, on occasion. "I knew," said Curtis, "that we thought alike in all the great interests of society."

The light had failed in Washington, in the second term of Ulysses S. Grant. A country in the grip of hard times was confronted with thievery and fraud in nearly every department of the federal government, including the President's own staff. Scandal had followed scandal. A Secretary of the Navy had somehow profited by $300,000 beyond his apparent income. A giant Whiskey Ring had robbed the Treasury of an estimated $4 million. From Boston, Charles Francis Adams warned that unless strong action was taken the entire political system could collapse, and he was deadly serious as only an Adams could be.

When a Republican Reform Club was organized at the Union League at the start of the new year, Theodore joined at once and was soon looked to for leadership. In February, Adams' son Professor Henry Adams of Harvard put out a call for a special conference of reformers, a very high-toned affair, he stressed, to be held in New York in advance of the national conventions. It was to be by invitation only, "for about 200 of the most weighty and reliable of our friends." And when the conference got down to business at the Fifth Avenue Hotel the afternoon of May 15, Theodore was among those prominently mentioned to indicate how "weighty and reliable" a group it was. Others included Theodore Dwight Woolsey, former president of Yale, E. L. Godkin of *The Nation*, Frederick Law Olmsted, Brooks Adams, William Graham Sumner, Mark Hopkins, New York's two most esteemed ancients, William Cullen Bryant and Peter Cooper, and the very young Henry Cabot Lodge of Boston, who, as secretary of the meeting, did most of the work. Nothing of consequence was accomplished—"Oh, they reenacted the moral law and the Ten Commandments for a platform, and have demanded an angel of light for President," said a Tammany observer—nonetheless, it was as important a gathering of truly distinguished citizens as New York had seen in a long time, and if they took themselves a little too seriously as the "saving element" in politics, so too did many others. One out-of-town reporter, picking his way past the potted palms in the lobby of the hotel, observed for his readers, "Men whose names ring through the country and round the world were to be encountered at every step through the crowd, and upon every face not familiar was the plain stamp of intelligence and character."

General Grant was himself the issue no longer, since by this time he had declined to run again. He wanted a third term, Grant said, no more than he had wanted a first and no one doubted that he meant it. What loomed now was an even more worrisome prospect, the candidacy of Senator Roscoe Conkling of New York, a man of Theodore's own generation, who was among the most fascinating, outrageous men of the era and the one Republican against whom every reformer could gladly join ranks. Conkling, a Stalwart (one steadfastly loyal to Grant), was considerably larger than life —tall, beautiful, enormously talented in the art of politics—and in the eyes of the "saving element," evil incarnate. From the moment he let his presidential aspirations be known, there seemed to be a smell of brimstone in the air. Schurz, addressing the Fifth Avenue Conference, declared unequivocally that no machine politician could ever be the Republican standard-bearer, however brilliant he might be. And by the time he departed for the Republican National Convention, at the head of a sixty-man reform delegation, Theodore had instructions to "fight Conkling at all events."

The essential, underlying corrupting force in public life, the evil of "practical" politics, the reformers insisted, was the party system and its sacrosanct creed of party loyalty. Public policy must be above party; the ideal candidate, as Henry Adams lectured young Lodge, was the man who cared nothing for party. And it was thus that the reformers were so ardently opposed to Conkling. Conkling was not a crook; his name had been linked with no scandals; nor had he any personal crudities of the kind associated with a reprobate like Tweed. What was so objectionable about Conkling was his utterly masterful, arrogant use of the very system they deplored. He was the ultimate professional. He loved power; he *believed* in power. He believed in "structure," and for the keystone of his empire he had the Customhouse on Wall Street, the largest federal office outside Washington. His most valued lieutenant, Chester A. Arthur, was Collector of the Port of New York; *all* the Customhouse "boys" were his; and it was thus that he ruled the Republican Party in New York. In Washington, largely through his friendship with Grant, he had achieved a grip on patronage second to none. "Which one is Conkling?" visitors to the Senate gallery would ask, wishing to see the most powerful man in Washington City.

Conkling's scorn for all reformers was monumental, which naturally endeared him to the party professionals and made him all the easier for the reformers to hate. To him they were "the dilettanti" and beneath contempt. At his most charitable, he called them "leaders without followers." More often, he scoffed at their "snivel service" reform, ridiculed their idealism. "When Dr. Johnson defined patriotism as the last refuge of a scoundrel," Conkling once observed, "he ignored the enormous possibilities of the word reform." Curtis and his kind were "the men-milliners" of politics, the goody-goodies; their masculinity was questionable.

Conkling himself, the picture of conspicuous manhood, stood six feet three, and was solidly formed beneath his extravagant clothes. He had built himself up with hard exercise, boxing and horseback riding. A leader ought to look the part, he believed. He walked as though he owned the world, stomach in, his great chest swelled. A worshipful reporter said it was the walk of a prince, but Congressman James G. Blaine, a fellow Republican, called it his "grandiloquent swell, his majestic, super-eminent, overpowering, turkey-gobbler strut," words that had stunned the House and that Conkling would refuse ever to forgive or forget.

Women thought Conkling gorgeous, which he was. He carried a sun umbrella and favored bright bow ties, fawn-colored vests and trousers, English gaiters, and gleaming pointed shoes. His beard was the color of burnished copper and it too was pointed. His hair was a darker red, thick and wavy, and he combed it to produce a single Hyperion curl at the center of his forehead. The curl—everything—was done for effect. His voice was rich and beautifully modulated. His thrilling stump speeches, delivered without notes, were all carefully memorized in advance and rehearsed on long walks in the country. He was a detail man, like every great performer. Had he chosen a career on stage, it was commonly agreed, he would have been a sensation.

Even his private life had about it a kind of forbidden, theatrical glamor. Though a married man with children he had for years been carrying on an affair with a fellow senator's wife, the beautiful, ambitious Kate Chase Sprague. It was the sort of thing that simply was not done, but that everybody knew about. The explanation sometimes heard was that he was too good-looking to be pure.

For a master politician Conkling was an odd combination. He had little humor, no patience with those he thought beneath him intellectually. He remained haughty and insufferably vain, anything but a man of the people. He deplored the use of tobacco and whiskey and said so. He disliked reporters and crowds; he hated ever to be touched. But his gift for leadership was surpassing and he had a mind approaching genius.

To Theodore virtually everything about him was repugnant, and the fact that Conkling was a man of education and polish, the son of an eminent upstate jurist and scholar, the fact that Conkling's man "Chet" Arthur was regarded as a thorough gentleman, belonged to the Union League and the Century, made Conkling's power and treachery seem the more hateful. Also, Conkling represented something new in Theodore's experience. Mr. Greatheart had done battle with ignorance and poverty and the Giant Despair, with cruelty and crippling disease; he had waded into unpleasant, unsung work of the sort others shunned; but nowhere along the line does he appear ever to have faced an individual adversary, and certainly none like "the Lordly Roscoe."

Probably he and Conkling had met each other in times past, perhaps even as early as the war when Conkling was a young congressman and Theodore was making his rounds on Capitol Hill lobbying for the Allotment Commission. In any event, the prospect of taking the field against the seemingly impregnable giant of New York politics cheered Theodore tremendously. As his friend Howard Potter once observed, this most "lovable," "tenderest" of men had a decided instinct for a fight.

· 2 ·

IN HINDSIGHT it would become clear that Conkling never had a chance for the nomination at Cincinnati and many would wonder what all the fuss had been about. But only in hindsight. Conkling himself, as shrewd a political judge as any, thought his hour had arrived. Further, his candidacy was based on the kind of precept that any serious politician would take to heart: he could carry New York against all comers, including Governor Tilden, who seemed certain to be the Democratic nominee.

As a matter of policy, Conkling never attended national conventions and he refused now to break that rule. He sent Chester Arthur to work in his behalf and to nobody's surprise the official New York delegation, largest of all the state delegations, went "solid for Conkling," with the single exception of George William Curtis. A Pennsylvania delegate, seeing the Conkling people file into their hotel, remarked that it was a mystery to him "where the Customhouse got bail for all those fellows." In fairness it ought also to be noted that *The New York Times* and the *Sun*, both openly admiring of Conkling's candidacy, were impressed most by the perfect decorum and obvious "quality" of the Conkling people. "It is conceded [said the *Sun*] that the men who are here urging the claims of 'the noble statesman from Oneida' are the best dressed, the best-looking, and the best behaved of any of the outside deputations . . ." The total number of Conkling "shouters" on hand was estimated at fifteen hundred.

Theodore and the New York Reform Club reached Cincinnati on June 10 and stretched their banner across the front of the Gibson House. They had agreed upon a candidate, Benjamin H. Bristow of Kentucky, Grant's former Secretary of the Treasury, a man of impeccable record who had been responsible for uncovering the Whiskey Ring. Bristow clubs had cropped up around the country and the one in Cincinnati numbered three thousand people or more. So for the first few days things looked somewhat promising.

"You would never recognize your father in his new guise," Theodore wrote enthusiastically to Bamie. He was doing all in his power to "work conversions," discovering how it felt to be a "colporteur," and not without results. "I have really brought one very important man to think with me and his action will be productive of much good. Several more are helpful and I fully appreciate how desirable and indeed necessary for the moral effect it was that we [the Reform Club] should come." Richard H. Dana and James Russell Lowell of Cambridge were "perhaps the pleasantest additions" to his list of new friends, but then the number of friends already made was "legion."

According to other accounts, he and his club worked "day and night" against Conkling and there is reason to believe Theodore was paying a large part of the club's expenses while in Cincinnati. Temperatures were in the nineties, their hotel rooms "stewing hot," as Lowell said. Lowell and others complained of the dirt and grime in the air. But nothing seemed to bother Theodore.

The leading contender for the nomination, as he explained to

Bamie, was James G. Blaine, Conkling's old nemesis. Blaine was an entirely different kind of man from Conkling—warm, captivating, a "magnetic" personality—yet no less the professional politician and scarcely less objectionable to Theodore and his fellow crusaders. Further, in light of events now only weeks old, it appeared Blaine was not exactly incorruptible. The sensation of the Mulligan letters had burst upon Washington. A Boston bookkeeper named Mulligan had produced letters in Blaine's hand indicating that Blaine had once used his position as Speaker of the House to profit secretly in the sale of some western railroad bonds. On June 5, only nine days before the convention was to open, Blaine denied everything in an emotional speech before the House, and to the great rank and file of the Republican Party, and especially among Westerners, he stood vindicated; he was "Blaine of Maine," the most exciting man in public life.

Strolling with Carl Schurz in Lafayette Square, just before Schurz left Washington for the convention, Blaine threw an arm about Schurz's shoulder and said, "Carl, you won't *oppose* me, will you?" But Schurz had no intention of supporting Blaine, whatever happened, nor did any of his followers. Some, in fact, like James Russell Lowell, had come to Cincinnati for the express purpose of stopping Blaine.

All the same, after less than twenty-four hours in Cincinnati, Theodore was sure Blaine stood far in the lead, a view he modified only somewhat with the news from Washington on Sunday, June 11, that Blaine had collapsed on his way to church and remained in a coma. A rumor swept the hotels that Blaine was dead and so the Conkling threat seemed greater than ever.

It was the following night, Monday, June 12, that Theodore made a speech from a balcony at the Gibson House. A band hired by the Reform Club "tendered a serenade" from the street below, where a large, friendly crowd had gathered. It was the first such speech he had ever made, and taking his instructions to fight Conkling quite to heart, he delivered the most vivid, biting attack on Conkling of the entire week, enjoying every moment—the whole noisy, torchlight spectacle, the excitement and approval in the faces below. It was "altogether like a scene from one of those electioneering Irish rows," he told Bamie happily, "but all perfectly good [and] natural."

"Mr. Roosevelt of New York, a Bristow man, got the floor of the balcony," wrote a local reporter, "and made such a strong hit at Conkling that a convenient [Conkling] band put him down." With the music blaring below, Theodore simply paused, waited his turn, then when the band stopped, he told the crowd it had just been treated to a perfect demonstration of how the forces of political corruption sought always to drown out every honest expression of respectable opinion. "The crowd cheered violently," he reported to Bamie. "We were all in perfect harmony . . ."

We have no text of his speech, which is a shame, but it was the conviction and vigor with which he spoke, more than any one thing he said, that had the greatest force. Such was the force of the speech, in fact, that it earned him the everlasting enmity of the man at whom it was directed. The absent Conkling, upon learning what had been said, was not to forget or to forgive him, any more than he had James G. Blaine.

FRIENDS OF CANDIDATES WORKING WITH HEROIC ENERGY, read one headline. SUBLIME DISPLAY OF CONFIDENCE ALL AROUND . . . THOUSANDS OF PEOPLE IN THE STREETS AT NIGHT.

The actual convention got under way at noon Wednesday, June 14, inside the giant wooden Exposition Hall, and that afternoon George William Curtis, the only official reform delegate from New York, berated the "odious" Conkling machine as a menace to "the very system of our Government." The one memorable oration of the convention, however, was delivered the next day—Colonel Robert G. Ingersoll's famous nominating speech for Blaine, which, with its impassioned portrayal of the "plumed knight" of the party, sent delegates and spectators into paroxysms of approval and very nearly put Blaine over. Blaine's recovery from his mysterious attack had been confirmed, and had the balloting begun after Ingersoll finished, Blaine almost certainly would have been the nominee. But it was turning dark outside and the gas lighting in the hall was said to be unsafe, so the vote was put off another day.

As it was, neither Blaine nor Conkling nor Bristow was chosen. A compromise candidate, the dark-horse governor of Ohio, Rutherford B. Hayes, uninspiring but respectable, won on the seventh ballot. The party professionals at once lined up behind the nominee. ("How is New York?" a Hayes delegate is said to have asked Conkling's man Arthur. "All right," was the answer, "all the time for Hayes.") And among the reformers the outlook was equally cheery, if not ecstatic, the Hayes people having convinced Schurz and Curtis that "the Governor" was one of them.

For his part, Theodore came home from Cincinnati thoroughly satisfied. Conkling had been stopped and he himself had had the grandest kind of time. He felt, he told a reporter, like the Israelites after crossing the Red Sea, so thankful was he for the narrow escape from the disaster of a Conkling nomination.

By the time summer rolled around and the Democrats had proclaimed Governor Tilden their nominee, Theodore was once more immersed in life at Oyster Bay and probably as much at peace with himself and his prospects as he was ever to be. Ellie was home from Texas and thriving by all appearances. Teedie had been accepted at Harvard and would start in the fall. A letter he wrote to Bamie, who was with friends in Maine, provides one of the best pictures we have of the summer life that had become so dear to him, and the setting in which the family was to remember him best.

Oyster Bay
August 9, '76

My Own Dear Little Bamie,

I actually have a few minutes to myself by refusing a sail with Elliott. Annie Gracie has gone with him, your mother is preparing for the Reading Class, Conie is at her lesson and Theodore out shooting specimens. I took answers to the Smiths at Laurelton this morning on my ride, accepting for a hop for the boys' account. The ride was lovely. The morning delightful, and I did enjoy the woods intensely. I have just paid George his wages and parted with him so you will scarce recognize the family below stairs when you return. The cause of the suddenness of his departure is the appearance of a jealous wife to whom the servants have described in glowing terms his intimacy with Sophie, but I had already dismissed him to go as soon as I could find a good man. Davis will now be above until I find one.

Your mother is learning to swim and our baths are becoming the feature of the day, all else gives way to them. The competition between your mother and Aunt Annie runs high, your aunt is a little in advance. Conie and [Cousin] Leontine dive from Ellie's boat after swimming out to it. The summer is passing delightfully away and my only regret is the rapidity with which it is going. Theodore's departure for Cambridge is one of the straws that show that the time is approaching when the birds will leave their nest and I am very glad for them all to have such pleasant memories connected with this summer. Our pleasures tie us all so much together . . .

He was worlds away from politics, one might gather, and perfectly contented to have it so. But then late in September, in a letter to Teedie, who had departed for college, he mentions how a crowd of Oyster Bay Republicans came out from the village that evening to serenade him. He would have liked very much to make them a "Hayes speech," he said, but Mittie locked the front door.

CHAPTER EIGHT

Father and Son

· 1 ·

THEODORE SAW HIS SON OFF to Cambridge—off to become a
"Harvard man"—from the little station stop at Syosset, Long Island, on September 27, 1876.

At seventeen the boy was as tall as he would grow, five feet
eight inches, and he weighed at most 125 pounds. His voice was
thin and piping, almost comical. The blue-gray eyes squinted and
blinked behind thick spectacles, which, when he laughed or
bobbed his head about, kept sliding down his nose. The sound of
his laugh was described by his mother as an "ungreased squeak."

In conversation he spewed words with a force that often startled people not accustomed to him, and this, with his upper-class
New York accent, would be enough to set him off as something out
of the ordinary at Harvard—even at Harvard—from the time he
arrived. To many it seemed he had a speech impediment, and
possibly the problem may have been associated with his asthmatic
condition, physiologically that is; but it appears also to have been
such an integral part of his make-up, so established a trait, that
those within the home circle took no notice of it. They were as
oblivious to this, apparently, as they had been earlier to his myopia.
If he talked "funny," they never thought so.

At Harvard, classmates soon learned to goad him into an argument for the sheer fun of hearing him. His large, extremely white
teeth appeared to chop sentences to pieces. Words tumbled over
one another. "At times he could hardly get them out at all," remem-

bered a friend, "and then he would rush on . . . as skaters redouble their pace over thin ice."

The teeth and glasses were the outstanding features, though he preferred his ears, which were unusually small and close to his head. ("I don't think my features separately are very good with the exception of my ears," he would one day tell a sculptor. "I like my ears, they are good. I always notice the ears of everyone.") His hands and feet too were unusually small, his feet actually dainty, a mere size five or six. The slippers he took with him to Harvard were his mother's and they fit perfectly.

The great reformation of physique to which he had devoted so many hours would have been judged a flat failure by anybody unfamiliar with the circumstances. A classmate named Richard Welling, seeing him for the first time during a workout at the Harvard gym, could hardly believe his eyes. He confronted, Welling said, a "youth in the kindergarten stage of physical development" who was standing between two upright poles, gripping them with both hands and swaying forward and back, rising nicely on tiptoe at each forward thrust. "What a humble-minded chap this must be," Welling thought, "to be willing to give such a ladylike exhibition in a public place."

In a "Sporting Calendar" that he had kept at Oyster Bay the summer of 1875, it is recorded that he could do the hundred-yard dash in 12.25 seconds, broad-jump 13 feet, and clear the bar in the pole vault at 5 feet 8.5 inches—in all nothing very special for a boy of his age, but apparently better than his cousins could do and attainments of much pride to him. His health, though unquestionably improved over what it had been earlier, was still a worry and a burden. He was no more a model of good health than he was a strapping physical specimen. His health, like his physique, was impressive only in contrast to what it had been. Some of his sieges of colic, his headaches, the vomiting and diarrhea (his dreaded cholera morbus), appear to have been quite serious. In March, preparing for the Harvard examinations, he worried that he "lost so much time in my studies through sickness."And after he had been accepted at Harvard, it was decided that for reasons of health he could not possibly live among other students in one of the dormitories. He was to have private rooms of his own and no roommate. Bamie—Bamie "the Major Generaless," as Ellie called her—was sent on in advance to Cambridge that summer to find suitable quarters off campus. She chose his furniture, had the rooms painted, papered, saw that there was coal for the fireplace.

Except for the time in Dresden, he had never lived apart from the family, and even at Dresden he had Ellie and Conie with him, two cousins and an adoring aunt nearby, and lived with a German family. Harvard was to be his first solo venture into the world, as his father said, and the fact that his father had such faith in him probably counted for more than anything else. "As I saw the last of the train bearing you away," Theodore wrote, ". . . I realized what a luxury it was to have a boy in whom I could place perfect trust and confidence . . ."

His preparation for Harvard under Arthur Cutler had been rigorous. The hardest work had been in mathematics, which was Cutler's specialty and the subject in which he himself was most obviously deficient. In two years he had accomplished what would normally have taken three and did well on the entrance exams, but like so much else in his life, his tutoring had all been custom-tailored for him and experienced in the privacy of his own home. He was in all things still—in all save his imagination—"a great little home-boy," as Bamie called him. He had never faced a real professor. He knew little about academic competition, to say nothing of the unwritten rules by which classmates determine who the good fellows are. Most freshmen could count on a certain number of ready-made friends from previous schools, and those from the Boston area—the great majority of the class—were already soaked in Harvard custom and tradition. He came knowing one other boy and that one not very well—John Lamson, of the family that had helped Bamie get out of France the summer of 1870. He apparently had never seen Harvard, knew nothing of Cambridge until the night he found his way to Number 16 Winthrop Street and the rooms Bamie had arranged on the second floor.

The picture we get from his summers at Oyster Bay is of a slight, tousled boy browned by the sun, clothes in disarray, who could barely keep still. As the tutor Cutler would write proudly in remembrance, "the young man never seemed to know what idleness was." The collecting continued in earnest. ("At present I am writing in a rather smelly room," he tells Bamie, "as the fresh skins of six night herons are reposing on the table beside me.") He was busy with his field notes and scientific essays, including one remarkable composition titled "*Blarina talpoides* (Short-Tailed Shrew)," which appears to have been written sometime shortly before he left for Harvard. He had captured a male shrew and kept it in a wire cage for study, feeding it insects at first, then a live mouse, which the tiny shrew instantly attacked and killed. Fasci-

nated by such ferocity in something so very small, the boy then put
in a garter snake.

> It did not attack at once as with the mouse [he observed] but
> cautiously smelt his foe . . . then with a jump the shrew seized
> it, low down quite near the tail. The snake at once twisted
> itself right across the shrew's head and under one paw, upset-
> ting him; but he recovered himself at once and before the
> snake could escape flung himself on it again and this time
> seized it by the back of the neck, placing one paw against the
> head and the other on the neck, and pushing the body from
> him while he tore it with his sharp teeth. The snake writhed
> and twisted, but it was of no use, for his neck was very soon
> more than half eaten through and during the next twenty-four
> hours he was entirely devoured.

"Certainly a more bloodthirsty animal of its size I never saw,"
he wrote in wonder.

Socially he was generally ill at ease. With girls of his own age
he could act theatrically superior—Fanny Smith would recall how
he tapped her lightly on the top of her head with his riding crop—
or become painfully shy and self-deprecating. At such times he
would talk pointedly of Ellie's superior attainments. Yet he rarely
missed a chance to show off, with his shotgun or his memory for
things he had read. As Fanny Smith observed, the summer before
he left for Harvard, "If I were writing to Theodore I would have to
say something of this kind, 'I have enjoyed Plutarch's last essay on
the philosophy of Diogenes excessively.' "

To family and servants he was young lord of the manor, father's
"noble boy," and in spirit he hungered for visions of noble quests
and high valor. *The Saga of King Olaf*, the Longfellow epic, had
been discovered and devoured by now. He adored *The Song of
Roland*, read and reread the whole of the *Nibelungenlied*, taking it
all very much to heart.

Another Oyster Bay youngster, Walt McDougall, later a well-
known political cartoonist, remembered him as studious, nervous,
and "somewhat supercilious besides." But Fanny Smith confided
to her diary that he was "such fun, the most original boy I ever
knew," and a lifetime later she would remember how, at formal
dinners, she dreaded being seated next to him for fear he would
get her laughing so uncontrollably she would have to leave the
table.

The limits of his social world had been defined by Oyster Bay summers and the Monday dancing classes in New York under a dancing master named Dodsworth. The "ladies" at these sessions were only those of whom Mittie approved, naturally, and if anything, his own concern over decorum seems to have been greater than hers. Besides Fanny Smith his "great favorites" were Annie Murray, whom he judged both pretty and "singularly sweet," and Edith Carow, for whom he had lately named his rowboat. When Edith "dresses well," he observed, "and don't frizzle her hair, [she] is a very pretty girl." Fanny, he judged pure, religious, bright, well read, "and I think a true friend." "The dancing class went off very well," he noted one evening, "and was very orderly except that Mr. Dodsworth once had to stop the ladies from talking."

Any expressions of endearment, however, were reserved for his "Darling Motherling," as he and Ellie had begun calling her, and for Conie, now fifteen and flirtatious, who adored parties and to moon with him over "serious" poetry. Her health, like his, remained "delicate." She was "Baby Conie" or "Little Pet Pussie," a nickname in fashion among their "set" (Edith Jones, the future Edith Wharton, was another Pussie). They shared eager "intimacies" and in private correspondence with her, as with his mother, he could slip into a cloying baby-love-talk that no one in that pre-Freudian household thought a thing of. "Little Pet Pussie," he would write from Harvard, "I want to pet you again awfully! You cunning, pretty, little, foolish Puss. My easy chair would just hold myself and Pussie."

In the first letter he wrote to Mittie from Harvard, he told her how he had put her picture on his mantelpiece, "where I can always see Motherling." He emphasized how "cosy" everything was, with a bright coal fire burning in the grate. "The table is almost *too* handsome, and I do not know whether to admire most the curtains, the paper or the carpet."

His tone with her was very different from what it was with his father. With Father he must measure up, show the progress he was making along approved paths. But with Mittie, or with Conie, he could relax, ramble, even be "frivolous," sounding at times very much the mama's boy, or somebody's parody of a preposterous little Harvard snob. He had been "down to New Haven" to see the Harvard football team play Yale; Harvard had lost, he explained to his mother, "principally because our opponents played very foul." Yale was not at all to his taste. "The fellows too seem to be a much more scrubby set than ours."

He tells her he is wearing her slippers, "which remind me of you all the time."

In pursuing his new social career, he wished all at home to know, he was choosing his acquaintances exclusively from the "gentleman sort" and it was slow going, since he knew so little of anyone's "antecedents." "On this very account, I have avoided being very intimate with the New York fellows."

Then, to his amazement, he discovered that numbers of his classmates had come to Harvard with no intention of getting an education. John Lamson, he reported indignantly, was there only to enjoy himself.

"Take care of your morals first, your health next, and finally your studies," the elder Theodore wrote.

They all wrote to him, the letters going off at a rate of two, three, sometimes four a week. One from Liverpool from Uncle Jimmie Bulloch touched him so that it was all he could do to keep from weeping. Like his father, he reserved Sundays for correspondence. "Sundays I have all to myself, as most of the fellows are in Boston on that day. . . . Our ideas as to how it should be spent . . . are decidedly different . . ." They must understand that he was not in the least homesick. Ignoring the countless nights he had suffered from asthma, forgetting the fears and loneliness and terrible feelings of inferiority he had lived with for as long as he could remember, he told his Beloved Motherling: "It seems perfectly wonderful, in looking back over my eighteen years of existence, to see how I have literally never spent an unhappy day, unless by my own fault! When I think of this, and also of my intimacy with you all (for I hardly know a boy who is on as intimate and affectionate terms with his family as I am), I feel that I have an immense amount to be thankful for." To Theodore he wrote, "I do not think there is a fellow in college who has a family that love him as much as you all do me, and I am *sure* that there is no one who has a father who is also his best and most intimate friend, as you are mine. . . . I do not find it nearly so hard as I expected not to drink and smoke . . ."

He was signing himself Thee, Jr., or Theodore, or, as time passed, Ted or Teddy or Tedo. He seemed not to know what he should be called.

On October 27, from Philadelphia, where he had gone to see the Centennial Exposition, his father wrote as follows, addressing him as Theodore:

I must write a few lines to my oldest boy on his eighteenth
birthday. I cannot realize that you really are so old, and still it
is a great comfort to find that you are approaching man's estate.
I have worked pretty hard all my life and anticipate passing
over to you many of my responsibilities as soon as your shoulders are broad enough to bear them. It has always seemed to
me as if there was something peculiarly pleasant in the relations between a father and a son, the enjoyment of the father is
so great as he cares for the boy and sees him gradually become
a reasoning being, his mind and his physique both developing
under his care and training, and above all his religious views
becoming more fixed. As he approaches manhood the boy en-
joys relieving the father of first the responsibilities which he
has borne until that time, and those cares prepare the boy to
take the father's place in the great battle of life.

We have both been fortunate so far and have much cause
for thankfulness to that one who has guarded and made our
lives so much more happy than those of the many by whom we
are surrounded. Indeed, it seems strange how few great sor-
rows I have been called upon to bear and you scarce one.

He wanted the boy to send him a complete description of his
daily routine. How much exercise was he getting and of what sort?
Did he find he was keeping up his health as well as at home?

The wonder was his health had never been better. It was quite
the most remarkable development since leaving home. He was "in
beautiful health," he exclaimed to Mittie after having been away
nearly two months; and he added confidently, "I do not think I
shall have any difficulty at all on that score . . ." His eyes had bothered him a little, but it was nothing to worry about. Most amazing
of all, his asthma had disappeared. There had not been a sign of it
since leaving home. Nor would there be that entire freshman fall,
other than a brief flare-up in November, on the eve of his return for
Thanksgiving, but it was so slight an attack that he never bothered
to mention it until weeks afterward. To Bamie, at the time, he said
it would be mistaken to picture him in anything other than perfect
health, "entirely free of asthma," and without a worry. His real
troubles, he said, were math and "my rug, which *will* curl up at the
edges, although I devote a half hour every day to stamping it back
into shape."

Not even a typically miserable, raw Cambridge winter set him
back. Cambridge in January and February might have been a
health resort, to judge by the state of his health. He wanted the

name of a doctor, "in case of accidents," and through Professor Henry Adams was put in touch with a local man, Dr. Morrill Wyman—an interesting choice, since Dr. Wyman happened to be a leading specialist in pulmonary ailments—but all he was ever treated for was a mild case of measles, a condition he found amusing.

His health was good, his outlook was good. There was too much going on to leave time even to be homesick, he wrote in February. "I have been very much astonished at this, and also at my good health. Excepting a little asthma in November, I have not been sick at all."

The picture that emerges, sketchy as it may be, is of an almost miraculous transformation, an improvement of the kind often seen among present-day asthmatic children who are treated by removing them temporarily from their home lives and environments. Away from his family for the first time, he had a year of health like none he had ever known. He was "astonished."

There was to be a misconception in later years that he conquered his childhood infirmities mainly through will power and body building, that he rid himself of asthma by making himself a strong man. But that is not quite the way it happened. First of all, he never would be rid of asthma entirely, and if there was a point at which he clearly found reprieve from suffering of the kind he had known, it came well before he attained anything like rugged manhood. It came when he went to Harvard, when he left home and was on his own in ways he had never been.

Returning to New York for the Christmas holidays, he sported a new beaver hat, a cane, and "English" side-whiskers. Several classmates came on for the New York parties—the first guests of his own choosing to be brought into the house. Mittie and Theodore put on a party in his honor. "We all like his friends so much," reported Aunt Annie to Elliott, who was back in Texas for more Wild West therapy. "They seem to be such manly gentlemen. . . . Teedie is a lovely boy . . ."

His last day home he spent sleighing in the park with his father. The snow and the day were perfect, the horses in peak condition. "He went off most cheerfully to Cambridge again," Theodore wrote. "He has had a glorious time . . ."

At Cambridge, he came suddenly to life socially. He was being asked to friends' homes for dinner. He wrote now of an assembly dance at Brookline, of a sleighing party with "forty girls and fellows, and two matrons in one huge sleigh. . . . dragged by our eight horses rapidly through a great many of the pretty little towns which form the suburbs of Boston." Another dance at Dorchester was "quite a swell affair." He was playing cards, drinking coffee, taking dancing lessons. A Miss Wheelright, a Miss Richardson, a Miss Andrews, and a Miss Fisk began to appear in his letters. He was having a "pretty gay time" and happened also to be needing some money. A hundred dollars ought to do, he thought, though "by rights" it should be more. (A year at Harvard then could cost anywhere from about $500 to $1,500, depending on the style in which the student chose to live. The average was about $800. But for this first year the elder Theodore would pay $1,700—or roughly $17,000 in present-day money—and it was to be the boy's most economical year of the four.)

He and another boy, Henry Minot, were already planning a collecting trip to the Adirondacks once classes ended in June. Henry Minot was his one close friend, the son of a prominent Boston family (the "antecedents" were quite acceptable), who, at seventeen, had already published a book on New England birds. He would bring Henry home one day, he wrote in a long letter to Mittie and Theodore; he was sure they would approve.

> By the way, as the time when birds are beginning to come back is approaching, I wish you would send on my gun, with all the cartridges you can find and my various apparatus for cleaning, loading it, etc. Also send on a dozen glass jars, with their rubbers and stoppers (which you will find in my museum), and a German dictionary, if you have one.

He was in a world of his own, absorbed, bookish, happy. He had a manservant to black his boots and light his fire in the morning. A large black woman looked after his laundry. To please his father he began teaching Sunday school at Christ Church, opposite the town common, just outside Harvard Yard. Of Cambridge life in general, however, he cared nothing. Of the whole workaday world, or those happenings that filled the newspapers, he appears to have been oblivious. That fall, just before the national elections—if we are to believe the reminiscences of one or two classmates—he had marched in a demonstration for Rutherford B. Hayes. It was supposedly his first show of political interest and he is described responding with characteristic, theatrical anger, fists thrashing in the air, when a potato came flying from an upstairs window. But his own letters from that freshman year contain no mention of such an event, no mention of politics or of the election and its bizarre outcome—which is odd mainly in view of how greatly such events filled the thoughts of his beloved father.

· 2 ·

THE ELDER THEODORE had first seen the Republican candidate in the flesh at the Philadelphia Exposition, during one of Hayes's rare campaign appearances; and having seen him, Theodore felt even better about what had happened in Cincinnati.

"He talked very pleasantly," Theodore wrote to his Harvard son, "and impressed one as being perfectly honest." Most people found Hayes disappointing, dowdy. A reporter for *The New York Times* covering the same occasion despaired over the candidate's "dreadfully shabby coat and shockingly bad hat, all brushed up the wrong way." But Theodore concentrated on the face, finding in it no sign of "divided character."

Theodore took most of what he knew of the campaign from his morning paper, the *Tribune*, as ardent a Hayes paper as any in New York, and his faith in Hayes held steady, even afterward, during the drawn-out winter months when nobody knew who—whether Hayes or Tilden—had been elected President. At first it seemed Tilden had. Tilden swept New York and nationally held a clear majority. But the votes in four states—Oregon and three in the Deep South—were in dispute, states that, if carried by the Republicans, would swing the electoral vote to Hayes. Republican "statesmen" rushed south to confer with election boards. Through February a special committee met daily in Washington to appraise the conflicting tallies, and outraged Democrats from all walks spoke of violence should the Republicans try to steal the election. In Columbus, Ohio, somebody fired a shot at Hayes's house as he sat down to dinner.

Given the conscience he had, it is somewhat hard to picture Theodore wholly at ease with the declaration on March 2 that Hayes was the winner by a single electoral vote, but like countless others (including Hayes), he appears to have accepted the proposition that the Republicans really did carry all four of the disputed states and that claims to the contrary were but further evidence of the usual Democratic calumny. Like peaceable men of both parties he breathed a sigh of relief at Tilden's refusal to contest the deci-

sion, and like every true liberal Republican he brightened at the
news that Carl Schurz was to be the new Secretary of the Interior
and that William Evarts, the eminent New York attorney and old
Conkling foe, had been named Secretary of State. Even James Russell Lowell was to be rewarded with the post of minister to Spain.

Hayes's inaugural address carried the memorable line, "he
serves his party best who serves his country best." And in another
month came word of a full-scale investigation into the affairs of the
New York Customhouse. A blue-ribbon investigating commission
was announced, with John Jay, an old friend of Theodore's, at its
head. By the time Hayes made his first visit to New York as President in May, the hearings were under way downtown at the Customhouse and causing a stir wherever politics were talked. Quite
obviously the Administration had decided it was time to cut Conkling down to size.

The record of what was going on behind the scenes is far from
complete, but from all available evidence it appears that William
Evarts was in charge of the assault. It was Evarts who proposed to
Hayes that Chester Arthur be removed and that the new man at the
Customhouse be Theodore Roosevelt.

Evarts was the law partner of Theodore's close friend Joseph
Choate, himself a crusading liberal Republican and somebody who
had had ample opportunity to appraise Theodore's executive abil-
ities at close hand over many years. (It was Choate who, at Theodore's request, had drawn up the original charter for the Museum
of Natural History, for example.) And Evarts, too, had had his own
dealings with Theodore only the year before, when Evarts headed
a committee to raise the money for a pedestal for a promised gift
from France of a giant *Statue of Liberty*. Theodore had served on
the committee and served well, seeing at once the importance that
so great a work—like his museums or the bridge to Brooklyn—
would have to his beloved city.

At what point Theodore's name was first broached for the Customhouse is impossible to determine, but judging by the attention
he received during the days that the President was in town, it could
have been as early as May. One gets the impression certainly that
he was being looked over or lined up for something and it took no
great acumen to see what an ideally suited choice for the post he
was. Few men stood higher in the estimate of the community—*or*
of those high-toned, high-placed liberals upon whom the Administration must count for support in any fight with Conkling. Theodore, moreover, had already proved himself admirably in a

somewhat analogous situation at Vienna in 1873 when he stepped
in as a commissioner at the Exposition. The authorized commissioner had been found to be dishonest and Theodore, at a moment's notice, had righted a confused and embarrassing situation
with both dispatch and tact, and the home papers had taken
note.

His very name bespoke rectitude. Great wealth—supposedly
—placed a man above such crass temptations as were traditional at
the Customhouse. As a merchant and importer, he had ample
knowledge of customs procedures. Yet with the Roosevelt family
now divested of the glass trade, there could be no charge of conflicting allegiances. The point that Collector Arthur happened to
be doing a rather respectable job, all things considered, was immaterial since the real target was Conkling.

Beyond all that there was William Evarts himself, who was not
without his own ambitions concerning future control of party machinery in the state. A strong, reliable, honest man in the Customhouse—his man—would be as valuable to him as "Chet" Arthur
was to Conkling. And the fact that Theodore had shown himself to
be such a fiercely outspoken foe of Conkling meant he was not just
a worthy ally but one whose appointment was guaranteed to enrage
the unforgiving Conkling.

The Collectorship of the Port of New York was a government
post like none other. Politically it was the ultimate plum. The
power and responsibility attending the job were enormous, greater
than those of most Cabinet officers; and the pay, as things were
constituted, could exceed even that of the President.

Everything about the Customhouse was mammoth. If considered as a business operation, it stood in a class by itself, doing
an annual dollar volume approximately five times that of the largest
business office in the country. The revenues collected exceeded
those of all the other American ports of entry combined. Roughly
two-thirds of the country's total tariff revenue was taken in at New
York. Employees numbered more than a thousand. The building
itself was colossal.

Customs collectors and clerks, importers, and customs brokers
carried on their transactions in an echoing rotunda beneath a huge
dome supported by marble columns, the desks of the collectors and
clerks being arranged in concentric circles around a large four-
faced clock at the center of the floor. Messengers darted in and out
while visitors, there to enjoy one of the "sights" of downtown,
watched from the periphery. Collector Arthur, tall, radiant, invari-

ably dapper, paraded through to his private office usually around noon, ready for his official day.

The Collector had direct authority over the majority of employees. The next highest ranking officials were the Naval Officer, who was primarily a backup for the Collector; the Surveyor of the Port, who ran a staff of inspectors, weighers, gaugers, and "keepers of storage places"; and the Appraiser, whose people decided what incoming goods were worth and therefore determined the size of the duty to be paid. These officials had their deputies and the deputies had their deputies, and as previous investigations had shown, "overemployment" was standard down the line. Indeed, the customs service was notorious as an asylum for nonentities and has-beens, a kind of warm, dry dumping ground for failed merchants and broken-down sports with political connections, and for every kind of political hack. Numbers of customs service people were, of course, honest and hardworking. One, we know, was a genius, Herman Melville, who was finishing out his life in dreary anonymity as a customs inspector at a Hudson River wharf at $4 a day. But the opportunities for personal "rewards" in addition to salary—for emoluments, gratuities, and for plain bribery—were so great that almost any job could be made to pay handsomely.

Of greatest importance, and especially to those at the top, was the moiety system, as it was known, a practice deep in the grain at the Customhouse and quite within the law. It was the chief reason why the Collectorship was known as the best-paying job "within the gift of government."

Instituted as early as 1789, the system provided that employees share in all fines and forfeitures. The idea had been to inspire perseverance among inspectors, but the temptation, naturally, was for inspectors to find discrepancies where there were none, in order to collect their share of the fine and also win favor with those at the top—the lieutenants of the New York machine—whose own shares would be substantial. Every importer resented the system but it was not until Chester Arthur's first year as Collector, with the sensational Phelps, Dodge case, that their feelings turned to outrage. Theodore, with his ties to the Dodge family, could hardly have been more stunned, one imagines, had his own firm been the victim.

The case can be summarized briefly as follows:

Phelps, Dodge and Company, importers of copper, lead, zinc, and other metals, was among the most respected firms in New York. It was headed by William E. Dodge, Sr., and by his son,

William E. Dodge, Jr., Theodore's lifelong friend. In 1872 the senior Dodge was summoned to the office of a special agent at the
Customhouse, a man named Jayne, and was informed privately that
by undervaluing certain shipments his firm had been defrauding
the government. Dodge, who had been an outspoken critic of Customhouse mores, was impressed with the extreme seriousness of
the situation and given a choice. He could either settle out of court
for the amount owed to the government, all of which had been
figured down to the penny ($271,017.23), whereupon the case
would be closed, or he could face a lawsuit and whatever costs and
publicity that might entail, in addition to an ultimate fine that conceivably could exceed a million dollars. Never bothering to question the authenticity of the charge, Dodge paid up, only to learn
that in actual fact the government had been cheated of nothing.
The few undervaluations committed by his firm had been minimal,
less than its errors of overvaluation. He had been the victim of an
extortion. He spoke out at once, a congressional investigation resulted, and in 1874 Congress put an end to the moiety system. But
the money paid by Dodge had been divided up meantime. The
Collector, the Naval Officer, and the Surveyor of the Port—good
Conkling men all—got some $22,000 each; special agent Jayne
received roughly three times that for his part; and for legal services
rendered, Senator Conkling received a sizable fee. Claiming he
knew nothing of the details of the case, Collector Arthur survived
the investigation untouched.

Though the fixed salary of the Collector was $12,000, which
was more than that of a Cabinet officer, Collector Arthur's real
annual income from his position ranged around $55,000. The
present-day equivalent would be $500,000 or more.

"We look back upon it, and we think . . . that we were fools,"
Dodge had told the congressional committee. The government, he
said, must have intelligent men in the Customhouse, men of high
character and standing.

Theodore, Collector Arthur, and both Dodges were present
with several hundred others at the lavish Chamber of Commerce
banquet given for the President at Delmonico's the night of May
14. Dodge, Sr., in fact, was seated with John Jay, Schurz, and William Evarts at the head table. The Jay Commission was in its third
week of hearings by this time and Schurz, the main speaker of the
evening, was at his rousing best. The time had come for a "thorough reform of the public service of the country [loud applause]—
the organization, I mean, of a public service upon sound business

principles [renewed applause]. . . . The public service ought not to be a souphouse to feed the indigent, a hospital and asylum for decayed politicians [great cheering]. . . ." The expression on Collector Arthur's face through all this is not recorded.

Then the following afternoon, May 15, a soft, lovely spring day in New York, Theodore and Albert Bickmore escorted the President on a preview tour of the American Museum of Natural History, which was in its final stages before being officially opened to the public. They peered together at cases of Cherokee beadwork, arrowheads, spearpoints, and silver ornaments unearthed from burial mounds in Georgia.

Mittie was included at the reception for the President and Mrs. Hayes given that same evening by former governor Edwin D. Morgan at his Fifth Avenue mansion. And the morning of the sixteenth, when the President went downtown for an official welcome at City Hall, Theodore was again part of the official entourage, riding in the second carriage with old Thurlow Weed and Webb Hayes, the President's son. At the conclusion of still one more opulent affair that night, this at the home of John Jacob Astor III, Theodore and Mittie were asked to stay on for a small, private gathering with the President and the First Lady, as the wife of the Chief Executive was now being called.

In another few weeks rumors were in the wind of Arthur's dismissal. Hayes refused to say anything officially until the Jay Commission completed its work, which consumed most of the summer, as witness after witness confirmed the worst suspicions of Customhouse corruption, inefficiency, waste, and stupidity. On June 22, however, Hayes issued an executive order forbidding party assessments of federal employees and forbidding federal employees any role in the running of party affairs—an order aimed squarely at Conkling and his "boys." Chester Arthur, for whom nobody seems to have felt any ill will, was invited to Washington and quietly offered the consulship in Paris if he would simply resign, but this he refused to do. Presently, when the newspapers learned before he did that his resignation was to be requested, Arthur felt he had no choice but to stand fast. The New York *Sun*, a Democratic paper, speculated that perhaps Secretary Evarts' real wish in bringing new management to the Customhouse was to foster some fresh Republican leadership in New York.

To date there had been no response from Roscoe Conkling, who had been abroad for the summer (Mrs. Sprague was currently living in Paris). It was not until September that he opened his attack, in a speech at a Republican state convention in Rochester, and with a savagery that appalled everyone, including many of his admirers.

Who were these men cracking the whip over him like schoolmasters, Conkling demanded, these man-milliners, these carpet knights of politics with their veneer of superior purity. George William Curtis, who had spoken in support of Hayes only moments before, sat muttering, "Remarkable! What an exhibition! Bad temper! Very bad temper!" Hammering on, glaring at Curtis, Conkling said no party was ever built on deportment or ladies' magazines or gush. The speech was taken to be an unfortunate emotional outburst, the senator having momentarily lost hold of himself. *The New York Times* said he sounded like a maniac. But in fact it had all been quite carefully prepared and memorized, every breath of it timed for maximum effect.

"We are all excited here about politics just now, everybody outraged at the late performances at Rochester," wrote Joseph Choate to his wife after spending the weekend with Theodore and the family at Oyster Bay.

For Theodore life went on all the same. He had become interested in a scheme to bring Cleopatra's Needle to New York. He was busy at the office, busy as always with his good deeds, and working too hard, the family felt. In May he had taken a break to escort Bamie, Conie, Cousin Maud, and Edith Carow on a weekend visit to Harvard, and again in midsummer he and Bamie went off to stay with friends at Mount Desert Island in Maine. Back at his office later, he observed that he, the gay butterfly, had been reduced once more to a grub. Elliott had returned from Texas to stay and young Theodore was embarking on prodigious expeditions up and down Long Island Sound by rowboat, covering in one day as much as twenty-five miles. The long summer was a "capital time," highlighted by a visit from Uncle Jimmie Bulloch. Then the first week in September Theodore went off to Saratoga to a State Board of Charities meeting to discuss the conditions of insane children.

The formal announcement that he was to replace Arthur at the Customhouse came in October. Two others—General Edwin A. Merritt and a lawyer with the majestic name of Le Baron Bradford Prince had been picked to fill the posts of Surveyor and Naval Officer. The nominations went to the Senate on the twenty-fourth, by which time it was obvious that more than the fate of the Customhouse or the Conkling machine was riding on the outcome. At issue was the power of the presidency as measured against that of the Senate, and the realities of Senate politics being what they were, and in view of the decline of presidential power since Lincoln, the chance for a Hayes victory looked slim. For one thing, the committee through which the nominations would first have to pass was the committee on commerce, of which Senator Conkling was chairman. Still, Hayes remained firm. "I am clear that I am right," he wrote in his diary. "I believe that a large majority of the best people are in full accord with me." Senator George Edmunds, Republican of Vermont, was delegated to warn Hayes of the risks he was running and to ask that he "cooperate." "We must cooperate in the interests of the country," Hayes responded.

To the reformers, of whom very few were members of the United States Senate, it had become a test case.

Conkling's committee sat on the nominations for another month and more, during which, to the delight of reporters, Conkling gave forth with some of the choicest invective of his career. Stopped one day in New York by a man from the *Herald*, Conkling observed that there were in total perhaps three hundred in the city who opposed him, "who believe themselves to occupy the solar walk and the milky way, and even up there they lift their skirts very carefully for fear even the heavens might stain them. . . . They would have people fill the offices by nothing less than divine selection."

Theodore, meantime, was appearing at City Hall before the New York Board of Apportionment to protest, in behalf of the State Board of Charities, scandalous conditions in the city's asylums for the indigent and the insane. (TERRIBLE CHARGES, read the headline in the *Herald* the morning after he had spoken his piece.) He denounced the mixing of criminals with the sick and the insane, deplored the wretched food, the rampant incompetence and "graver moral deficiencies" of the people employed to work in such places. The underlying problem, he insisted, was politics, the system by which every job was political and no one person could ever be held accountable.

To friends and admirers he seemed to have reached a new plateau of maturity and influence. The stature of the Collectorship would be raised to new heights the moment he took office, his admirers knew. One friend, D. Willis James, who had been away from the city for a year, wrote after seeing him again that fall that "he seemed to me another man," so great was the change. "I was astonished. I was amazed at the growth . . ."

At age forty-six he was, as said the *Tribune,* "in the prime of vigorous manhood" and stood ready to do his duty. Naturally he stood ready to do his duty. "I will take the office not to administer it for the benefit of a party," he told the papers, "but for the benefit of the whole people." If confirmed he would serve without pay. Editorials praised the appointment. "Mr. Roosevelt is a gentleman above reproach and would unquestionably inaugurate a new order of things at the Customhouse." George William Curtis said in *Harper's Weekly* that the President could have found no man "of higher character or greater fitness."

But the fight over the confirmation was one in which Theodore himself could take no personal part, conspicuous as he was made by the appointment; and his frustrations and worries compounded as weeks went by and nothing happened beyond talk and speculation. Greatly as he detested Conkling he was unable to speak out. He must bide his time, maintain perfect decorum and silence, and so passive a role did not sit at all well with him.

In secret he hoped he would be turned down, he later told young Theodore. To "purify" the Customhouse would be a task of unfathomable difficulty and he dreaded it. He knew what to expect at the hands of the politicians and the press.

To the rest of the family, meantime, he seems to have said as little as possible about the job or the changes it would mean for all of them; and to judge by the very little his son said about the subject in what he wrote from Harvard, none of them was overly concerned in any event. "Tell Father I am watching the 'Controllership' movements with the greatest interest," the boy added to the end of a letter to Bamie, suggesting he was ignorant even of the name of the job. But he also asked that his subscription to the *Tribune* be renewed and observed in another letter to Bamie in November that it looked as though their father would not get the Collectorship. "I am glad on his account, but sorry for New York." His own triumph of the moment was "The Summer Birds of the Adirondacks in Franklin County, N. Y.," his first published work, a pamphlet of three or four pages that he and Henry Minot had gotten up as a result of their trip the previous summer.

There was something in the papers about the Customhouse nominations nearly every day. On November 10, Senate Republicans caucused in "unusual secrecy" for five hours during which

Conkling argued against any nomination made to succeed an officer dismissed without cause. On November 30, Conkling's committee on commerce unanimously rejected the Customhouse appointments, and four days later when the Senate went into executive session to consider the full list of presidential appointments—circuit judges, Indian commissioners, postmasters—time was somehow never found to decide on any appointments to the customs service. Since the current session of Congress expired that same day, the Administration would thus be required to send those particular nominations to the Senate all over again with the start of the next session. Conkling was not merely stalling for time to line up the votes he needed, but giving the Administration opportunity to see the light and drop the matter altogether.

By now the story filled the front pages. Following a Cabinet meeting on December 4, it was reported that a compromise was in the making. Allegedly, to appease Conkling, Theodore Roosevelt would not be named again for the Collectorship. Conkling, it was understood, might accept some other nominee, but not Roosevelt under any circumstances. But on December 6, Hayes told a delegation of New York congressmen who had come to speak for Collector Arthur that his nominees were "good men" and he would make no changes. He sent his customs service list to the Senate later the same day and the Senate went into executive session at once.

Conkling challenged Hayes for not giving due cause for removing Arthur. He denounced Hayes personally, ridiculed the civil service passages in Hayes's annual message to Congress issued the day before. Conkling was "forcible, witty, and severely sarcastic." He also proved himself grandly inconsistent by supporting the nomination of a new customs Collector at Chicago to replace someone being removed without explanatory cause.

"I am very much afraid that Conkling has won the day," young Theodore wrote to his father.

On December 11, the committee on commerce confirmed the appointment of Edwin A. Merritt and rejected those of Theodore Roosevelt and Le Baron Bradford Prince. The vote in the Senate came the afternoon of the twelfth, when the doors of the Senate were again swung shut for another executive—secret—session. Conkling's speech this time was one of his major orations, reputedly one of the three most brilliant performances of his political career. He spoke last and for nearly an hour and a half. From an undisclosed source a reporter put together a vivid picture of the scene, of Conkling striding up and down the aisle as he spoke, his voice gathering strength until he was shouting "and [he] clinched every sentence with violent gestures." He tore into the Administration, as before; he defended his dear and loyal friend Arthur. He denied "in an excited manner" that the Customhouse was in any way a political machine. But the climax came with his attack on Theodore Roosevelt. "He said Mr. Roosevelt was his bitter personal enemy, who had lost no opportunity of denouncing him, and he appealed to Senators to protect him and the four millions of people he represented." It was because Roosevelt was his enemy that the Administration had picked Roosevelt for the job in the first place. The appointment, Conkling said, had been made solely to destroy and humiliate and dishonor Roscoe Conkling and he would not have it.

The vote came at eight that evening and of the Republicans a mere six refused to go along with Conkling. The nominations of Theodore and Le Baron Bradford Prince were rejected by a count of 31 to 25. "In the language of the press," wrote Hayes in his diary, " 'Senator Conkling has won a great victory over the Administration.' . . . But the end is not yet. I am right, and shall not give up the contest."

Theodore, who is not known ever to have kept a diary, wrote to his older son the following Sunday evening.

6 West 57th Street
December 16, 1877

Dear old Theodore,

As usual I sit down to my desk in my little room after the others have gone to bed. You know that it is not the want of the will that makes me a poor correspondent, but even tonight when I had passed over the newsboys to Mr. Blagdon's care and anticipated a quiet evening we have been obliged to devote ourselves to others.

People have been calling, including Mr. [Albert] Bierstadt, who came in late to ask me to dine with him and gave some very interesting descriptions of the manner in which he made his studies of the buffalo.

A great weight was taken off my shoulders when Elliott read the other morning that the Senate had decided not to confirm me, no one can imagine the relief. To purify our Customhouse was a terrible undertaking which I felt it was my duty to undertake but I realized all the difficulties I would encounter and the abuse I must expect to receive. I feel now

so glad I did not refuse it. The machine politicians have shown
their colors and not one person has been able to make an ac-
cusation of any kind against me. Indeed, they have all done
me more than justice. I never told your mother but it would
have practically kept me in the city almost all the time in summer and that would be no joke. I feel sorry for the country,
however, as it shows the power of the partisan politicians who
think of nothing higher than their own interests. I fear for your
future. We cannot stand so corrupt a government for any great
length of time.

What he failed to mention was that in the final weeks of the
battle he had been stricken with severe intestinal pains, of which
he apparently wished the boy to know nothing. Bamie, however,
had already sent word on and in a letter to her written from Cambridge that same Sunday he said he was "very uneasy about Father." Did the doctor think it anything serious, he asked. "Thank
fortune, my own health is excellent, and so, when I get home, I can
with a clear conscience give him a rowing up for not taking better
care of himself . . . The trouble is the dear old fellow never does
think of himself in anything."

· 3 ·

THEODORE DIED less than two months later. He had his good days,
mornings when the pain subsided as if by miracle and he and
Bamie would go for a drive. Through one long remission—the
week after Christmas, with young Theodore home—he actually
seemed to be recovering. But even then his confidence and cheer
were a front. When the American Museum of Natural History had
its grand opening on December 22, he was too ill to attend. Again
President Hayes took part and Charles W. Eliot, president of Harvard, was the main speaker. It was described in the papers as "one
of the most brilliant daylight assemblages that New York has ever
seen," and for Theodore, by all rights, it should have been a day of
days, a moment of acclaim and restitution after what he had been
through since October. Of his defeat at the hands of Senator Conkling, he had been willing to say only that he remained "definitely
hostile" to machine politics in any form.

The first sign that there was something seriously wrong with
him had come less than forty-eight hours after he had written the

long letter to young Theodore, his final letter to the boy so far as is known. The diagnosis then was acute peritonitis, which was regarded as extremely alarming. As one of young Theodore's friends would write, "You couldn't have your appendix out then, you didn't know the word, you got something they called peritonitis, or inflammation of the bowels, and usually died." But as later determined, he was, in fact, dying of cancer of the stomach—of a malignant, inoperable tumor of the bowel that was growing rapidly.

The anxiety that swept through the family may be felt even in such brief entries as to be found in a diary kept by Anna Gracie.

Tuesday, December 18
Ellie stopped on his way downtown, said his father was taken very ill about 4 o'clock this morning. Bamie's party tonight. I saw Thee before I went into [the] drawing r[oo]m, *very* ill. Conie sat with him until two o'clock.

Thursday, December 20
All day at 57th St. Thee desperately ill.

Friday, December 21
First ray of hope, dear Thee will be better of this attack of peritonitis, but the disease is no better.

Sunday, December 23
Took tea at 57th St. Thee so ill but more comfortable.

Monday, December 24
Spent tonight at 57th, arranged table and stockings of children's things. Thee more easy but very weak.

Tuesday, December 25
Saw dear Thee a short time before we went to church. Afternoon sat with him while Bamie rested. He made us all but Mittie go in to Xmas dinner . . .

"Can *I* do anything for you and Mrs. Roosevelt?" asked Louisa Schuyler in a note to Bamie. "I mean by way of sitting downstairs to answer messages and notes—or anything of the kind?" "Xmas. Father seems much better," wrote young Theodore, who was keeping a "Private Diary" of his own once again and who left for Harvard after New Year's convinced his father had passed the crisis.

They said goodbye to each other January 2, and according to later entries in the new diary, Theodore told him he was the dearest of his children and had never caused him a moment's pain. There had been a heavy snowfall. The city was a winter scene from *Harper's Weekly* and the boy and the family coachman, bundled to the ears, were not a hundred feet from the door, heading for the boat, when their sleigh tipped over and they were dragged off down the street by the horses like a snowplow—all "rather good fun," as the boy said. He expressed no particular concern for his father in the letters that followed from Cambridge, nor in his diary, but then neither was he being told anything of the actual situation. It had been decided that he should be spared any worry. With Henry Minot, he had now joined the Nuttall Ornithological Club of Cambridge, before which, on the evening of January 28, 1878, he presented a paper on certain aspects of the English sparrow problem.

As the days passed, Theodore's physical pain became excruciating. Mittie seldom left his side. But they all took their turns watching over him—Anna Gracie, James Alfred, who came in from next door, Bamie, Elliott, Conie, the maid Mary Ann. They sat and read aloud to him, or they just sat. "I have sat with him some seven hours," Conie told Edith Carow. "He slept most of it but at times was in fearful agony. Oh, Edith, it is the most frightful thing to see the person you love best in the world in terrible pain . . ." He was suffering so, she said, that his hair was turning gray.

The morning of February 7 he was either sufficiently free from pain or sufficiently sedated to be taken for a sleigh ride, Bamie riding in the seat beside him; and that afternoon there was a letter from young Theodore that pleased him enormously. "I was with your dear father when your mother read your letter to him out loud," wrote Anna Gracie. "You would have felt more than repaid for the exertion of writing such a cheery, long letter to him, if you could have seen the expression of his face. . . . His whole face lighted up with a beautiful smile when she read the figures out of the two examinations you have just passed. . . . I have not seen him look so pleased and like himself for a long time."

The next morning, early, he and Bamie went off again, though this time, on return, he was again in agony. The doctor was sent for. Carriages came and went through the rest of the day as friends called to express their concern and to ask if there was anything they could do. Word of his condition had also reached the newspapers by now and the day following, Saturday, February 9, a crowd gathered on the sidewalk outside. It was there hour after hour as the day passed. Conie would remember it as a "huge" crowd, which perhaps it was, and most heartrending to her, as to all those who came and went, were the numbers of ragged children who stood waiting—his newsboys and orphans. The scene, as recalled, seems so very Victorian as to be not quite real, like some sentimental deathwatch from Dickens. One imagines the wind whipping the snow. (Actually it had turned warm and rain fell several times during the day.) But the children *were* there at the steps to the house waiting for news of the man who doubtless meant, just as Conie said, more to them than any other human being.

A telegram was sent telling young Theodore to return at once. Three doctors were rushed to the house. James Alfred and Aunt Lizzie stood by on the first floor. Cornelius and Laura arrived, as did Anna and James Gracie. Counting the servants there were at times as many as twenty people in the house.

The end did not come until nearly midnight. Of the long day itself, there is only one firsthand account. It was written by Elliott, whose devotion to his father over the past week or more had been heroic. He had hardly taken time to eat or sleep. He was ill, close to a complete collapse, his "young strength . . . poured out," as Conie remembered, even before the day began. The account, given here with only a few minor deletions, appears to have been written soon after Theodore died, possibly the following day, the "terrible Sunday" when young Theodore arrived by the night boat from Boston.

Feb. 9, 1878
This morning at ten while I was sitting in my room smoking, Corinne ran in and said, "Ellie, Father wants to be moved, will you come upstairs?" I went immediately and found Father still under the influences of sedatives, sitting in the rocking chair in the morning room. As I came in he beckoned to me. I ran to him and . . . my arms about him, he got up and with my help tottered to the mantel. Here suddenly his face became distorted with pain and he called out loud for ether. I left him, got the bottle and taking him in my arms put him on the sofa and drenching the handkerchief I held it on his nose. Mother, Bamie, and Mary Ann came up and we sent for the doctor. This was 10:15. From then until 11:30 all the strength I had could barely keep him on the sofa. He never said anything but "Oh! My!" but the agony in his face was awful. Ether and sedatives were of no avail. Little Mother stood by with a glass of water which I drank at intervals, being deathly sick. Pretty soon Fa-

ther began to vomit after which he would be quiet a minute,
then with face fearful with pain [he] would clasp me tight in
his arms. . . . The power with which he would hug me was
terrific and then in a second he would be lying, white, panting,
and weak as a baby in my arms with sweat in huge drops
rolling down his face and neck. . . . At 11:30, thank God, the
doctor came. I ran up to the Ellises, found Dr. Thomas and
returned to find the doctor about to give Father chloroform. On
its application Father became quiet instantly but the two doctors despaired of his life and from then until 1:30 Mother sat at
his head and I by him with the chlo[roform] and handkerchief.
We put him from one chlo[roform] sleep into another . . . Dr.
Polk relieved Mother and I at 1:30 when we tried to take a bit
of lunch. The afternoon Dr. Polk, Mother, Uncle Jim, [Dr.]
Thomas, and I were by his side all the time. . . . At 6:30 Mother
and I went down and tried to eat dinner. I felt so sick I stayed
to smoke a cigar and after felt well and more myself. I sat in
the little room with Uncles Corneil and Jim and Aunts Laura
and Lizzie and little Mary Ann. Going upstairs at 7:30 I found
the servants in the hall waiting with scared faces in Corinne's
room, Aunt A[nna], B[amie], and C[onie] all in tears. Mother,
Dr.'s Polk and Goldthwait and Uncle Jimmie by the bedside.
Father seemed the same but his pulse much feebler. Dr.
P[olk], Bamie, and C[onie] went to bed. Uncle Jim came up
and Mother and the two uncles and Dr. G[oldthwait] and
watched. Oh, my God, my father, what agonies you suffered.
. . . So it went on. At eleven fifteen he opened his eyes. I mo-
tioned to the Dr. who applied the tube and brandy to his
mouth. He did not make an effort to suck even. We put the
glass up and dropped it [the brandy] down. He turned sharp to
the left and throwing up his arms around, he gave one mighty
clasp and then with a groan of pain turned over and with his
right hand under his head and left out over the side of the sofa
began the gurgling breathing of death. "Call the doctor."
"Bamie—Corinne." "Mother, come here for God's sake
quick." And then Dr. Polk sitting by his side. Mother kneeling
by him. Bamie by her. The little Baby [Corinne] trembling and
crying, kneeling by me on his left side and all the rest standing
near. His eyelids fluttered, he gave three long breaths. It is
finished. No, my God, it cannot be. "Darling, darling, darling,
I am here," cried my little widowed mother. I knelt down and
prayed, "Our Father which art in heaven, hallowed be Thy
name, Thy will be done, Thy will be done." As the last
breath left his body the little clock on the table struck one—
one half past eleven. Thirteen and a quarter hours of agony

it took to kill a man broken down by three months' sickness.

We got the girls and Mother to bed. The uncles watched
the dead. I lay down on the sofa in Father's dressing room but
not to sleep . . .

· 4 ·

HE WAS EXTOLLED from a half-dozen pulpits and by the editorial
pages of nearly every newspaper in the city, by lifelong friends,
fellow philanthropists, and political reformers during memorial
tributes at the Union League and the State Charities Aid Association. He was praised for his "high moral purpose" (in the *Tribune*),
his "singular public spirit" *(Evening Mail)*, his "generous public
spirit" *(Telegram)*, his contributions to science and art *(Evening
Post)*, for "using great opportunity for the best end" and preserving
the honor of a great family name *(The New York Times)*.

George William Curtis, in what he wrote for *Harper's Weekly*,
called him "an American citizen of the best type—cheerful, hearty,
sagacious, honest, hopeful, not to be swerved by abuse, by hostility
or derision." Godkin, in *The Nation*, said New York should take
heart in such a life: "We believe, the mere fact that New York
could even in these later evil years produce him, and hold his love
and devotion, has been to hundreds of those who knew him and
watched his career a reason for not despairing of the future of the
city."

His "sweet strong influence," his "magnetic power in influ-
encing others," the "stirring summons" of his example, were all
mentioned repeatedly. "What a glorious example!" a friend wrote
to Bamie. And in the other sympathy notes that poured into the
house most people seemed to be saying in one way or other that
they felt better for having known him.

At the family's request there were no flowers at the funeral.
Eight pallbearers—William E. Dodge, Jr., and Howard Potter
among them—carried the plain rosewood coffin out of the house
after a brief family service in the front parlor. The Fifth Avenue
Presbyterian Church was filled to overflowing. There were two
thousand people, perhaps more, within the huge nave as the coffin
was borne down the sloping center aisle to the altar. Two preachers
officiated, John Hall and the venerable William Adams, Theodore's
former pastor at the Madison Square Presbyterian Church and now
head of the Union Theological Seminary, whose voice broke several times in the course of his remarks. Burial was at Greenwood

Cemetery, in the family plot, beside Mittie's mother, the funeral procession crossing the East River to Brooklyn by ferry under a cold winter sky.

Secluded once more at 57th Street, the devastated family hardly knew which way to turn, let alone how to face what Conie called "the blank" of life without Father. Anna Gracie was staying on, to be near Mittie. Everyone drew nearer. Conie was to remember "something infinitely inspiring" about those days. Father had preached that one must live for the living, and so "[we] felt that our close family tie must be made stronger rather than weaker by the loss . . ."

What Mittie felt we cannot begin to know. A month later she would write to young Theodore simply, "It is so hard to have parted with him. I think of him daily and almost hourly . . . long to have him with us. It must be a comfort to you to know that you never gave your dearly loved and prized father anything but pleasure."

Years later Bamie would say only that "Of course, after his death we all had to work out our own salvation."

Elliott, we know, was shattered. It was as if, in the convulsive grip of his father's arms, he had had something crushed irreparably within. Theodore's death was the ultimate disaster from which he would never quite recover.

To young Theodore it was all a "hideous dream." His mother and sisters were suffering the worst, he wrote to Henry Minot, and "it was best that Father's terrible sufferings should end." But in his Private Diary he let go, pouring out pain and bewilderment and presently a torrent of longing and loneliness and angry self-judgment. He began within hours after the funeral, describing the suspense of his ride home on the night boat, the "bitter agony when I kissed the dear, dead face and realized he would never again on this earth speak to me," the sound of the first clod of earth striking the casket.

"He was the most wise and loving father that ever lived: I owe everything to him."

His anguish spills across pages, for weeks, months. Back at Harvard, alone in his room, he wrote of little else:

Sunday, March 3
Have been thinking about Father all evening, have had a good square breakdown, and feel much better for it.

Wednesday, March 6
Every now and then there are very bitter moments; if I had
very much time to think I believe I should go crazy . . .

Saturday, March 9
It is just one month since the blackest day of my life.

Sunday, March 10
. . . had another square breakdown.

Sundays, with all their memories, were the hardest for him. It
had been a Sunday, "that terrible Sunday," that he had "kissed the
dear, dead face."

In the margin of his Bible he writes "February 9, 1878" beside
a verse of the 69th Psalm: "*I am weary of my crying: my throat is
dried: mine eyes fail while I wait for my God.*"

Twice, in different letters, he reaches out to Bamie. With Father gone, he says, she must help him. She must take Father's place
in his life. "I know only too well the dull, heavy pain you suffer,"
he wrote, "and I know too that it . . . has been easier for me . . . for
here I live in a different world . . . I am occupied busily all the
time." Still, she must stand by him. She must tell him what to do.
"My own sweet sister, you will have to give me a great deal of
advice and assistance, now that our dear father is gone, for in many
ways you are more like him than any of the rest of the family."
Henry Minot, his closest friend at Harvard, has "left college!" he
reports in dismay to her that spring. "His father has taken him away
and put him in his office to study law." To Henry himself he writes
of how greatly he misses "someone to talk to about my favorite
pursuits and future prospects."

With Father gone, nothing seems to have any purpose. "Am
working away pretty hard," he reports in May; "but I do not care
so much for my marks now; what I most valued them for was *his*
pride in them."

Other times he seems insistent that Father has not "gone." "I
almost feel as if he were present with me," he tells his mother; and
it is emphatically in the present tense that he writes, "Every event
of my life is tied up with him." Father's words keep coming back
with a vividness that is "really startling. During a brief visit to
Oyster Bay just before exams, he picks up the journal he kept during the winter on the Nile and finds that "every incident is con-

nected with *him*." He walks about the empty house and "every nook and corner . . . every piece of furniture . . . is in some manner connected with him." "Oh, Father, Father, how bitterly I miss you, mourn you and long for you," he writes June 7, still at Oyster Bay. "All the family are wonderfully lovely to me," reads the next entry, "but I wish Mother and Bamie would not quarrel among themselves."

Then Sunday, June 9, in the dim light of the little Presbyterian church at Oyster Bay, he sees Father sitting beside him in the corner of the pew, "as distinctly as if he were alive."

Father was the shining example of the life he must aspire to; Father was the perfect example of all he himself was not. Grief turned to shame and a sense of futility. He felt diminished by the memory of the man. "Looking back on his life it seems as if mine must be such a weak, useless one in comparison." He was engulfed by self-doubt. Self-reproach bordered on self-contempt. How could such a wonderful man have had a son of so little worth, he asked. One especially difficult Sunday he brooded over "how little use I am, or ever shall be . . . I am as much inferior to Father morally and mentally as physically." He had failed his father when his father had needed him most and for this, in the light of his own conscience, he stood condemned.

> He did everything for me, and I nothing for him. I remember so well how, years ago, when I was a very weak, asthmatic child, he used to walk up and down with me in his arms . . . and oh, how my heart pains me when I think I never was able to do anything for him during his last illness!

"Sometimes, when I fully realize my loss," he writes, "I feel as if I should go mad."

Conie would recall sitting with him by moonlight on a high point called Cooper's Bluff, overlooking Long Island Sound, and listening while he recited Swinburne in a high-pitched singsong voice:

> *In a coign of the cliff between lowland and highland,*
> *   At the sea-down's edge between windward and lee,*
> *Walled round with rocks as an inland island,*
> *   The ghost of a garden fronts the sea.*

But there were notable chinks in all this gloom, moments even in the diary when he was unable any longer to deny his own good cheer or outright exuberance. It was only a few weeks after Theodore's death when he confided to Conie that he felt not nearly so sad as he had expected to. He is "astonished," he says later in the diary, at how readily he goes about daily life "as if nothing had happened." And as summer begins he is feeling so very good at times, his spirits so high, that he can no longer hold back. "I could not be happier," he writes, but then immediately feels obliged to justify this. It would be *"wrong,"* he says, for him to be anything other than cheerful; ". . . and besides, I am of a very buoyant temper, being a bit of an optimist. Had a glorious 20-mile ride on Lightfoot, cantering the whole time."

It was a summer of tremendous highs and lows. At Harvard, the week before his final examinations, his asthma had returned. (It was from "being forced to sit up all night with the asthma," he explains, that he did so poorly in French.) He had yearned as never before for the "wilds" of Oyster Bay, to be in the woods again, to be on horseback, to be out alone on the water in his rowboat. One day in July he rowed alone all the way across the Sound to Rye Beach and back again. Elliott was the sailor, as Conie explained, while "Theodore craved the actual effort of the arms and back." He "loved to row in the hottest sun, over the roughest water, in the smallest boat . . ."

He ran, he hiked, rain or shine; he blasted away with a new Sharps rifle at birds, bottles, almost anything in sight. On one "tramp" he went twenty-five miles "through awful places."

Some days in the diary he seems about to burst with his joyous outdoor freedom. He turns to one of his father's favorite passages in the Bible: *"For ye shall go out with joy, and be led forth with peace: the mountains and the hills shall break forth before you into singing . . ."* "Oyster Bay is the perfection of a place for fellows," he declares. "I wonder if anyone could have a happier time than I . . ." It is August 9, a date he has marked heavily in black, as it is now six months since Theodore's death.

Yet one senses a darker undercurrent, a kind of desperate, underlying frenzy bespeaking anger and fear. The pace of his activities is punishing, sometimes cruel. It is as if he is striking back at something, taking it out on Lightfoot, his horse, taking it out on himself—do or die, literally. Annoyed by a neighbor's dog on a morning ride, he shot and killed it, "rolling it over with my revolver very neatly as it ran alongside the horse," he reports in the diary. The horse he rode so hard day after day that he all but ruined it.

From one or two comments he and others made long afterward, it appears there was also a romance that summer with Edith Carow, and that it too blew up in a fit of anger. The diary says nothing of any of this, but years later he would tell Bamie how close he and Edith had been, and that "we both of us had . . . tempers that were far from being of the best."

By midsummer he was down with stomach troubles (his dreadful cholera morbus), then hit "pretty hard" by an attack of asthma in early September en route to the genuine wilds of Maine. He went with cousins West and Emlen and a doctor named Thompson. "Look out for Theodore," the doctor is said to have advised their Maine guide. "He's not strong, but he's all grit. He'll kill himself before he'll even say he's tired."

His father's fatal illness, it had been concluded among the family, stemmed from a hike he had taken in Maine the previous summer. Theodore had strained himself somehow mountain climbing, during the stay at Mount Desert with Bamie. Beyond that there seemed no possible explanation why someone of such vigor—such a "splendid mechanism"—could have been brought down. With his Maine guide, a large, bearded, kindly man named William Sewall, a man as large as Theodore had been, the boy now hiked twenty, thirty miles a day, all such feats being recorded in his diary, just as during another summer in the mountains of Switzerland when he was ten.

"I feel sorry for the country . . ." Theodore had told the boy in his last letter. "I fear for your future. We cannot stand so corrupt a government for any great length of time." He would keep his father's letters always, the boy vowed. They were to be his "talismans against evil."

Death and political defeat had coincided in the life of "the one I loved dearest on earth." It is not known for certain that he or others in the family made a direct connection between what had happened at the hands of Senator Conkling and the tragedy that befell Theodore and thus to all of them so soon afterward. But it is almost inconceivable that they would not have made such a connection and have felt it deeply.

President Hayes, true to his word, had refused to concede defeat over the Customhouse. That same summer of 1878, with Congress in recess, he simply fired Chester Arthur and put Edwin Merritt in his place. The appointment was subsequently endorsed by the Senate (the Democrats had since gained a majority), the

Conkling forces were rolled back. So had Theodore lived, he would have been made Collector after all, and his political fortunes thereafter might have been considerable. Instead, he had died a loser. If not exactly killed off by Conkling, he had been unhorsed, made to look foolish and impotent in a battle known to the entire country.

So what should a noble boy and namesake make of that? How should one respond to the downfall of Greatheart?

It is easy enough to speculate about all this, tempting to see an edge of vengeance in the career that was to follow. Allegedly, the family resolved to have nothing more to do with politics. But in fact we really do not know what was resolved, if anything. The future was very much on the young man's mind; this we do know from the Private Diary. "I should like to be a scientist," he declared only a few months after Theodore's death. He felt he had aged since the tragedy. He tried to picture himself a man, as head of a family of his own. "I so wonder who my wife will be! 'A rare and radiant maiden,' I hope; one who will be as sweet, pure, and innocent as she is wise. Thank heaven I am at least perfectly pure."

"How I wish I could ever do something to keep up his name," he would write in the diary. For the moment, however, having had a private talk with James Alfred, he decided to think only of his remaining two years at Harvard, resolving to study hard and to conduct himself "like a brave Christian gentleman."

Part Three

———————

CHAPTER NINE

Harvard

· 1 ·

"YOU BELONGED TO HARVARD, and she to you." The bond was everlasting, asserted William Roscoe Thayer, Harvard '81, who was a biographer and historian and for twenty-three years editor of the *Harvard Graduates' Magazine*, which lent certain weight to anything he said. Moreover, "she" in that day—Theodore's day—had been a "*crescent* institution . . . in the full vigor of growth" and this "crescent spirit," Thayer said, had been of enormous benefit to all fortunate enough to have been there at the time, however insensitive some were to what was happening to them.

Theodore, recalling his Harvard years, would credit Harvard mainly with providing him an especially good time.

The growth and change had begun well before either he or Thayer arrived on the scene. In 1869 Charles W. Eliot had been named president at age thirty-five and after that Harvard was not the same. Eliot insisted that Harvard become a modern university, and, by stages, instituted what has become known as the elective system. He enlarged the faculty, overhauled the Law School and the Medical School, raised money as never before, and commenced the greatest building boom in Harvard's long history up to that time. A scientist by training, he held that science and the humanities were not incompatible; further, that to be educated in science was to be educated for the future. He believed, as he had said in his speech at the opening of the Museum of Natural History in New York, that science was "the firm foundation" for man's faith in himself and in what he called "the present infinite Creator."

Eliot wished the Harvard student to be treated like an adult, to flourish in an atmosphere of academic freedom. He got rid of petty disciplinary rules, so that by Theodore's time the old rule book of nearly forty pages had been reduced to one of five. In back of his elective system was an unshakable faith in the instinctive capacity of free human beings to follow the path that was best for them. No one could master anything worthwhile "without a deal of drudgery," but then with so much that was so urgent and difficult in school life—in any life—it seemed "superfluous to invent other disagreeableness, whether for children or for men." "Do you think it is a wise parent who invents disagreeable tasks for his children, or enforces any observance simply because it is disagreeable?"

He was a turning point for Harvard and for American education, and as an example of serene, Unitarian, Boston sagacity and rectitude none could match him. To those like William Roscoe Thayer who viewed the college as one big family, he was the supreme father whose influence—whose outlook and standards— touched all. He was large and straight, "with the back of an oarsman," and unforgettable, since most of the right side of his face was covered by an ugly, liver-colored birthmark. He believed in public service and in duty. On a gate to the Yard he would have inscribed:

> Enter to grow in wisdom
> Depart better to serve thy country and thy kind.

His personal motto was a saying of one of his Overseers, Edward Everett Hale: "Look up and not down; look out and not in; look forward and not back, and lend a hand."

But generations of Harvard undergraduates would also remember him stalking through the Yard looking neither left nor right and recognizing no one. They did not like him, for all the new freedoms he brought. He would be remembered for the few rules he enforced more than for the many he did away with. Owen Wister, a freshman in Theodore's junior year, called him a "flagstaff in motion." To others he was New England's "topmost oak."

Along with his liberal reforms, Eliot also brought a variety of memorable personal views. He disapproved of sermons that mentioned "that *scoundrel* King David," for example, and he believed in the benefit to mind and body of strenuous physical activity in the open air. A morbid mental condition, he once told his own son, was of physical origin. He himself could work twelve hours a day and not feel tired. As part of his preparation for life, every boy ought to be able to row a boat and ride a horse, swim a mile and hike twenty-five miles. He approved of football, but had the odd idea that the ball carrier ought always to do the manly thing and hit the most resistant part of the enemy's line, not look for holes. Baseball he did not much care for because it depended too much, he said, on the pitcher and the pitcher resorted too often to deceptions. The curve ball, a recent innovation, was to his way of thinking a low form of cunning.

The Harvard campus then, like the enrollment, was still comparatively small. About fifteen dissimilar buildings, mostly of red brick, stood near or facing a main parklike quadrangle, the Yard, as it had long been known, which was crisscrossed with straight gravel paths, shaded by numerous elms, and loosely framed by a low rail fence. Massachusetts Hall, built several generations before the Revolutionary War, was the oldest building. Thayer, Matthews, and Weld halls were new since Eliot had taken over. And just beyond the Yard, set apart between Cambridge and Kirkland streets, stood the great red-brick Memorial Hall, the university's most magnificent building, which had been completed the year Theodore arrived as a freshman. It overtopped the trees with its turrets and pinnacles. Within was a huge central dining hall, or commons, hung with portraits, a theater, and a vaulted transept, the great marble-floored Memorial Hall proper, consecrated to the sons of Harvard—the Union sons only—who had fallen in the Civil War. The walls were lined with white marble tablets, each with the names of the war dead, student-soldiers fallen in battle, arranged by class and with eloquent inscriptions in Latin—"CONSUMMATI IN BREVE EXPLEVERUNT TEMPORA MULTA." There was no comparable memorial to the war anywhere in the country. "The effect of the place," wrote Henry James, "is singularly noble and solemn, and it is impossible to feel it without a lifting of the heart. It stands there for duty and honor, it speaks of sacrifice and example, seems a kind of temple to youth, manhood, generosity. Most of them were young, all were in their prime, and all of them had fallen; this simple idea hovers before the visitor . . ."

What, one wonders, was the effect on an impressionable youth whose father had hired a substitute?

The famous Museum of Comparative Zoology, the "Agassiz Museum," where Theodore spent a good part of his junior and senior years, was another several blocks beyond Memorial Hall, opposite the Divinity School.

That was all to the north of the Yard. To the south and southwest were Harvard Street (later Massachusetts Avenue), where the Boston horsecars ran, and Harvard Square (actually a triangular junction of Harvard, Boylston, and Brattle streets), where a variety of modest shops clustered about the University Bookstore, the telegraph office, and the Cambridge Bank.

Winthrop Street, where Theodore lived, was two blocks from Harvard Street, in the direction of the Charles River. The quickest route was down Holyoke. The two-story frame house —Mrs. Richardson's boardinghouse—stood on the southwest corner of Holyoke and Winthrop.

A student's room at Harvard, by tradition, was his sanctuary. "Its occupant for the time being is its master," we read in a contemporary account. "He can do as he will in it; lock his door and be not at home; admit all comers; sit alone and read or study, or sit with his congenial friend and talk out whatever he may have the good fortune to have in mind." One was expected to have a personal library in view ("nothing furnishes a room so well"), a few sporting prints, family tintypes on the mantel, a tennis racket on the wall, and sufficient furniture ("nothing need match") to suggest "solid comfort." A convenient spittoon was usually of polished brass, but the fancier kind, of porcelain with hand-painted rosebuds, was not uncommon.

Theodore's quarters, all four years, were those Bamie had picked for his freshman year and consisted of a living room or study and a small bedroom behind, to which various "improvements" had since been added. ("I had Harry Chapin in here the other day to look at the new bookcase," he had written Bamie in his sophomore year, ". . . and after he had examined it he exclaimed, 'Jove! Your family *do* act squarely by you!' ")

Harvard undergraduates numbered just over eight hundred, and at a time when only about one American in five thousand went to any college, let alone Harvard, they were an extremely privileged lot. They were not all the sons of rich men, as popularly supposed, and President Eliot's own particular interest was in those of modest means, who, in his view, constituted "the very best part" of Harvard. But then they were hardly representative of the country that, by Eliot's lights, they were supposed to serve. Judged by the color of their skin, the churches they attended, the number of syllables in their names, by almost any such criteria, they were

as homogeneous an assembly of young men—and as unrepresen-
tative of turbulent, polygot, post-Civil War America—as one could
imagine. It was not just the comparatively small scale of Harvard
that gave it a "family" feeling, they all *looked* alike. There was
virtually no diversity to be seen, except by the practiced eye, and
then it was usually measured by such things as money or "family"
or the cut of one's clothes. William Roscoe Thayer, warming to his
undergraduate memories, would write of the exceptional opportunity Harvard had afforded to meet students of many different views
and from all parts of the country, but in fact the decided majority
came either from Boston or from towns close by. A study of Theodore's Class of 1880 shows that nearly two-thirds came from within
a hundred-mile radius of the Harvard campus. Harvard, moreover,
was supplied year in, year out by the same New England schools.
In the case of Theodore's class, more than half had come from
Andover, Exeter, St. Paul's, Noble's, Hopkinson, Adams Academy,
and other such prestige training grounds. A high-school boy from
some point beyond New England was a rarity (there were about a
dozen among the 171 who finally graduated).

The same surnames appeared in class after class. In Theodore's there were a Blodgett and a Cabot, a Guild, a Morison, a
Quincy, and a Saltonstall. The Saltonstall, Richard Middlecott, was
actually the sixth of his line to attend Harvard; the first, Nathaniel,
graduated in the Class of 1695.

There were no blacks in the Class of 1880, suffice it to say, and
no foreign students. There were exactly three Roman Catholics,
but no Boston Irish, no Italians, Swedes, or Latin Americans, no
one with a name ending in an *i* or an *o;* and there were no Jews.
Full-page cartoons in the *Lampoon,* the undergraduate humor magazine, were sometimes crudely anti-Irish, anti-Semitic, or mocking
of Negro aspirations.

"If you asked me to define in one word the 'temper' of the
Harvard I knew," reflected a contemporary named Samuel Scott,
"I should say it was *patrician,* strange as that word may sound to
American ears. . . ."

> Birth of course counted for much, prominence in athletics was
> naturally a help, but scholarly attainments per se went for very
> little, I fear. A certain amount of money was necessary, for a
> man had to dress decently and share in the pleasures and con-
> vivialities peculiar to youth, but *wealth as wealth* was no pass-
> port to anything in that community. . . .

This code, unwritten yet all pervading and all powerful, is difficult to define. Over and above the copybook virtues, it insisted upon a composure of manner, a self-suppression and a sense of *noblesse oblige* that were in happy contrast with the blatant self-assertions, the unbridled enthusiasms and misconceived doctrines of equality that were characteristic of the country in general. It gave its approval to those who understood that modesty was compatible with manliness, who knew how to combine self-respect with respect for authority and for the opinions of others, and who were firmly convinced that it was truer sport to lose the game by playing fair than to win it by trickery.

I think I am not exaggerating this influence in the college life. . . . It was all rather narrow and provincial, perhaps, but I still believe that those who were really in sympathy with such a discipline greatly benefited by it, while those who were not, must have been in some way affected by it.

About the only remaining vestige of "old Harvard" in the way of rules was compulsory chapel every morning at 7:45, from which a student could be excused only for reasons of health—for an asthmatic condition, for example—an option Theodore never exercised. Otherwise the student could live much as he chose, so long as he performed up to the mark academically. The elective system had also evolved sufficiently by Theodore's time so that in his junior and senior years a student was free to pick just about any course he cared to.

The faculty, though still comparatively few in number, was strong in most areas, and when the names of the larger Harvard-Cambridge literary-intellectual community are included, the list is truly awesome.

Emerson, Phillips Brooks, and Charles Francis Adams were Overseers, as was the elder Theodore's friend from the Cincinnati convention, Richard H. Dana. Francis Parkman (then at work on his *Montcalm and Wolfe*) was a member of the Corporation, and Longfellow, former professor of Belles Lettres—Old Poems, as he was called—could be seen strolling on Brattle Street in his familiar brown overcoat. The renowned botanist Asa Gray, Darwin's chief spokesman in America, was officially retired from the faculty, but was still at work and also much in evidence. Nathaniel Southgate Shaler taught geology and zoology, and the younger faculty—all recruited since Eliot took over—included Charles Dunbar, Harvard's (and the country's) first professor of political economy; Wil-

liam James, who taught anatomy and physiology; and Charles Eliot
Norton (Eliot's cousin), who offered "Lectures on Modern Morals
as Illustrated by the Art of the Ancients." Recently, Henry Cabot
Lodge had been installed to teach a new course in the history of
the United States.

But by tradition Harvard students and Harvard professors were
a different species and in this at least tradition held sway. Contact
between them, apart from the lecture hall or classroom, was minimal. Henry Adams, who had given up teaching in 1877, found it
nearly impossible to get students to talk to him. Others on the
faculty, like the students, preferred it that way. To involve themselves in the lives or interests of undergraduates was simply not
part of their job.

"Don't take it upon yourself . . . to ask questions or offer observations in recitations," the undergraduate newspaper, the *Crimson*, advised lightheartedly in Theodore's freshman year. "Your
questions would bore the students, and your observations would
bore the tutors. And don't talk to the tutors out of hours."

In opposition to the Eliot ideals of academic freedom and individual initiative stood a modish student pose of indifference, not
to mention the plain laziness that came as naturally to Harvard
undergraduates as to any others. *"We ask but time to drift,"* sang
Theodore's friend George Pellew, class poet, in a Hasty Pudding
show during their senior year:

> *We deem it narrow-minded to excel.*
> *We call the man fanatic who applies*
> *His life to one grand purpose till he dies.*
> *Enthusiasm sees one side, one fact;*
> *We try to see all sides, but do not act.*
> *. . . We long to sit with newspapers unfurled,*
> *Indifferent spectators of the world.*

If everyone "flocked" to hear Charles Eliot Norton, it was because his course was a "snap"; while Henry Cabot Lodge, who was
known to be difficult, soon had almost no students. "My system
was simple," Lodge later explained, "to make the students do as
much work for themselves as possible and have them lecture to
me." His classes shrank from fifty students to three.

"A boy could go completely to pieces and there was no one
whose job it was to know anything about it," remembered a classmate of Theodore's, who, like many, viewed the Eliot Epoch as a

disaster. "There never was a worse time for a boy to be in Harvard."

In Washington a historic blow for temperance had been struck by Lucy Hayes, the first First Lady with a college degree. "Lemonade Lucy" had banned all alcoholic beverages from the White House. (At state dinners, said William Evarts, the water flowed like champagne.) But no such edict stood in the way of Harvard undergraduates in these years of the Hayes regime. "Students got drunk then" was the terse assessment of another in Theodore's class, John Woodbury. Even Charles Eliot, looking back, would concede that there had been "much intemperance," though he thought it had been mainly in the clubs and particularly the Porcellian, the summit of Harvard's social hierarchy. (He had thought the same of the Porcellian in his own undergraduate days and had refused to have anything to do with it.)

They drank whiskey, which was relatively cheap and easy to get. They drank French champagne and Burgundy, and endless quantities of beer and ale, which were cheapest of all, and shandygaff, a mixture of beer and ginger ale. (For Sunday mornings a concoction of ginger ale and rum was thought "just right.") The favorite local stop was a grogshop called Carl's below sidewalk level on Brighton Street.

There were at Harvard, said *Scribner's Magazine*, "lads of good morals and lads with an inclination toward unwholesome experiment." A Boston paper, angry over a student disturbance in one of the theaters, wrote that seeing the world to such young men meant only "gazing with watery eyes upon half-clad ballet girls and burlesque actresses, and hovering about them, later, like flies about a carcass."

One wonders if the elder Theodore may have known more of Harvard life than he let on when he advised his son to take care of his morals first. Or if the decision to postpone any thought of Ellie going to college suggests something more than concern for his health alone, if possibly the father had sensed even then what the boy's susceptibilities were.

The sharpest division within the undergraduate body was between those who were the sons of Boston's elite and those who were not, and the line between them was clearly understood. In Theodore's class the "set" or "high set," "the club crowd" as it was also known, was composed of perhaps twenty-five young men, or no more than ten percent of the class. They were mainly all Bostonians and thought to be very rich and quite impressed with themselves. Their clothes were English in cut. They carried slim canes or walking sticks and wore the heavy gold watch fobs of the kind customarily worn by men twice their age. Several—Robert Bacon, Ralph Ellis, Josiah Quincy, Richard Saltonstall, Minot Weld— parted their hair in the middle, which to the average American was the hallmark of the pampered snob. General Grant was only the best known of those who disliked on sight any man whose hair was parted in the middle.

"The set had a new suit of clothes for every day of the week," remembered a classmate named Rand, who because of Harvard's alphabetical seating system was able to observe one such higher being, Josiah Quincy, at close range. Rand sat beside Quincy in class through all four years, yet Quincy never "deigned" to speak to him once. Quincy may have been the worst example, Rand conceded. Bacon and Saltonstall, for instance, would say hello.

But for those few non-Bostonians whom the set found acceptable, the Harvard years could be quite pleasurable, for their society included not just the "right" clubs, but entrée to the "right" families. As Owen Wister, a Philadelphian, observed, "pleasant doors in Boston, and round about in Milton, Brookline, and Chestnut Hill, stood open" to a world of "gentlefolk" who were truly hospitable—"not mere entertainers"—who could talk of books and horses and winters in Rome. It made all the difference, he thought, in how one benefited from Harvard.

Those students—that small minority—who insisted on taking their studies seriously, who worked hard and made no effort to conceal their academic ambitions, were known as "digs" and were naturally outcasts. Socially, they had no chance. As the *Crimson* advised, only a little in jest, digs might be "eminently worthy" as people and it was "well to have a pleasant, bowing acquaintance with them, for they may turn out in the future to be very great men," but their manners, like their clothes, were "apt to be bad; and except at class elections, their friendship is of no sort of use."

Still, anyone who did not take seriously the academic side of life—or who did not *appear* to take it seriously—was expected to "go in" for something else (the air of indifference notwithstanding), and athletics rated above all. The late 1870s would be regarded afterward as among the most brilliant years in the history of Harvard athletics. Football, like so much else at Harvard, was new —still spelled as "foot ball"—but already great status attached to anyone who played. (The Harvard-Yale "match" that Theodore saw in his freshman year was only the second time the two colleges

had played each other in football and the first game in which the
teams were limited to eleven men each, rather than fifteen.) In
baseball Harvard was "repeatedly victorious" and Harvard's eight-
oar crew defeated Yale three years running—in '77, '78, and '79.
Harvard's color, as of 1875, had been officially designated as crimson—rather than magenta as before—and to wear the crimson on
the playing field or as an oarsman on the Charles was the quickest
way to notoriety and acclaim. In Theodore's time there was never
any question as to the most popular man in the class. He was Robert Bacon, "the manly beauty," captain of the football team, heavy-
weight boxing champion, winner in the hundred-yard dash and the
quarter mile, number seven on the crew. The Class of 1880 was
known then and later as Bacon's class.

· 2 ·

THE DIFFERENCE between Theodore's final two years at Harvard
and the first two was enormous. In the first two he had discovered
he could handle the work and function reasonably well socially.
His name, background, all that comprised his own "antecedents,"
had also proved an advantage, something that was not to occur very
often again in his life. He had fallen in immediately and quite
naturally with the young Brahmins and their respective families,
after which, with the death of his father, he had become a subject
of great sympathy among them. But it was not until his junior year
that he found himself a social success all at once. "People knew
who he was," as said William Roscoe Thayer. Indeed, he enjoyed
a celebrity of a kind, for the first time ever. He knew things were to
be different almost from the day he arrived at Cambridge that fall
of 1878 and the feeling was heady.

"All the fellows greeted me with enthusiasm," he writes in his
diary, September 27. "Funnily enough, I have enjoyed quite a
burst of popularity since I came back," he tells Mittie a little later,
"having been elected into several different clubs."

In no time he belonged to nearly everything one was supposed
to—the Hasty Pudding Club, the "Dickey" (DKE), the lofty Porcellian—and several others as well. The night of his initiation into
the Porcellian, which occupied several rooms over a store on Harvard Street, he got " 'higher' with wine than I have ever been."
"Of course" he was "delighted to be in," he reported to Bamie;
"there is a billiard table, magnificent library, punch room, etc., and
my best friends are in it."

Apart from the drinking, he embraced the new life with open arms. (He suffered so from a hangover the morning after the Porcellian rites—his "spree"—that he drank but sparingly, if at all, from then on. Besides, he noted, "Wine always makes me fighty.") He was savoring partridge suppers at "the Porc," served by a dignified liveried black man named George Washington Lewis. He was picking up expressions like "Jove" and "dear old boy." "Porc men" were "perfect trumps."

"Roosevelt was right in this group in every way," recalled classmate Rand. Roosevelt would talk to others if the occasion arose, Rand said, "though such did not often occur."

"Please send my silk hat *at once*," he demanded in a letter to Mittie written on Porcellian stationery, "why has it not come before?"

He was regarded as a "little fellow" and richer even than his elegant friends, and while this may have been no guarantee of success, it did lend an aura. Henry Jackson, one of the Bostonians who had gone to New York for the Christmas parties their freshman year, would remember for the rest of his life the splendor of the "Roosevelt establishment" on 57th Street. (Real-life butlers and footmen were not ordinarily part of domestic life among Boston's best families.) In his junior year, furthermore, Theodore kept his own horse in Cambridge, something few could afford, and during his senior year he drove a smart little tilbury, or "dog cart," which pleased him no end. With horse, cart, whip, and lap robe, he had, he said, "as swell a turnout as any man."

He spent his money in grand style, as he would never have dared were his father alive. His inheritance from his father, he had been informed by Uncle James Alfred, was $125,000, and from this he could expect an annual income of approximately $8,000 a year, a princely sum. It was, for example, considerably more than the salary of the president of Harvard. On $5,000 a year Charles Eliot kept a comfortable home, entertained, owned a summer house, a boat, and put his own two sons through Harvard. But Theodore, as he wrote in his diary, judged himself only "comfortable, though not rich," which may have been the way Uncle James Alfred had expressed it to him by way of encouraging a degree of financial caution.

For additions to his wardrobe in his junior year, we know from his neat accounts, he spent $685.80 (in a day when the best suit cost about $35); in his senior year, he spent a whopping $761.59 more on clothes. This was more for clothes than some students had to cover all expenses. And clothes and club dues combined for those same two years added up to $2,400, a sum the average American family could have lived on for six years.

Just to stable the horse cost more than $900 a year. In present terms it would correspond to spending an annual $12,000 on clothes and clubs, plus another $9,000 or more to have a car at college.

But while it is hard to imagine him daring to live quite so lavishly under his father's eye, it is also obvious that, consciously or not, he was actually behaving very like his father—that side of the father that was the dandy, the lover of fine horses, expensive clothes, the best clubs. Once, as Theodore would later relate, his father had given him a brief lesson in economy—this in view of his possibly entering a life of science wherein he could expect to earn little or no money. The great trick was to "keep the fraction constant," his father had said. If one could not increase the numerator, then he must reduce the denominator. But it would have been an extremely unobservant boy indeed who failed to sense the kind of figures the father himself had to be working with in his own "fraction." Expenditures on the order of those the family was accustomed to obviously added up to a very large denominator indeed, but they also implied an equally large or larger numerator. The elder Theodore was a rich man who knew how to spend money—to *enjoy* his money—and the son, thus far, was doing the same. And extravagant as he might appear, he was still spending less than his income.

He could hardly have been more conspicuous, it seems—or more energetic. He was a figure of incessant activity (as he himself said), of constant talk, constant hurry, a bee in a bottle. He rowed on the Charles in a one-man shell (and posed for a photographer wearing rower's skullcap and knee breeches, barefoot and barechested, arms folded and his whiskered face set in a defiant scowl). He took boxing lessons and enrolled in Papanti's Dancing Class. (". . . am very fond of dancing," he would note in his diary; "it is my favorite amusement, except horseback riding.") He wrestled and went off on long hikes of the kind President Eliot approved. "He was always ready to join anything," remembered Richard Saltonstall, who became the nearest thing to a close friend. He was "forever at it," said another man. There was no one who possessed such an amazing array of interests, said John Woodbury, who came to be one of his most steadfast admirers.

He joined the Rifle Club, the Art Club, the Glee Club. (Even if unable to carry a tune, he could help raise money.) He was vice-president of the Natural History Society, helped start a Finance Club, and was named to the editorial board of the *Advocate*, the undergraduate magazine, which in turn "opened the door" to the O.K. Society.

His grades were excellent. In his junior year, his best academically, he carried nine courses—German, Italian, themes, forensics, logic, metaphysics, Philosophy 6 (as Dunbar's course in political economy was known), Natural History 1 (geography, meteorology, and structural geology), and Natural History 3 (elementary zoology)—and finished with an 87 average. During his senior year, in addition to his thesis, he began work on a book, his study of the naval side of the War of 1812; and though his grades were down some from the year before, he finished with an overall average high enough to qualify him for Phi Beta Kappa.

It was hard for others to imagine how he could possibly do all that he did, quite aside from his social schedule, which with the advent of Alice Lee in his life consumed as much of his time—or more—than everything else. There was always the possibility, of course, that his involvement with the extracurricular activities and organizations was something less than met the eye. The editor of the *Advocate*, for example, could not recall that Theodore ever attended a board meeting and knew of only one article he had written.

Nor, for all his joining, did he seem to belong in the way others did. There was always something "different" about him. The "unchastened eagerness" that one was supposed never to show was what showed most of all. He was wholly—constitutionally—incapable of indifference. He was the kind who spoke up in class. The strange, shrill manner of speech persisted. George H. Palmer, his professor of metaphysics in his junior year, remembered that he "sort of spluttered" as he spoke, his thoughts charging on faster than his mouth could handle them. The sound, said Palmer, was something like water coming out of a thin-necked bottle. Yet he would be heard and at length if necessary. Shaler, the geologist, a man of tremendous bearing and his own expansive enthusiasms, is said to have exclaimed on one such occasion, "See here, Roosevelt, let me talk, I'm running this course."

Crossing the Yard between classes, he scurried when one was supposed to saunter. At the gymnasium some afternoons he could be seen skipping rope (!) and his rooms on Winthrop Street were said to contain live lizards, snakes, and other such "loathsome" creatures, so intense was his passion for natural science. In fact, he may have kept nothing of the kind at Winthrop Street—Richard Saltonstall, who lived on the floor below, remembered no caged animals, or anything, for that matter, which was the least out of the ordinary about Theodore's rooms, and a photograph said to be of his living room looks not unlike any number of others from the time, except for a few mounted birds in bell jars to be seen on top of a bookcase. But the story was one everybody liked (then as later), which was more important. It was "Teddy exactly," off to himself with his books and bird skins and creepy live things, and it became standard. Robert Bacon is supposed to have been so repulsed by the mere thought of Theodore's quarters and all therein that he refused to go near the place.

Forty years later, sorting out his own personal recollections of "Roosevelt at Harvard," William Roscoe Thayer remembered thinking of him as chiefly comical, "a joke . . . active and enthusiastic and that was all." Thayer had certainly perceived no portents of greatness, though one spring day in Theodore's senior year, they had talked about the future. They were sitting in a window seat in Charles Washburn's room in Holworthy, overlooking the Yard, and Theodore had said something to the effect that he might try to help the cause of better government in New York, though he hardly knew how. Thayer's only reaction, as he remembered, was to look hard at Theodore and ponder to himself " 'whether he is the real thing, or only the bundle of eccentricities which he appears.' "

The ever-admiring John Woodbury seems to have been alone in his forecast of distinction. Woodbury, as he said later, figured Theodore might amount to something—as a professor of history perhaps—if only because he seemed to know what he wanted.

To most others he remained likable but peculiar ("queer"), and much too intense for comfort. "Some thought he was crazy," said Woodbury.

Martha Cowdin, a Boston debutante known to all the class because she was engaged to Robert Bacon, described Theodore as "not the sort to appeal at first." He was too eccentric, she said, too ambitious, while Bacon, by contrast, was "a wonderful normal human being."

"He danced," said Rose Lee, sister of Alice, "just as you'd expect him to dance if you knew him—he hopped." Charles Washburn remembered how he ate chicken "as though he wanted to grind the bones."

Washburn was one of the relative handful of classmates "good and true" whose friendship mattered most to Theodore. The others were Saltonstall, Bacon, Harry Chapin, Henry Jackson, Harry Shaw, Jack Tebbets, and Minot Weld. They were Boston to the bone, and following graduation, with but few exceptions, they would settle happily in good, predictable Boston careers in banking, finance, or the law. (Jackson, who chose medicine, returned to a position on the Harvard faculty.) Their names figure time and again in Theodore's letters and in the pages of his diaries. Saltonstall—"Old Dick"—a large, well-fed young man with a big, soft, bland face, is certified "my most intimate friend," with Harry Shaw coming second. And since Saltonstall was also Theodore's entrée to the Lee household at Chestnut Hill, and thus to Alice, he would always be regarded in a different light from the others. By their senior year Saltonstall qualified for the highest rating possible: "Old Dick I place on par with the Roosevelts."

There were also two acknowledged "dig friends" who should be mentioned, both New Yorkers—George Pellew, the class poet, who afterward became a writer for the New York *Sun*, and Richard Welling, later a prominent New York attorney and reform crusader. Welling was a particularly interesting young man, a serious student and a powerful physical specimen. It was he, during their freshman year, who had been so astonished by Theodore's namby-pamby workout at the gymnasium, and once, sometime later, during a skating expedition to Fresh Pond, he had discovered how very mistaken he had been in that first impression.

The day was bitterly cold, with a furious wind blowing, and the ice was much too rough. Any sane man would have given up and gone home, Welling recalled, but Theodore had kept exclaiming his delight as they beat their way across the pond, arms flailing, neither knowing how to skate very well. The harder the wind blew, the more miserable Welling felt, the greater Theodore appeared to be enjoying himself. (Welling actually remembered him shouting, "Isn't it bully!" but then Welling wrote his account of the incident a very long time afterward.) "Never in college was my own grit so put to the test," Welling said, "and yet I would not be the first to suggest 'home.'"

They were out on the pond nearly three hours. Only when it became too dark to see did Theodore at last say that perhaps they ought to stop. Had there been a moon, Welling surmised, they might have gone on until midnight.

Like some of the other stories, this one could be taken two ways, as proof either of an indomitable will—what Welling called Theodore's amazing vitality—or of mental imbalance.

He would be remembered reading by the fire in a room full of friends, unmindful of their talk or the fact that his boots were being singed. In another story he flies into a rage when a drunken club-mate does an imitation of his facial contortions—the teeth, the thrusting jaw. In still another he becomes so flustered on entering Eliot's office that he announces, "Mr. Eliot, I am President Roosevelt."

The truth of such anecdotes is hard to gauge. Even the best-known of the Harvard stories may be largely apocryphal. It appeared first in *The Saturday Evening Post* some twenty years later, in an article by Owen Wister. Alice Lee, "pretty . . . in nice furs," is said to have been watching from the balcony as Theodore fought for the Harvard Athletic Association's lightweight boxing cup in the spring of his junior year. The setting was the Harvard gymnasium—the "old" gymnasium, as it would be known, since it was shortly replaced by a larger, more up-to-date building—and his opponent was the defending lightweight champion, a senior named C. S. Hanks. When the referee called time at the end of a round and Theodore dropped his guard, Hanks is said to have landed a smashing blow on the nose that produced a great spurt of blood and angry booing and catcalls from the crowd—whereupon Theodore raised an arm for silence. "It's all right," he said, "he didn't hear him." Then, with bloody face, Theodore stepped over to Hanks to shake his hand and we are left to imagine the effect on the girl in the balcony.

That Theodore fought Hanks and lost on March 22, 1879, is a matter of record. Hanks was entered at 133½ pounds, Theodore at 135, and Hanks was much the better of the two, "punishing Roosevelt severely," according to an account that appeared in *The New York Times*. But the old gymnasium had no balcony and no women were present. In his diary, where he never let modesty stand in the way if there was something of which he was proud, Theodore states only the fact that he was beaten. The *Times* reports no display of high sportsmanship, nor does the *Advocate* in its comments on the event, and to picture a reporter of that day passing up a scene such as Wister described is a little hard to imagine. Fiction was Wister's specialty and the mere thought of his friend Theodore seems at times to have inspired the Parson Weems in him. Another eyewitness to the Hanks-Roosevelt bout, a man named George Spalding, who was sitting beside Wister, called Wister's account "the most barefaced egregious manufactured history ever conceived."

Theodore never became a champion boxer at Harvard, never distinguished himself at any sport. He was not a good or natural athlete. He had no interest in organized athletics, played on no team and shunned—because of his poor eyesight—any game that involved a moving ball, with the exception of lawn tennis, the new game, which he played socially only and poorly.

He was, to be sure, a rabid competitor in anything he attempted. He was constantly measuring his performance, measuring himself against others. Everybody was a rival, every activity a contest, a personal challenge. "As athletes we are about equal," he wrote the summer between his junior and senior years, comparing himself to his brother; "he rows best; I run best; he can beat me sailing or swimming; I can beat him wrestling or boxing; I am best with the rifle, he with the shotgun, etc., etc." On another expedition to Maine later that summer, he climbed Mount Katahdin carrying a forty-five-pound pack and noted in his diary that both Cousin Emlen and Arthur Cutler had given up in exhaustion long before reaching the top.

Theodore, his cousin Maud Elliott had once observed, "always thought that he could do things better than anyone else." But the impression is more of somebody who wants to prove, who *must* prove, he could do things better than anyone else.

Of course, one had to maintain a certain perspective. All rivals were not equal. Writing Bamie about his academic record the fall of his senior year, he put the matter succinctly and, apparently, in total seriousness.

"I stand 19th in the class, which began with 230 fellows," he said. "Only one gentleman stands ahead of me."

The memory of his father could still leave him "desolate and heartsore." Those lone spells of brooding, however, the painful diary entries, were far fewer now, confined almost exclusively to special or commemorative calendar days—the eve of departure for Christmas vacation, an anniversary of his father's death, or his own birthday.

"Oh, how little worthy I am of such a father," reads the most anguished of such passages in the diary from his junior year. "I feel such a hopeless sense of inferiority to him; I loved him so. . . . But with the help of God I shall try to lead such a life as he would have wished, and to do nothing I would have been ashamed to confess to him. I am very . . ."

The next page, consisting of seven lines, has been carefully blotted out in heavy black ink. Apparently, he had gotten drunk again, or was still sorely distraught over what had happened the night of the Porcellian initiation. For under laboratory conditions, by back-lighting the page, it has been possible to determine two and a half lines of the seven he chose to censor: "angry with myself for having gotten tight when . . ."

"May God help me to live as he would have wished," he repeats one more time, this in his senior year, as he turns twenty-one.

Morally, he had tied himself to the mast. He did not smoke— and never would—and he remained preeminently "pure," as he said. He abhorred foul language, and humor smacking of what he called smut. One expression of righteous indignation to be found in the diary, this on the news that Cousin Cornelius had married a French actress, might be a line from an English drawing-room farce: "He is a disgrace to the family—the vulgar brute."

The Sunday-school classes at Christ Church continued regularly each week for a total of three and a half years. He quit only in January of his senior year when it was discovered that he was a Presbyterian, not an Episcopalian. He must either join the church, he was informed by the rector, or go.

"I told the clergyman I thought him rather narrow-minded," he wrote Mittie. He then started teaching a mission class in the poorest section of Cambridge.

His health was superb, better even than during the first two years. Apparently he had but one bout with asthma all his junior year and none his senior year.

The attack during his junior year had again coincided with a trip to Maine, another arduous hunting expedition like the one before, again under the guidance of Bill Sewall, only this time in the dead of a Maine winter. "The first two or three days I had asthma," he reported to his mother, "but, funnily enough, this left me entirely as soon as I went into [the logging] camp." Beyond that he said no more on the subject. It was his joy in the wilds that he wanted to share with her. He had never beheld anything so beautiful as the Maine woods in winter. He had killed a buck and trapped a lynx, he also told her proudly.

He was a steadfast correspondent, certainly, however busy he was, and as he liked to remind those at home, writing was slow work for him. The words never came easily, a letter always took more time than they would ever suppose. His longest letters were to his "own sweet Motherling" and he signed himself now as his father had, as Thee.

Of the world at large, of events in the daily papers, he apparently thought no more than in previous years. The one odd note was a passing remark in an eight-page letter to Mittie written early in his junior year. He was enjoying especially Dunbar's lectures in political economy, as well as Palmer's course in metaphysics. These, he wrote, were even more interesting than his natural-history courses.

· 3 ·

LONG AFTERWARD, looking back, he would say he had left Harvard little prepared for "the big world." He thought what he had learned at Harvard of considerably less value than what he had learned at home. Further, he blamed Harvard for killing the old boyhood dream of a career in science. The emphasis, he said, had been entirely wrong for him, almost exclusively on laboratory work and the minutiae of biology, none of which appealed. ("I had no more desire or ability to be a microscopist and section-cutter than to be a mathematician.") Had Harvard encouraged the active life of a field naturalist, a career like those of his boyhood heroes—Audubon, Baird—things might have gone differently, he implied.

On the surface this would seem a sad and ironic commentary and especially if, as appears, Harvard had been chosen in the first place for its strength in the natural sciences. But there is little reason to believe that the young man at Harvard would have given anything like the same explanation, had he been asked. To judge again by what he said in the diary, he enjoyed particularly the time in the laboratory; and if grades are a fair index, it was in the sciences that he did his very best work at Harvard, scoring in the 90s in three of his four science courses in his junior and senior years, and an 89 in the fourth.

His boyhood dream, he later charged, had been the victim of a "total failure" on the part of the science department "to understand the great variety of kinds of work that could be done by naturalists, including what could be done by outdoor naturalists." Yet a more outgoing outdoor naturalist, a more inspirational teacher than Na-

thaniel Southgate Shaler would have been extremely difficult to
find. Shaler was the antithesis of the laboratory recluse and Shaler
was the dominant spirit of the Natural History Department, which
had all of three professors. His geology field trips were famous. ("If
he hears you call him old man," said a student, "he'll walk your
damned legs off.") Reporters sometimes went along to describe the
experience—the huge love of nature he exuded, his humor and
unending intellectual enthusiasm. In the Agassiz tradition Shaler
was "thoroughly human"; he wrote, he traveled, he was refresh-
ingly outspoken. "He was much like what Roosevelt later became," remembered President Eliot, "very energetic and large
hearted."

Indeed, every sign is that the boyhood vision of a lifework in
natural history faded for Theodore in spite of the way science was
taught at Harvard, rather than as a consequence. Not even Shaler
could hold him. The fact that he had no praise for Shaler in later
years, no Shaler stories of the kind so many of his contemporaries
told, may not mean much, since he was often to be silent on people
who had mattered in his life, and particularly, it would seem, if he
felt they had somehow abandoned him, or he had abandoned them.
The only Harvard professor he was to remember fondly, A. S. Hill,
in the English Department, was also the only one he was known to
have openly disliked as an undergraduate.

The fairest judgment seems to be that he had found other interests—such as the Dunbar lectures and Alice Lee. If Harvard
failed him, or let him down, it was in other ways.

He never found any real intellectual excitement there, for all
his good grades. He was never inspired to reach or push himself
academically. At no point did he churn with intellectual curiosity
or excitement. He was conscientious about his work and could give
it all his concentration when need be. Like his father, he had the
power of being "focused," and because of this—and because he
very carefully organized his time—he gave the impression of working relatively little. Richard Saltonstall, for one, was under the
impression that he was pretty much coasting.

When President Eliot was asked long afterward if there was
anything he could say as to the influence of Harvard on Theodore,
he responded "No." Eliot's recollection of Theodore as an undergraduate was vague. He could recall only a "feeble" youth with
prominent teeth, a boy who probably read a good deal but never
got "to the bottom of things."

He had had no real contact with Eliot, as almost no one did.

William James, from whom he had taken anatomy in his sophomore year, made no apparent impression. The names of Emerson or Dana or Parkman fail to appear anywhere in his letters and diaries. Also, for someone supposedly enthralled by the works of Longfellow—someone so deeply moved by the heroic theme of *King Olaf* —it seems odd that he never reports sighting the Great Man himself, or makes any effort to go see him.

Nor, as time would tell, did Harvard provide him with any lasting male friendships. He was never anything but proud of his Harvard affiliations. He liked being known as a Harvard man. He would return for reunions. He would report dutifully on his career for class biographies and recall with conspicuous pride—and, on occasion, with something less than strict regard for the truth—his various undergraduate accomplishments. He would claim, for example, to have held Harvard's lightweight boxing crown; and in describing his academic record, he would remember finishing in the top ten percent of his class, which was also inaccurate, since at graduation he stood number 21 out of 171.

Of his Porcellian connection he was proudest of all. The day would come when, in a letter from Washington, he would inform Kaiser Wilhelm II of the engagement of his daughter Alice, his own firstborn, and include the wonderful news that it was to be a match with a Porcellian man.

But his Harvard friendships were to become peripheral very rapidly. Except for Henry Minot, the departed friend from his freshman year, he had found no one with whom he shared common interests, beyond the social or athletic. Years later, having interviewed a number of those who had known him best, another Harvard man, the writer Hermann Hagedorn, would conclude that Theodore must have been lonely as an undergraduate. Several said they thought he had had few real friends. "I have discovered no one who was intimate with him and few who were sympathetic," Hagedorn noted privately. "Most of his classmates simply did not like him," he was told by Mrs. Robert Bacon.

It is certain, however, that Theodore had an extremely good time at Harvard, just as he remembered. When, midway through his junior year, he writes, "Truly these are the golden years of my life," he means every word. He "can't conceive of a fellow possibly enjoying himself more." "I doubt I shall ever enjoy myself as much again" is the emphatic declaration as his junior year ends. If he knew others thought him peculiar or "bumptious," as one professor said, he never let on.

For Mittie, in the fall of his senior year, he provided this memorable social log:

Cambridge, October 20, 1879

DARLING MOTHERLING,

I have just returned from spending Sunday with the Guilds, cousins of Harry Shaw, who live out at Forest Hills near the Minots. I drove over there in my cart, and the ride home this morning was delicious. Yesterday (Sunday) Harry Guild and I drove over to the Whitneys' to take tea.

Last Monday I drove Jack Tebbets over to call on the Miss Bacons, who are very nice girls. Wednesday I dined at the Lees', and spent the loveliest kind of an evening with Rosy, Alice, and Rose. The two girls [Bamie and Corinne] must come on to Boston next month if only to see Chestnut Hill; and, by Jove, I shall be awfully disappointed if they don't like it. Mamie Saltonstall's birthday was on Friday; I gave her a small silver fan chain. Saturday I spent all the morning playing tennis with the two Miss Lanes; I forgot to say that on Thursday they took Dick and myself to call on the Chinese professor. We had a most absurd visit.

This afternoon I am going to drive Van Rensselaer over to Chestnut Hill; tomorrow he and I take tea and spend the evening at the Lanes'. Wednesday Harry Shaw and I give a small opera party to Mr. and Mrs. Saltonstall, Rose, and Alice. Thursday six of us—Harry Shaw, Jack Tebbets, Minot Weld, Dick Saltonstall, Harry Chapin, and myself—are going to take a four-in-hand and drive up to Frank Codman's farm, where we will spend the day, shooting glass balls, etc.

He did have fun, time after time. And he did fall in love, head over heels.

"I have certainly lived like a prince for my last two years in college," he begins one of the most candid and heartfelt entries in the diary, a summing up written shortly after graduation.

I have had just as much money as I could spend; belonged to the Porcellian Club; have had some capital hunting trips; my life has been varied; I have kept a good horse and cart; I have had a dozen good and true friends in college, and several very pleasant families outside; a lovely home; I have had but little work, only enough to give me an occupation, and to crown all infinitely above everything else put together, I have won the sweetest of girls for my wife. No man ever had so pleasant a college course.

He counted himself a success, and that too was an altogether new feeling.

CHAPTER TEN

Especially Pretty Alice

· 1 ·

THEY MET the first time on October 18, 1878, which is to say they met early that same heady autumn of Theodore's junior year when suddenly everything seemed to be going so right for him. He had his "burst of popularity" and found the girl of his dreams, his " 'rare and radiant maiden,' " all within about ten days.

The eighteenth was a Friday. Classes were over for the week and in the afternoon Dick Saltonstall had driven him out to Chestnut Hill in a buggy to meet his family and spend the weekend. It was a ride of only six miles, but through open country most of the way, hills brilliant with fall color, and Theodore's first impression, almost from the hour they arrived, was of coming home.

The two great neighboring homesteads of the Saltonstalls and the Lees might have been Oyster Bay mansions and the two large, active families into which he was at once gathered might have been Roosevelts.

The houses were within calling distance of each other, about fifty yards distant, with hayfields and orchards and woodland falling away down the hillside. A connecting path ran from the Saltonstall back door on a gradual uphill slope to the Lee place, past the Saltonstall barn. The Saltonstalls faced east, the Lees south; but the houses were of the same vintage and much the same in scale and appearance—huge and Victorian, with clapboard siding and an endless number of windows, high porches, high, peaked gables, tremendous red-brick chimneys, and long kitchen wings. The kitchen alone at the Saltonstalls' was as big as a barn (quite large enough to serve as an additional Saltonstall dwelling, years later, when it was cut off and removed from the main house). And the Lee house was larger even than the Saltonstalls'.

Leverett Saltonstall, Dick's father, and George Cabot Lee, the father of Theodore's heart's desire, were two wealthy, important, middle-aged Bostonians, dignified, good friends, brothers-in-law, and as steeped in Harvard as one could possibly be. (Leverett had been in the Class of 1848; George, in the Class of 1850.) Leverett, an attorney, had given up his regular practice to dabble in one thing and another, including politics; George was a Lee of Lee, Higginson and Company, the Boston banking and investment firm. Indeed, there was no more exemplary figure of good, old, Boston financial stability than George Lee, he being the keeper of the famous vaults at Lee, Higginson. Another of the firm, Colonel Henry Lee, some fifteen years before had hit upon the idea of a safe-deposit vault beneath the State Street headquarters, the first such vault in the country, but George had become its manager. A small, compact man with a high forehead, high color, and a white mustache, he was known to be "prudent, assiduous, a lover of detail," a little gruff in manner but kindly withal, and totally reliable. To have your money securely invested, in the Boston vernacular of that day, was to be "as safe as Lee's vaults."

They were men certainly of whom the elder Theodore would have approved. The one notable difference in their outlook and his was political, since both were Democrats, and Saltonstall, in particular, harbored bitter enmity toward almost all Republicans as a consequence of the 1876 election. Sent by the National Democratic Committee to witness the tally of disputed votes in Florida, he had seen the presidency being stolen before his eyes and refused ever to forget it.

Saltonstall's wife was George Lee's sister, Harriett Rose, which made the Saltonstall and Lee children first cousins. Dick was the oldest of five Saltonstall children, followed by Rose, Mary, Phillip, and eight-year-old Endicott. Alice—Alice Hathaway—was the second of six Lee children, five girls and one boy. Rose, or Rosy, Lee was her older sister. Then followed Harriett, Caroline, Isabella, and George, who was nine. Their mother was Caroline Haskell Lee.

So together the two households comprised what amounted to one very large family of fifteen, and with five or six full-time servants for each house, with horses to ride, surrounding countryside to explore, fireplaces in every room for chill October nights, this was everything Theodore could have wished for, the whole atmosphere being "so homelike," as he said.

Alice was seventeen. Theodore was nineteen, the same age his father had been when he first reached Roswell and found his Princess from Afar in another large country house on a hill. What Alice was wearing when he first saw her, whether they were at the Saltonstalls' or the Lees' house, or somewhere along the path between, we do not know; but as he told her later, she affected him in a way he had never experienced before. The feeling was instantaneous. He loved her, he later wrote, as soon as he saw her. And she was "my first love, too."

She was, by every surviving account, extraordinarily attractive, slender, graceful in her movements, and "rather tall" for a girl of that era, five feet seven, which meant that with shoes on she was as tall as he. Her hair was a honey-blond and done in fashionable "water-curls" about her temples, in "the Josephine look." Her eyes were extremely blue, her nose just slightly tilted. She is described repeatedly as "radiant," "bright," "cheerful," "sunny," "high-spirited," "enchanting," "full of life," the same words one finds in descriptions of Mittie Bulloch at that age. She loved games, as Mittie did; she wore white; she was full of humor and flirtatious ("bewitching," Theodore said); her birthday was in July, as Mittie's was.

Saturday morning, accompanied by Dick and one of his sisters, she and Theodore walked in the woods together. In the afternoon they all drove to Milton, to the Ellerton Whitney estate, for dinner and tea. "We spent the evening dancing and singing, driving back about 11 o'clock," he reports in his diary. Sunday, after church, just the two of them went "chestnutting" and three weeks later he was back again for another Sunday, to see the Saltonstalls ostensibly.

Invited for Thanksgiving, he could write proudly at the day's end, "They call me by my first name now."

As time passed they were to cover countless miles in country walks together, she more than keeping up with him with her "long, firm step." They played tennis, at which she was quite good; they went to dances, dinners, and endured what appears to have been an unending quantity of tea and talk and always in the best company.

"Snowed heavily all day long," reads one Saturday entry in the diary. "But in spite of the weather I took a long walk with

pretty Alice . . . spent most of the remainder of the day teaching
the girls the five step and a new dance, the Knickerbocker. In the
evening we played whist and read ghost stories." He had a rug
made for her from the lynx he trapped in Maine. She made him a
pair of slippers (to replace Mittie's presumably); and it was that
spring that he had his horse shipped on to Cambridge so he could
ride to Chestnut Hill on his own whenever he chose. ("It was the
best stroke I ever made getting him on here.")

To judge by what he said in his letters home, he was having a
"capital time" with any number of Boston girls—Jennie Hooper,
Nana Rotch, Lulu Lane, Bessie Whitney—and when he mentioned
Alice, even in the supposed privacy of the diary, it was usually in
the same breath with Rose Saltonstall, as if there were no difference in their appeal to him. Nor did he neglect to include periodic
references to others from his "past." "Remember me to Annie and
Fanny, and give my love to Edith—if she's in a good humor," he
wrote to Corinne; "otherwise my respectful regards. If she seems
particularly good-tempered tell her that I hope that when I see her
at Xmas it will not be on what you might call one of her off days."

Once he ventured to declare in the diary, "The more I see of
Rose Saltonstall and Alice Lee the more I like them, especially
pretty Alice." By spring he felt up to saying the same thing (and in
almost identical words) to Bamie, adding quickly, "All the family
are just lovely to me."

"I want you particularly to know some of my girl friends now,"
he wrote to Corinne, expecting that she, Mittie, Bamie, and Aunt
Anna might show up for Class Day. "They are a very sweet set of
girls," he assured her.

Through that summer, until he left for Maine (and to see Alice
en route), he appeared to have little or nothing on his mind, exactly
as if Alice Lee did not exist. Her name never appears in the diary
rendition of his days at Oyster Bay. He writes instead of "the same
active, out-of-door life that I always enjoy so much." He is thinking
mainly about "getting into beautiful condition," spending "the
whole time out in the open air; and at night am always tired enough
to sleep like a top. Naturally I am in magnificent health and spirits." A "pretty little Miss Hale" from Philadelphia turns up as a
guest of Uncle James Alfred and family. "I take her out rowing
quite often." Another of "the prettiest girls in Oyster Bay" is a Miss
Emily Swan, with whom he has had "several very pleasant rows
and rides." He walks with Bamie and "Pussie," he walks with
Mittie, who is "just too sweet and pretty for anything." On August

11 he reports, "I am teaching pretty Miss Emily Swan to play lawn tennis."

But it was all an elaborate deception, according to what he revealed later. In truth he had already proposed to Alice. He had made up his mind to marry her as early as that Thanksgiving at Chestnut Hill. He had even recorded the decision in the diary at that time, but then, thinking better of it, carefully removed the page with a straight razor. The proposal came sometime in June, to judge by things he said later, and from the diary, one gets the impression it was on the evening of the twentieth, Class Day, for which none of the Roosevelts had made an appearance. There were parties most of the day—an afternoon tea dance at the new gym, a dinner at the Hasty Pudding Club—and after dark, from about eight o'clock until ten, he and Alice sat together in a window at Hollis Hall "looking at the Yard beautifully lighted and listening to the Glee Club." He had "never seen her look so lovely," he wrote. "We then went and danced at Memorial [Hall]."

But whatever the time or setting, she turned him down, or at least put him off.

As he wrote later to Henry Minot, he had "made everything subordinate to winning her." His entire last two years at Harvard, as he saw them, were in "eager, restless, passionate pursuit of one all-absorbing object."

"See that girl?" Mrs. Robert Bacon would remember him saying at a Hasty Pudding function. "I am going to marry her. She won't have me, but I am going to have *her!*"

The showy little dog cart was acquired as his senior year got under way and it was now that the expenditures on clothes took their biggest jump. His campaign was rolling. He enlisted all the help he could get. Early in November, he arranged for Mr. and Mrs. Lee, Alice, and her sister Rose to visit Mittie at 57th Street. Two weeks later Bamie and Corinne made their appearance at Chestnut Hill, where they were given dinners at both the Lee and Saltonstall houses. On November 22 he put on a lunch in their honor at the Porcellian, complete with wine and flowers, the table set for thirty-four guests, including Alice and her mother.

He escorted Rosy Lee to a tennis party and had "lovely fun" dancing with her at a Harvard Assembly. He took "dear and honest" (and very homely) Rose Saltonstall driving in his "swell" dog cart. He talked poetry and theology with the rather august Leverett Saltonstall most of one long evening.

Other young men, meantime, circled about Alice as moths to a flame (in the words of another of her cousins), and with the return of winter Theodore was beside himself. He is described wandering sleepless through the woods near Cambridge "night after night." Obsessed with the idea that somebody else would run off with her, he sent abroad for a set of French dueling pistols, which it is said he actually succeeded in getting through the Customhouse "after great difficulty." One winter night when he was off on another of his wanderings in the woods, somebody telegraphed New York and Cousin West, now a medical student, had to come on immediately to see what could be done for him.

Then, over the Christmas holidays, the course of the romance took an abrupt turn. Alice came back to New York for a second visit, accompanied by Rosy and Dick and Rose Saltonstall. It becomes "an uproariously jolly time." There is a theater evening. Parties are given in Alice's honor by Aunt Anna and Aunt Lizzie next door. New Year's Day Elliott stages a lunch and a dance at Jerome Park. It is a sparkling winter day with fresh snow on the ground and everyone rides to and from the party in three big sleighs.

On Sunday, January 25, 1880, again at Cambridge, he could announce unequivocally in his diary, "At last everything is settled . . ."

> I drove over to the Lees' determined to make an end of things
> . . . and after much pleading my own sweet, pretty darling consented to be my wife. Oh, how bewitchingly pretty she looked! If loving her with my whole heart and soul can make her happy, she shall be happy; a year ago last Thanksgiving I made a vow that win her I would if it were possible; and now I have done so, the aim of my whole life shall be to make her happy, and to shield her and guard her from every trial . . .

He was off at once on a flying visit to New York to "tell the family," all of whom were "very much surprised," according to his impression. By February 2, he had bought her a diamond ring.

> *Feb. 3* Snowing heavily, but I drove over in my sleigh to Chestnut Hill, the horse plunging to his belly in the great drifts, and the wind cutting my face like a knife. My sweet life was just as lovable and pretty as ever; it seems hardly possible that I can kiss her and hold her in my arms; she is so pure and so innocent, and so very, very pretty. I have never done anything to deserve such good fortune. Coming home I was upset

in a great drift, and dragged about 300 yards holding on to the reins, before I could stop the horse. . . .

Feb. 4 Superb sleighing, took Dick out for a long drive. The engagement is not to come out till a week from Monday; it is awfully hard to keep away from her.

Feb. 13 . . . I do not think ever a man loved a woman more than I love her; for a year and a quarter now I have *never* (even when hunting) gone to sleep or waked up without thinking of her; and I doubt if an hour has passed that I have not thought of her. And now I can scarcely realize that I can hold her in my arms and kiss her and caress her and love her as much as I choose.

He began sending advance notices to a few select friends, to Hal Minot, to Edith Carow and Fanny Smith. To Mittie, who seems to have been greatly distressed, he wrote, "Really you mustn't feel melancholy, sweet Motherling; I shall only love you all the more."

The formal announcement was made February 14. When Mittie, Bamie, Elliott, and Corinne arrived three days later, he drove them to a "great family dinner at the Lees'." Later, at the Hasty Pudding Club, too excited to sleep, he played billiards until dawn.

"Alice," said Mrs. Robert Bacon long afterward, ". . . did not want to marry him, but she did."

Alice, in her own words, felt as if in a dream, to have "such a noble man's love." She loved Theodore deeply, she wrote to Mittie, in answer to a letter welcoming her into the Roosevelt fold, "and it will be my aim both to endear myself to those so dear to him and retain his love. How happy I am I can't begin to tell you, it seems almost like a dream."

A date for the wedding was a subject no one had broached as yet, and when she told Theodore she wanted to be married the following autumn, he anticipated a "battle royal" with her father, who apparently thought she was too young to be in any rush and would have welcomed a long engagement. "I most sincerely wish I had you here to assist me," Theodore wrote Bamie. But then Mittie proposed that he bring Alice home to live at 57th Street, once they were married, and it was thus that he "carried the day" when the confrontation took place. "Indeed," he told Corinne, "I don't think Mr. Lee would have consented to our marriage so soon on other terms."

To Mittie he now announced, "I wish to send invitations to *all*

Theodore Roosevelt (now "Teddy") at Harvard.

The room Bamie chose and furnished for Theodore off campus.

BOTH PHOTOS: THEODORE ROOSEVELT COLLECTION, HARVARD

Theodore in rowing attire.

Opposite top, Theodore as yachtsman.

Opposite bottom, Theodore the hunter, in Maine with Bill Sewall (left) and Will Dow.

Raining hard; I drove over in a buggy to the Lees to dinner and, thanks to the storm, spent the night there. In the evening I was all the time with my darling Little Sunshine; she is so marvelously sweet, and pure and lovable and pretty that I seem to love her more and more every time I see her, though I love her so much now that I really *can not* love her more. I do not think ever a man loved a woman more than I love her; for a year and a quarter now I have <u>never</u> (even when hunting) gone to sleep or waked up without thinking of her; and I doubt if an hour has passed that I have not thought of her. And now I can scarcely realize that I can hold her in my arms and kiss her and caress her and love her as much as I choose.

A page from Theodore's diary, junior year.

Alice Lee.

The young politician with some Albany allies. The "best friend," Isaac Hunt, is seated at left, and behind stands Billy O'Neil. At center seated is George Spinney of *The New York Times*. At right is an assemblyman from Brooklyn, Walter Howe.

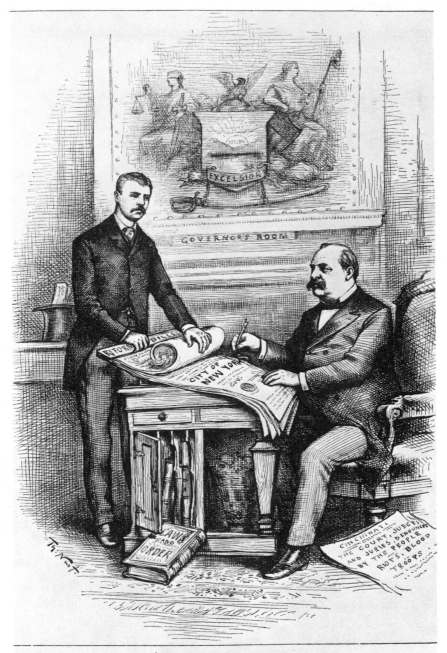

REFORM WITHOUT BLOODSHED.
GOVERNOR CLEVELAND AND THEODORE ROOSEVELT AT THEIR GOOD WORK.

The gentleman reformer is paired with New York's new reform governor,
Grover Cleveland, in a cartoon by Nast in Harper's Weekly.

The Roosevelt brothers (Elliott with pipe) pose in a photographer's studio in 1880, the summer of their hunting trip in the West.

Parlor of the Roosevelt mansion at 6 West 57th Street, with Elliott's tiger as centerpiece.

Anna Hall.

Elliott at the Meadowbrook Hunt.

Henry Cabot Lodge.

Theodore in the Bad Lands in full cowboy regalia.

THEODORE ROOSEVELT COLLECTION, HARVARD

TWO PHOTOS: STATE HISTORICAL SOCIETY OF NORTH DAKOTA

Above, Madame de Mores, the former Medora von Hoffman.

Right, the Marquis de Mores in the Bad Lands.

Opposite top, Theodore's Elkhorn Ranch, as sketched by Frederic Remington.

Opposite bottom, studio portrait of Theodore as "the plainsman," made to help promote one of his books. (The buckskin suit cost $100 —the equivalent of $1,000 or more today. Knife and scabbard were custom-made by Tiffany.)

Edith Carow.

Opposite top, Bamie with Baby Alice, about 1886.

Opposite bottom, Sagamore Hill, soon after completion.

Theodore Roosevelt, age 27, at the time he ran for mayor of New York.

my friends and *acquaintances* in New York; so couldn't you send me on a visiting list of all the people I know or ought to know? I want to include everybody, so as to rub up their memories about the existence of a man named Theodore Roosevelt, who is going to bring a pretty Boston wife back to New York next winter."

· 2 ·

6 West 57th Street

MY DEAR MRS. WARD,

Will you take a cup of tea with me on Monday next, the 12th, at 4 o'clock.

I wish to present to you Miss Alice Lee of Boston who with her mother will be visiting us then.

Miss Lee is a very lovely young girl of eighteen and is just engaged to my oldest son, Theodore, who does not graduate from Harvard until June.

I think I can rely upon your interest, my dear Mrs. Ward, in my son's engagement and I am anxious to welcome you to my home among a few of my friends. . . .

Hoping to welcome you then, my dear friend, on April 12th. I am faithfully yours—

M. B. ROOSEVELT
April 5, 1880

The note was one of the many Mittie sent off in her own hand on her monogrammed cream-colored stationery that spring of 1880 and there were to be a very great many more, several hundred at least, before the year ended. It was as if time and circumstances and all those rites of passage expected by proper society had conspired to put her at center stage as she had not been since her own engagement. And with so much expected of her—her particular grace and "example" often critical to the success of an occasion— she appears to have played her part with nothing but pleasure, and flawlessly. One New York paper was to write of her "brilliant prowess" as a hostess. "All the entertainments that she gave . . . were stamped with the spirit of good cheer, high breeding, and elevating conversation. Few houses have entertained so many guests and none has made of guests so many friends."

Her small tea of April 12 had been preceded by a family reception for Alice on April 8 and was followed by a large evening affair on April 13 at which she and Alice made a striking picture receiving their guests in front of the ornate mantelpiece in the dining room at 57th Street. In December she would stand in the same spot, Corinne on her right this time, Alice on her left, at Corinne's coming-out party, hothouse flowers banked on all sides, rooms so full of people it was difficult to move about.

Between these two occasions, in about seven months' time, she would give perhaps twenty dinner parties and an equal number of teas; she would see the 57th Street house closed for the summer—silver packed, furniture shrouded with slipcovers—and move to Oyster Bay (on May 29). She would attend Theodore's graduation at Cambridge (June 30); entertain a steady stream of guests at Tranquillity through the summer; settle issues among her servants; fret over Theodore's health; see Theodore and Elliott off to the West for a hunting trip; have Tranquillity put in order for Theodore's honeymoon; reopen the 57th Street house and arrange an "apartment" for Theodore and Alice on the third floor; attend the wedding at Chestnut Hill; plan Corinne's party; issue the invitations for Corinne's party; and adjust to the idea that Elliott was going off to hunt big game in India.

Theodore's romance, moreover, was but one of several with which she must play a part.

It was at one of her April dinner parties at 57th Street, a week or so after the reception for Alice, that Bamie's friend Sara Delano first met James Roosevelt of Hyde Park, a dignified member of the Hudson River "branch," who was twice Sara Delano's age and a widower. "He talked to her the whole time," Mittie remarked to Bamie when the evening was over. "Why, he never took his eyes off her!" Sara, like Bamie, had resigned herself to the probability of lifelong spinsterhood and would credit Mittie ever after for the way things turned out. On May 7, following up on an invitation from "Squire James," Mittie took Bamie and Sara for a visit to Hyde Park, a day Sara was to remember as among the most important in her life. "If I had not come then," she would tell her son years later, "I should now be 'old Miss Delano' after a rather sad life!"

Sara Delano and James Roosevelt were married at Algonac, the Delano estate on the Hudson, that October, a few weeks before Theodore and Alice were married. In November Sara and James sailed for a European honeymoon, taking the *Germanic*. On the same ship was Elliott, who was en route to India by way of London.

Cousin West was in love with Fanny Smith (she turned him down when he proposed), and Corinne, too, was being actively courted by a large, demonstrative, florid young Scot, a friend of Elliott's named Douglas Robinson, heir to a real-estate fortune, who, like Alice, spent part of that summer with the family at Oyster Bay, his booming voice adding a new note—like that of a calliope, Theodore thought—to the usual sounds of summer.

Corinne was thought "clever" (Fanny Smith said she had "genuine intellectual power") and though no beauty she had, at eighteen, a certain vitality and natural femininity that appealed to men and women. Beside Alice or Mittie, Corinne looked rather plain, but between her and Bamie, she was much the more attractive to the eye and her two brothers and her male cousins made a great fuss over her. She was a little taller than Mittie, with tiny hands and delicate features. For her summer reading this year she had undertaken Gibbon's *Decline and Fall.*

The same big porch rockers tilted back and forth at Tranquillity as in years past. The blue bay and sunshine were no different from other summers, or any less a tonic. The familiar, noisy games went on in timeless fashion and in the midst of it all Mittie herself often seemed a timeless summer note, "the mother in white . . . seated in state on the lawn," a book usually in hand, or talking on in her easy, unchanged Georgia way to Sister Anna or Lucy Elliott. Only the strong-willed Bamie seems to have lost patience with her on occasion.

Nothing could ruffle Mittie. Corinne, who treasured especially her mother's warmth and spontaneity, saw in her also a steady enduring strength—of a kind different from Bamie's, but strength all the same. A "perfect readiness to meet all situations," Corinne called it.

Mittie approved of Douglas Robinson, it appears; and having accepted Theodore's decision, she had taken Alice to her heart quite literally as one of her own. Elliott may have become a worry by now; it is impossible to know for certain.

Elliott had begun working for Uncle James Gracie at a bank downtown and in summer commuted to and from Oyster Bay. As some writers have said, Elliott may also have begun already to drink more than was good for him, and so the trip west in August could have been as much for his benefit as for Theodore's. Returning to Chicago after a week's hunt in Iowa, Theodore would write to Corinne of their brother's joy in "the change to civilization."

As soon as we got here he took some ale to get the dust out of
his throat; then a milk punch because he was thirsty; a mint
julep because it was hot; a brandy smash "to keep the cold out
of his stomach"; and then sherry and bitters to give him an
appetite. He took a very simple dinner—soup, fish, salmi de
grouse, sweetbread, mutton, venison, corn, macaroni, various
vegetables and some puddings and pies, together with beer,
later claret and in the evening shandygaff.

But the letter is so plainly Theodore's idea of humor—tall-tale
humor out of the Wild West—that it suggests there was no "problem" as yet. That he would treat a subject of such seriousness in so
open and bantering a vein would seem a sign that neither he nor
Elliott nor any of them was very concerned.

As Elliott and Theodore proceeded on their western expedition, it was Elliott who got on most readily with the people encountered—male and female—some of whom, according to Theodore,
were "pretty rough." Elliott's natural, easy way with people cut
across barriers of class or background, an attribute Theodore could
only admire, and doubtless Elliott's past experiences in Texas gave
him confidence of a kind Theodore lacked.

"Last Sunday night we got this motley crew together to sing
hymns," Mittie read in one of Theodore's letters, this dated August
25, 1880, from a farm in Illinois; "thanks to Elliott it was a great
success. It was all I could do to keep a sober face when I saw him
singing from the same book with the much-flattered Mrs. Rudolf
and Miss Costigan."

The trip had been badly planned. With no clear idea where to
go, they kept trying different spots, first in Illinois, then Iowa and
Minnesota, taking time out in Chicago between each foray to re-
cuperate and figure their next move. The flies were dreadful in
Illinois and on a lake in Iowa they both nearly drowned when their
rowboat capsized. But they saw it as their last chance for an adventure together, entirely on their own, which probably would have
been reason enough for going in the first place, quite aside from
Theodore's health. "I enjoy being with the old boy so much,"
Theodore said. "I am so glad . . . we two brothers have been able
at last to be together," wrote Elliott. "All the happier we are solely
dependent on each other for companionship . . ."

Theodore had become violently ill during a midsummer visit
to Bar Harbor with Alice, Rose, and Dick Saltonstall. He had
weathered his final examinations at Harvard, Class Day, gradua-

tion, the excitement of having Alice as a guest at Oyster Bay, all with no ill effect, only to be struck down in embarrassing fashion in far-off Maine. He was hit by violent diarrhea, his old cholera morbus ("very embarrassing for a lover," as he told Corinne), and to Mittie he declared a trip west would be just the thing to put him back on his feet and build him up.

What he did not tell her—or Alice or Elliott, so far as we know —was that he had also received some extremely disquieting news from the college physician as far back as March. He had gone for a routine physical examination, at the conclusion of which Dr. Dudley A. Sargeant told him he had "heart trouble." Of what variety, or whether that was even discussed, we do not know and it was only years later that Theodore ever talked about the incident. But apparently he was warned he must live a quiet life, choose a relatively sedentary occupation. He was to avoid strenuous physical exertion—he was not to run up stairs, for example. He responded at once and defiantly, telling the doctor he could never live that way, that he would do exactly the opposite.

He was sick again in Minnesota, at the Red River bordering on Dakota Territory, their farthest point west. An attack of asthma had him gasping so that he spent the night sitting up in order to breathe. The day after he was in such pain with colic he could hardly walk. Yet only a few days before, writing from Chicago, Elliott had described him as looking like a new man, "as brown and well as can be," the picture of health. "I think he misses Alice, poor dear old beloved brother. But I try to keep him at something all the time and certainly he looks a hundred percent better than when he came out."

For all the grouse, geese, snipes, sharp-tailed plovers, ducks, and grebes they managed to kill—in excess of four hundred birds —the shooting was "not as good as expected." They had hunted on foot, not horseback. There had been no whirlwind rides over the prairie as in a Mayne Reid adventure. They had never reached the "real West," the Far West," as Theodore called it. The whole episode had been very tame and colorless in contrast to what Elliott had experienced in Texas or what he could expect in the wilds of India.

As once Theodore had stayed safely at home with his studies while Elliott went off to Fort McKavett, so now he would settle in with his "little pink wife" while Elliott circled the world. But plainly there was an element of escape to Elliott's forthcoming adventure. He was getting out before Theodore returned, abdicating his place as man of the house, and to "a far better man," he assured Bamie in another letter from the western trip.

> Thee is well able and no mistake—shrewd and clever, by no means behind the age. What I have often smiled at in the old boy are I am now sure some of his best points—a practical carrying out in action of what I, for example, am convinced of in theory, but fail to put in practice.

Theodore wanted Elliott to be his best man at the wedding and declared further that if, because of his India plans, Elliott was unable to be there, then he wanted no best man—all of which pleased Mittie greatly.

"Theodore is in the city now . . . wild with happiness and excitement," wrote Fanny Smith in her diary on October 15. "I went with him to see the wedding presents he is going to give Alice. I hope she is very fond of him."

He had spent several thousand dollars on a sapphire ring, other jewelry and more gifts for her. He would begin saving, he vowed, once they were married. Two days ahead of the others, he departed for Boston.

They were married on a perfect New England fall day, the height of Indian summer, Wednesday, October 27, 1880, Theodore's twenty-second birthday, at noon in the Unitarian Church at Brookline. Mittie had invited Fanny Smith and Edith Carow to come on to Boston with the family and so they were both in the pew beside her, along with Bamie and the Gracies. Corinne was a bridesmaid. Elliott stood beside his brother with the ring and Theodore, when it came time for his vows, responded, as Fanny Smith said, "in the most determined and Theodorelike tones."

One of the servants in the Lee household, Alice's nurse from childhood (recorded only as Christina), ran the two miles from the house to the church, having missed the last carriage when it departed, and arrived just in time for the ceremony.

Alice made a stunning bride. Some weeks before, on a flying visit to Boston after his western trip, Theodore had found her "the same as ever and yet with a certain added charm" he was unable to describe. "I cannot take my eyes off her," he wrote in his diary; "she is so pure and holy that it seems almost profanation to touch her, no matter how gently and tenderly; and yet when we are alone I cannot bear her to be a minute out of my arms."

The reception was in the grand tradition—at home, with

music, food, dancing, servants with trays of champagne, the bride the center of everyone's attention, the big house where she had grown up bright with sunshine streaming through long windows.

On their wedding night the couple stayed in Springfield, at the Massasoit House, and from there the following day went directly to Oyster Bay for a honeymoon of two weeks. A proper European honeymoon had been postponed until summer, Theodore having since decided, at the urging of Uncle Robert, to enter the Columbia Law School.

Early the first week of November, a few days before Elliott sailed, Mittie received word that they were "living in a perfect dream of delight" at Tranquillity, waited on hand and foot by two faithful Roosevelt servants—the ever reliable Mary Ann, the groom Davis—and by a local woman named Kate, who did all the meals. "The house is just perfection," Theodore told her; "Kate cooks deliciously, and Mary Ann is exactly *the* servant for us; and Davis does his part beautifully too, always sending in his respects in the morning to 'the good lady' as he styles Alice."

Breakfast was at ten, dinner at two, tea at seven. Except for the servants and a big black-and-white collie named Dare, they had the place to themselves. The summer "crowd" had long since departed. The big summer houses stood silent in the golden autumn light.

They played more tennis, went on more walks and for long drives over the hills in the family buggy. At night they read aloud from Keats and Sir Walter Scott before a log fire. Their one contact with the outside world was the morning paper. Once, on November 2, Theodore had Davis drive him over to East Norwich so he could cast his first vote in a presidential election, for the Republican, James A. Garfield, and his running mate, none other than Chester Arthur.

"There is hardly an hour of the twenty-four that we are not together," he wrote in his diary a few days later. "I am living in a dream land; how I wish it could last forever."

Saturday, November 13, Mittie welcomed them home at 6 West 57th Street.

· 3 ·

THAT WINTER in New York was the busiest and possibly the happiest time Theodore had ever known. Even the most frenetic days at Harvard had never been quite so full. For Alice, after the pace of life at Chestnut Hill, the change must have been overwhelming.

Theodore at once took up the part of his father, presiding at the head of the family table, presiding Sunday evenings in his father's old place at the newsboys' dinner, beginning their first Sunday in New York. He was elected a trustee of the Orthopedic Hospital and the New York Infant Asylum. And for the Roosevelt women now, at least figuratively in his charge, he became the main source of news from "downtown," the perfect escort to the theater and the opera, the whip hand on sleigh rides through the park or along Riverside Drive. Reading aloud to them from Mark Twain's latest, *A Tramp Abroad*, he would laugh so uproariously that he could hardly go on, turning "literally purple," as Corinne said.

At meetings of the St. Andrews Society he chatted with Whitelaw Reid of the *Tribune* and with others who had known his father. He joined a Free Trade Club, organized a whist club, started to work seriously on the naval history he had more or less toyed with the year before. By mid-February Corinne could also report in a letter to Douglas Robinson that "he has been going to Republican meetings steadily this week, and gives us most absurd accounts of them."

And all of this, meantime, was only tangential to the new career in the law.

From 57th Street to the Columbia Law School, then located in the battered, old Schermerhorn house on Great Jones Street, was a distance of about three miles—fifty-four blocks down Fifth Avenue —and he walked it regularly every morning, leaving the house around 7:45, arriving in time for an 8:30 class. Classes over, he sometimes stopped in at the Astor Library, across Lafayette Place, to do research for the book, then walked home again. The six-mile round trip, he remarked apologetically, was the only regular exercise he was able to work into his day, given all he had to do.

"The law work is very interesting," he said in his diary; and again, "I like the law school work very much." Some afternoons, when not at the Astor Library, he read law in the offices of Uncle Robert, who was back in the news again as one of the new reform trustees of the Brooklyn Bridge, now in its eleventh year of construction and still unfinished.

Before dark, if there was snow, he would bundle Alice into the sleigh and strike off to the north, through the park or crosstown to the Hudson. "I love to take my sweet little wife up the Riverside Park," he wrote shortly before Christmas; "it is a beautiful drive now, with the snowy palisades showing in fine relief against the gray winter skies, as with the dark waters of the Hudson, covered with ice, at their feet."

Once, on a sleighing party along the Hudson, the elder Theodore and Mittie had gone as far as one of their summer "cottages," at Riverdale, where Mittie insisted on getting out to inspect the place. The snow was deep and Theodore had picked her up and carried her in his arms, only to step in a hole and over they had gone. "She enjoyed it like a child," he happily told the family afterward. "Your Uncle Jimmie and Mrs. Dodge looked shocked."

"When my sweetest little wife can't go," reads another of the diary entries, "I always take dear little Mother. It is lovely to live as we are now."

But the quantities of energy expended on his studies and sleigh rides, the historical research, the daily constitutionals in every kind of weather, or his clubs and meetings and charities, seem almost secondary to what went into "the season," the New York social whirl that dominated the winter and took front rank in the running diary account he maintained so conscientiously. From the night of Corinne's debut, December 8—the "great ball at our house" when Alice wore her wedding dress and white flowers in her hair—there was something going on, some reception, dinner, musical, or spectacular society ball, nearly every night of the week. He and "pretty Alice" were an immediate triumph as part of the ultrafashionable "young married" set, "taken up" and fussed over by what Edith Wharton called "the little inner group of people who, during the long New York season, disported themselves together daily and nightly with apparently undiminished zest."

There was a "jolly little dinner" at the Iselins', a "very pleasant little party" at Aunt Annie's, dinners at the Leavitts', the Griswolds', the Weekeses', the Keans', the Morans', the Tuckermans', the Stuyvesant Fishes', a musical at the Betts', a dinner for twenty-four at home, and several large dinners given by Mrs. William B. Astor, Jr.—*the* Mrs. Astor—who was homely and without charm and so laden with chains of diamonds as to be immobile, but who, with her social counselor, Ward McAllister, reigned over New York society. The Roosevelts and the Astors were "family" now, after a fashion, since Mrs. Astor's daughter Helen had married young James Roosevelt Roosevelt—"Rosy" Roosevelt—who was the son of Sara Delano's James by his first marriage.

There were theater parties and "small suppers" afterward, a box at the opera Monday nights, the Mendelssohn Concert series.

There were private dances by candlelight at Delmonico's that often lasted until three in the morning, the Patriarchs' Ball and the Family Circle Dancing Class (the F.C.D.C.), these latter two the inspiration of Ward McAllister and already regarded as time-honored social institutions.

"Dinner at Delanos'," reads the diary entry for Monday, January 11, 1881, at the start of a new week on the social calendar; "sat between Mrs. Astor and Mrs. Drayton." The night following came a "very jolly theater party and supper at Tuckermans';" the night after that, a "great ball" at the Astors'. On Friday, January 14, Theodore, Alice, and some thirteen others, including Bamie, Corinne, and Douglas Robinson, went off to Niagara Falls by private railroad car.

Saturday, January 15 Ideal day; perpetual spree. Saw falls, rapids, and whirlpool; took long sleigh rides, ended trip with every kind of dance in evening. Took hotel by storm. Everybody so jolly and congenial.

Sunday, January 16 Sleighed to church. Went under Falls; grand sight. Took night train for N.Y. Ghost stories and songs. Trip is *the* success of the season.

Monday, January 17 Went to Patriarch Ball.

It was "the greatest kind of fun." He knew how to pace himself, he said. "I never stay more than two minutes with any girl and so don't get talked out." Corinne, he claimed, was a "great belle" of the season, while Alice grew ever more dazzling. With her on his arm he could not help being the center of attention. "Alice is universally and greatly admired; and she seems to grow more beautiful day by day . . . and oh, how happy she has made me!" The attentions showered on her at every party seem only to have pleased and flattered him. The old wild jealousy, any thoughts of dueling pistols, were all in the past apparently.

For her own part, meantime, Alice had also joined a tennis club and the Fifth Avenue Presbyterian Church ("now we are one in *everything*," said Theodore emotionally), and formed a bond with her new mother-in-law that, from the evidence we have, must have been extraordinary. If one chose to marry a Roosevelt, Douglas Robinson was to remark, one ran the risk of being "bullied or ignored or hung on the family like a tail to a kite," but Alice is not known to have shared or ever to have expressed any such feelings

and the love she and Mittie had for each other would be talked
about for years.

There was no friction between them and it was not as though
Alice was an unfelt presence. Practicing at the piano in the corner
of the parlor, she played loud enough to be heard through the wall
of the adjoining Roosevelt house. She entered into conversation—
Mittie found her "so companionable"—and for all her sunny spirit
appears to have had no fear of expressing exasperation or impatience with some of her husband's ways. (In another of Owen Wister's vignettes involving the spilling of Roosevelt blood, Theodore
is described working away at his War of 1812 studies, alone in the
library, standing on one leg, checking through a book on navigation
while making little sketches, his desk a sliding panel that pulled
out from the bookcase. Alice bursts in on him and exclaims, "We're
dining out in twenty minutes, and Teddy's drawing little ships,"
whereupon "Teddy" charges to the third floor, cuts himself shav-
ing, and is at once attended by the adoring wife and other resident
female Roosevelts who "take measures" to save his collar from
being stained.)

At times, too, she questioned the need for such everlasting
activity in their lives. While Theodore and Bamie thrived on the
tightly packed schedule—"Oh, Energy, thy name is Bamie!" Theodore once hailed his adored sister—Alice seems to have felt something alien in the pellmell rush of New York life, just as Mittie had
when she first came to the city as a bride. Racing down the street
with Corinne to catch a horsecar one morning, Alice had panted
out, "Do you always have to run to catch anything in New York?"
And Corinne, writing reflectively to Elliott later in the day, had
agreed it was true, they were indeed constantly rushing to catch
something or other. "Sometimes we succeed," she said, "and
sometimes we do not, and it is not particularly satisfactory either
way." Only within the home walls was life "intensely satisfactory."

During the flurry of excitement surrounding Corinne's engagement to Douglas Robinson later that winter, Alice seems to have
remained largely in the background. The engagement was a peculiar business—eagerly supported by Theodore and Bamie and
looked upon by Corinne as a great mistake from the moment she
agreed to it. She had no wish to be married. She had a horror of
marriage, as she told her ardent Douglas in a variety of ways, one
letter after another, he having departed from New York almost immediately after the announcement to check over some landholdings in West Virginia.

She had interests other than marriage, she insisted, interests she knew he regarded as "unwomanly." Her favorite nights at home were those when Theodore came bursting in from one of his political meetings "full of it all." Douglas was her "dear old fellow," to be sure, but she was utterly unable to say she loved him and would not until she did. But following an afternoon ride with Theodore up Riverside Drive, she wrote, "Such a lovely long talk as we had. . . . He is very fond of you, Douglas, and said there was not a single other man he knew except you that he would like me to marry." "Sometimes," she wrote later, "I think if I could have one talk with my father it would be all right."

Alice and Corinne became close companions, shopping together, making social calls, reading aloud to each other. With Bamie, Alice seems to have acted with a certain restraint, that same edge of respect, even deference, shown by others toward Bamie since childhood. If at a party she found herself caught in conversation with some formidable someone whose mind ranged beyond her own, she wished always, Alice said, that Bamie could be there to take her place. One rainy evening toward spring, when Mittie was not feeling well, the three young women—Alice, Corinne, and Bamie—sat with Mittie in her room talking at length of their own lives and ambitions. Bamie would have preferred to live in more stirring times, she said, and to have taken a prominent part. "What a splendid queen she would have made," wrote Corinne to Douglas. "With you and Teddy as prime ministers and Elliott as master of ceremonies, you might have ruled the world!!"

The one false note in the picture was the inclusion of Douglas Robinson—a gesture of kindness on Corinne's part—for there could never be but one prime minister to Queen Bamie; no one could possibly be regarded on a par with Theodore in the eyes of his two sisters, then or ever. Their love for him was a force, a presence precluding, as it would turn out, any feelings of comparable intensity for any other man—as Corinne herself had all but said already to her long-suffering, distant suitor.

And possibly, everything considered, it was Alice's acute awareness of this, her seemingly instinctive understanding of how very much Theodore meant to the other Roosevelt women and her pleasure in their presence in her married life, that speaks most for her character. As Corinne herself observed long afterward, Alice was wholly unselfish about sharing Theodore with his adoring, now entirely female family. It was this that endeared her most to them and made her at once one of them.

CHAPTER ELEVEN

Home Is the Hunter

———————

· 1 ·

SOME YEARS AFTERWARD, reflecting on the personality of Theodore Roosevelt, a friend and fellow politician by the name of John S. Wise wrote that it would be mistaken to picture Theodore as resembling his father. He had never known the father, Wise acknowledged. "But from all accounts of him he was one of the gentlest, most lovable, public-spirited and popular men that ever lived in New York City." Theodore, however, had not inherited "the gentler traits" of the father. "In his sturdiness and love of life's battles and enterprises, he much more resembled his uncle, Mr. Robert Roosevelt, who had been my friend and associate these many years."

Then Wise spoke of the Roosevelt he liked best, about whom the general public knew little or nothing, Elliott, "the most lovable Roosevelt I ever knew."

He was one of my earliest acquaintances in New York and our attachment grew from the moment of our first meeting until his death. Perhaps he was nothing like so aggressive or so forceful a man as Theodore, but if personal popularity could have bestowed public honors on any man there was nothing beyond the reach of Elliott Roosevelt.

Little that counted for "home news," the news he hungered for, was lost on Elliott during his time away, so thoroughly, so

conscientiously was he posted by Mittie, Bamie, Theodore, Corinne, and by the ever sympathetic Aunt Annie, whose affection for
him surpassed even what she felt for the other three of her sister's
children. "At present I have thirty-two! letters to answer," he declared at one point in his travels. Aunt Annie alone, we know,
wrote him a total of sixty-one times.

He was apprised of the ups and downs of Corinne's romance
and from four or five different perspectives. Word of her engagement left him "flabbergasted." ("Is Bamie showing any signs of the
same thing?" he asked Theodore excitedly from Hyderabad.) He
was posted on the departure of "the two innocents" (Alice and
Theodore) for their summer abroad. He heard how Theodore had
climbed the Matterhorn.

"I have tried to make Corinne understand she's not to marry
unless she is sure," Mittie was still writing in August.

Theodore's reunion with Uncle Jimmie Bulloch in Liverpool
had been a huge success . . . Theodore and Alice were home again.
("Teddy brought out from London with his dress suits two or three
satin waistcoats—purple, pale yellow, and blue, and one rich black
silk one," wrote Mittie. ". . . Emlen has been quite contemptuous
about them, and you should hear Douglas standing up for Teddy.")
Theodore was "going in" for politics, as a candidate for the State
Assembly. . . . Theodore was elected by a margin of fifteen
hundred votes. . . . Uncle Jim's new house at Oyster Bay was up to
the second story. . . . Father's old friend Theodore Bronson had
died in Paris. . . . Edith Carow had given Theodore and Alice a
party and Theodore led an impromptu cotillion. . . . Theodore's
book was finished and delivered to the publisher.

"Has not our dear Thee done well," Elliott wrote Bamie from
Kashmir.

Their letters took anywhere from two to three months to catch
up with him, once he got to India, and there was no little frustration
in hearing things so long after the fact, and particularly since other
news often reached him astonishingly fast. When James A. Garfield
was shot in Washington in July, much of the world knew about it
in a matter of days. Word of Garfield's death in September—and of
the ascension, incredibly, of Chester A. Arthur to the presidency
—reached Elliott in Delhi not much after it did Theodore in Liverpool.

Of his own adventures he could hardly say enough. His travels
became ultimately a trip around the world.

Through social contacts in London made possible by the James

Roosevelts and with the help of a letter he carried from Secretary of State Evarts, introducing him as the son of the eminent Theodore Roosevelt of New York, he had no trouble making himself welcome among Her Majesty's forces in India. Arriving at Bombay in mid-January he was put up at the Byculla Club and provided with a full-time servant who slept outside his door. There were lunches ("tiffins") in his honor, a round of elaborate dinners.

"I would not trust myself to live here," he wrote Mittie. "There is no temptation to do anything but what you please . . .

"At seven Aya brings me my coffee and cigarette," he went on, describing a typical day, "and I sit on the veranda lazily taking in all the beauties of the early morning—

At my feet directly under me is the race track and the horses are being taken round for a morning spin. Some of them, beautiful Arabs, bounding by with that long easy stride so sure an indication of the dash and go of the breed. Over the field, beyond the belt of green waving trees yonder, stretches the ocean; as the mist slowly rises, see the boats lazily drift along. To sit and read and think for an hour here is perfect happiness. But the bath is ready by eight, I am dressed for nine o'clock breakfast with Mr. Clark of the Bombay Club, where I go in a buggy or gig, the "hansom" of the city. "Stewed sole—egg toast—prawn curry and beer cup" does not make a bad beginning for the day. A little business, a good deal of sporty talk, and the papers bring a fellow very quickly to M. Vouillon's two o'clock tiffin in my honor. I cannot describe it, it was all too Arabian night-like. The rich peacock feather hand *punka*, the delicious perfume, the delicate dishes and still more delicate wines, the quiet service—no sound of boots for the boys go without them, and the clothes make no noise. They are certainly wonderful servants. The afternoon, a call on the Governor of Bombay—and a visit to the Appollo Bunder [a popular rendezvous for fashionable Bombay]—to pay my respects to Mme. Vouillon, who drives in a handsome C-spring landau, two Sikhs, a coachman in scarlet and gold and she herself a beautiful woman, beautifully dressed, looks particularly well, as she is set off by the odd contrast—though there are many other as perfect turnouts and pretty women. Kittredge drives me to the Club, I dress and sit on his right at a dinner he gives me. A fairly fitting ending to the eastern day, a dinner of six, each man his own servant to wait on him and a boy to keep him cool. Then bed—almost in the open air. . . .

To his hosts he was a refreshing novelty—an American sports-man of impeccable taste and manners, a good shot, handsome, high-spirited, a born gentleman. The hard-drinking, polo-playing officers wished only "to give me the best of times."

En route to Kashmir, as the guest of Sir Salar Jung, regent of the Nizam of Hyderabad, he was escorted to an evening banquet through lines of black men holding flaming torches, dined in the open court of a palace beside a fountain filled with floating candles. He was shown a room made entirely of china, furniture as well. On another day, in company of his British host, Colonel Hastings Fraser, he was received by Sir Salar as though he were a visiting prince—the colonel in full uniform, Elliott in black coat and top hat. "Just fancy your young brother talking, aye, and advising with two of the most celebrated men in these parts," he wrote Bamie.

On a tiger hunt south of Hyderabad, arranged by Sir Salar, he traveled by horse, by elephant, and by palanquin, a large, covered litter carried on poles by sixteen men. Camp gear was transported by forty camels and there were horses enough to mount the full party of about two hundred men. It was "roughing it" of a rather different kind, he wrote. The usual evening meal "in camp" con-sisted of soup, salmon, various chicken or veal cutlets, broiled chicken, tongue, wild duck, "gulow" and rice, six or seven differ-ent curries, then possible snipe or Welsh rarebit, cheese, and cof-fee. "And a big pitcher of cooled beer and soda water, which has been in a wet blanket and fanned all day. Each one of us has his pitcher and it *is* good. The heat gives one an awful thirst . . ."

The tiger he shot was one of the largest ever seen locally and he was at once a great hero. "Three hours after the blood had been running she weighed 280 lbs.," he wrote Theodore in a state of utter euphoria. "Her length was 9 feet 1½ inches, height, 3 ft., 7 in." The "brute" had been "glorious" in her final agony as she made her last charge and he "finished her . . . with a spare shot from the Bone Crusher—by George, what a hole that gun makes."

If only his "brave, old Heart of Oak Brother" could have been with him. Here was "sporting work worthy of the Roosevelt name."

"It is the life, old man. *Our* kind. The glorious freedom, the greatest excitement. . . . How everything here would have pleased your fondness for the unusual and the dangerous."

In the parlor at 6 West 57th Street, watching her husband's reaction to such letters, Alice worried he might at any moment drop everything and leave for India himself. "Poor dear Teddy . . . longs to be with you and walks up and down the room," wrote Mittie, ". . . when Alice appealed to him, he smothered her with kisses."

"This is your last hunt," Theodore advised solemnly, "so stay as long as you wish . . ."

Dora, Mary Ann, Daniel the butler, were thrilled by his letters, Mittie told him, and so pleased to be remembered by him. Alone of all the family, he regularly inquired for the servants in his letters.

The claws of the tiger would be made up for her as a necklace, Mittie was told. Skin and head were being shipped to London, where Sir John Rae Reid, "the mighty hunter," would see that a proper rug was prepared. In other letters came word that three crates of skins, heads, and horns were on the way, two crates of painted woodwork from Kashmir, another of silver and gold works, tea sets.

But a siege of fever at Srinagar had also left him feeling and looking like a "perfect bag of bones." And he was upset terribly by the human wretchedness to be seen everywhere. How could beings created in the image of God be brought so low? "And how easy for the smallest portion to sit down in quiet luxury of mind and body—to say to the other far larger part—lo, the poor savages. Is what *we* call right, right all the world over and for all time?"

In Europe, at virtually the same moment, traveling by boat with Alice on the Rhine, Theodore puzzled over the numbers of castles on shore. The Age of Chivalry, he speculated, must have been lovely for the knights, but gloomy indeed for those who had to provide the daily bread.

On hearing that Theodore and Alice had purchased land at Oyster Bay on which to build their dream house, Elliott told Theodore wistfully that he too might build something there one day. "We will *all* live there happily as in old times . . ."

"It delights me beyond bounds to see the way you have 'gone in' for everything as a son of the dear old father should," he went on, "and I will come back ready and eager to put my shoulder by yours at the wheel, Thee."

"How proud of you [I am], Thee, in your life so useful and so actively led at home," he wrote another time. "Will it be any help to have me one of these days go round with you to back you in your fights, old man?"

Do take care of yourself now for everybody's sake, the little wife's (to whom give my best love), the family's, and mine. I

tell you, Thee, I shall need you often in your good old strong
way to give a chap a lift or for that matter if I am on the wrong
road a *blow* to knock me back again.

For the sheer pleasure of living, he said in another letter, this
to Bamie, he had never known anything to equal his time in India.
But a life lived solely for pleasure was not in the cards; it was not
" 'our way,' for that means life for an *end*."

In Ceylon he brought down two elephants, killing the second
only after it had chased him through the jungle for two and a half
hours, Elliott running as fast as he could the whole time. He had
hit it in one eye with his first shot, but that had not slowed the
animal in the slightest: ". . . it was only after I had put sixteen
bullets into him that his great, crushing weight fell down in the
bamboos."

From Ceylon he went to Singapore and from there to Saigon,
in the teeth of a typhoon. Saigon had "the quaint air of old France
. . . much shipping and an air of thrift and quiet comfort that reminded one more than anything else of a prosperous southern city
in the old days, say in Louisiana." At Hong Kong he took a side trip
to Canton, riding an "ordinary American river steamboat" up the
Pearl River, "really into China proper."

That was late in December 1881, or about the time Theodore
was making ready to leave for his first session in the Albany legis-
lature. In January, from the neat, curtained privacy of Aunt Anna
Gracie's house on West 36th Street, Aunt Ella Bulloch, in New
York for a brief visit, wrote Elliott of the long conversation she and
"Teddy" had just had, "mostly about you, darling."

"The dear old fellow is back from Albany on a short leave and
spent an hour with me . . . and we *gloried* in you together, Teddy
exclaiming, 'What a fellow that is!' "

I was so glad to find that Teddy too thinks so highly of your
power of influence with others. He spoke of the differences
between you in this respect with such noble generous warmth
and said that where he would naturally wish to surpass other
men, he could never hold in his heart a jealous feeling toward
you. Then we talked of his book and his political interests.
Thee thinks these will only help in giving him some fame, but
neither he says will be of *practical* value, or giving him ad-
vancement, but says he must begin again at the beginning. . . .
So that you will *both* in point of fact start your career together,
he having gained this intermediate experience while you gain

yours in a different way during your travels. Thee is a dear "grand" old fellow in very truth. . . . Sometimes he reminds me so much of you . . .

Then the morning of March 11, 1882, having been gone a year and four months, Elliott walked through the front door at 6 West 57th Street and a week or so after that, having dined privately with him, having listened to his stories, Aunt Annie, we know from her diary, was in church, head bowed, praying to God "to cure him" —but of what, whether of some mysterious Oriental fever or of his old "nervous" seizures or of drinking, is not known. "Ellie is very ill" is all she says in another entry.

Whatever the problem, it does not seem to have held him back. He was asked by the James Roosevelts to be a godfather for their infant son, Franklin Delano, an honor that touched him deeply, as he wrote in reply, and one he would have declined had not "my dear mother . . . persuaded me that I should accept." (The small ceremony took place at Hyde Park's St. James Chapel on March 20, just nine days after his return.) And when Corinne was at last married that April, he performed his supporting part admirably, convinced like everyone else—everyone but Corinne—that Douglas Robinson was the ideal match, "a good fellow . . . worthy of our bright, innocent little girl." Theodore gave her away before a flower-banked altar at the Fifth Avenue Presbyterian Church; the reception followed at 6 West 57th Street; Corinne, it is said, spent the better part of the day weeping.

"My little heart," Elliott had written her from India, "if I could only take you in my arms and kiss you this evening, pet you and love you. . . . Ah! My little love . . . I smile to myself now as I recall the old dreams about you, Baby Sister, now a big woman going to be married . . ."

"Why if you don't take him [Douglas Robinson]," reads another letter, "you and Old Nell will keep house in some cozy country corner all by ourselves . . ."

"Dear Elliott has been such a loving, tender brother to me," Corinne once told Douglas. Elliott was so much more sensitive than other men, so much more understanding and considerate of her feelings and of her shortcomings, never dogmatic or judgmental. "How different people are," she mused; "there is Teddy, for instance, he is devoted to me too, but if I were to do something that he thought very weak or wrong, he would never forgive me, whereas Elliott no matter how much he might despise the sin, would forgive the sinner . . ."

"If you were my brother or cousin," she explained to Douglas, "how freely I could say I love you dearly. That kind of love I give absolutely . . ."

In time Elliott joined with Theodore and Douglas, Poultney Bigelow, and Cleveland Dodge (the son of William, Jr.) to start a New York Reform Club, the first meeting being held in the library at 57th Street. ("The respectable, educated, refined young men of this city should have more weight in public matters," Theodore told a reporter somewhat pompously.) Elliott also joined Douglas and Archibald Russell in the real-estate business downtown at 106 Broadway. The firm was renamed Robinson, Russell, and Roosevelt, new stationery printed. So at twenty-two, Elliott appeared to be on his way in the world of serious affairs, his adventuring over.

He lived at home, meantime. Indeed, having faced the beasts of the jungle, having seen and doubtless experienced more of the "big world" than any at home—or that they could have even imagined, one expects—he now found himself quartered at Mittie's insistence in a small room just off hers, exactly as though he were a small boy in need of watching and mothering.

She called him her "comfort child." He was the son who had given her greatest solace and who, until his travels, had stayed closest to her. She adored him, openly, happily. She spoiled him. And he as openly welcomed her love and attention. "My special charge," he called her, since his father sometime in his final agony had charged him to look after her.

"Ah! dear one, if you love me, your son, does he not love you?" he had written her from Madras. "I tell you yes, little Motherling, and so tenderly." She was never to worry over a thing. "Tell me *all*, I have broad shoulders and am amply strong. When I come back, dear, I come to see you alone. Not to leave you again . . ." And another time: "Remember Father left me particularly to care for you and at any time you want me no other mortal thing shall keep me from being with you. Trust Nell."

Among the reasons he liked Douglas Robinson as much as he did was Robinson's fondness for Mittie, who of late, Elliott conceded privately, was showing a "slight unevenness." A few of her long-standing peculiarities—her chronic tardiness, her need for order and cleanliness—had become considerably more pronounced. To judge by some accounts she was becoming really quite odd. In an exchange that took place many years later, a recorded conversation between a daughter of Corinne's, Mrs. Joseph Alsop, Jr., and Bamie's son, W. Sheffield Cowles, Jr., the situation was portrayed as follows:

> MRS. ALSOP: Then, she [Mittie] had an absolute passion for cleanliness. Well, it was a phobia. . . . Mother would, with peals of laughter, tell me things she would do, and it would sound to me exactly as though she were talking about a crazy person. Not to be able ever to be on time. . . . Then she had a library closet where she tied and untied bundles of different kinds. She and the maid worked all the time in the library closet. . . . She had a white chenille net that she wore on her hair to keep the dust out. She always took two baths—one for the soap, and then she got out and it was run again by the maid and she then got in again, so as to wash the soap off. Then when anybody came to see her if she was in bed a large sheet was put down, particularly if the doctor came. And when she said her prayers a sheet was put down so that she wouldn't touch the floor.
>
> MR. COWLES: She was crazy!
>
> MRS. ALSOP: Oh, yes, of course, she was; but crazy, according to my mother, in a perfectly delightful, charming and companionable way. . . . The whole thing is very fascinating.

But what makes it still more "fascinating" is the very contrary impression Mittie made on so many others at the time who found her anything but odd or laughable. Most notably there was Sara Roosevelt, Cousin Sally, a woman of strong mind and will who was never known to suffer fools. She thought the world of Mittie, invited Mittie to visit her at Hyde Park, where Mittie sometimes stayed for as long as a week, Cousin Sally obviously preferring her company to that of almost anyone else of that generation. "I was very proud when she came and stayed with me," Cousin Sally would recall. (Her diary entry from the time reads, "I love having her. We have read together, admired Baby, driven with James, tea'd at Mother's.")

Theodore, too, was proud to bring his political friends to the house, sure of the impression she and Alice both would make. To Elliott oho romainod "tho boautiful oontor of our homo worohip." If she babied him, he accepted that with good grace and with what Fanny Smith called a "caressing" kind of humor. Describing his new sleeping arrangement, he would say, "Now when my little mother feels cold at night, she comes in and puts an extra blanket on me, so that I wake up perfectly roasted, and when she is warm, she comes in and takes the covers off me so that I wake up frozen."

The great tiger-skin rug was stretched before the parlor fireplace, where it dominated the entire room. The front hall now was lined with the heads of other animals Elliott had shot. Once, as he was about to leave India, Mittie had written, "I am very jealous that you gave some of your trophies away in Bombay, when I value even a tail of a mouse that is my darling Elliott's trophy!" Her interest in every detail of his letters describing the tiger hunt had been, as she said, quite as intense as that of Theodore.

Those nights when he came in late from parties, or not at all, she left little penciled notes. "My darling son, I have missed you *all* evening. Sleep well, darling, and call Mother if you wish her."

· 2 ·

WHILE THEODORE WENT churning back and forth to Albany, making speeches, railing against corruption in high places, getting his name in the papers day after day, Elliott was preoccupied principally with becoming a man-about-town. He was drinking more than he should—but then so did many others of his set and there is nothing to suggest that anyone found him offensive.

In appearance, he was a taller—by two inches—and only somewhat handsomer version of his brother, not the Apollo-like figure portrayed in some later accounts. He and Theodore had each grown a mustache by this time—Elliott's being the thicker, more successful effort—both were parting their hair in the middle, or nearly so, and Elliott, too, now wore metal-rimmed spectacles. Seen from a distance, in riding attire, say, or waving from a sailboat out on the Sound, either could easily be taken for the other. Appearing at the Newsboys' Lodging House for the first time, immediately after his honeymoon at Oyster Bay, Theodore had been amazed when the boys started stamping and cheering. "As soon as they saw me, they mistook me for you," he had explained to Elliott. "I thought it pretty nice of them; they were evidently very fond of you."

It was Elliott's effortless charm, his generosity and humor, his way of talking to people—as if he had never found anything quite so fascinating as what the other person had to say—that made him so very attractive. He was glamorous in much the way his father had been—and as Theodore most obviously was not—and this, with the aura of his recent adventures, plus a certain bravura and suggestion of decadence, made him enormously appealing to women especially. He had none of the self-righteousness which in his brother put some people off; and little or none of Theodore's combativeness or bombast. Isaac Hunt, a friend of Theodore's in the legislature, described Elliott as "a smooth, quiet [compared to Theodore], nice fellow." Unlike Theodore he had not an enemy in the world.

Reading through surviving reminiscences, one senses that Elliott was very like some of his Bulloch forebears, that he would have been quite at home with the young bloods at the Savannah Club in days past. And it was not simply the women in the family who fawned and fussed over him, or melted before his attentions. "If he noticed me at all," wrote Fanny Smith, "I had received an accolade and if on rare occasions he turned on all his charm, he seemed to me quite irresistible."

("He drank like a fish and ran after the ladies" was Edith Carow's less charitable summation, years later. "I mean ladies not in his own rank, which was much worse.")

As befitting a gentleman and a Roosevelt, he gave time to the Orthopedic Hospital, took an occasional turn Sunday evenings at the Newsboys' Lodging House. He was also understood to be "working up" his travel notes, compiling his letters and journal entries, with the thought of doing a book on big-game hunting. Few Americans had been to India, or experienced all he had, and since he did write well, the possibilities in the idea were genuinely promising. But somehow nothing ever came of this. He seemed incapable of pulling things into focus, or of seeing a piece of work through to completion, as his brother could. To write his *Naval War of 1812*, Theodore had forced himself to master every nuance and technical term of seamanship—Theodore, who never particularly cared for sailing, who disliked long sea voyages. Theodore had plowed through everything in print on his subject, tracked down original documents to amass volumes of statistics on fighting ships, armaments, crews. He had started out knowing no more about his subject than anyone else and with no experience or training in historical research. At times he felt he had taken on more than he could handle. "I have plenty of information now, but I can't get it into words; I am afraid it is too big a task for me," he had written Bamie from The Hague, where, in the midst of his European honeymoon, he was still hammering away at the book. And had he not been able to spend several weeks soon after that soaking up "advice and sympathy" from the "blessed" Uncle Jimmie Bulloch in Liverpool, he might not have brought it off. But persist he would, and though the end result, his first published opus, was often dry and tedious in the extreme—much of it virtually unreadable to anyone without a prior interest in the subject or in the author (one can only sympathize with poor Alice or Mittie trying to make headway in such a book)—it was also scrupulously thorough, accurate, fair, and would remain a definitive study.

"'It's dogged as does it,'" Theodore liked to say, quoting a line from Trollope. He admired "staying power" in anyone. It was a hunter's virtue, he said. Yet the most celebrated hunter of the moment seemed not to have it, as he himself recognized. He was lacking, said Elliott, "that foolish grit of Theodore's."

Long afterward, when Elliott did at last try his hand at serious writing, it was in fiction, a well-handled, revealing short story that was never published. It is about a New York society figure living abroad—a woman he calls Sophie Vedder—who is described as having "so many friends, so many good and lovable qualities," but who is also plainly bound for a tragic end. "Live and let live" is her motto. "Never miss an opportunity of enjoying life, no matter at what cost, and when the end comes, well, take it cheerfully." There will be no dirges played at her funeral, she boasts, only Strauss. "My life has been a gamble. I have lived for pleasure only. I have never done anything I disliked when I could possibly avoid it. . . . I hoped against hope that something would turn up and pull me through. It was the hope of a gambler." "Poor Sophie, what a frivolous, useless thing you are," he has her say to herself at the last, as she is about to pull the trigger in front of her mirror. "Still, you never did anyone any harm but yourself . . ."

When Elliott began spending time with a society belle named Anna Hall, the whole family took heart. The Halls were Hudson River gentry, with Ludlows and Livingstons in their background. Anna, the oldest of four Hall sisters, had been raised at Tivoli-on-the-Hudson, twenty miles above Hyde Park, where she was schooled by a painfully pious, self-absorbed father who never worked and who for years, before an early death, required that she walk up and down the lawn with a stick pressed against the small of her back to instill the "carriage" of a lady. She was tall, golden-haired, like Alice Lee, but unlike Alice, prim and cool, and where Alice was lovely-looking, fresh, radiant, Anna was something more. She was stunning, regal, with a magnificent figure and large, haunting blue eyes. She was "made for an atmosphere of approval," as a friend said. In London a few years later, the poet Robert Browning became so infatuated with her beauty that he asked if he might just sit and gaze while she had her portrait painted.

Elliott was dazzled. A courtship proceeded. Letters were exchanged, his addressed to "My dear Miss Hall," hers to "My dear Mr. Roosevelt." He sent flowers, took her driving in the park.

They were seen at parties. They knew the same people; their families, of course, knew one another and all about one another. One Sunday evening she went with him to meet his newsboys, and according to Fanny Smith, it was at a house party at Algonac, the Delano estate on the Hudson, over Memorial Day in 1883, that he asked her to marry him. Apparently she accepted, though no one was told for another several weeks.

"I am honestly delighted," wrote Theodore to Corinne from Richfield Springs, where he was convalescing, taking the waters as he had as a child. Alice had announced she was pregnant and Theodore had been hit by an attack of asthma as bad as any in years, in addition to a siege of cholera morbus worse even than that of the summer before their marriage. But Ellie's news was something they could all be glad about. It would do "the dear old boy" great good, said Theodore, "to have something to work for," "to marry and settle down with a definite purpose in life." In measured brotherly fashion, Elliott was told it was "no light thing to take the irrevocable step," while Aunt Annie reminded him, "You must be very pure and very true now that you have secured the right to guard, love and cherish so sweet a girl as Anna."

When, at summer's end, Theodore picked up and went west again for his health and some shooting, to Dakota Territory this time, for two weeks in the "real West," he went alone, Elliott being preoccupied. Anna, not Mittie, now wore the tiger-claw necklace. Elliott was riding to hounds at Hempstead, on Long Island, playing polo at Meadow Brook. At Tivoli one weekend he suffered some kind of relapse or seizure—"My old Indian trouble," he explained to Anna—and had a difficult time getting back to New York on the train. He was injured at polo several times. He played extremely well, but with an ardor bordering on recklessness. Some nights, nursing a sprain or a "beastly leg," he would sit alone brooding and smoking in his room at 57th Street, and Anna worried that he was keeping something from her. "I know I am blue and disagreeable often," he wrote, "but please, darling, bear with me and I will come out all right in the end, and it really is an honest effort to do the right that makes me so often quiet and thoughtful about it all."

Theodore and Alice had moved into a house of their own, on West 45th Street, next door to Corinne and Douglas, who in April had become the parents of a son, Theodore Douglas Robinson, the first of the new generation. Theodore by now had also purchased more than a hundred acres of prime land at Oyster Bay, on Cooper's Bluff, then sold parcels to Bamie and Aunt Annie, so they could build beside him. His stable was already going up on the ninety-five acres he had kept for himself.

Theodore had any number of irons in the fire. He had taken a flier in cattle in Wyoming, investing $10,000 in a ranch run by a Harvard classmate. Theodore had put another $20,000 into G. P. Putnam's Sons, the publisher of his *Naval War,* in order to make himself a limited partner. And though he had gone to the Dakota Bad Lands ostensibly to shoot a buffalo while there were still a few left to shoot, he returned to announce he had launched a cattle venture of his own. He talked proudly now of "my ranch in Dakota."

As a politician, Theodore was already seen as a phenomenon, often abused or made a laughingstock by the opposition papers, but a somebody nonetheless and a bright, rising star in the eyes of the men his father had set such store by. Theodore, as everyone said, was on his way, his life had taken hold, while Elliott had only Anna Hall.

Their wedding, "one of the most brilliant social events of the season," took place at Calvary Church downtown, in the neighborhood of the old house on East 20th Street, on December 1, 1883. Theodore was best man and it was the last such occasion at which the whole family was present.

CHAPTER TWELVE

Politics

· 1 ·

IT WAS, AS WOULD BE SAID, no ordinary thing for a young man of wealth and social position, a son of the "solid, old quiet element," to go of his own accord down into the great bear pit of politics— thrash it out, survive or fall, in "the rough hurly-burly of the caucus, the primary, and the political meeting." But the impression that Theodore was virtually the *only* such young man of his day, or that he did what he did against the wishes of family and friends, is mistaken—as mistaken as was the doctrine so earnestly espoused then that any such young man would automatically raise the level of political morality and serve as inspiration for more of his kind to join the good work. New York already had a sterling example of such high ambition in Seth Low, the young reform mayor of Brooklyn, who was a Columbia College graduate and heir to the Low shipping fortune; nor should it be forgotten that another recent Harvard graduate was Boies Penrose of Philadelphia, who had been in the class behind Theodore's. Penrose too was descended from a wealthy, distinguished line. He was a "lover of vigorous outdoor sports," an aspiring author, and he too started off exactly as Theodore, by running for the state (Pennsylvania) legislature as a gentleman champion of reform. But Penrose was to become another of the era's flagrant political bosses, overbearing, power obsessed, the antithesis of the reform spirit. Penrose was a perfect, Harvard-cultivated, Harvard-sounding aristocrat—and when among his political cronies, to quote one biographical sketch, "capable of conduct and utterances which caused the judicious to grieve and moved the pious to indignation."

Theodore said later it was a combination of curiosity and "plain duty" that led him into politics, and that "I intended to be one of the governing class," which may be taken as another way of saying he wanted power. In the novel *The Bostonians* (1886), Henry James would portray a leading character as "full of purpose to live . . . and with high success; to become great, in order not to be obscure, and powerful not to be useless." The description would apply perfectly to Theodore. Obscurity, one imagines, would have snuffed him out like a candle.

He claimed also, years later, that a "young man of my bringing up and convictions could join only the Republican Party," a curious observation in view of the large number of Democrats within his own "intimate" circles—Uncle Robert, father-in-law George C. Lee, the Saltonstalls, the Delanos, the Hyde Park Roosevelts, his friend Poultney Bigelow. Nor does it suggest how tenuous old party ties had become among Republicans of comparable social background and moral sensitivities as a result of the Grant scandals, the stolen election of 1876, or the dominance of such figures as Conkling and Blaine.

In any event, no one in the immediate family objected to his trying for the Assembly. Rather, it was quite the opposite. He received their most enthusiastic support and from Bamie especially, whose interest in his career was to serve him well. She and Corinne clipped everything written about him, filling large scrapbooks as time passed. Corinne told her devoted Douglas that he too had better begin taking part. "If there is one thing I like particularly," she said, "it is public spirit."

In afteryears Theodore would remember the prominent clubmen, businessmen, and lawyers who had "laughed at me," warning that political parties were composed of riffraff, "saloon keepers, horsecar conductors, and the like." But at the time, he happily talked politics with William Waldorf ("Willie") Astor, who had served in the state legislature and was then running for Congress. And the fact is his strongest backing came from the most influential of his father's friends—the ultimate clubmen, businessmen, lawyers—who lent their immediate support, attesting publicly to his "high character . . . honesty and integrity." Among his very prominent backers were Joseph H. Choate, J. Pierpont Morgan, William Evarts, Elihu Root, and Morris K. Jesup, and it was support he gratefully acknowledged at the time. "I feel that I owe both my

nomination and election more to you than to any other one man,"
he wrote Joseph Choate, for example, following his initial run for
the Assembly. At a testimonial dinner at Delmonico's attended by
three hundred leading figures in white tie and tails, he was praised
to the skies by none less than Chauncey Depew, *the* after-dinner
speaker of the day, who described himself as a "cordial friend" of
the late Theodore (and who mused privately that the son looked
about eighteen).

Robert Roosevelt approved emphatically and, despite party
differences, asked the powerful Democratic assemblyman Michael
C. Murphy, chairman of the City Affairs Committee, to keep an eye
out for the young man once he reached Albany, and it was thus that
Theodore was put on Murphy's committee first thing.

Within his own social set he was a hero. "We hailed him as the
dawn of a new era," remembered Poultney Bigelow, "the man of
good family once more in the political arena; the college-bred tribune superior to the temptations which beset meaner men.
'Teddy,' as we all called him, was our ideal."

As near as can be determined all of three people disapproved
—Uncle James Alfred, cousins Alfred and Emlen. "All my friends
stand by me like trumps," he says in his diary, "except for Al, Em,
and Uncle Jim."

"We thought he was, to put it frankly, pretty fresh," recalled
Cousin Emlen, who added the ultimate condemnation: "We felt
that his own father would not have liked it . . . The Roosevelt circle
as a whole had a profound distrust of public life." But this recollection—frequently quoted later—was offered long after the fact,
when Emlen, a somewhat stuffy man to begin with, had become
considerably more so. Writing to Bamie in that earlier day, as he
began work as a bookkeeper at Roosevelt and Son, Emlen said he
wished he might do something for his country. "It is very plain that
our young men must take a more active interest in our government,
something more than mere voting and talking." For a while, he
trailed along with Theodore to meetings at Morton Hall, the district
Republican headquarters, but dropped out because, as he later
said, "I did not relish the personnel of that organization."

Unaccountably, Theodore did. He was fascinated by the likes
of big Jake Hess and Joe Murray, two machine "pols" if ever there
were. Hess, the district leader, was a German Jew and a City Commissioner of Charities and Corrections (who, as a consequence,
knew not only of the work done by the elder Theodore, but appreciated the political value of the young man's name). Murray, a Hess

lieutenant, was an Irish Catholic and onetime Tammany heeler
who had worked his way up from the very bottom of the political
heap in time-honored fashion, by being resourceful, loyal, and, on
occasion, good with his fists. Murray appealed strongly to Theodore. Murray's vision of the spoils system—as different from what
Theodore had been raised on as were Murray's religion and his
background—was unequivocal. As Theodore later explained, "Not
to insist on the spoils when you get into office and share them
equitably among your political friends seemed [to Murray] almost
as dishonorable as not to pay your debts."

The membership of the Twenty-first District Republican Association was a "mixed lot," Morton Hall itself nothing more than
a big, dingy room over a saloon on East 59th Street. Some wooden
benches, brass spittoons, and framed pictures of General Grant and
Levi P. Morton comprised the principal "appointments." Jake
Hess ran things from a dais at one end, seated at a small table upon
which rested a single pitcher of ice water.

"They rather liked the idea of a Roosevelt joining them,"
Theodore recalled when talking some years afterward with a visitor
from England who was gathering material on the "good government" movement. "I insisted on taking part in all the discussions.
Some of them sneered at my black coat and a tall hat. But I made
them understand that I should come dressed as I chose. . . . Then
after the discussions I used to play poker and smoke with them."
His intent, he said, had been to get inside the machine.

It was only when he reached Albany, however, that he realized
what an extraordinary world he had entered. A new "Legislative
Diary" was begun, filled with a whole new cast of characters, some
as closely observed as various rare birds in the boyhood field journals. There was much the same feeling of wonder and discovery, a
little as though he were back on the Nile seeing fauna of unimagin-
able shapes and kinds and plumage.

The other 127 members of the Assembly consisted of farmers,
mechanics, a half-dozen liquor dealers, a cooper, a butcher, a to-
bacconist, a compositor, a typesetter, three newspapermen, thirty-
five lawyers, and a pawnbroker. Roughly a third of these he judged
to be crooked. Approximately half the Democrats came under the
category of "vicious, stupid-looking scoundrels."

Appraising his fellow members on the City Affairs Committee,
he found his Uncle Rob's friend, Chairman Murphy, to be a tall,
stout Fenian, "with a swollen, red face, a black mustache, and a
ludicrously dignified manner; always wears a frock coat (very

shiny) and has had a long experience in politics—so that to un-
doubted pluck and a certain knowledge of parliamentary forms he
adds a great deal of stupidity and a decided looseness of ideas as
regards the 8th Commandment." Another Democrat named Shan-
ley was shrewder than Murphy and easier to get along with, "being
more Americanized," but equally dishonest. Higgins was "a vicious little Celtic nonentity from Buffalo"; Gideon, "a Jew from
New York who has been a bailiff and is now a liquor seller."
Dimon, a country Democrat, was "either dumb or an idiot—probably both," and still another notable Democrat, a physical giant
named McManus, he described as "a huge, fleshy, unutterably
coarse and low brute . . . formerly a prize fighter, at present keeps
a low drinking and dancing saloon . . . is more than suspected of
having begun his life as a pickpocket."

The leading lights in his own party were hardly less objectionable. One senior Republican, the veteran Thomas Alvord from
Syracuse, was a "bad old fellow." Of another, John Rains, he wrote,
"he [has] . . . the same idea of public life and civil service that a
vulture has of a dead sheep."

He liked a gigantic, one-eyed Civil War general named Curtis,
and a German from Cattaraugus County named Kruse was a "capital fellow." Peter Kelly, a young Democrat from Brooklyn, was an
ardent believer in Henry George and thus much else in the way of
doubtful "abstract theories," but on "questions of elementary morality, we were heartily at one."

His favorites were two freshmen Republicans named Isaac
("Ike") Hunt and William ("Billy") O'Neil. Hunt, a tall, thin, melancholy young man, was a lawyer from Watertown and "thoroughly
upright." O'Neil, who kept a crossroads store in the Adirondacks,
became "the closest friend." Both were as untried and as ambitious
nearly as Theodore, and would take his side on issues again and
again.

Nothing seemed to intimidate him. Though all of twenty-three,
though unmistakably the youngest member of the Assembly, he
plunged ahead, deferring to no one, making his presence felt. It
was a spectacle not to be forgotten. Whatever astonishment or in-
credulity he felt concerning his fellow members was more than
matched by their response to him. One Albany reporter of long
experience, seeing him on the floor of the Assembly, watching him
wipe his eyeglasses, thought to himself, "What on earth will New
York send us next?"

"We almost shouted with laughter," recalled Ike Hunt, "to think that the most veritable representative of the New York dude had come to the Chamber."

Hunt had seen him first at a Republican caucus held one evening in a committee room at the State House.

> He came in as if he had been ejected by a catapult. He had on an enormous great ulster . . . and he pulled off his coat; he was dressed in full dress, he had been to dinner somewhere. . . . [Later] I was standing right by the fireplace, and Teddy got up and looked around and bolted over to where I was. He said, "You are from the country"—which was the most crushing thing he could have said to me . . . I was standing there and was laboring under the hallucination that nobody would ever think I was from the country, but that is what he said to me. And he proceeded to go into all the details of how we got along and how we managed our affairs . . . and how we did everything in the country.

As at Harvard, the impression among many was that he had a speech defect of some odd kind. Hunt was sure of it. "He would open his mouth and run out his tongue and it was hard for him to speak." The New York *Sun* called it a Dundreary drawl, to go with his English side-whiskers. When, in his maiden speech, he used the expression "rather relieved," it was printed in the *Sun* as "r-a-w-t-h-e-r r-e-l-i-e-v-e-d."

Wishing to gain attention on the floor he would stand at his place, stretching far forward over the desk, calling, "Mr. Spee-kar! Mr. Spee-kar!" his voice often shifting suddenly from tenor to penetrating falsetto.

"I do not speak enough from the chest," he told Mittie, "so my voice is not as powerful as it ought to be."

The new gold-rimmed spectacles and their fluttering black ribbon, his gold watch fob, the part in his hair, the narrow cut of his clothes, made him known at once. For reporters for the *Sun*, the *World*, and other Democratic papers, he was the fairest kind of game and they went right after him. He was called a "Jane-Dandy," "his Lordship," "weakling," "silly," "Oscar Wilde," "the exquisite Mr. Roosevelt," "little man," the fun always at his expense. The *World* reported that his trousers were cut so tight that when making his "gyrations" before an audience "he only bent the joints above the belt."

Yet despite all this, and a trivial, patronizing maiden speech, he left no doubt that he was there to accomplish something—"to do the right thing." The Republican papers also gave him every chance and he made friends steadily. As his Maine guide, Bill Sewall, once observed, "wherever he went he got right in with people." Some at Albany, like Hunt and O'Neil, and two reporters, George Spinney of *The New York Times* and William Hudson of the Brooklyn *Eagle*, quickly perceived how much more there was to him than the bizarre mannerisms and foppish clothes. They saw something in the glittering gray eyes. They listened to what he was actually saying. If he was "green as grass," said Spinney, he was also "a good-hearted man to shake hands with, and he had a good, honest laugh . . . not an affected laugh . . ." He worked hard; he obviously cared and wanted to learn. "You could see that here was an uncommon fellow," said Spinney, "distinctly different."

The great question was whether he would prove to be what Tammany Hall's leading political philosopher, George Washington Plunkitt, would call a "mornin' glory"—the usual high-principled, blue-blooded amateur who "looked lovely in the mornin' and withered up in a short time."

The eagerness with which he had approached Hunt the first night, firing questions about Hunt's experiences in the country, was only a light warm-up. Spinney called him a walking interrogation point. Theodore would literally stand a man against a wall, "boring in," as Spinney said, for half an hour. At breakfast in the dining room of the old Delavan House, down the hill from the Capitol, he would sit talking and reading a stack of morning papers, going through the papers at tremendous speed. "He threw each paper, as he finished it, on the floor, unfolded," remembered William Hudson, "until at the end there was, on either side of him, a pile of loose papers as high as the table for the servants to clear away. And all this time he would be taking part in the running conversation of the table. Had anyone supposed that this inspection of the papers was superficial, he would have been sadly mistaken. Roosevelt saw everything and formed an opinion on everything . . ."

The Assembly was elected annually. Theodore's first term, in 1882, ran five months, from January 1 to June 2; his second term, in 1883, just four months, from January 1 to May 4. So in those two years he was actually in Albany a total of only nine months. Yet the change in him was amazing. Even by the close of the first term, according to Spinney, he knew more about state politics than nine

out of ten members. He was chronically impatient, impulsive, and
could be inconceivably impolitic (a "perfect nuisance"), but he
grew steadily. "He made me think of a growing child," said Hunt.
"You know you take a child and in a day or two their whole character will change. They will take on new strength and new ideas,
and you can see them growing right up. . . . He would leave Albany
Friday afternoon and he would come back Monday night and you
would see changes that had taken place. . . . New ideas had taken
possession of him. He would run up against somebody and he got
a new perspective. . . . He would be entirely changed, just like a
child."

He and Theodore boarded at the same house. Hunt always
knew when it was Theodore returning from a weekend, because
Theodore would swing the front door open and be halfway up the
stairs before the door swung shut with a bang.

· 2 ·

MUCH OF WHAT HAPPENED in the beginning was unexceptional.
He had won his seat about as handily as expected, the Twenty-first
being New York's safely Republican "brownstone" district. (His
opponent had also helped. He was a former director of the Blackwell's Island Lunatic Asylum who had been dismissed for incompetence, exactly the sort of political hack the elder Theodore had
tried to drive from office in his campaigns for asylum reform. Even
the man's name sounded like one specially contrived for some low
character out of the nightmare world of the madhouse, Dr. W. W.
Strew.)

And many of the positions he took on issues his first term were
about as would have been expected, conservative, unspectacular
—that is until the Westbrook Scandal. He opposed salary increases
for New York policemen and firemen, opposed a bill that would
have set the minimum wage for municipal workers at $2 a day, and
for such stands he was hailed as a "watchdog" over the people's
money. He favored supplying New York with pure water.

But it was also in his first term, even before the Westbrook
affair, that he became involved with the Cigar Bill, as it was known,
and though his part in the issue was to receive none of the notoriety
of the Westbrook affair, the experience was one from which he
learned a great deal.

The Cigarmakers' Union had introduced a bill to outlaw the

manufacture of cigars "at home" in the tenements of New York, a system of long standing and the sole livelihood for thousands of the city's poorest families. The bill was referred to the City Affairs Committee and Theodore found himself named to a subcommittee of three to look into the matter. Of the other two members, one, a Republican, had little use for the bill but intended to vote for it, he said, because of labor strength in his district. The second member, a Tammany man, confided candidly that he would vote no because that was what was required of him by "certain interests." This left Theodore the deciding vote, and as yet none of them had been to see the conditions the bill was designed to stop.

"As a matter of fact, I had supposed I would be against the legislation," Theodore remembered, "and I rather think that I was put on the committee with that idea, for the respectable people I knew were against it; it was contrary to the principles of political economy of the *laissez-faire* kind."

There had been cigarmakers' unions in New York since the Civil War and they had accomplished almost nothing. A prolonged strike in 1877 had been a complete failure, and the unions, bankrupt and without discipline, would have remained little more than debating societies had not a few determined young men taken charge, the most able of whom was Samuel Gompers. It was Gompers who had drawn up the new bill, the first important law against the exploitation of workers, and it was Gompers who prevailed on Theodore to make an inspection tour and see for himself, an invitation Theodore at first refused, because, in Gompers' words, "he disbelieved the conditions which I portrayed to him." Gompers had previously gathered his own information by going from tenement to tenement posing as a book salesman offering a set of Dickens.

Gompers was short, squat, almost gnomelike, opinionated and a good talker. He also believed in action, quite as much as Theodore, and at thirty-two was practically a contemporary. But he came from an entirely different world. He had been born in a London slum, the son of a cigarmaker. He was a Jew and had known only work and deprivation his whole life. So the two of them, going the rounds of the sweatshops, made an improbable pair. Once Theodore had seen for himself, Gompers remembered, "his whole manner toward me changed."

Nothing had prepared Theodore for the wretchedness he beheld, the stench and filth. Some scenes would stay with him the rest of his days.

I have always remembered [he would write nearly forty years later] one room in which two families were living. . . . There were several children, three men, and two women in this room. The tobacco was stowed about everywhere, alongside the foul bedding, and in a corner where there were scraps of food. The men, women, and children in this room worked by day and far into the evening, and they slept and ate there. They were Bohemians, unable to speak English, except that one of the children knew enough to act as interpreter.

It was because so few legislators knew of such conditions, Gompers said, that nothing was done to change the system or alleviate the distress. Simply to survive, such people had to work twelve to eighteen hours a day. Infectious disease was rampant among them. The manufacturers owned the tenements and so for the majority of workers there seemed no way out.

His rounds with Gompers were enough to settle Theodore's mind. It made no difference how many theories of economics or of the rights of the individual might argue against the bill, he would back it. He returned for two further inspection tours, once with his two subcommittee colleagues in tow, another time by himself. When the Cigar Bill came out of committee, he spoke for it on the floor, and when it failed to come up in the Senate—because a lobbyist for the manufacturers stole the official copy—he resolved to carry the fight in the next term. He had by no means been converted to a union sympathizer, he was no "sentimentalist," as he would say, but for possibly the first time in his life he had come face-to-face with certain extremely unpleasant realities that struck him as intolerable, a side of American life he had been unwilling to believe existed until seeing with his own eyes.

Gompers would remember his "aggressiveness and evident sincerity."

But the Cigar Bill, really everything he took a hand in that first session, was put in the shadows by his sudden call, on March 29, for the investigation and impeachment of a State Supreme Court judge, T. R. Westbrook, who, it appeared, was in league with the notorious Jay Gould.

The resolution was, as Hunt said, a bombshell. It was not that Theodore was exposing some awful new truth—Gould's "association" with this particular judge had been dealt with in the papers, and in *The New York Times* in some detail—but that he, a very small fry in the legislature, was challenging not only the judiciary but the likes of Gould, who was understood to have more power than any man in the United States; Gould, who controlled something like ten percent of the country's railroads; who now also controlled the Western Union Telegraph Company, and through it, the Associated Press; who owned the New York *World,* which published or withheld news however he wished; who had his own spies and agents and whose personal fortune was of a kind to make those of such "old money" aristocrats as the Roosevelts appear minuscule. (On a March day in 1882, when word began circulating that he was broke, Gould had called Russell Sage and one or two others into his office and spread before them on his desk a few of his securities—$23 million of Western Union stock, $12 million of Missouri Pacific Railroad, $19 million of "other stocks.") Furthermore, few men had such a long-standing, proved reputation for largess in and about the corridors of the State House at Albany.

That the "best society"—Theodore's constituency—scorned the whispery little Gould was no secret. He had been refused membership in the New York Yacht Club; he was never seen at Mrs. William Astor's balls because he was never invited. It is even said James Alfred Roosevelt personally threw Gould out of his office on one occasion. Indeed, Gould was held contemptible by a great variety of decent people and was so despised by some whom he had destroyed along the way that he required plainclothes police protection day and night.

But scorn also had its limits, and while no gentleman could condone such shady dealings or ruthlessness of the kind Gould practiced, or accept him as a social equal, few prudent, ambitious men would ever openly attack him. Further, several of the city's most important business people saw no reason not to join him in his ventures if it was to their advantage. They could make their peace with Gould in a purely business way readily enough and without apparent qualm. Having gained control of the Western Union Company the year before by the most blatant kind of piracy, Gould had had no trouble bringing in as board members such figures as John Jacob Astor and J. Pierpont Morgan. As head of his more recently acquired Manhattan Elevated Railway Company, the centerpiece of the Westbrook Scandal, Gould had installed Cyrus Field, who was famous as the promoter of the first Atlantic Cable and was one of New York's most socially prominent "good citizens."

Theodore had happened on the Westbrook affair through his

friend Hunt. In conjunction with work he was doing on an investigative committee, Hunt had learned that certain lawyers, assigned by the courts as receivers for insolvent insurance companies, were taking exorbitant fees and with court approval. Hunt had gone down to New York to the county clerk's office and searching through the files found that such fees not only amounted to hundreds of thousands of dollars, but that they had all been allowed by the same judge, T. R. Westbrook. When Hunt returned to Albany and recounted his findings to Theodore, the name rang a bell—*The New York Times* had earlier charged Westbrook with complicity in Gould's sudden acquisition of the huge Manhattan Elevated—so Theodore now went to New York to talk to the city editor at the *Times,* Henry Loewenthal, and to ask to see what the *Times* had in its files. This turned out to be quite a lot. Theodore was at the newspaper's offices much of the day and afterward invited Loewenthal back to 57th Street, where they talked until well after midnight.

In his book, *The Naval War of 1812,* Theodore had devoted a large part of his energies to refuting the recognized authority on the subject, an English author named William James, whom Theodore found to be much in error and attacked on point after point. Often, he seemed more intent on destroying James than in telling his story. But he did it by going to documentary sources, seeing for himself, and here the situation was the same. He was attacking a figure of established authority, but only after having done the necessary spadework.

In the picture that emerged, Westbrook was plainly Gould's pawn, even to the point of holding court in Gould's private office at the Western Union Building. As Westbrook said himself in a letter to Gould—a letter the *Times* had somehow obtained but not published—he was "willing to go to the very verge of judicial discretion" to protect Gould's interests.

Recognizing the tremendous future in store for any rapid-transit system in New York, Gould had decided he needed the Manhattan Elevated. His scheme, as usual, was to harass and intimidate the existing owners at every opportunity, drive the stock down below its true value, then begin buying. He was joined in the venture by Russell Sage, possibly the shrewdest of all Wall Street freebooters, and all the while his editors at the *World* kept up a running attack on the owners of the Manhattan Elevated, implying they were corrupt, the company insolvent. But even more effective for Gould's purposes was his judge, Westbrook, who at the proper moment declared the company bankrupt and appointed two of Gould's people as receivers. The stock fell to a fraction of its previous value and once Gould had taken over a major share of the stock and the price suddenly rebounded, the judge as suddenly reversed himself, declaring the company miraculously solvent. He ordered that its affairs be removed from the hands of the receivers and entrusted to management, which appeared to be Cyrus Field but which in fact was Gould. In the *World*, the editors said they "never believed but that Manhattan would be rescued by men who have the brains and the means to make the most of it."

In days gone by, when Gould had been starting out on his rise to power, his first lawyer was T. R. Westbrook.

Theodore had been warned to tread lightly and no sooner was his call for an investigation put before the Assembly than it was stalled through parliamentary maneuver (tabled for further discussion), the leadership on both sides manifestly wishing no part of it.

He was warned again, only now, too, by an old family friend, someone he never identified except as a "member of a prominent law firm." Theodore was taken to lunch and was advised patiently that while it had been fine of him to make the "reform play," he had done enough. It was time he left politics and identified himself with "the right kind of people," those who in the long run "controlled others" and reaped rewards "worth having." Theodore was appalled. Did this mean, he asked, that he must give in to the "ring"? It was naïve, said the friend, to imagine a mere political ring of the sort the newspapers pictured. The real "inner circle" was one of businessmen, judges, lawyers, and politicians all "in alliance," and this was the point: the successful man had to win his success by the backing of these same forces, whatever his field.

Late the afternoon of April 5, the official day nearly over, "the exquisite Mr. Roosevelt" was up again calling, "Mr. Spee-kar! Mr. Spee-kar!" He wanted his resolution debated and voted on with no further delay. "No! No!" shouted "bad old fellow" Tom Alvord. But Theodore kept talking, "clearly and slowly," for another ten minutes, his voice filling the huge chamber. He went through Westbrook's conduct step by step, attacking Gould by name, calling him a shark and a swindler whose dishonesty was a matter of common knowledge. The members sat in absolute silence, listening to every word. As the *Times* commented the next morning, for any public man to speak so, "calling men and things by their right names in these days of judicial, ecclesiastical, and journalistic subservience to the robber-barons," required "some little courage."

I am aware that it ought to have been done by a man of more experience, and, possibly, an abler source than myself, but as nobody else chose to demand it [the investigation], I certainly would in the interest of the Commonwealth of New York . . .

There was no applause when he finished, only the hum of great muffled excitement. Ten minutes remained until closing time at five, and had Theodore known how to bring the issue to vote right then, it might have carried. As it was, Tom Alvord very smoothly intervened. Alvord had been Speaker of the Assembly the year Theodore was born. He stood now in the aisle, leaning on his cane, recalling slowly how often in his career he had seen good men shattered by irresponsible, unsubstantiated charges. Possibly there should be an investigation, possibly he would support such an investigation, he said. But there need be no hurry—indeed, "the young man from New York" would be well advised to take a little time to reflect on the wisdom of his actions.

So the clock ran out, nothing was accomplished.

The issue could be ignored no longer, however. There had been an immediate response in the press to what Theodore had said and, except for the *World*, nearly all laudatory. With his first major speech he had made himself known throughout the state. Gould's representatives in Albany were also busier than usual. A special messenger from John Kelly, head of Tammany Hall, came on from New York at once by night train.

Theodore tried again the next morning and again he was outmaneuvered. He forgot to specify the kind of vote he wanted. The Speaker called for a standing vote and the whole body started bobbing up and down so rapidly nobody could keep count. The clerk's tally, the only one that mattered, was 50 for, 54 against.

Another try in the afternoon fared better. Theodore waited for a lull, when many members had wandered away from their seats. "I demand ayes and nays," he remembered to say this time, and though the count was still short of the two-thirds majority needed for such an investigation, there were now more members voting with him than against, and from then on his support gathered rapidly. Public indignation had been roused and as a consequence the change of heart among his colleagues was astonishing. On April 12, the Assembly voted the investigation by a margin of 104 to 6.

For most of what remained of the session, the matter was in the hands of the Judiciary Committee, and when the committee presented its report at the end of May, it was a whitewash. The judge was said to have done nothing for which he should be impeached. Apparently the committee had been "turned" by three bribes of $2,500 each, a reasonable sum, it was thought, for decisions of such large import.

Theodore was up on his feet once more, expressing himself as forcefully as he knew how. The effect, said Hunt, was "powerful, wonderful," and to no avail. The vote sustained the committee report; the judge was not to be touched.

The pressures brought to bear on individual members had been enormous. Virtually the entire Democratic Party had lined up behind Westbrook, and the afternoon of the final vote the lobby was crawling with "prominent men from all over the state," there to see exactly who voted which way. Ike Hunt had been called on by a fellow lawyer from his hometown and reminded of how once Westbrook had decided a case in his, Hunt's, favor. "Now you don't want to go to work and destroy a good judge like Judge Westbrook," Hunt was told. Years afterward, Hunt would concede that Westbrook had been a respectably good man, until he "got in that thing and sharpers got him . . ." And Theodore, too, in retrospect, said he never knew if Westbrook was corrupt or not. "He may have been; but I am inclined to think that, aside from his being a man of coarse moral fiber, the trouble lay chiefly in the fact that he had a genuine . . . reverence for the possessor of a great fortune as such. He sincerely believed that business was the end of existence, and that judge and legislator alike should do whatever was necessary to favor it."

The Assembly disbanded two days later. The Westbrook Scandal faded into the background. Westbrook himself was later found dead in a hotel room in Troy, whether by suicide or natural causes remained a mystery. Gould and Russell Sage held on to the Manhattan Elevated, but disposed of Cyrus Field, leaving him financially ruined. The distinguished Field, unlike Gould or Sage, actually knew something about the elevated system and thought it should be run as an institution of public service. Gould had needed Field's name and his money, and the trusting Field had foolishly concluded that Gould was his friend.

For Theodore, prospects had never looked so bright. It was said, by the *Evening Post*, that he had accomplished more good than any man of his age and experience had accomplished in years. (The *Evening Post* at the moment was being edited by Carl Schurz.) George William Curtis singled him out for national attention in *Harper's Weekly*.

It is with the greatest satisfaction that those who are interested
in good government see a young man in the Legislature who
. . . does not know the meaning of fear, and to whom the blus-
ter and bravado of party and political bullies are as absolutely
indifferent as the blowing of the wind.

More important, no one in Albany could dismiss him as a lightweight any longer. Henceforth, as Hunt recalled, he was to be
"considered a full-fledged man worthy of one's esteem." He had
worked an almost miraculous change.

Running again the fall of 1882, he carried his district by better
than two to one, and in the face of a victorious Democratic ticket
headed by a reform candidate for governor, the mayor of Buffalo,
Grover Cleveland. Back at Albany again, he was made the Republican nominee for Speaker, a somewhat empty honor in view of the
overwhelming Democratic majority, but one which put him at the
head of his party in the Assembly at the age of twenty-four. It was
almost inconceivable prominence for one so young and inexperi-
enced, let alone so unconventional. The papers began writing
about the Cleveland Democrats and the Roosevelt Republicans.
Theodore now was called to the governor's office to confer on
pending legislation. Remembering the two of them together, William Hudson of the Brooklyn *Eagle* would write, "The Governor
would sit large, solid, and phlegmatic, listening gravely to the energetic utterances of the mercurial young man, but signifying neither assent nor dissent. Not infrequently taking silence for
acquiescence, Roosevelt would go away thinking he had carried
everything before him."

"There is great sense in a lot of what he says," Cleveland
would remark of Theodore, "but there is such a cocksuredness
about him that he stirs up doubt in me all the time. . . . Then he
seems to be so very young."

He was seldom out of sight, seldom still. "Such a super-abun-
dance of animal life was hardly ever condensed in a human being,"
said Hunt. If Theodore had a failing, in Hunt's estimate, it was
only that he wanted to set everything to rights instantly, and it was
because of this that the second term was not what either of them
anticipated. Success had gone to his head, Theodore later said,
though the second term was hardly the disaster he felt it was, and
in what it revealed about him as a human being, it was, if anything,
more interesting than the first.

His sudden rise may be explained in part by other, earlier developments involving his father's old enemy, Conkling. An unexpected dissolution of power had occurred just before Theodore ran for his first term and again the Customhouse was the issue. Early in 1881, the newly elected President, Garfield, had refused to follow Conkling's dictates concerning the appointment of a Collector. In a fury Conkling resigned from the Senate, his friend and ally, New York's other senator, Thomas C. Platt, going along with him. Both men had expected to be quickly vindicated and reinstated by a compliant legislature at Albany and thus to return to Washington stronger than ever. But it had not worked out as planned. Most people thought Conkling had made a fool of himself; the legislature turned on him and chose another in his place. Inconceivable as it seemed, the giant Conkling had come crashing down; his political career was ended. "I am done with politics forever," he announced, and he meant it. He resumed the practice of law on Wall Street, his clients including Jay Gould. In Albany his minions were left "wandering around like wild geese without a gander." Conceivably Tom Platt might have stepped in then, instead of later—Platt being a "great man for organization"—but Platt had been discovered in a compromising position with a young woman and was forced to retire from the scene in disgrace. Very possibly he had been framed. To quote Ike Hunt, "Jimmy Husted and some of them peeked over the transom and saw Tom one night in the hotel."

All this left the old party machinery in disarray and provided opportunity of a kind not known for years for ambitious newcomers. The game had opened up just as Theodore commenced to play. Moreover, the reform spirit was gathering momentum on all sides —it was what had swept Cleveland into office—and so for someone like Theodore the timing could not have been better. In Washington that January, as Theodore started his second term, Congress was passing the Pendleton Act, the country's first civil service reform legislation, which, irony of ironies, would be signed into law by ex-Collector Chester A. Arthur. When the bill went before the Senate, not a single Republican voted against it.

His first months back in Albany Theodore lashed out at the New York City Board of Aldermen ("miserable and servile fools") and went after Jay Gould again, calling on the Attorney General to bring suit to dissolve the Manhattan Elevated. Sounding much like his Uncle Robert, he warned of a great popular uprising unless legal action was taken against such corrupt corporations. A bill comparable to the Pendleton Act was before the Assembly and this too he championed, gladly joining forces with the Democrat Cleveland.

He never doubted the moral virtue of any of his own positions or of the need to punish the wicked. (At one point he called for the return of the public whipping post as punishment for any man who inflicted brutal pain on a woman or a child.) Every issue was seen as a clash between the forces of light and dark. His side was right; the other was the side of corruption or self-interest. Among the several hundred clippings being pasted into the scrapbooks at 6 West 57th Street was one containing a remark by a New York editor that "there is an increasing suspicion that Mr. Roosevelt keeps a pulpit concealed on his person."

So when suddenly he reversed himself on still another issue involving Jay Gould and the Manhattan Elevated, then took the floor to deliver an emotional apology for his earlier stand, he was the talk of the Capitol.

The Five-Cent Bill, as it was called, had been introduced to reduce by half the ten-cent fare on the elevated railway. It was seen as a way to strike a blow at the haughty Gould, who was supposedly reaping huge concealed profits, and, of course, to please the many thousands who rode the elevated railway. Theodore, like nearly everybody else in Albany, gave the bill his support—until Governor Cleveland, in a brave, forceful message, insisted it was unconstitutional, since it violated commitments made by the state in the company's original charter. Cleveland vetoed the bill and sent it back, expecting the decision would prove ruinous for him politically.

The day the message was read in the Assembly, Theodore got the floor as quickly as possible. Like others, he realized Cleveland was right and that his own position had been wrong. He said this, which was somewhat remarkable in itself, but then he went on:

I have to say with shame that when I voted for this bill I did not act as I think I ought to have acted, and as I generally have acted on the floor of this House. . . . I have to confess that I weakly yielded, partly in a vindictive spirit towards the infernal thieves and conscienceless swindlers who have had the elevated railroad in charge and partly to the popular voice of New York.

For the managers of the elevated railroad I have as little feeling as any man here. If it were possible, I would willingly pass a bill of attainder on Jay Gould and all of Jay Gould's associates. . . . I regard these men as furnishing part of that most dangerous of all dangerous classes, the wealthy criminal class. Nevertheless, it is not a question of doing justice to ourselves. . . .

We have heard a great deal about the people demanding the passage of this bill. Now, anything the people demand that is right it is most clearly and most emphatically the duty of this Legislature to do; but we should never yield to what they demand if it is wrong. . . . If the people disapprove our conduct, let us make up our minds to retire to private life with the consciousness that we have acted as our better sense dictated; and I would rather go out of politics having the feeling that I had done what was right than stay in with the approval of all men, knowing in my heart that I had acted as I ought not to.

It was a speech that was to be published and quoted widely as illustrative either of his rank duplicity and opportunism or of his innate decency. It was a wrenching confession, a little sermon, a crystallized declaration of political philosophy; noble and self-serving. To profess shame in oneself was something a politician did not do if he liked his job and it was something Theodore found personally distasteful and almost never indulged in, even among those closest to him. Any ostentatious baring of one's transgressions smacked of self-pity or a desperate craving for attention, he thought. "Never indulge yourself on the sinner's stool," he would lecture his friend Owen Wister. "If you did any harm, that won't undo it, you'll merely rake it up. The sinner's stool is often the only available publicity spot for the otherwise wholly obscure egotist." Yet here he was doing exactly that.

His expression "the wealthy criminal class" was new and original and would not be forgotten. The righteousness he bespoke was the old Roosevelt family theme, the burden and spur of "our way." ("I know I am blue and disagreeable often," Elliott had told Anna Hall, "but please, darling, bear with me and I will come out all right in the end, and it really is an honest effort to do the right that makes me so often quiet and thoughtful about it all.") Probably Theodore had not the least idea how arbitrary and self-righteous he sounded.

The reaction in the press and among other members was immediate and almost entirely adverse. The *Tribune* and one or two papers upstate said it took a special kind of courage to confess a lack of courage, but elsewhere he was dubbed a weakling and a bogus reformer, which doubtless hurt very much. Even the loyal *Evening Post* found it strange that he could think so little of the views of the people unless those views coincided with his own; and though ridicule in the *World* was to be expected, the remarks published there must have been the most painful of all. "It is quite bad enough that a son of Theodore Roosevelt could have brought this discredit upon a name made honorable by the private virtues and public services of the father," said the *World;* friends of the late Theodore could only take satisfaction that at least he had been spared seeing the boy make a public spectacle of himself.

When the Five-Cent Bill was put before the Assembly, Theodore voted against it, with the majority as it turned out, but in doing so was parting company with Hunt, O'Neil, and others of his closest allies.

He was acting as though he were under some kind of emotional strain, seemed not to know how to handle himself. A day or so later he made another grandstand play on the floor, suddenly tendering his resignation from a committee when the Assembly refused to go along with the committee's recommendation. The speech turned into a wild, childish diatribe against the whole Democratic Party. It was as if, like the tiny shrew in the cage, he would fling himself at the great Democratic snake and tear it to pieces before anyone knew what happened.

"The difference between our party and yours," he shouted across the aisle, "is that your bad men throw out your good ones, while with us the good throw out the bad." The entire history of their party was rotten.

> You can run down the roll from Polk, the mendacious, through Pierce, the Copperhead, to Buchanan, who faced both ways. You can follow the record of their party from its inception down to this time. . . . You can take the record made by their party now in this House; the shameless partisanship they have displayed; the avidity they have shown for getting control of even the smallest offices . . .

When in an interview held in the quiet of the Harvard Club in New York, many years later, Ike Hunt referred to Theodore as "the most indiscreet guy I ever knew," it was moments such as this that he had in mind. "Yesterday, in a speech," reported the New York *Observer*, "Mr. Roosevelt got up and said in effect that he couldn't have his own way in that House and he wouldn't stand it, so there!"

As it was, the Assembly merely refused to accept his resignation and passed on to other matters.

"Billy O'Neil and I used to sit on his coattails," remembered Hunt. "Billy O'Neil would say to him: 'What do you want to do that for, you damn fool; you will ruin yourself and everybody else!'" Even Michael C. Murphy, the questionable guardian chosen by Uncle Rob, he of the swollen red face and shiny frock coat, could be heard from his seat nearby saying in fatherly fashion, "Now, Theodore, now, Theodore . . ."

But toward the end of the session another, smaller incident occurred, a different kind of apology having more to do with his make-up as a human being than with any question of moral principle. In his scathing attacks on the Democrats he had been concentrating on a particular member from Staten Island, the elderly Erastus Brooks, whom he picked on repeatedly. Brooks finally spoke up in his own defense and with great feeling, hitting hard at Theodore. When the speech ended and Brooks's friends gathered about to congratulate him, Theodore came pushing through, tears in his eyes, holding out his hand. "Mr. Brooks," he said, "I surrender. I beg your pardon."

Success had come to him too fast, he later said; he had lost his perspective, "and the result was I came an awful cropper and had to pick myself up after learning by bitter experience the lesson that I was not all-important and that I had to take account of many different elements in life."

All the same, his legislative record surpassed that of the first term. The civil service bill was enacted. And so also was the Cigar Bill—by both houses this time—though after a protracted battle in the courts the Cigar Bill was to be found unconstitutional. The judges sided with the manufacturers, whose counsel, former Secretary of State William Evarts, argued that socialism and communism were in back of the bill and that such home industry was actually beneficial to the "proper culture of growing girls." In its final judgment, in 1885, the New York Court of Appeals asked how possibly a cigarmaker's health and morals could be improved by forcing him from his home and its "hallowed associations."

Theodore had spoken for the bill both in the Assembly and at a hearing in the governor's office. Conceding at one point that the measure was in a "certain sense a socialistic one," he said the terrible growing extremes of poverty and wealth in the cities demanded something be done, even if it meant modifying certain doctrines and principles. No children raised under conditions such as he had seen in the tenements would ever be fit for citizenship, he argued, echoing the old theme espoused by Charles Loring Brace and by his own father. In the end, however, he had resorted to the plea that the measure be passed if for no other reason than hygiene, an appeal which seems to have had no small influence on the preponderant number of cigar smokers among his colleagues.

· 3 ·

ELECTED A THIRD TIME in the fall of '83, he returned to Albany in advance of the new session, late the December of Elliott's wedding, determined to be named Speaker. The Republicans had gained a majority in the Assembly, largely because of what he and his Roosevelt Republicans had accomplished the session before, and so it seemed his time was ripe. But he lost when John J. ("Johnny") O'Brien, Republican boss of New York City, an old Conkling henchman, once one of the Customhouse "boys," withdrew his support at the last moment. Senator Warner Miller (Platt's replacement in Washington) had shown Johnny "the valuables in the Treasury" that could become available were he to see his way clear to voting the right way. O'Brien had been the first powerful figure among the "regulars" to line up behind Theodore, and a main reason for Theodore's confidence. Many of Theodore's admirers had been skeptical at the time, sure that something was afoot.

The defeat was a bitter blow. He had wanted the job badly and felt he had earned it. The day after Christmas he had hired a suite at the Delavan House, the somewhat seedy hotel where he often took breakfast and where in years past so many other political fortunes had been won or lost. Old Thurlow Weed and William Seward, Tweed, Conkling, Chester A. Arthur, had all practiced their craft in the lobby and corridors and private suites of the Delavan, cajoled and traded, entreated, listened, charmed, bribed, threatened, flattered unmercifully, all in the endless give-and-take of political maneuver. And Theodore, as he said, had managed "a stout fight."

The problem was the prospect of the political year ahead. A presidential election was in the offing, a Republican national convention less than six months away. Rivalry in the party, along the old Stalwart–Half-Breed lines, was as intense as ever, the Blaine people feeling it was their turn at last. And given the importance of New York at the convention, not to say in the general election, there was abnormally high interest in who was to occupy the Speaker's seat at Albany. To the professionals it was business of the most serious kind. Scouting the lobby of the Delavan just after Christmas, one reporter remarked on the numbers of "friends of the Administration in Washington" who were present, "friends of United States Senator Miller . . . representatives of the Customhouse . . . friends of the corporations."

Refusing to align himself with any faction, Theodore had declared, "I am a Republican, pure and simple, neither a 'Half-Breed' nor a 'Stalwart'; and certainly no man, nor yet any ring or clique, can do my thinking for me." But he was called "unsound" by the professionals—"That young fellow might go off like a rocket," one of them warned. The Stalwarts and the Half-Breeds joined ranks against him and that decided it. At the party caucus New Year's Eve the position of Speaker went to a "regular," an underwear manufacturer from Little Falls named Titus Sheard.

Theodore knew in advance he was beaten and it was he who moved that Sheard's nomination be made unanimous. Allowing that the defeat left him "chagrined," he would claim later that by waging his own fight he had assured his standing as floor leader and consequently accomplished more than he would have as Speaker. Achievement was "the all-important thing," position mattered "only in so far as it widened the chance of achievement."

His Cousin Emlen, recalling the eagerness with which Theodore persisted, said he was "the most ambitious man I ever knew . . ."

As recompense he was named chairman of the City Affairs Committee. Within days he had issued three major bills, one to reduce the power of the New York City aldermen and strengthen the office of mayor, another to put a limit on the city's debt, and a third to raise the license fee for the sale of liquor. None was designed to please the "regulars," but the first, the Reform Charter Bill, as he called it, was the one aimed directly at what he, like many others, saw as the fundamental cause for big-city political corruption. The aldermen, the legislative side of city government, were an amorphous and anonymous body to all but the professionals and those who did business with them. Yet the power wielded by the aldermen was tremendous, including, most importantly, the power of approval over the appointment of department heads. City government in New York had become an exceedingly big business, with a payroll of some $12 million and twelve thousand jobs, making it a larger employer, for example, than the Carnegie iron and steel works. But the aldermen, those who really ran the city (taking their orders from the bosses), were cloaked in very carefully maintained obscurity. Scarcely any voter could name even one alderman or explain what his duties were. Who was to tell who was accountable, let alone remember at election time. Which was exactly as the machine wished to have it.

The remedy, according to reform theory, was to simplify and concentrate power; *and* to make power as conspicuous as possible: give someone the responsibility and hold him responsible, that someone being the mayor. And the model was the business corporation. "Some one man must be given the power of direction," preached Mayor Seth Low of Brooklyn; ". . . they [the public] understand that power and responsibility must go together from the top to the bottom of every successful business organization."

The arrangement by which Seth Low ran Brooklyn was exactly what Theodore hoped to attain in New York. Theodore knew a good deal about Low, not only from what had appeared in the papers, but through Uncle Robert, who had worked with the young mayor as part of his duties concerning the Brooklyn Bridge, that great work now having been finished at last. Low functioned under a new Brooklyn city charter put in effect in 1882 and unlike any other. It made the mayor of Brooklyn the real, as well as the nominal, head of government, with absolute authority over the appointment of police commissioner, fire commissioner, health officers, treasurer, tax collector, and on down the line. This, said Low, was "a great and direct gain . . . because it creates and keeps alert a strong public sentiment, and tends to increase the interest of all citizens in the affairs of their city." And by "all citizens," he, Theodore, and other high-minded gentlemen concerned with municipal reform had specifically in mind the hordes of immigrants who, like Theodore's cigarmakers, spoke little English, who were illiterate, bewildered by the political system, and thus easily manipulated by the political bosses (who, as it also happened, knew considerably more about these same people and what their real needs were than did the high-minded gentlemen concerned with municipal reform). It was not that the system must be simplified merely for the average citizen, but for what Seth Low called "the simplest citizen."

In Brooklyn the results were astounding. In Brooklyn more

people had voted in the election for mayor than in the election for governor. And having such power as Seth Low had, said Low himself, "appeals to the best that is in a man as strongly as it exposes him to the fire of criticism if he does not do well."

To strip the New York aldermen of their power—those "creatures" of the bosses, as Theodore called them—and give New York a mayor like Seth Low struck nearly everybody but the bosses as eminently sensible, and so with his Reform Charter Bill Theodore had placed himself squarely in the forefront of a very popular cause. Quite rightly he saw it as his most important effort since entering politics.

Samuel Gompers had been impressed by his aggressiveness. On January 15, or less than a week after introducing the Reform Charter Bill, Theodore was made head of a special committee to investigate New York City government. Four days later, at the Metropolitan Hotel in New York, he opened hearings into the affairs of the city's Department of Public Works, which of late, under the direction of Commissioner Hubert O. Thompson, had shown an increase in expenditures of some sixty-five percent and with no discernible benefit to the city. Thompson was well known in Albany, where he spent a disproportionate amount of his time "conferring" at the Delavan House. Early in his first term, Theodore had picked him out as among the most blatantly odious and fascinating political "creatures"—"a gross, enormously fleshly man with full face and thick, sensual lips; wears a diamond shirt pin and an enormous seal ring on his little finger." And though Thompson, who had had prior experience with investigative hearings, succeeded in making the first session something of a joke at Theodore's expense, it was Theodore's intention to keep the hearings going at the hotel every Friday, Saturday, and Monday until the job was done.

It was a chance at last to do battle, good against evil, in New York itself and in what he liked to call "the full light of the press," light he very obviously loved. He relished the publicity and he relished the battle itself. He loved a fight, more even than his father had. It was possibly the chief reason he loved politics, needed politics. He was never more pleased with himself than when he had made a "stout fight." The political allies he cared most for were those who were fighters, who were "fearless," like Joe Murray. He loved the camaraderie of such men. Of Billy O'Neil, the "best friend," he would write, "we stood shoulder to shoulder in every legislative fight."

Experience, moreover, had already taught him a grudging respect for the rogues who fought against him, who, too, were fearless and forthright in their fashion. Indeed, he preferred them to what he called the "parlor reformers," "the timid good men" who stood on the sidelines. Unhappily, "blamelessness and the fighting edge are not always combined." It was exactly because politics was a bear pit that he wanted in.

"A man should never put on his best trousers when he goes out to battle for freedom and truth," advised Henrik Ibsen in his 1882 play, *An Enemy of the People*. Theodore never wore anything but his best trousers; he was every inch the "dude" the newspapers portrayed; he made no pretense by word or dress at being anything other than wellborn, never resorted, as Boies Penrose did, to being "one of the boys" by talking or acting like one of the boys. But in a political fight he fought tooth and claw. As the journalist Mark Sullivan would observe, "Roosevelt did not regard politics as a gentleman's sport, to be played in the spirit of a private duello, with a meticulous code about choice of time and place. Roosevelt had a trait of ruthless righteousness.'"

Years later, writing about his father's old friend John Hay, Theodore made an acutely revealing observation—revealing of his own nature. The problem with Hay, he said, was his unwillingness to "face the rather intimate association which is implied in a fight."

One must never shrink from what was "rough in life"; one must never recoil or flinch in the face of a Jay Gould or a Hubert O. Thompson. He had marked another verse in his Bible: *The wicked flee when no man pursueth: but the righteous are bold as a lion."*

Also, as Charles Eliot once observed, a man in a fight had little chance to be lonely.

CHAPTER THIRTEEN

Strange and Terrible Fate

· 1 ·

HE FELT FINE. He felt better, in fact—about his work, about himself, his future—than he had in a long while.

At his worst, he got what he called his "caged wolf feeling." To be confined, hemmed in, to have nothing to do, was unbearable. Boredom was something he had had to deal with so rarely in life that when he had to he hardly knew how to respond. The hotel at Richfield Springs the summer before had been torture. He complained of it more than the asthma that sent him there. "I have a bad headache, a general feeling of lassitude, and am bored out of my life by having nothing whatever to do," he told Corinne, "and being placed in that quintessence of abomination, a large summer hotel at a watering place for underbred and overdressed girls, fat old female scandal mongers, and a select collection of assorted cripples and consumptives."

Of late in Albany he had even begun boxing again, taking sparring lessons for the first time in five years. "I felt much better for it," he wrote Alice January 22, 1884, "but am awfully out of training. I feel much more at ease in my mind and better able to enjoy things since we have gotten under way; I feel now as though I had the reins in my hand."

The winter of his first term she had come with him to "that dear, dull, old Dutch city," but the year after, for his second term, she remained behind in New York, in the brownstone on West 45th Street, and more recently, because of her advancing pregnancy, she had moved back with Mittie once more. So now with the hearings in session at the Metropolitan Hotel, he was staying on at 57th Street three or four nights a week.

In all regards the personal, domestic side of his life was wholly satisfactory. Uncle James Alfred worried that he was spendthrift, but appears also to have been the only one who did. His income was substantial, not quite $14,000 a year, or nearly twice what it had been before he was married. James Alfred had been looking after his "affairs" exceedingly well. The income from Roosevelt and Son alone had been nearly $8,000 the previous year. In addition there were returns from a variety of railroads in which James Alfred was himself actively involved (the Mobile and Ohio, the Rochester and Pittsburgh, the Shenango and Allegheny). There were dividends from Uncle Jimmie Gracie's J. K. Gracie Company, from the Union Trust, and from his own Wyoming cattle investment. His salary as an assemblyman, his only earned income, was $1,200 a year.

What Alice contributed, from money or investments of her own, was never spoken of, but considering her background it was probably a respectable sum; and in any event, they knew there was a great deal to fall back on, if need be, in both families. By the way he was spending—buying the 45th Street house, buying property at Oyster Bay, sinking no small amounts in this and that—he obviously felt there was plenty to spend, plenty more where that came from. At the time he decided to buy in as a partner with George Haven Putnam he handed Putnam a check for $20,000, which, as he did not seem to understand, was approximately twice what he had in his account. But the difficulty was smoothed over at once by James Alfred, who borrowed the difference out of Theodore's "expectations."

To return from the political battlefields to his "own sunny darling" was all he had dreamed marital bliss might be. He knew no greater happiness than to be with her in his own sitting room at 45th Street, playing backgammon "before a bright fire of soft coal, my books all around me." The house, since rented to Elliott and his bride, had been the first and only home of their own, and for the benefit of the two maids who ran it, Aunt Anna Gracie had drawn up a detailed program for cleaning, cooking, and so forth, a manuscript of several pages that included one directive Theodore thought memorable. " 'Every morning the cook should meet the ashman with a pail of boiling water,' " he would read aloud to friends, then question what the ashman might have done to deserve a scalding.

Seeing old friends on the street, he would insist they come home with him to see Alice. He was sure she was a great asset to him in his political career and told her so. Now, when the hearings broke up at week's end, he would bring two or three others from the committee home to 57th Street. "All of the men were perfectly enchanted with their visit to our house . . ." he wrote her from Albany January 28, after one such occasion. "They could hardly believe that Mother was really our mother; and above all they praised my sweet little wife." One man, Tom Welch, a Niagara Falls Democrat whom he liked particularly, told him he had never seen anyone look prettier than Alice, a remark Theodore thought she would enjoy since she was then a little more than eight months pregnant.

Her confinement precluded any social life of the kind that had once occupied so much of their time, and this suited him perfectly. Such a life led to nothing, he had decided.

He had shaved off his side-whiskers, given up keeping a diary. The Newsboys' Lodging House and the other good works of his father's no longer interested him and he gradually gave them up also. He had gone into such activities, he would explain, in the same spirit as the Sunday-school classes at Harvard, because of his father, but it had not worked. He had no patience with simple, unsung altruism. "I tried faithfully to do what Father had done," he later told the author Jacob Riis, "but I did it poorly . . . in the end I found out that we have each to work in his own way to do our best; and when I struck mine, though it differed from his, yet I was able to follow the same lines and do what he would have had me do."

He had also abandoned the law. It was not just that his political life was growing larger, crowding out other things, but that other things seemed to be falling away as in some very natural process. Part of the previous summer had been spent in Uncle Robert's office, but Theodore was not to return there again and he had not been back to the Columbia Law School in more than a year. He had become, he later said, sadly disillusioned by the law. In the careers of the corporation lawyers one was supposed to admire and emulate he saw little that was "compatible" with his own ideals. Lawyers, it appeared to him, were trained to serve clients, not justice. "The *caveat emptor* side of the law, like the *caveat emptor* side of business, seemed to me repellent; it did not make for social fair dealing," he wrote long afterward in his memoirs.

There is the possibility, of course, that he simply found the law dull and had too much else he would rather be doing. The philosophical conclusions may have been those of the older man, a career's-end distillation of accumulative disrespect for certain kinds of legal giants, and thus as open to question as his subsequent views on the teaching of natural history at Harvard. The few specific references he made to his law work at the time are actually quite positive. Still, the thesis offered by the old family friend at lunch, the unnamed member of the prominent law firm who appeared in the midst of the Westbrook Scandal, was more than just "incompatible" with his idealism; it revolted him. And if that were not sufficient, the spectacle soon after of the vaunted William Evarts mouthing nonsense about the sanctity of the home as cause for perpetuating the cigar sweatshops must have made very clear the priority of client over "social fair dealing." Theodore then, as later, equated a law career with moneymaking, not with social service, and as he also said then, as later, his inheritance had liberated him from moneymaking.

Oddly, for all his quick success in politics, the passion and energy he exuded, he was still unable, or unwilling, to accept politics as his lifework. He never spoke of it as a career or calling. To have announced he was a professional politician, or openly aspired to that, would have been awkward, to be sure, since "professional" was considered synonymous with "corrupt." It was only as a gentleman doing his part in the public interest—as a temporary volunteer, so to speak—that he could maintain a reputation for independence and integrity. A degree of disinterest in a political future had obvious political value; it was part of what made him "different," less vulnerable to the ways by which the obviously ambitious are bought or held in check. But even among the few with whom he was most candid, he admitted to no clear vision of a lifework. In the parlance of later-day psychologists he had still to find an occupational identity, and it troubled him. His plight was nothing like that of his brother, but, by the same token, he was by no means as resolved and focused as implied by his soaring performance.

It was only within the last six months, for example, that he and Alice resolved to build on the land he had bought at Oyster Bay. At one point, earlier, he thought seriously of settling upstate at Herkimer, in the Mohawk Valley, where Douglas Robinson's family had a large estate. "I hardly know what to do about taking a place up here," he wrote Bamie in the fall of 1882, she being the one to whom he still invariably turned for serious counsel on serious questions; "it would be lovely to have a farm, and fortunately Alice seems enchanted with the country. The only, or at least the chief, drawback, is the distance from New York. Still, if I were perfectly certain that I would go on in politics and literature I should buy the farm without hesitation; but I consider the chances to be strongly favorable to my getting out of both . . ."

The Oyster Bay house, once decided on, was his first commitment to the future. And certainly there was nothing equivocal or tentative about the plans that evolved—once he, Alice, Mittie, Bamie, Aunt Anna Gracie, and architects Lamb and Rich had hiked over the site, savored the view, and picked the spot. He knew too little of architecture, he said, to say what ought to be done on the outside, but on "inside matters" he was "perfectly definite." As he later told an editor for the magazine *Country Life in America*, "I wished a big piazza . . . where we could sit in rocking chairs and look at the sunset; a library with a shallow bay window looking south, the parlor or drawing room occupying all the western end of the lower floor . . . big fireplaces for logs . . . I had to live inside and not outside . . ."

The house was to be enormous, suggesting a future for Alice, at least, of unending pregnancies. Along with his other wishes, the plans called for ten bedrooms, excluding maids' rooms.

Everything bespoke solidity, permanence, comfort, security, *family*. The foundations were to be nearly two feet thick. There were eight fireplaces, four on the first floor, four above, twenty-two rooms in all. The materials, interestingly, were to be of the most ordinary kind. No fine paneling or costly plasterwork was called for. Doors, windows, doorframes, and the like were all of the common, inexpensive variety. Frills were dispensed with. Size, command of the hill, were what seemed to matter. It was the way he liked his food, simple but plentiful, heavy on the plate.

The "outside cover" supplied by the architects was Queen Anne—brick on the ground floor, then shingles and a slate roof. The final cost was to be something just under $17,000.

It should be called Leeholm, he decided. From the front piazza they would be able to see a whole, long sweep of Long Island Sound and, on clear days, Connecticut beyond. Now, in winter, the trees bare, the water dominated the panorama and was a deep vivid blue, different from summer. In summer, after dark, they would be

able to see the lights of the Fall River steamers as they passed in
the distance.

Albany, February 6, 1884

DARLING WIFIE,

How I did hate to leave my bright, sunny little love yesterday afternoon! I love you and long for you all the time, and
oh *so* tenderly; doubly tenderly now, my sweetest little wife.
I just long for Friday evening when I shall be with you again.

Today I sparred as usual; my teacher is a small man and in
the set-to today I bloodied his nose by an uppercut, and
knocked him out of time.

In the House we had a most exciting debate on my Reform
Charter Bill, and I won a victory, having it ordered to a third
reading. Tomorrow evening I am to dine at the Rathbones', at
half past seven; it was very kind to ask me, but I do not anticipate much fun.

Goodbye, sweetheart.

Her pregnancy appears to have been without incident. Mittie
had once remarked how "very large" she looked, but no one seems
to have been concerned about her, and with the baby expected any
time, he apparently had no misgivings about being away from her.
Albany was five hours by train.

In another letter also written February 6, he told her he had
given one of his "best speeches" the day before, and if she was
looking in the papers that day, she saw that others agreed. "Mr.
Roosevelt's argument . . . was conclusive and unanswerable," said
the *Times.* "Mr. Roosevelt," according to the *Evening Post,* had
made "a speech admirable both in clearness and force." A headline
in the *Herald* spoke of "MR. ROOSEVELT'S BRILLIANT ASSAULT ON
CORRUPTION."

"I propose to put the power in the hands of the men the people
elect," he had said. "At present the power is in the hands of one or
two men whom the people did not elect." It was being called the
Roosevelt Bill now. A rally in its support was to be held at Cooper
Union the next week.

· 2 ·

ON FRIDAY, when he returned to 57th Street, he found that Mittie
was "quite sick" with what appeared to be a cold, and that Corinne

and Douglas had left their infant son in Bamie's charge while they went off to Baltimore for a long weekend.

The weather was miserable, chill and damp. There had been no sign of the sun for days. Monday, Mrs. Lee arrived on a morning train. Theodore put in another day at the hearings downtown, then left for Albany first thing Tuesday morning.

Later that day, Tuesday, the twelfth, Alice went into labor and some time that night a baby girl was born. Telegrams went off the next morning announcing the news that mother and child were doing well. Ike Hunt would remember Theodore, "full of life and happiness," accepting the congratulations of his friends. But then a few hours later a second telegram arrived and Theodore, looking suddenly "worn," rushed for the next train.

The *Times* that morning called it suicide weather. It covered most of the Northeast—rain, unending fog, rivers over their banks. In New York, traffic barely moved on the rivers, so thick was the fog. Trains were hours behind schedule. Corinne and Douglas, who had received a telegram at Baltimore and started for New York, would remember crossing through thick fog by ferry from New Jersey, then taking the elevated train uptown, everything moving at a crawl.

They were the first to reach the house. Corinne would remember walking from the elevated station to 57th Street and seeing a single light through the fog in a third-story window. She went up the front steps a little ahead of Douglas. The door was thrown open and Elliott stood in the doorway, the light from the hall behind him, a terrible look on his face. If she wished to see her baby, he said, she should do so before coming in. The baby was at Aunt Annie's. "There is a curse on this house! Mother is dying, and Alice is dying too."

The time was approximately 10:30. Mittie, the doctor said, was dying of typhoid fever; Alice, of Bright's disease. Theodore did not arrive for another hour.

By the time he reached her bedside and took her in his arms, Alice barely knew who he was. He stayed there, holding her, until some time just before three in the morning when he was told that if he wished to see his mother again, he must come at once.

Mittie died at three o'clock the morning of February 14, her four children at her bedside. Alice lingered on another eleven hours. Alice died at two that afternoon, Theodore still holding her.

•   •

The first man to rise when the Assembly convened the next day said he had never in his years at Albany stood in the presence of such sorrow. Six others spoke, including three of Theodore's most hostile opponents, all visibly shaken. In an unprecedented gesture of respect, the Assembly voted to adjourn until the following Monday.

Saturday in New York, the morning of the double funeral service, skies were clear, the temperature back down in the twenties. Theodore, his face a mask, sat in the front pew with Elliott, Bamie, Corinne, and Alice's father. Again, as six years before, the enormous church was full; except that now two rosewood coffins stood at the altar. The familiar faces scattered among the more than two thousand who had gathered included Astors, Vanderbilts, Harrimans, but also Speaker Titus Sheard, Johnny O'Brien, and Mayor Seth Low. They sang "Rock of Ages"; Dr. John Hall prayed for the bereaved and for the four-day-old baby, weeping openly as he spoke. Then two hearses clattered off down Fifth Avenue, followed by carriages carrying the immediate family. Burial was at Greenwood, beside Grandmamma Bulloch and Theodore.

Again disease had struck and destroyed and changed everything. The life of the family had seemed an unending, tragic struggle against one cursed disease after another—Pott's disease, asthma, cancer, whatever nameless disorder plagued Elliott—and now came typhoid and nephritis, or Bright's disease, chronic inflammation of the kidneys. Mittie, whose precautions against dirt and contamination had seemed silly and obsessive, died of contaminated food or water, of the acutely infectious bacteria *Salmonella typhosa*. Typhoid fever, an ordeal of usually several weeks, had killed her in five days. It had appeared at first as though she had only a cold, because that is how typhoid begins. Little that mattered was done for her, because there was little anyone could do, given what was known, what was available. And it had been the same for Alice. Two summers before, the country had learned about Bright's disease when the Associated Press carried a story saying President Arthur was ill with it. The story was denied, on authority of the President, but the feeling remained that Arthur was a dying man, since Bright's disease in adults was almost inevitably fatal. That it had gone undiagnosed in Alice all that winter seems odd. Plainly neither she nor any of the family had any idea there was something the matter with her. And though none of the family was to challenge or investigate the part played by her doctor, some of her friends would later contend that the doctor had been guilty of criminal negligence.

No one knew how possibly to justify or explain such tragedy. There were no answers save "God's will" or fate, "strange and terrible fate," Theodore said. The sole, overwhelming lesson was the awful brevity of life, the sense that the precipice awaited not just somewhere off down the road, but at any moment. An asthmatic childhood had shown that life could be stifled, cut off, unless one fought back, and all Papa's admonitions to get action, to seize the moment, had the implicit message that there was not much time after all. Father had died at forty-six; Mittie had been only forty-eight; Alice, all of twenty-two, her life barely begun. Nothing lasts. Winter waits.

· 3 ·

"HE DOES NOT KNOW what he does or says," wrote his old tutor, Arthur Cutler, the day of the funeral. Yet three days later Theodore was back in Albany, and the day following, at ten in the morning, he was in his seat as usual and that afternoon he took up where he had left off, arguing for his Reform Charter Bill. In one of the speeches given in sympathy the week before, an old Republican named Lucas Van Allen, a man who had opposed Theodore time and again, prayed Theodore be given the strength "to work bravely in the darkness."

Now week after week, on into March and April, he did little but work, shunting back and forth from Albany to his hearings by night trains. He reported a flood of bills out of his City Affairs Committee—seven, nine, fourteen a day. His outpouring of work, of words printed and spoken, of speeches delivered, of witnesses grilled, of interviews, of inspection tours (of conditions at New York's infamous Ludlow Street jail), of headlong, concentrated energy was utterly phenomenal, surpassing anything he had ever done before and causing those close at hand to wonder how much longer he could maintain a hold on himself. One day in March he reported fifteen bills out of committee, then six more at a night session; and even then his work for the day had only begun. Dissatisfied with a report on his hearings that had been drafted by counsel for the committee, he wrote an entirely new version at a single sitting, working through until morning.

He didn't want to [Ike Hunt recalled], but he did it. He started
in at night and he wrote all night long and he got his breakfast
and still continued to write. The House opened and he came
up to the House and he wrote that report, and as soon as he got
a sheet of foolscap written in long hand the page was right
there to take it down to the printer because the committee had
got to report that morning. But Teddy would get up and say,
"Mr. Speaker, that bill so-and-so with reference to so-and-so is
all right," and then he would sit down and commence to write
again. Finally, he said, "There it is, I am finished." I sat right
in front of him. I said, "There won't be any continuity to that
report, I don't believe." He said, "Don't you worry." In a little
while the printer came up with the report all printed and
Teddy went out and read it to the committee and they signed
it and that was the report that was handed in.

Of his personal tragedy, he would say nothing. "You could not
talk to him about it," Hunt remembered. " . . . He did not want
anybody to sympathize with him."

"I have taken up my work again; indeed, I think I should go
mad if I were not employed," he wrote in answer to a sympathy
note from Carl Schurz, who a number of years before had survived
the death of his own wife by pouring himself into his work in just
such manic fashion.

"Teddy was as sweet and gentle as ever on Sunday," wrote
Corinne after one of his weekends in the city, "but he feels the
awful loneliness more and more, and I fear he sleeps little for he
walks a great deal in the night and his eyes have that strained red
look."

Within days after the funeral, it had been decided to sell 6
West 57th Street. It was put on the market and snapped up at once
by an immensely wealthy old friend of the elder Theodore's, a
fellow director of the Museum of Natural History, John S. Kennedy, who, with his banking firm, J. S. Kennedy & Company, was
closely involved with James Alfred in the financing of the Great
Northern Railroad. The family had until May to be out of the house.
Theodore left it to Bamie to handle the details and to sell his own
place on West 45th Street. "That year seems a perfect nightmare,"
she would recall, "parting with all the places we had cared for,
dividing everything that had always meant home and deciding how
to recommence life."

Several hundred condolence letters had to be answered, and
again it was Bamie who bore the major burden. There were letters

from Bullochs in Savannah, recalling "the beautiful, angelic and active girl I knew and loved so well"; from friends made abroad ("It seems such a short time ago when we were together on the Nile . . ."); and from people like Aunt Lucy Elliott, who must be answered at length. "If baby is living who will take it?" wrote a cousin from Charleston.

In the interval between her mother's death and the hour when Alice died, Bamie had sent off a wire to Liverpool and in a strong, clear hand Uncle Jimmie Bulloch had written in reply, "The cable has never carried through the depths of the sea a sadder message than it has brought us today. . . . Our anxiety about dear Alice adds to our unhappiness, but we will doubtless learn how it fares with her."

I always believe in showing affection by doing what will please the one we love, not by talking, her father had drummed into her. Faced with the decision of whether to proceed as planned with the house at Oyster Bay, whether to sign with the contractor, Theodore decided to go ahead with it, but wanted Bamie to supervise the job, to tend to all details. He wished no part of the project, only to have it finished.

Nor was he interested in his baby, Alice, as she had been christened the Sunday after the funeral, and so she too was entrusted to Bamie, who now bought a house of her own on Madison Avenue, "furnishing it with my share of the 57th Street things." Theodore, for the house at Oyster Bay, was to have the furniture from the master bedroom.

"It seems," wrote Conie, remembering her mother, "as if there were so few that one really cared for." She longed for Mittie. Even her joy in her own child seemed changed somehow, depreciated with Mittie gone.

Baby is lying on the bed taking his lunch by me [she wrote Elliott]. Though he is my greatest comfort and delight, still so much of my pleasure in him is changed, for I never was so happy as when I saw her with him. She loved him so extravagantly . . .

On the day Alice died, Theodore had made a large X on the page for February 14 in an otherwise empty diary for the year 1884, and beneath he wrote only, "The light has gone out of my life."

Later in the year, working at a small table in a cabin in the Dakota Bad Lands, he wrote a memorial for private publication.

She was born at Chestnut Hill, Massachusetts, on July 29, 1861; I first saw her on October 18, 1878, and loved her as soon as I saw her sweet, fair young face; we were betrothed on January 25, 1880, and married on October 27th, of the same year; we spent three years of happiness such as rarely comes to man or woman; on February 12, 1884, her baby girl was born; she kissed it, and seemed perfectly well; some hours afterward she, not knowing that she was in the slightest danger, but thinking only that she was falling into a sleep, became insensible, and died at two o'clock on Thursday afternoon, February 14, 1884, at 6 West 57th Street, in New York; she was buried two days afterward, in Greenwood Cemetery.

She was beautiful in face and form, and lovelier still in spirit; as a flower she grew, and as a fair young flower she died. Her life had been always in the sunshine; and there had never come to her a single great sorrow; and none ever knew her who did not love and revere her for her bright, sunny temper and her saintly unselfishness. Fair, pure, and joyous as a maiden; loving, tender, and happy as a young wife; when she had just become a mother, when her life seemed to be but just begun, and when the years seemed so bright before her—then, by a strange and terrible fate, death came to her.

And when my heart's dearest died, the light went out from my life for ever.

CHAPTER FOURTEEN

Chicago

· 1 ·

May 31, Chicago—Fast and thick the delegates to the convention are flocking into this city . . . a canvass of the members of the convention here shows Blaine to be in the lead. . . .

In the gilded, mirrored comfort of the Palmer House barbershop, where, as every visitor to Chicago learned soon enough, the floor was inlaid with silver dollars, they sat waiting for a morning shave, smoking their first cigars of the day, or, if not that, spitting tobacco juice with amazing accuracy, some among the Californians —those newly arrived by the "Blaine Train"—looking, as one man said, as if they had walked in from the Pacific Coast. They talked of Blaine's strength in the West, of the send-off they had had at San Francisco, of stops the day before, Memorial Day, at places like Marshalltown, Iowa, where several thousand people were waiting at the depot to cheer them on. They studied the plan of the convention floor published in the morning *Tribune* or read aloud a quote from Tom Platt that "for every kicker who does bolt, Blaine will get two Irish votes in exchange." Such observations as "It's Blaine's turn now" and "Arthur can't carry New York" were also exchanged as the long line of barbers went about their business. Then shaved, combed, made fragrant with a splash of bay rum, their bright red-and-white BLAINE badges in place, they went out to join the fun.

In the marble lobby of the hotel there were still more of them, talking, reaching for outstretched hands, huddled in threes and fours. At the Grand Pacific Hotel, four blocks away, they were even more numerous. At Blaine headquarters upstairs Titus Sheard of New York was already claiming 341 Blaine votes on the first ballot, a mere 70 shy of what was needed to nominate, and by midday in the bar and the main dining room, they were clinking green glasses in toasts to the next President of the United States, James Gillespie Blaine.

Reporters were struck by their exuberance, their confidence, and the contrast with the Arthur people, who were so plainly downcast and uninspired. "Whenever you meet a Blaine man," complained the correspondent for *The New York Times*, "he seizes you and pours into your ear the same old story. 'Everybody wants him. The great West cries for him. The Middle States yearn for him.' " "All were filled with enthusiasm," noted another reporter, "and the most enthusiastic were filled with whiskey." Some ambitious orators liked to climb up on the lobby furniture in order to make known their theories for the salvation of the country.

They were the rank and file of the party, as they were fond of saying, from city and country alike, as Tom Platt stressed. Theodore, in a letter to Bamie, would describe them as mainly "good, ordinary men, who do not do very much thinking, who are pretty honest themselves, but who are callous to any but very flagrant wrongdoing in others, unless it is brought home to them most forcibly, who 'don't think Blaine any worse than the rest of them' . . ."

It was their feelings for Blaine that made them such a force to reckon with. Blaine's only power was the devotion he inspired through force of personality (demagoguery, Theodore and his friends called it). Blaine controlled no patronage, no machine, held no keys to the Customhouse or the Treasury. His home state of Maine had no political importance nationally. And though in recent years he had served quite ably as Garfield's Secretary of State, and could be thus fairly described as a "statesman," he did not even hold public office any longer. Blaine was adored for being Blaine —for his very real human warmth and love of people, his brains and loyalty, and "that gorgeous surplus of personal grace called magnetism." He remained, since the Ingersoll speech at Cincinnati eight years before, the "Plumed Knight" of the party, the Republican's Republican whose mere presence on a platform could work magic wherever Republican fortunes were in trouble. At the last national convention, also held in Chicago, his forces had carried their fight through thirty-six ballots before Garfield was named. It had been Blaine who handed his friend Garfield the nomination at the last and it had been Conkling who kept the nomination from Blaine; and now with Conkling out of the picture, Blaine's people were bound to let nothing stand in the way.

The famous visage—the long, pale face with its luminous dark eyes and silvery beard—was to be seen everywhere about the hotels and in store windows, but the idol himself, like President Arthur, remained in Washington. Ironically, with the prize closer to his reach than at any time before, Blaine no longer craved it as he once had.

Also, in April, only weeks before the convention, the old burden of the Mulligan letters had been resurrected in brilliant, vicious fashion by a famous full-color cartoon that the opposition was busily passing out in Chicago, just in case there was anyone left who had not seen it. It had appeared in *Puck*. Blaine was displayed as "The Tattooed Man," stripped to his undershorts before a tribunal of his Republican peers. The tattoos were all his old sins— "Mulligan Letters," "Little Rock RR Bonds," "N Pacific Bonds," "Corruption"—and his famed personal magnetism was revealed to be nothing more than a cheap "magnetic pad" worn about the neck.

Nor was the old "saving element" of the party any less adamant in its opposition to Blaine than in times past. Virtually everyone from the Fifth Avenue Conference who was still active in politics was lined up against him—Schurz, Curtis, Godkin, Lodge —and some, like Schurz, talked openly of bolting the party if Blaine was the nominee. They saw him as morally obtuse and the most "venal" of apologists for the spoils system. He had been too close all his career to "the wealthy criminal class," and to Jay Gould in particular. About the only thing they would not do to stop him was support Chester Arthur. Theodore, writing to Lodge shortly before leaving for Chicago, described the choice as between the Blaine devil and the Arthur deep sea, though of the two, Blaine was "the most dangerous man."

The puzzling thing about Arthur was that he had turned out to be quite a respectable President. Since Garfield's murder in 1881, he had been a surprise to almost everybody. His record was a good one. He had conducted himself with great dignity, denied old cronies special license. ("He isn't 'Chet' Arthur any more," Johnny O'Brien observed wistfully, "he's the President.") He had supported the Pendleton Act, the national indebtedness had been cut, the cost of domestic postage reduced. At his urging a decrepit wooden navy was being phased out, new steel cruisers built. The country was prospering. Times were so good that when General Grant's Wall Street firm of Grant and Ward failed that spring, it "created only a temporary disturbance" in the overall business picture.

With his height and elegant tailoring, Arthur also looked more like a President than any of his Republican predecessors. He had insisted that the somewhat dowdy old Executive Mansion be brought up to standards (according to the taste of the day), and that official hospitality be raised from the depths of the Hayes years. Modern plumbing was installed in the White House, and the first elevator. Louis Tiffany of New York had done over the Red, Blue, and East rooms, and the showpiece of the new look was a jeweled Tiffany glass screen, fifty feet in length, that now divided the main corridor from the public north vestibule. At Arthur's invitation, Madame Christine Nilsson and other opera singers performed at state dinners, where, customarily, there were flowers in abundance, as well as small bouquets of roses at every lady's place, boutonnieres for the men, and gilt-edged place cards embossed with the national coat of arms in gold. There could be as many as fourteen courses with seven or eight wines, each with its proper glass. It was said that Arthur had brought more tact and culture to the White House than anyone in memory, and if such influential figures as Schurz and Curtis thought little better of him than in days gone by, Mark Twain and Henry Ward Beecher thoroughly approved. "I can hardly imagine how he could have done better," Beecher was quoted as saying. More important for the moment, he was liked by businessmen and could count on strong support from those on the federal payroll and from black politicians and party workers from the South. Of the 820 accredited delegates converging on Chicago, something over 100 were government employees.

Arthur had made little effort to get the nomination and professed he did not want it. His representatives on the scene were badly organized, poorly financed. When a New Yorker showed up with a suitcase full of cash amounting to $100,000, all for the Arthur cause, Arthur, by cable from Washington, ordered that the money be returned. But Arthur's forces also included such able men as Elihu Root, such thorough professionals as Johnny O'Brien, who had no doubt that he wanted another term.

Besides Arthur and Blaine, there were a half-dozen different dark horses and favorite sons whose strength, if combined, could conceivably stop Blaine. There were John Sherman of Ohio and

John A. Logan of Illinois, both United States senators, dainty little Benjamin Harrison of Indiana, and Robert Todd Lincoln. There was talk of Senator Sherman's more famous brother, William Tecumseh Sherman, and of George William Curtis. But the only one with any substantial support, other than the two front-runners, was the candidate the reformers had settled on, the man upon whom Theodore was banking his fortunes, Senator George Franklin Edmunds of Vermont. Edmunds was the Bristow of this season's crusade. He was bearded, scowling, capable, incorruptible, eligible, contentious, colorless, devoid of humor, and the very one, it had been decided, to rescue the party and restore it to the high ideals of the founders. (That Blaine, too, had been among the founders was a point left unsaid.) Theodore, so far as is known, had never met Edmunds, nor does he appear to have been aware that it was Edmunds, back at the time of his father's nomination for the Customhouse, who made a special trip to the White House to urge Hayes to compromise with Conkling and choose another, more acceptable man.

The drumbeat for Edmunds had begun as far back as January, when *Harper's Weekly* described him as "in full sympathy with the intelligent progressive spirit," an "inflexible Republican of spotless personal character," and it had been Curtis who led the campaign thereafter, joined by George Jones of *The New York Times*, Godkin of *The Nation*, President Eliot of Harvard, Andrew D. White, who was president of Cornell, and Henry Cabot Lodge. Of the bare handful of actual politicians who announced for Edmunds the two most frequently mentioned were John D. Long of Massachusetts, who was a congressman and former governor, and Theodore, who in that spring of furious, headlong work and sleepless nights had done all he could to further the Edmunds cause, and with notable results. At the state convention at Utica in April, working at fever pitch, he had neatly outmaneuvered the Blaine and Arthur forces and seen that the four who were elected as delegates-at-large to the national convention were all Edmunds men, he himself and Andrew D. White receiving the most votes. Henry Cabot Lodge, also newly elected as a delegate-at-large from Massachusetts, had written to suggest that they combine forces at Chicago, and that in the meantime they make a run down to Washington to see what Edmunds support could be found. The Washington trip proved nothing, except that Theodore and Lodge got to know each other. Lodge stopped over in New York, spending a weekend at 6 West 57th Street amid packing boxes and bare floors. "We are breaking up house," Theodore had warned, "so you will have to excuse very barren accommodations."

When Theodore departed for Chicago on the *Pennsylvania Limited* the evening of May 30, he traveled in a private car with the same two who had led his father's one political crusade in 1876, Schurz and Curtis. (Again as in 1876, Schurz was going to the convention as an observer.) And when Theodore and Curtis were seen checking in at the Grand Pacific Hotel the next morning, amid the swarming Blaine crowd, they were at once the subjects of much talk and speculation. Curtis, with his white bangs and sallow, priestly look, was a face everyone knew. Theodore, according to the New York *Evening Post*, was "more specifically an object of curiosity than any other stranger in Chicago." He was the boy wonder of Albany, New York's "Cyclone Assemblyman," the youngest delegate at the convention. Curtis and his cartoonist, Thomas Nast, had been giving Theodore handsome attention in *Harper's Weekly* that spring. In one Nast cartoon he had been shown holding a whole sheaf of reform bills as Governor Grover Cleveland signed them into law.

They were there to work for Edmunds, Theodore told reporters. He was carrying a bamboo cane and wearing a "clipper" straw hat, the brim of which, on the underside, was bright blue. He talked extremely fast. He had "a mouth full of regular white teeth like a young lady," it was noted, and his gold-rimmed spectacles kept sliding down his nose. He was asked by a man from the Chicago *Tribune* what he might do should Blaine be the nominee. Would he bolt the party? "I will not speak for the others, but for myself I say freely that under no circumstances will I cast a vote for either Blaine or Arthur in this convention. But I am a Republican, and should one or the other of them be nominated, then I will support him."

Curtis, who was standing at his side, let the remark pass, but by saying what he had to the *Tribune*, Theodore had guaranteed that in a matter of hours it would be available in print for every delegate in town.

Later in the day, when Theodore, Curtis, and Schurz walked into the main dining room and stood waiting for a table, they looked, said one man, "as if the fate of the nation was in their keeping. Perhaps it is."

Lodge, who arrived from Boston that same day, seems to have known from the start that there was no way to stop Blaine. And indeed to any experienced observer it looked as though the convention was already decided, three days before it officially opened. By nightfall New York reporters were cabling their home offices that the Blaine boom had "burst all bounds."

Bits of good news . . . came thick and fast to cheer the partisans of Blaine and keep their enthusiasm at the boiling point. . . . To sum it all up, the drift today has been decidedly toward Blaine. He was never so near the nomination. . . .

Thousands more poured into the city the following day, Sunday, June 1, and it was emphatically "ANOTHER BLAINE DAY." As a Boston correspondent observed, few people went to church. In New York the *Times* gave notice that if Blaine was nominated, the *Times* would abandon the Republican Party.

Monday, the papers were saying Arthur was clearly beaten and the word from the Arthur people was that if the nominee could not be their man, then it must be Blaine, which was about the same as saying Blaine was nominated. If noise and cheap enthusiasm were to be the deciding factors, said *The New York Times* indignantly, then Blaine was a certain victor. A sure sign, supposedly, was the swing to Blaine by the Ohio congressman William McKinley. No one talked of issues or programs, only of winning in November.

The first news of consequence came Monday night, and it was then that Theodore and Lodge went to work. Theodore, almost alone of the delegates, it would seem, was sure Blaine could be beaten.

The National Committee, dominated by Blaine people, had announced that the name to be placed in nomination for the honor of temporary chairman, the name to be put before the convention first thing in the morning, was that of Powell Clayton, a former Arkansas governor and Grand Army general who had lost an arm in the war and whose personal reputation was very low. Clayton, who had come to Chicago uncommitted, had offered his fourteen Arkansas votes to the Arthur people in trade for a Cabinet seat. "Not for forty nominations," Arthur responded by wire, and so Clayton went immediately to see the Blaine people. He and Tom Platt, it was known, had been closeted most of that afternoon. (His Conkling past behind him, his "bit of scandal" in the Albany hotel fading from memory, Platt had "thrown in" with Blaine and as head of the New York Blaine delegates was realistically viewed as one of the two or three most important men at the convention.)

Naming Clayton had been a silly move by the Blaine people,

the crudest kind of arrogance, and insulting to a large number of delegates. Even the most case-hardened veterans of political compromise were visibly stunned. Chauncey Depew is said to have received the news with his mouth hanging open, speechless for perhaps the first time in his career.

Theodore saw it at once as a chance to force a fight and test Blaine's strength at the outset. Lodge came rushing to him with much the same idea and so the two "pulled together and went in for all we were worth," as Theodore said. They were up most of the night, working the hotel corridors, seeing everyone they could. To challenge a decision of the National Committee at the start of a convention was unheard of. "Many of our men were very timid," Theodore reported to Bamie, and chief among the "weak-kneed ones" was George William Curtis.

Just finding somebody willing to stand as a candidate against Clayton proved difficult and apparently it was Theodore's personal appeal that made the difference. The volunteer was former Congressman John R. Lynch, a black delegate from Mississippi, who was pledged to Arthur.

When, at ten the next morning, the different delegations began forming up in the hotel lobbies for the march to the convention hall, Theodore had had perhaps two hours' sleep. The day, June 3, 1884, marked his debut in national politics, his first chance on the national stage.

· 2 ·

PROBABLY HE HAD HIS MIND on business only as the march began —out of the hotel into the glare of the morning. But the day was spectacular, clear and surprisingly cool for June, and Chicago itself on such a day, and at that particular moment in history, could be a tonic. Four years earlier, when stopping there with Ellie, he had called "Chicagoe," as he spelled it, a "marvelous city." Chicago was the new America, the real thing, full of "go-aheadism," as everyone heard from its outspoken citizenry. It exuded "a sense of big things to be done." If Chicago had faults, it was because Chicago was "young yet"; Chicago was the "Phoenix City of America," risen out of its own ashes, as the saying went. One could take heart in Chicago, from new life, energy, enterprise, even grandeur, springing forth from tragedy.

The parade to the Exposition Hall was under way by eleven,

the crowds falling back and making way for the delegates to pass. They marched two by two in the glaring sunshine, everybody adorned with his proper badge. Their party, for all its failings, its scandals and fallen idols, was still the party of Lincoln, the party that saved the Union, freed the slaves, restored the national credit. Even to so sensitive a moralist as George William Curtis it remained "the party of the best instincts, of the highest desires of the American people." Many men were Republicans as they were church elders or lodge brothers. It was as if one belonged to an order. Their loyalties, their faith and pride in party, were often deeper, more vital to their self-respect and sense of worth than they could express. Delegates to Republican national conventions, as Mark Sullivan noted, sometimes had their official badges cast in gold and passed them along in their wills as precious relics. When a man like Tom Platt talked about the depth of James G. Blaine's loyalty to the party, he did so knowing full well the emotional content in those words—"loyalty" and "party." He felt it himself, even Tom Platt. They all did, or nearly all. "What I liked about him [Blaine] then, as always," Platt remembered, "was his bold and persistent contention that the citizen who best loved his party and was loyal to it, was loyal to and best loved his country."

The line of march was east, toward the lake, along Adams Street to where it joined wide, wood-paved Michigan Avenue. The Exposition Hall, pale green with much glass and a red roof, stood straight ahead on the other side of the avenue, and from all its turrets, domes, and gable ends, a hundred or more flags and banners were flying in the breeze, flying and floating exactly as flags are supposed to, against a clear blue sky. The hall had been built expressly to show that Chicago could rise from the disaster of the Great Fire. It stood at the edge of a broad park and beyond the park was the lake, at the moment nearly violet in color and flat as a tabletop. Above the main portico hung a single, tremendous sign: NATIONAL REPUBLICAN CONVENTION.

The crowd converging from all directions, stopping traffic, backing up at six or seven different entrances, was estimated at ten thousand. The scalpers' price for tickets was $50.

The parading delegates entered through the main door, then moved along a passage beneath the back gallery which opened all at once on to several acres of faces turned in their direction. The Iowans came in first, followed by Rhode Island. Congressman McKinley—short, solid, close-shaven—walked at the head of the Ohio delegation.

The Pennsylvanians wore brilliant blue neckties and cream-colored plug hats and matching cream-colored silk handkerchiefs in their coat pockets, a spray of lily of the valley on the lapel. The New Yorkers, seventy-two in all, largest of the delegations, had white badges with gold fringe and as they started down the aisle the band struck up "When First I Put This Uniform On." A Chicago reporter thought them "fine-looking fellows" and observed that nearly all were wearing the latest low-cut shoes. "The leader was Mr. George William Curtis with his handsome white whiskers. . . . He had on his arm Theodore Roosevelt who bowed right and left to delegates and newspapermen." Theodore was wearing his straw hat. Immediately behind walked Andrew D. White and bringing up the rear was Tom Platt.

They had the priority position, four rows front and center. Curtis sat on the aisle, beside the New York pennon. As the others were getting settled, Theodore was seen to vault lightly over several chairs to sit directly in front of Curtis, after which Andrew D. White negotiated a seat beside Theodore. Platt, meantime, sat at the far end of the row from Curtis and appeared to have nothing more on his mind than the slow, rhythmic stroking of his beard.

The setting looked like nothing else so much as a tremendous, dressed-up railroad terminal. An enormous vaulted ceiling was carried overhead by iron girders, these springing upward from long clerestory windows through which great shafts of sunshine slanted onto portions of the crowd like theatrical spotlights. The ironwork was painted red; the ceiling, pale blue; and red-white-and-blue bunting, state flags, and shields of every color banked the galleries.

The stage was at the west end of the hall and back from the stage was a still higher platform reserved for a thousand or more who qualified as "distinguished persons." Directly above this point, suspended at an angle of about sixty degrees, was a colossal sounding board, hung from the ceiling, a duplicate of which could also be seen at the other end of the hall. The combined surface of these two devices was twenty-five thousand square feet, about half the area of a football field, and their combined acoustical effect was quite amazing. A speaker on stage, talking in a normal voice, could be heard anywhere in the hall and the hall sat about twelve thousand people.

The stage itself was a big semicircle with a long, curving prow now all but buried in still more bunting. A speaker's stand was flanked with battle flags. There were potted palms and several large bouquets of flowers and two large portraits of Washington and Lincoln.

Members of the press, of whom there were no less than eight hundred in attendance, were arranged behind a line of tables on a raised platform immediately in front of the stage. Then across the entire main floor, from the press section to midpoint in the hall, were the cane-seated oak chairs for the delegates, row after row, divided into three equal sections. The pennons marking each reserved section were of blue silk lettered in gold, one for each of the thirty-eight states, eight territories, and the District of Columbia. The boundary line between the delegates and all other ticketholders was a white picket fence running across the center of the hall, from which point the floor sloped steadily uphill to the bleachers at the very back. At the center of the bleachers, directly below the second sounding board, was a thirty-piece band under the direction of "Professor" Johnny Hand. The overhead galleries, running the length of the hall on two sides, were perhaps fifty feet above the main floor.

The opening gavel of the Eighth Republican National Convention fell at 12:28. A slender young clergyman with yellow hair stepped to the rostrum and with hands behind his back thanked God for Plymouth Rock, Yorktown, Appomattox, the Declaration of Independence, the Emancipation Proclamation, and the Republican Party, then prayed for—in vain, as it happened—"dignity of temper" in the forthcoming campaign. The chairman of the National Committee, a senator from Minnesota named Sabin, spoke of Chicago as sacred ground (Lincoln, Grant, and Garfield had all been nominated in Chicago), after which he put Powell Clayton's name before the convention.

Immediately, Lodge was on his feet calling to substitute Lynch of Mississippi. Lodge, tidy, prim, full-bearded, and close-buttoned, spoke without passion, as though he wished merely to express a polite difference of opinion. He offered the name of Lynch, he said, with no view of attempting to make a test vote, but simply to strengthen the party. His manner was described as "supercilious."

Others demanded to be heard. The Blaine people claimed that any challenge to the National Committee would subject the party to needless divisiveness. The opposition insisted that the convention had a right to do as it pleased. Meantime, if we are to believe one of those observing the scene from the press section, the "rather dudish-looking" Roosevelt and the "properly English" Lodge "applauded with the tips of their fingers, held immediately in front of their noses."

Then it was Theodore's turn. "Up from the midst of the Empire State Delegation rose a slight, almost boyish figure," wrote the admiring correspondent for *The New York Times*. "Everybody knew the man, for there is not a State headquarters which he had not visited in his canvass for Edmunds, and scarce an individual delegate with whom he had not conversed in a straightforward, manly way, carrying conviction even when he could not convert." He had handed someone his hat and climbed onto his chair. It was said he looked like a college boy.

"It was the first time I had ever had the chance of speaking to ten thousand people assembled together," he would tell Bamie.

He had one hand on his hip. A reporter described how his "slight frame shook with the effort to make himself heard."

"Mr. Chairman . . . I hold it to be derogatory to our honor, to our capacity for self-government, to say that we must accept the nomination of a presiding officer by another body; and that our hands are tied . . ." He asked that the vote on the temporary chairman be taken by an individual poll of the delegates. "Let each man stand accountable . . . let each man stand up here and cast his vote, and then go home and abide by what he has done."

> It is now, Mr. Chairman, less than a quarter of a century since, in this city, the great Republican Party for the first time organized for victory and nominated Abraham Lincoln, of Illinois, who broke the fetters of the slave and rent them asunder forever. It is a fitting thing for us to choose to preside over this convention one of that race whose right to sit within these walls is due to the blood and treasure so lavishly spent by the founders of the Republican Party. And it is but a further vindication of the principles for which the Republican Party so long struggled. I trust that the Honorable Mr. Lynch will be elected temporary chairman of this convention.

Then, as quickly, he was back in his seat again, the "warmest applause" ringing in his ears, and once five or six others had spoken, the roll was called. Lynch won—Blaine had lost—by a margin of forty votes.

So for the moment, for one exhilarating, fleeting afternoon, it looked as if Blaine might be stopped after all. Certainly, he could not be nominated on the first ballot. In New York the *Evening Post* hailed the all-night efforts of Roosevelt and Lodge as a brilliant flanking movement. *The New York Times* singled Theodore out as not only the most conspicuous of the Edmunds men, but the most effective. But what the vote had actually done was to show that the balance of power was held by the reform contingent, the Edmunds people: the "Plumed Knight" could be stopped, but only if they were to give up on Edmunds and agree to Arthur, or resolve a way to unite the Edmunds and Arthur forces behind some acceptable alternative, such as John Sherman. It was clearly a case of Blaine against the field and the field could win only by uniting, which seemed just about hopeless, given the known preference of the Arthur people for Blaine as their second choice.

That night at the Grand Pacific, as a glee club hired by the Arthur forces paraded about the lobby singing the praises of the President, Theodore went back to work.

Wednesday, June 4, was taken up with routine business. The weather was cloudy and warm. "Young Roosevelt alone was buoyant . . ." The one bit of excitement was a resolution put forth by the Blaine people—an old Conkling resolution from the previous convention—calling for every delegate to pledge in advance his support of the nominee, irrespective of who it might be. It was aimed directly at George William Curtis and Curtis was instantly on his feet. The color was drained from his face, his hands clenched. Curtis had a magnificent voice—a famous voice—and he spoke now with what was described as "electric" intensity: "A Republican I came into this convention. By the grace of God, a Republican and a free man I will go out of this convention." The resolution was withdrawn.

Thursday, June 5, petitions for women's suffrage were read and referred to committee, there to die; the party platform, replete with praise for a high tariff and the gold standard, was read aloud in its entirety by William McKinley. Again the weather was correspondingly gray and dull, and again Theodore was extremely active, "quick, watchful, rather enjoying his brief lease on public life." An Ohio delegate, Joseph Foraker, would later relate that he had found one conference with the indefatigable New Yorker "so trying upon the strength and the mental operations" that he was barely able to make it back to the convention hall that evening for the nominating speeches.

Sixteen nominating speeches were delivered, beginning at 7:35 and lasting more than five hours. Every seat was taken, every

foot of standing room. The night was hot and close and thousands
of little fans were moving in the mellow gaslight. Outside, thousands of people crowded about the building, waiting for whatever
news was shouted down from those inside who were seated in the
last rows of the galleries, up along the line of clerestory windows.

Senator Shelby Cullom of Illinois nominated his colleague
Logan; the principal speaker for Arthur was an elderly unknown
from Troy, New York, named Martin Townsend, who was obviously unprepared; John Sherman was nominated by Foraker of
Ohio; and the two speeches for Edmunds were delivered by John
D. Long, a noted speaker, and George William Curtis. Theodore
thought the speech by Long the finest he had ever heard. It struck
the old theme of the Hayes inaugural: country before party. "We
are here as Republicans, and yet . . . not in the interest of the Republican Party alone. Even in this tumultuous excitement, we feel
that . . . we are here in the interests of the people and all the people—of the country and the whole country." And then Long said,
"Gentlemen, I nominate the Honorable—aye! the *Honorable*—
George F. Edmunds of Vermont."

But the overwhelming, unforgettable event of the night was
the nominating speech for Blaine and what it did to the audience.
No one could remember having witnessed anything comparable. It
was one of the most memorable events in the whole history of
national political conventions. To some it was appalling. Andrew
D. White called it a scene "absolutely unworthy of a convention of
any party, a disgrace to decency." Godkin, from what he was told,
would dismiss it as "a mass meeting of maniacs." Theodore, in a
moment of calm reflection afterward, would concede to Bamie that
it had been "most impressive."

The speaker was a blind man, Judge William H. West from
Bellefontaine, Ohio, a tall, gaunt, white-bearded figure in an ancient blue cloak that reached nearly to the floor, who was led to the
stage and up the steps by a small boy. He "stood looking with his
sightless eyes towards the vast throng," wrote Theodore, ". . . his
voice rang like a trumpet . . ."

He had been in Chicago in 1860, said the speaker. He had
been there when they nominated Abraham Lincoln.

Four and twenty years of the grandest history in recorded
times have distinguished the ascendancy of the Republican
Party. The skies have lowered and reverses have threatened,
but our flag is still there, waving above the mansion of the

Presidency. . . . Six times, in six campaigns, has that symbol of union, freedom, humanity, and progress, been borne in triumph . . .

The cadence was Biblical and he looked as if he might have been present at the Creation.

Gentlemen, the Republican Party demands of this convention a nominee whose inspiration and glorious prestige shall carry the Presidency. . . . Gentlemen, three millions of Republicans believe that the man to accomplish this is the Ajax Telamon of our party, who made and whose life is a conspicuous part of its glorious history. Through all the conflicts of its progress, from the baptism of blood on the plains of Kansas to the fall of the immortal Garfield, whenever humanity needed succor or freedom needed protection or a country a champion, wherever blows fell thickest and fastest, there, in the forefront of the battle, was seen to wave the white plume of James G. Blaine, our Henry of Navarre. . . . Nominate him, and the campfires and beacon lights will illuminate the continent from the Golden Gate to Cleopatra's Needle. Nominate him, and the millions who are now waiting will rally to swell the column of victory that is sweeping on. In the name of the majority of the delegates from the Republican States and their glorious constituencies who must fight this battle, I nominate . . .

But he never completed his sentence. It was as if the huge auditorium had been rocked by an explosion. The noise was horrendous. Delegates were cheering, screaming, stamping their feet, shouting at the tops of their lungs. They climbed onto chairs, leaped and danced about in the aisles, grabbed one another in great bear hugs and went spinning around in circles. There were hats spinning on the tops of canes held overhead, hats flying into the air. Bonnets, coats, canes, umbrellas, thousands of white handkerchiefs, were waving frantically. People were singing, weeping. Flags and banners were being stripped from the walls. The noise went on and on. It was "pandemonium universal and all-pervading," a scene "never equaled and utterly indescribable." And just when everyone's energy seemed to have been spent, somebody came down the aisle and onto the stage carrying a huge American flag on a long staff at the top of which rode a helmet of pink and white roses surmounted by a waving snow-white plume, "the helmet of Navarre."

". . . James G. Blaine of Maine," Judge West was able to exclaim at last, a half hour later, and then "another great roar went up like the noise of many waters, sweeping in great waves of sound around the hall, and the crowd without . . . answered in a muffled roar, which echoed within."

Here and there on the floor, chiefly among the Massachusetts and New York delegations, could be seen small islands of silent men who sat with their arms folded and who, from the looks on their faces, might have been at a funeral.

Nothing said in the other speeches mattered greatly. Everything after the West speech was anticlimactic and by the time it was decided to adjourn, the hour then being past midnight, there was little doubt as to what would happen the next morning.

Yet once again Theodore and Lodge worked through the night. As a last-ditch effort they tried to unite the Arthur and Edmunds forces behind John Sherman, working behind closed doors with an Ohio delegate, a political nobody who was also attending his first convention and learning a great deal, Mark Hanna. Another idea was to stampede the convention for Robert Lincoln.

"It is a life or death struggle for the Republican Party in Chicago," wrote the editor of *The New York Times* as the paper was put to bed that night in New York. ". . . [Blaine's] nomination means a disastrous defeat for the Republican Party, and from that defeat the party would never recover except under other leaders and perhaps another name. The party has assuredly fallen upon evil days." The *Times* had decided at this late hour to support Robert Lincoln.

"It quickly degenerates into 'anything to beat Blaine,' " said a Chicago reporter who was on the scene.

It is eager, bitter, and peculiar. Dudes and roughs, civil service reformers and office-holding bosses, shorthairs and college presidents—many men of various kinds of ambition or selfishness join in midnight conferences. . . . Logan refuses all combination. The Lincoln boom collapses. . . . To throw Arthur to Edmunds is impossible. To transfer Edmunds to Arthur is merely to send Logan and Sherman to Blaine. Logan will not have Edmunds; the Edmunds men do not want Logan. Arthur also prefers Blaine to Sherman . . .

The balloting began the morning of the fourth day, Friday, June 6, the hall as packed as the previous night. "It was a tumultuous crowd, but a very good-natured one [noted a Chicago reporter]. . . . Tally sheets are ready, pencils are out, the delegates who are still toiling with the weak and weakening the stubborn, hurry to their places, while the gavel keeps up its heavy staccato."

Blaine did not win on the first ballot, nor the second, nor the third, but he kept gaining, while Arthur held steady and Edmunds kept slipping, so that by the end of the third ballot Blaine needed only thirty-six votes for the nomination. The opposition could only fight for time. Foraker moved to recess, and when a delegate from Pennsylvania challenged him, Theodore was up shouting that the motion was not debatable or amendable. Blaine people pushed their way across the stage to the chairman, surrounding him. Theodore and the Pennsylvania delegate stood on their chairs shouting at each other, but the noise of the crowd was so great it was impossible to hear what they were saying. Theodore, thrashing his arms in the air, "vociferated and gesticulated in a dramatic manner amid the cheers and jeers of the vast audience . . ." No one was seated any longer, most people were standing on their chairs. Theodore was trying to get on stage to ask a question, and getting nowhere until he thrust aside "several officious persons who were attempting forcibly to exclude him." But then William McKinley, the convention's great conciliatory figure, emerged from the crowd on stage, raised a small, pale hand, and "lo! as if Canute had found the sea obedient, the Blaine men drop into their seats, wipe their brows and puff out their short breath. . . . The storm is over."

"The gentlemen representing the different states here have a right to the voice of this convention upon this subject," said McKinley in a resolute voice, "and, as a friend of James G. Blaine, I insist that all his friends shall unite in having the roll of states called . . ."

A vote was taken on the move to adjourn and the Blaine forces voted it down.

So it was on the fourth ballot that Blaine carried the day. Logan released his Illinois delegation, 34 votes, to Blaine. Minutes later Ohio made it final.

The final vote for Blaine was 541; for Arthur, 207. Edmunds ended with only 41. In one of the galleries Carl Schurz took out his watch and remarked to a neighbor, "This is the hour and minute which will go down in history as marking the death of the Republican Party."

The crowd was euphoric, as the night before, "crazy with rapture . . . sheer ecstasy." The band was playing and somewhere in the distance a cannon boomed. There was a motion to make the nomination unanimous and William McKinley came pushing down the aisle to where Theodore and Curtis sat. He urged one or the other to go to the platform and speak for Blaine, but neither would budge. When Curtis shook his head, wrote one of the many reporters who were watching the whole interchange, it was not in anger but in sorrow. A reporter took hold of Theodore by the arm as he started toward the exit. He had nothing to say, Theodore insisted. His face was crimson, his "eyes flashed with indignation behind his gold-rimmed spectacles as he contemplated his first real defeat."

"I decline to say anything . . ."

"But you will certainly support Blaine, will you not?"

"That question I decline to answer. It is a subject that I do not care to talk about."

"Will you not enter the campaign in the interests of the Republican Party?"

"I am going cattle ranching in Dakota for the remainder of the summer and part of the fall. What I shall do after that I cannot tell you."

He brushed off another reporter by telling him to wait a week. To the man from the *Times* he said that by tradition he was expected to support the nominee, but refused to say more.

"A grave would be garrulous compared to me tonight," he told still another man, this one from the Boston *Transcript,* but then suddenly he said that picking Blaine was the greatest possible blunder—*and* that he would support him.

Lodge and Curtis were being besieged with the same questions. "Don't hit a fellow because he's down," Lodge responded. "I think on the whole I may join the machine and keep in politics. This country is in such a hurry it can't stop for reform."

Curtis, in Theodore's presence, said he had been a Republican too long to break from the party now.

The convention ended that evening with the naming of John A. Logan as Blaine's running mate. Logan, a profane, contentious figure, had been an excellent commander in the Union Army and in politics a "thick-or-thin" Grant supporter. He was on the ticket to please the old Conkling crowd and to bring in the soldier vote. It was Logan who, in 1868, had conceived the idea of Memorial Day. Blaine, like Cleveland, had hired a substitute during the war.

•   •

At the White House Chester A. Arthur sent off a cable pledging his "earnest and cordial support." Two weeks later, he would confide to a friend that he was indeed suffering from an advanced case of Bright's disease and did not have long to live.

Jubilant crowds surged through the streets of Chicago most of the night, tying up traffic for blocks around the main hotels. Bonfires burned at several street corners; one, in front of the Vickers Theater, gave off such heat that passing horses were injured. Rockets flashed from housetops; "people—young and old—formed impromptu processions and marched . . . howling like madmen: 'Blaine, Blaine, hurrah for Blaine!' "

Bulletins reported similar demonstrations for Blaine in Pittsburgh, Dayton, Princeton. In San Francisco all business was suspended. The city had "gone wild."

It was also that night, about midnight, according to one of the editors of the *Evening Post*, Horace White, that Theodore came into the Independent committee room at the Grand Pacific, where White was busy composing a dispatch to the New York office, predicting a revolt among the Independent Republicans. Theodore sat down, according to White's account, and White read aloud what he had written, asking at the end if he had made it strong enough. No, he had not, said Theodore, his fury and fatigue having caught up with him. "If I were writing it, I would say, 'any proper Democratic nomination will have our hearty support.' " He thought the best Democrat would be Cleveland.

By midmorning the following day, Saturday, June 7, however, Theodore had packed and checked out. "ROOSEVELT TAKES TO THE WOODS," scoffed a headline in the *World*. Roosevelt and Curtis, alone of all the delegates, had pouted and sulked like whipped schoolboys, said a Midwestern paper.

But then two days later came a report from St. Paul, Minnesota, quoting Theodore as saying, "I shall bolt the nomination of the convention by no means. I have no personal objections to Blaine . . . I believe Blaine will be elected. . . . I have been called a reformer but I am a Republican . . ." He had been interviewed by a reporter for the St. Paul *Pioneer Press* during a stop en route to the Bad Lands. The story was picked up all over the East—the New York *Tribune* carried it on the front page—and so suddenly whether he was in or out of the party, with Blaine or against him, was cause for an uproar.

"ROOSEVELT'S RECANTATION REGARDED AS HIS POLITICAL

DEATH WARRANT," announced the *World*, while the *Evening Post* insisted the whole thing was a hoax and sent off a wire to Medora, in the Bad Lands, calling for a denial. The *Times* decided to say nothing of the reported statement, so certain were the editors that it was false.

"Theodore, beware of ambition!" observed the *Daily Globe* in Boston. The *Evening Transcript* speculated that the story was the work of "some bungling Western reporter" (a remark some readers of the *Transcript* probably considered redundant). "If Mr. Roosevelt's remarks are reported aright," declared the author of a letter to the Boston *Daily Advertiser*, "they are among the most startling effects of modern practical politics."

The so-called repudiation from Medora was dated June 12, an enigmatic telegram saying, "To my knowledge had no interview for publication; never said anything like you report. May have said I opposed Blaine for public reasons not personal to myself."

So cheered were the editors of the Boston *Transcript* by this news that they put out an extra edition.

On June 16 came another telegram, but again there was no telling where he stood on Blaine, whether he was bolting the party or not.

"Just saw my alleged St. Paul interview for the first time. It is wholly fictitious. I never was interviewed on this subject, and never said anything even approximately resembling what was reported."

To the editors of the *World* it was all becoming wonderfully ludicrous.

> The gallant young man rushed away from the Chicago convention full of heat and bitterness. Now that he has expanded his lungs with the rarefied air incident to the high altitudes of the earth and cooled his intellectual brow in the streams which flow down from regions of virgin snow he might confer a favor on mankind by simply saying explicitly whether he is for or against Blaine.

In Boston, meantime, the revolt had begun in no uncertain terms. A meeting of the Massachusetts Reform Club had been called at the Parker House the very next day after the nominations in Chicago. Blaine was denounced, and a committee was organized to work for his defeat in November. Charles W. Eliot and Theodore's old classmate Josiah Quincy were principals in the movement. Most of those Theodore had known on the Harvard faculty were bolting the party (with the exception of Shaler, who was already a Democrat). Both James Russell Lowell and Richard H. Dana, his father's two friends from the '76 convention, were bolting.

In New York the *Times* ran columns of letters from Republicans who were joining the exodus. Schurz, Godkin, and the editors of the *Times* had already renounced Blaine, and so, too, by now had Curtis, who, in spite of what he said at Chicago and for all that the party had meant to him, was unable to go along with such a nominee. On June 14 *Harper's Weekly* came out against Blaine. On July 5, in an editorial, Curtis put the magazine squarely behind Grover Cleveland, and when at Chicago the next week, the Democrats made Cleveland their candidate, the effect among influential Republicans exceeded anyone's expectations. The staunchly Republican *New York Times* announced its support for Cleveland. Henry Ward Beecher was leaving the party. So was Mayor Seth Low of Brooklyn. So was Theodore's senior partner in the publishing business, George Haven Putnam, who called the Republican nominations "a farce and an absurdity, not to say an anachronism." Even J. Pierpont Morgan was bolting. And along with Curtis, Schurz, Godkin, Lowell, Dana—all those with whom the elder Theodore had worked with such verve and conviction in '76— there was even added the name of Benjamin H. Bristow.

Henry Cabot Lodge, who continued to say, as he had at Chicago, that he would stand by the nominee, was being denounced by old friends and admirers as little better than a traitor. He was no longer invited to dinner. Some in Boston who had known him all their lives were refusing even to speak to him. "Mr. Lodge maintains that he has changed his mind," remarked one man. "I call it not a change of mind but a change of soul." Schurz, in a kindly letter of advice, urged Lodge to come to his senses.

You are a young man. You have the great advantage of affluent circumstances. You have the promise of an honorable and useful career before you. . . . The course you are now in danger of following . . . will unite you more and more in fellowship with . . . the ordinary party politicians. The more you try to satisfy them the less you will satisfy yourself.

"Whatever the result of the election, the parties will remain," Lodge answered Schurz with cold logic. "By staying in the party I can be of use. By going out I destroy all the influence for power and good I may possess. . . . If I am to be banned because I vote according to what I believe . . . I will fight against such treatment with all my strength."

Lodge said later that he and Theodore had made a pact before Chicago to stand by the nominee even if it was Blaine, which is precisely what Theodore had told the Chicago *Tribune* he would do, the first morning at the Grand Pacific. It was also what he had told the Boston *Transcript* he would do within an hour after Blaine was nominated. But the last week in June, Lodge received a letter from the Bad Lands dated the seventeenth. "I am absolutely ignorant of what has been said or done since the convention," wrote Theodore, "as I have been away from all newspapers for ten days. I hope soon to be back when I will see you and decide with you as to what we can do."

A day or so later a second letter reached Lodge. He was heading east in another week, Theodore wrote, "as I wish to see you at once. You are pursuing precisely the proper course; do not answer any assaults unless it is imperatively necessary; keep on good terms with the machine, and put in every ounce to win." He was writing under certain difficulties, Theodore said, being in a cattleman's hut and having just spent thirteen hours in the saddle. In a postscript he repeated again that he had not seen a newspaper since leaving Chicago.

· 3 ·

WITHOUT QUESTION, the Chicago convention was one of the crucial events of Theodore's life, a dividing line with numerous consequences. He had carried the fight against Blaine with all that was in him, and if he had lost, if, as he told Bamie, it had been "an overwhelming rout," no one could fault him for not trying, and the impression he had made in this first appearance on the national political stage was phenomenal. He was still all of twenty-five years old; it had been his first national convention. Yet from the first day he had proved himself a force to reckon with, by friend or foe, and the attraction he had for newspaper attention was the kind every politician dreams of. He was a natural politician. He had a born genius for the limelight, for all the gestures and theatrics of politics. In his undersized, overdressed way he had presence. Unquestionably, he had nerve.

He understood the part reporters play and knew exactly how
to play to them. He was wonderful copy, easy—a pleasure—to
write about, however one felt toward him. Also, for many who
wrote about him, there was the underlying excitement of discovery: here was somebody with a future. In his best "notices" he was
portrayed as "fearless," "courageous," "manly," "tireless,"
"plucky and unyielding," as "the most interesting" man on hand,
the "young chief," as "an earnest direct speaker, who will be listened to whenever he speaks." The Chicago *Tribune*, a Blaine
paper, had called him "brilliant" and lauded his gallantry, placing
him alongside Curtis as a standard of moral rectitude and character.
He had been "young Casabianca Roosevelt [who] 'stood on the
burning deck whence all but him had fled' . . ." The Chicago *Times*
called him very simply "the most remarkable young politician of
the day," and then made the point that he had had to get where he
had in politics *despite* his background. "The advantage of being a
self-made man was denied him. An unkind fortune hampered him
with an old and wealthy family."

Those who had fought for Edmunds with him—Lodge, Andrew D. White, John D. Long—had been enormously impressed.
Andrew D. White, the Cornell president, would remember the rest
of his life this "first revelation of that immense pluck and vigor . . .
nothing daunted him."

Possibly the most fervent of all admirers through the week at
Chicago had been George William Curtis, who at lunch one day at
the Grand Pacific is said to have pushed back from the table, placed
his napkin beside his plate, waited a few seconds, then responded
as follows to a reporter's question about "young Roosevelt."

You'll know more, sir, later; a deal more. . . . He has integrity,
courage, fair scholarship, a love for public life, a comfortable
amount of money, honorable descent, the good word of the
honest. He will not truckle nor cringe, he seems to court opposition to the point of being somewhat pugnacious. His political life will probably be a turbulent one, but he will be a
figure, not a figurehead . . . or, if not, it will be because he
gives up politics altogether.

As important as anything, as time would show, was the bond
formed with Lodge. Chicago marked the beginning of the first lasting male friendship Theodore had ever made outside the family;
and like another friendship also formed at that same convention—

between McKinley and Mark Hanna—the political consequences were to be far-reaching.

In some respects Lodge was an improbable choice. Eight years Theodore's senior, he struck most people as unbearably superior and fastidious, cold, calculating, a man who appeared to find any but his own patrician kind extremely distasteful. But Lodge was also fiercely loyal to his friends. He had tremendous energy, wide-ranging interests, a keen mind. He was a scholar, wellborn, wealthy. He loved history and literature, long walks, horses, and Harvard University. He was a fellow member of the Porcellian. By 1884 he had already published five books and yet was ambitious for a political career, despite his obvious handicaps. (He was called "Lah-de-dah Lodge," among other things, and the sound of his voice was once compared to the tearing of a bed sheet.) Furthermore, he liked Theodore and let Theodore know it. They were fellow spirits in many respects and the difference in age made Lodge something of the big brother Theodore had never had. "I can't help writing you," he would tell Lodge some years later in a letter from New York, "for I literally have no one here to whom to unburden myself; I make acquaintances very easily, but there are only one or two people in the world, outside my own family, whom I deem friends or for whom I really care."

And beyond all that Lodge was a fighter. "I have never been able to work so well with anybody before," Theodore would tell him.

So . . . he had been in the roughest political fight of his experience and though beaten badly he had fought in a way no one would forget or that he need ever be ashamed of. He had commanded attention. He had found a friend, given a speech before the largest crowd he had ever seen, heard one speech he thought brilliant, heard another by a blind man whose voice "rang like a trumpet" and swept the convention. He had seen the voice of the people in action and had been both awed and a little appalled. But he had also perceived that Arthur failed because, as he wrote Bamie, Arthur had "absolutely no strength with the people." Probably, he had drawn from the experience the lesson that in politics "strength with the people" is what ultimately counts. He was glad to have been present, he also told her; it had been a "historic scene."

Interestingly, neither he nor any of those who wrote about him at such length ever mentioned the tragedy of February or the burden of grief he carried.

But the overriding importance of the Chicago convention for Theodore was that it marked the point at which he chose—*had* to choose—whether to cross the line and become a party man, a professional politician. He made no formal announcement of his support for Blaine until he had seen Lodge that July, but from all he had already said it is clear he knew what he would do even before leaving Chicago; he only needed, as he later said, time to cool down and think things over. Like Lodge, he was opening himself to heavy abuse from friends and from those admiring members of the press whose favor counted so much to him. Like Lodge, he could be accused of gross ambition, of moral backsliding, of betraying his own high-minded kind. And such condemnation could be extremely painful. Still, as he had said in a letter to Bamie soon after leaving Chicago, Blaine had been the "free choice of the great majority" of Republicans. It had been a fair fight, and while he found Blaine repellent, there was something about stalking off, quitting the game because he lost, that was even more repellent, quite apart from whatever personal ambition he harbored. He had no sentimental attachment to majority rule. "It may be," he told Bamie, "that 'the voice of the people is the voice of God' in fifty-one cases out of a hundred; but in the remaining forty-nine it is quite as likely to be the voice of the devil, or, what is still worse, the voice of a fool." But voice of God, devil, fool, whatever it was, he must abide by it, both out of some fundamental sense of fair play and out of plain determination to have a stake in political power. If he bolted, he knew, he would be finished, out of politics except in some chance or peripheral fashion. He would be an outsider, devoid of that "inside influence" he knew to be essential if he was ever to accomplish anything. He had arrived at the point where he must decide whether he was to be a "mornin' glory" or the real thing.

A writer of the day, Joseph Bucklin Bishop, who kept close watch on Theodore's career and became a later-day confidant, said that with the nomination of Blaine, Theodore confronted "what in many respects was the most serious crisis of his career. . . . He insisted upon deciding the question himself, and in his own way and time."

Similarly, a kinsman, the author Nicholas Roosevelt (son of Cousin West), was to write years later, "After watching American party politics closely for more than half a century, I am of the opinion that if TR had run out on the party in 1884, his political career would have been finished then and there."

Yet apart from the more obvious difficulties of the decision, there was the break it meant for Theodore with so much that his father had stood for. He was severing himself from his father's approach to public service, deserting his father's old friends, all the people his father had so admired. It was now, far more than when he entered the legislature, that he was taking the step his father would almost certainly have disapproved. Had Blaine or Conkling been nominated at Cincinnati in '76, there is little doubt what his father would have done.

Two years before, in February 1882, Theodore had written what, in the context of his decision on Blaine, is a very important letter. It was addressed to an old friend and admirer of his father's, the noted philanthropist and reformer Josephine Shaw Lowell.

I honestly mean to act up here [in the Assembly] on all questions as nearly as possible as I think Father would have done, if he had lived. I thoroughly believe in the Republican Party *when it acts up to its principles*—but if I can prevent it I never shall let party zeal obscure my sense of right and decency. What my success as a politician may be I do not care an atom; but I do wish to be able to end my work here with an entirely light heart and clear conscience.

The most striking and appropriate example of what would most likely have happened to him, had he bolted, is the case of Seth Low. Low refused to support Blaine, maintaining he was not a Republican mayor but the mayor of all the people in Brooklyn. As a consequence he never again received the wholehearted backing of the Republican organization, and his political career never came to much.

Theodore spent three days in New York with Bamie and his child, then several days at Chestnut Hill with the Lees before going to Lodge's summer home at Nahant on Boston's North Shore. The two of them spent a warm Friday evening sitting on a porch looking at the sea and talking until quite late. The following day, Saturday, July 19, Theodore made his statement to the Boston *Herald*.

I intend to vote the Republican presidential ticket. While at Chicago I told Mr. Lodge that such was my intention; but before announcing it, I wished to have time to think the whole matter over. A man cannot act both without and within the party; he can do either, but he cannot possibly do both. . . . I went in with my eyes wide open to do what I could within the party; I did my best and got beaten; and I propose to stand by the result. . . .

I am by inheritance and by education a Republican; whatever good I have been able to accomplish in public life has been accomplished through the Republican Party; I have acted with it in the past, and wish to act with it in the future . . . I am going back in a day or two to my western ranches, as I do not expect to take part in the campaign this fall.

People like William Roscoe Thayer felt "dumbfounded." "We thought of him as a lost leader," Thayer remembered. Owen Wister was convinced Theodore had come under the maleficent influence of Lodge, "his evil genius." At the State Street offices of Lee, Higginson and Company, where he was working as a clerk in the vaults, Wister overheard Henry Lee remark to George C. Lee, "As for Cabot Lodge, nobody's surprised at *him;* but you can tell that young whippersnapper in New York from me that his independence was the only thing in him we cared for, and if he has gone back on that, we don't care to hear anything more about him."

In New York he was denounced as "a crank and a nuisance."

Young men like Mr. Roosevelt owe all their force in politics not to party fidelity [wrote the *Evening Post*], but to popular confidence in their absolute integrity. . . . In fact, the function of such men is to stand firm against bursts of party folly or baseness, until the popular conscience has time to act. . . . There is no ranch or other hiding place in the world in which a man can wait for Blaine and the Mulligan letters to "blow over," for they will never blow over until justice is done.

Alone of those who had bolted, George William Curtis admitted privately that Theodore, in staying with the party, had "played the game fairly."

Theodore seemed immensely relieved, once the step had been taken. "Most of my friends seem surprised to find that I have not developed hoofs and horns," he wrote Lodge jauntily from New York before leaving again for the West. Next, he was writing from his ranch. "You would be amused to see me, in my broad sombrero hat, fringed and beaded buckskin shirt, horsehide chaparajos or riding trousers, and cowhide boots, with braided bridle and silver spurs." He had changed his mind about the fall campaign, he said. Lodge could count on his help.

CHAPTER FIFTEEN

Glory Days

·1·

THE COWBOY AS FOLK HERO was still an emerging phenomenon in the 1880s, at the time Theodore went west. The mythic figure of present understanding had yet to take shape in the popular mind —the success of the dime novel and the new Wild West shows notwithstanding—largely because Owen Wister's novel *The Virginian,* the first true "western," was still in the future, as were the magazine illustrations and paintings of Frederic Remington and Theodore's own books and articles. For it was these three upper-class "Ivy League" easterners, Wister and Roosevelt of Harvard, Remington of Yale, in their efforts to catch "the living, breathing end" of the frontier, who produced what in most respects remains the popular vision of the "real West" and its leading player, the cowboy. In New York, meantime, as Clarence Day relates in *Life with Father,* a small boy of proper upbringing could still be informed by an all-knowing parent that cowboys were no better than tramps, wild fellows who put up with dreadful food and the worst possible accommodations.

But a ranchman (also called cattleman or stockman) was quite another matter, as Theodore was to stress in the first of two books on his time in the West, *Hunting Trips of a Ranchman,* which was to be published in a limited, exceedingly elegant quarto-sized edition priced at an unheard-of $15, and dedicated "To that keenest of sportsmen and truest of friends, my brother Elliott Roosevelt."

Part of the mark of the ranchman was his attire, which, though similar to that of a cowboy, was of considerably finer materials, as Theodore explained. A ranchman's saddle, bridle, spurs, revolver, and the like were all of the first quality. A ranchman spoke (or wrote) of his men, his herds, and the quantity of horses he maintained ("on my own ranch there are eighty"). A ranchman had ample time for hunting and good books. ("No ranchman who loves sport can afford to be without Van Dyke's *Still Hunter*, Dodge's *Plains of the Great West*, or Caton's *Deer and Antelope of America* . . ." Theodore wrote. "As for Irving, Hawthorne, Cooper, Lowell, and the other standbys, I suppose no man, East or West, would willingly be long without them.") It was a life, he said, closely akin to that of the old southern planters.

The great appeal, of course, was the freedom and "vigorous open-air existence." It could do wonders for the spirit, wonders for one's health. It was also quite fashionable at the moment, a point he need not stress to those who would pay the $15 for his book, and it could be extremely profitable, which he did mention in the second and far better book, though with a cautionary reminder that financial disaster, too, was possible. The danger was a severe winter, he wrote prophetically, in advance of the winter of 1886.

Theodore's interest in the Dakota Bad Lands probably began with Commander Henry Honeychurch Gorringe, the former naval officer and audacious entrepreneur who in 1880 masterminded the transporting of Cleopatra's Needle (a 69-foot monolith weighing 220 tons) from Egypt to Central Park, a daring, difficult, and justly celebrated feat. Gorringe had bought up an abandoned government cantonment located on the Northern Pacific Railroad where the railroad crossed the Little Missouri in upper Dakota Territory, just east of the Montana line, in the heart of the northern Dakota Bad Lands. The idea had been to establish a hunting camp for eastern sportsmen, along the lines of Paul Smith's in the Adirondacks. And when Theodore made his initial trip to the Bad Lands in 1883, to get his buffalo, he was to have gone with Gorringe, who for some unknown reason backed out at the last moment.

But it could have also been his publishing partner George Haven Putnam who first told Theodore about the Bad Lands and/or about Gorringe, since it was Putnam who put out *The Great Northwest* for the Northern Pacific Railroad, the book containing the first glowing account of the Bad Lands and their charms. Or if not Putnam, it could have been any of a number of others with an interest in cattle and the West, including his own father-in-law, George C. Lee, since Lee, Higginson and Company, like many eastern banks and investment firms, was much involved in the "beef bonanza." Eastern and European money was going into cattle in a grand way and among those jumping in were numerous Roosevelt family friends and fellow Harvard men. The Wyoming ranch Theodore invested in earlier was known as the Teschemacher & DeBillier Cattle Company. Hubert E. Teschemacher and Frederic DeBillier were in the Class of '82 at Harvard, Owen Wister's class, and their partner Richard Trimble, a classmate of Theodore's and fellow New Yorker, was probably the one who enticed Theodore into that venture and schooled him on the potential profits involved. Teschemacher had decided to become a ranchman after reading a newspaper article in Paris. Trimble was to be long remembered in Wyoming strolling among his cattle with a pet poodle.

A classmate named Sanford Morison was also "pioneering" in Dakota Territory near Edmunds. Robert Bacon, now employed at Lee, Higginson, had put money in the Teschemacher & DeBillier venture, as well as in another Wyoming outfit called Riverside Land and Cattle, which was currently paying dividends of nine and a half percent. Henry L. Higginson himself was involved with the great Union Cattle Company, as was Alexander Agassiz. In New York the Seligmans were major backers of the immensely profitable Pioneer Cattle Company, and Poultney Bigelow's father, the diplomat John Bigelow, was another of those tied into Teschemacher & DeBillier. Abram Hewitt was involved in the Gorringe venture and the biggest and most publicized splash of all in the Bad Lands was being made by a young French aristocrat, one Antoine-Amédée-Marie-Vincent Manca de Vallombrosa, the Marquis de Mores, recently of the French cavalry, who was the husband of Medora von Hoffman, daughter of the Wall Street banker Louis A. ("Baron") von Hoffman.

To be off to one's ranch in the Wild West, or the ranch one had taken a "flier" in, or better still, to be just back from one's ranch, full of stories, looking brown and fit, was all the rage. Ranching was in the aristocratic tradition—requiring courage, horsemanship, offering deliverance from the tedium and pettiness of trade. It was adventurous. It was romantic. Ranching, wrote Theodore, had "little in common with the humdrum, workaday business world of the nineteenth century . . . the free ranchman in his manner of life shows more kinship to an Arab sheik than to a sleek city merchant or tradesman." The cowboys happened also to be much better fel-

lows and pleasanter companions than, say, farmers or farm workers;
"nor are the mechanics and workmen of a great city to be mentioned in the same breath." Cowboys, "except while on . . .
sprees," were "quiet, rather self-contained men, perfectly frank
and simple, and on their own ground treat a stranger with the most
whole-souled hospitality . . ."

Hundreds, possibly as many as a thousand, "dudes" were scattered over the West and more would follow, drawn often by what
Theodore was to write of the life and by his warning that it was a
life soon to vanish. He wrote of the adversities to be prepared for
(broiling heat, hailstorms, rattlesnakes), the kinds of horses to expect (very different from eastern mounts), of the stars at night and
endless reaches of prairie, of the guns to bring.

> Of course every ranchman carries a revolver, a long .45 Colt or
> Smith & Wesson, by preference the former. When after game
> a hunting knife is stuck in the girdle. This should be stout
> and sharp, but not too long, with a round handle. I have two
> double-barreled shotguns: a No. 10 chokebore for ducks and
> geese made by Thomas of Chicago; and a No. 16 hammerless
> built for me by Kennedy of St. Paul, for grouse and plover. On
> regular hunting trips I always carry the Winchester rifle, but in
> riding round near home, where a man may see a deer and is
> sure to come across ducks and grouse, it is best to take the little
> ranch gun, a double-barrel No. 16, with a 40–70 rifle under-
> neath the shotgun barrels.

His description of his own ranch "home" on the Little Missouri was every man's dream of a place in the West.

> In the hot noontide hours of midsummer the broad ranch ve-
> randa, always in the shade, is almost the only spot where a
> man can be comfortable; but here he can sit for hours at a time,
> leaning back in his rocking chair, as he reads or smokes, or
> with half-closed, dreamy eyes gazes across the shallow, nearly
> dry riverbed to the wooded bottoms opposite, and to the pla-
> teaus lying back of them. Against the sheer white faces of the
> cliffs, that come down without a break, the dark-green treetops
> stand out in bold relief. In the hot, lifeless air all objects that
> are not nearby seem to sway and waver. There are few sounds
> to break the stillness. From the upper branches of the cotton-
> wood trees overhead—whose shimmering, tremulous leaves
> are hardly ever quiet, but if the wind stirs at all, rustle and

quiver and sigh all day long—comes every now and then the soft, melancholy cooing of the mourning dove, whose voice always seems far away . . .

Wister called it a "perfect picture." Wister himself would be on his way in 1885, in search of health and big game in Wyoming, as guest of Teschemacher, DeBillier, and Trimble. "This life has a psychological effect on you," Wister would write to his mother. ". . . You begin to wonder if there is such a place as Philadelphia anywhere." His impression of cowboys at that time was that they were "a queer episode in the history of the country" and "without any moral sense whatsoever."

The picture Theodore had given Lodge of his own ranchman's costume was understated. He had spent a small fortune to look the part. Besides the big hat, the buckskin shirt, chaps, bridle, and silver spurs, he had fancy alligator boots, a silver belt buckle, beautifully tooled leather belt and holster, a silver-mounted bowie knife by Tiffany. His silver belt buckle was engraved with the head of a bear; the silver spurs had his initials on them. His Colt revolver was engraved with scrolls and geometric patterns and plated with silver and gold. On one side of its ivory handle were his initials; on the other side, the head of a buffalo to commemorate the one he shot in 1883. The buckskin shirt, all beautifully patterned and fringed, had been made to order by a woman in the Bad Lands and was part of a complete buckskin suit. He gloried in dressing up in his regalia and posing for pictures. He was in the saddle all day, he had told Bamie in June, "having a glorious time here."

Returning from the East in midsummer he brought Bill Sewall along and Sewall's nephew, Wilmot Dow, a rugged and resourceful man in his twenties, who, like Sewall, was an old companion from past hunting trips in Maine. They were to help out, now that he was expanding his operations. Looking the Bad Lands over, the large, homespun Sewall told Theodore it was no country for cattle. Theodore told him he was wrong and knew nothing about it. Sewall, in the privacy of a memorable letter to his family in Maine, described it as "queer country," "a dirty country and very dirty people on an average" (so much for his impression of cowboys). "Tell the boys," he continued, "they are better off there than here unless they could get hold with some rich man as we have and that is hard to do . . . tell all who wish to know that I think this [is] a good place for a man with plenty of money to make more, but if I had enough money to start here I never would come here."

· 2 ·

THE BAD LANDS cattle boom had begun in 1883, the year Theodore
made his first visit and his initial $14,000 investment there. Several
big Texas cattle companies, pushing their herds farther and farther
north in search of new rangelands, had discovered the Bad Lands,
and because the Northern Pacific Railroad had also penetrated the
area just then, and was eager to see it developed, the buildup of
cattle and money came quickly. Experienced cattlemen and eastern and European money people alike saw at once that the Bad
Lands were not all the name implied.

To French-Canadian fur trappers exploring the area a hundred
years before, it had been *les mauvaises terres à traverser*—bad
lands to travel through. It was as if the rolling prairie land suddenly
gave way to a weird otherworld of bizarrely shaped cliffs and hum-
mocks and tablelands, these sectioned and sliced every which way
by countless little ravines and draws and by the broad, looping
valley of the Little Missouri River, which, unlike the Big Missouri,
flowed north and in summer was not much more than a good-sized
stream. It was a region of "startling appearance," "of strange confusion," extending some two hundred miles along the river, a kind
of Grand Canyon in miniature, the work of millions of years of
erosion on ancient preglacial sediments. Stratified layers of clay,
clays as pale as beach sand, were juxtaposed against brick-red
bands of scoria or sinuous dark seams of lignite. Some formations
had the overpowering presence of ancient ruins. The leader of an
early military expedition against the Sioux described the landscape
as hell with the fires out—though in some places, where seams of
lignite had caught fire, the ground literally smoldered.

George Armstrong Custer, who spent several days snowbound
in the Bad Lands en route to the Little Big Horn in 1876, called it
worthless country, and Frederic Remington, when he arrived for a
first look some years after Theodore, saw it as "a place for stratagem
and murder, with nothing to witness its mysteries but the cold blue
winter sky."

In an effort to make it a tourist attraction, the Northern Pacific
tried renaming it Pyramid Park and described the geological curiosities to be found, along with the bracing air, the good shooting,
and opportunity for some real "rough riding."

But the cattlemen saw it differently from everyone. Unlike the other Bad Lands to the south (those of present-day South Dakota, which are geologically quite different), these were green along the river bottoms and green above, on the tops of the tablelands. "What a wondrous country it was for grass!" remembered the veteran cattleman John Clay of his first visit in the summer of '83. There was "grass and more grass" in the bottomlands and up along sweeping valleys: little blue-stem grass, "good as corn for fattening," and curly buffalo grass, "making unexcelled winter feed." Men like Clay and greenhorn money people alike were "dazzled by the prospects." The land was all public domain. The grass was free for the taking. There was water; and the very outlandishness of the terrain promised shelter from winter storms. Possibly fifty thousand cattle were driven into the Little Missouri basin that first summer alone.

The big Texas outfits included the Berry-Boice Cattle Company (the "Three-Sevens" brand), Towers & Gudgell (the "OX"), and the still larger Continental Land and Cattle Company (the "Hashknife"). These were "the real cattlemen." The smaller ranchers were nearly all from the East or from Canada and Europe. They were primed on such newly published authoritative works as *The Beef Bonanza: or How to Get Rich on the Plains,* and they were mostly all young (Bill Sewall, who was not yet forty when he arrived, would be known as "the old Mennonite"). There were the four Eaton brothers from Pittsburgh, who had been among the earliest arrivals; A. C. Huidekoper was from Meadville, Pennsylvania, and was a kinsman of a Harvard classmate of Theodore's, Frank Huidekoper. Gregor Lang and his teenage son, Lincoln, were from Scotland and had the financial backing of Sir John Pender of London. Lloyd Roberts was from Wales; Alfred Benson was an Englishman; Laval Nugent was the son of an Irish baronet; J. A. Van Eeghan, son of a prominent Dutch family, was "wayward but attractive," a fine musician, and could supposedly wire New York for money anytime he wished.

It was at Gregor Lang's ranch that Theodore had put up during his initial visit in '83, and it was from conversations with Lang, Howard Eaton, and two young Canadians named Sylvane Ferris and Bill Merrifield that he had decided to join forces with the Canadians, whose rude cabin beside the Little Missouri was known as the Chimney Butte or, alternatively, the Maltese Cross Ranch. Theodore had handed over a check for $14,000 to buy 450 head of cattle, a small start, but the direct, trusting way he did it

made an impression. "All the security he had for his money," remembered Sylvane Ferris, "was our honesty."

He bought no land, then or later. Like everybody in the area
but the young Marquis de Mores, he was a squatter. And then, after
just two weeks, he had been on his way home, having killed his
buffalo and all but killed his guide, Joe Ferris, a brother of Sylvane.
The chase had carried them pell-mell for seven days over some of
the wildest, most difficult terrain in the Bad Lands. Twice they
found a buffalo and each time Theodore had shot and missed. Exhausted by the pace Theodore set, Ferris kept praying things
would get so bad they would have to give up. It rained incessantly,
but Theodore's joy was not to be extinguished; every new adversity
seemed a refreshment. It was Fresh Pond all over again, Theodore
exclaiming, "By Godfrey, but this is fun!" For two days they had
nothing to live on but biscuits and rainwater. Remembering the
expedition long afterward, Ferris would be no less incredulous.
"You just couldn't knock him out of sorts. . . . And he had books
with him and would read at odd times." When at last he shot his
buffalo, just over the Montana line, Theodore broke into a wild
facsimile of an Indian war dance and handed Ferris a hundred
dollars. "I never saw anyone so pleased in all my life," remembered Ferris.

The dominant figure, the dominant force and center of attention in the Bad Lands, however, was the Marquis de Mores, who
on April Fools' Day in 1883, or six months before Theodore first
appeared on the scene, cracked a bottle of Mumm's champagne
over a tent peg to found the town of Medora, named in honor of his
wife. He had plans far more ambitious than mere cattle ranching,
as he announced; he had come to found an enterprise unlike any
in the West. "It takes me only a few seconds to understand a situation that other men have to puzzle over for hours," said the deadly
serious Frenchman in his nearly perfect English.

He was just Theodore's age and like Theodore a passionate
lover of hunting and the outdoors. Other than that, they had little
in common. The Marquis was tall, spare, and supremely fit, a prod-
uct of St. Cyr and of Saumur, regarded as the finest cavalry school
in the world. He was a superb horseman, a crack shot. Included
with his baggage the day he arrived on the Northern Pacific was a
silver-headed bamboo walking stick filled with ten pounds of lead
—to exercise his dueling arm, it was explained. One held the stick
straight out at arm's length for several slow counts, "thusly." He

was black-haired, dark-eyed, his handsomeness the most obvious thing about him, but it was a handsomeness of the Victorian stage-villain variety, to judge by the pictures we have. His tremendous black mustache was waxed to perfection.

In duels in France, he had already killed two men. Seen heading off on one of his forays along the Little Missouri, he looked like a mounted arsenal—weighed down with two huge Colt revolvers, two cartridge belts, a heavy-caliber rifle cradled in one arm, a bowie knife strapped to one leg. He was as well a professed anti-Semite, a devout Roman Catholic, and a royalist who liked to tell his new neighbors of his aspirations to the French throne and how the fortunes he would pile up in the Bad Lands were to be applied to that purpose.

Theodore seems not to have encountered the Marquis in person until his return in 1884, by which time the Marquis's town and enterprise were much in evidence.

His plan was to revolutionize the beef industry by butchering cattle on the range, there in the Bad Lands beside the railroad, and thus eliminate the cost of shipping live animals all the way to Chicago. That dressed meat could be transported almost any distance in the new refrigerator cars without spoilage had already been demonstrated. So, the Marquis reasoned, why not put the packing plant where the cattle were? It would do away with the Chicago middlemen, which would mean lower prices for the consumer, which in turn would produce an ever greater demand for beef.

He had picked the eastern side of the river for his site, just back from the Northern Pacific's bridge, and directly across from the old cantonment. His wife, it appears, had been provided by her father with an income of $90,000 a year, and this plus backing from his own family gave him, as he said, little worry over finances. He himself would head the Northern Pacific Refrigerator Car Company, while his father-in-law, Baron von Hoffman, was listed as treasurer.

He brought in hundreds of carpenters and masons to build his town and packing plant. He drew up plans, ordered equipment. Within a year or less he had bought up twenty-one thousand acres of land. He bought cattle, brought in twelve thousand sheep, and announced plans to raise cabbages, these to be fertilized with offal from the packing plant and shipped east in his refrigerator cars. He was not wanting in imagination. Another idea was to produce pottery from Bad Lands clays. Yet another was to ship Columbia River salmon from Portland to New York, at a profit of $1,000 a carload according to his estimates.

He had intended originally to make do in a tent until his own house was ready, but finding the tent a bit more inconvenient than expected, he had a private railroad car delivered and put on a siding. "I like this country," he remarked to one of his employees, "because there is room to turn around without stepping on the feet of others."

But in fact he seemed incapable of doing anything without stepping on feet or sensibilities. The West, despite its aura of freedom, its apparent absence of rules and regulations, was a place— an economy, a way of life—based on very definite rules, mostly all unwritten. If there was nothing illegal or even illogical about bringing in sheep or buying up land in country where nobody else owned any or believed in owning any, it conflicted with local custom and was thus, by the prevailing ethic, extremely dangerous. Worst of all, he had begun fencing his land, and when fences were cut, as he had been warned they would be, he as quickly replaced them. When three drunken cowboys shot up the town and vowed to kill him on sight, he prudently took a train back to Mandan to ask the territorial justice of the peace what he ought to do. "Why, shoot," he was told.

The next time the same threesome went on a rampage, the Marquis and his men were waiting by a bend in the river outside of town. It may have been an ambush—cold-blooded murder as Theodore's friends the Langs said—or it may have been self-defense as the Marquis pleaded in court. Either way, one of the three cowboys, a skinny, long-legged nineteen-year-old named Riley Luffsey, was dead with a bullet in his neck. The Marquis was acquitted after two highly publicized hearings in Mandan and resumed his projects as before, acting as though he were unaware of how many now despised him. Medora grew by leaps and bounds, becoming overnight one of the wildest cow towns in the West, the sort of place, as Theodore once remarked, where pleasure and vice were considered synonymous. But it also had a hotel and a brick chapel built for Madame de Mores, a brick house with a picket fence to accommodate father-in-law von Hoffman during his visits, and a breezy little newspaper, *The Bad Lands Cow Boy,* the mission of which was "to preach King Cattle to all men."

"Again and again is the fitness of the Bad Lands for a cattle country brought to our notice [declared the paper in an early issue]. . . . We have yet to hear of a solitary head ever having died in the Bad Lands from exposure."

There are now in the Bad Lands many cattle men who have had experience in every cattle country in the United States [read another item]. . . . We have questioned many of them and the invariable answer has been that nowhere in the United States is there a better cattle country than the Bad Lands.

And what was good for beast was good for man, claimed the editor-publisher, twenty-two-year-old Arthur T. Packard, who was newly graduated from the University of Michigan. "There is a wonderful amount of electricity in this atmosphere," he explained. ". . . This prevalence of electricity is doubtless one cause of the great vitality of anyone who lives in this climate. It takes hard and continued labor to tire a man in this country, and then a rest of a few minutes is sufficient to completely restore his energies. No one feels that lassitude so common in the East."

Most important of all, by the summer of 1884, a gigantic, up-to-date packing plant was in operation. Cattle were being slaughtered; dressed Bad Lands beef was rolling east in the Marquis's new refrigerator cars. It was all but impossible not to be impressed. In New York, in an article about the Marquis and his efforts, the *Times* described Medora as a "thriving, bustling" town with nearly one thousand people and a big future. It had become obvious to everyone "that the foreigner was not so crazy after all." The Marquis, said the *Times*, was a man of "good sense" who ran a "wonderful business," and in time would become "one of the great millionaires of the country."

"Before long some of my wealthy friends in France will come over to build tanneries, glue factories and horn works, and so establish interests that will tend toward a speedy development of the country," a reporter for the *World* was told by the Marquis, who when not in the Bad Lands lived at the fashionable Brunswick Hotel on Fifth Avenue. "My neighbors are all wealthy American ranchers. . . . We all work together and are on the best of terms."

He had completed his own house, "the château," as everyone in Medora called it, and Madame de Morès was in residence much of that summer. In truth, the château was an oversized frame farmhouse. There was nothing especially grand about it, except that it was large (twenty-six rooms), and since it stood in full view of town on top of a bare promontory across the river, it looked even larger.

It was painted a light gray, with red shutters and a red roof. A deep porch stretched around two sides. And once the Madame's big square piano had arrived by train from St. Paul and a staff of twenty servants had taken up their duties, it became in the minds of the local citizenry as much a château as any on the Loire.

The Madame was small and pretty, with fine features and an abundance of dark-red hair. In country almost devoid of women, she would have been talked about endlessly and regarded as a great lady however modest her attainments. But she was a superb horsewoman, spoke several languages (seven, allegedly), painted in watercolors, played Liszt and Verdi on the big piano. A local woman remembered her as "one of the most dignified, stately, and aristocratic women I ever met." Perched sidesaddle on one of the magnificent mounts the Marquis had also had shipped from the East, with her face shielded from the fierce Dakota sun by a huge black "sugar loaf" sombrero, the Madame looked not much bigger than a child. Yet she was reputedly a better shot than her husband (he insisted she was), and on a hunting expedition with him in the Big Horns, she killed three bears, including a grizzly. He had a special hunting coach built for her, equipped with folding bunks, kitchen, china, silver, and linens.

Gregor Lang and his son, who detested the Marquis—it was they who buried Riley Luffsey the day after the killing—had warned Theodore about him, but Theodore maintained a cordial, if somewhat formal, relation, as was befitting two gentlemen. They had attended a meeting of the local stockmen's association held at the railroad depot that June and later took a few days out to go by train together to Miles City, Montana, to volunteer for a vigilante campaign against rustlers and horse thieves, but were turned down because their faces were too well known. Theodore was a dinner guest at the château on several occasions as time passed, and the Marquis and Madame de Mores, we also know, dined with Theodore and Bamie at Bamie's house in New York. Meals at the château were prepared by a French chef, served on the Madame's blue Minton china, and accompanied by selections from her husband's wine cellar. With her travels (she had met the Marquis in Cannes) and culture, not to mention her love of shooting, she must have been a very refreshing note for Theodore. Bamie, years later, would remark only that "Theodore did not care for the Marquis, but he was sorry for his wife . . ."

Theodore had told Bamie in June that the outlook for making a business success of ranching was *"very"* hopeful. "This winter I lost about 25 head, from wolves, cold, etc.; the others are in admirable shape, and I have about a hundred and fifty-five calves. I shall put on a thousand more cattle and shall make it my regular business." With such confidence and excitement in the air at Medora, with the buildup the Marquis was getting in the eastern papers, one could hardly blame him. Like his sisters and brother, he had also by now come into his share of Mittie's trust fund, some $62,500. So at a stroke he more than doubled his investment in cattle, sinking an additional $26,000 into another one thousand head. But while this represented a very serious commitment on his part—a full $40,000, or roughly twenty percent of his total resources—his was still a small operation compared to some others. According to the county census of the following year, he was running some forty-five hundred head of his own, while such outfits as Berry-Boice and Towers & Gudgell were running four to six times that number.

In August, with Sewall and Dow on hand, he established a second ranch, known as the Elkhorn, where he and they could live to themselves, rather than with Merrifield and Ferris at the Maltese Cross. Like the Eaton brothers' Custer Trail Ranch and the Langs' ranch, the Maltese Cross was south of Medora and only seven miles out. The new spot he had found was in the opposite direction, north, or downstream on the river, and more than thirty miles from town, the packing plant, and the railroad. His nearest neighbors would be ten to fifteen miles away. He wanted to be off to himself where he could write, and it was the ranch house Sewall and Dow built for him there, in a clump of cottonwoods by a bend in the river, that he was to describe at length in such passages as the one quoted earlier. It was begun in October, after Theodore had left again for the East, and by Bad Lands standards it was sumptuous, with eight rooms, numerous windows, a stone fireplace, and a cellar that Theodore was to use as a darkroom for processing his photographs. "I designed the house myself," Bill Sewall would remember proudly, "and it was a sizable place, sixty feet long, thirty feet wide, and seven feet high, with a flat roof and a porch where after the day's work Theodore used to sit in a rocking chair, reading poetry."

The other ranchers called him Theodore or Roosevelt; the cowboys, Mr. Roosevelt, as he wished, or Four-Eyes or Old Four-Eyes out of hearing, and their initial impressions were about what one would have expected. Once, in an effort to head off some stray

calves, he immortalized himself along the Little Missouri by calling to one of his cowboys, "Hasten forward quickly there!"

He was only an average rider and never learned to handle a
rope very well, as he would readily admit. But there came a moment one night in a bar across the Montana line in what was then
known as Mingusville (present-day Wibaux) when he stood up and
in quiet, businesslike fashion flattened an unknown drunken cowboy who, a gun in each hand, had decided to make a laughingstock
of him because of his glasses. Theodore knocked him cold with
one punch. As Theodore later explained, the man had made the
mistake of standing too close to him and with his heels close together.

After the "saloon incident," he was looked on with new respect—it "gained him some reputation," as Bill Sewall said. But
more important as time went on, he "did all the regular work of the
cowboy," "worked the same as any man," asking no favors and
never complaining. Sewall, who had known him since he was eighteen, spoke of him in letters home as "a very fair fellow" and "as
good a fellow as ever." "He worked like the rest of us," Sewall
would recall, "and occasionally he worked longer than any of the
rest of us, for often when we were through with the day's work he
would go to his room and write."

Once, seeing one of his ablest cowboys about to put the
Maltese brand on an unbranded stray found on Gregor Lang's
range, Theodore dismissed him on the spot. The cowboy could not
understand. "A man who will steal *for* me will steal *from* me,"
Theodore said. "You're fired."

Sometimes that first year, as Bill Sewall also remembered,
Theodore could become "very melancholy . . . very much down in
spirits." It made no difference what became of him, he told Sewall;
he had nothing to live for.

" 'You have your child to live for,' I said. 'Her aunt can take
care of her a good deal better than I can,' he said. 'She never would
know anything about me, anyway. She would be just as well off
without me.' 'Well,' I said, ' . . . you won't always feel that way . . .
you won't always feel as you do now and you won't always be
willing to stay here and drive cattle . . .' "

Whatever it was Theodore felt for the Bad Lands was quite
beyond Sewall. Anybody who preferred such a place to the East,
Sewall wrote his brother, "must have a depraved idea of life or
hate himself or both."

Theodore saw grandeur and mystery. The Bad Lands were

"dreary and forbidding," they were "as grim and desolate and forbidding as any spot on earth could be," and he felt he belonged. "The country is growing on me, more and more," he had written Bamie in June, "it has a curious, fantastic beauty of its own . . ." The Bad Lands looked, he decided, the way Poe sounds.

The words "loneliness" and "solitude" appear repeatedly in what he wrote. He writes again and again of "great dreary solitude" and "melancholy pathless plains," "the deathlike stillness." "Nowhere," he writes in 1884, "not even at sea, does a man feel more lonely than when riding over the far-reaching, seemingly never-ending plains; and after a man has lived a little while on or near them, their very vastness and loneliness and their melancholy monotony have a strong fascination for him. . . . Nowhere else does one seem so far off from all mankind . . ."

Loneliness and desolation, a sense of exile, were old themes in the literature of the West, literature he knew and loved. Parkman, to whom he would dedicate one of his own later works, wrote in *The Oregon Trail* of "something impressive and awful" about the prairie. Parkman, the first Harvard man to venture beyond the Mississippi and go home to write about it, had found "something exciting in the wild solitude of the place." Parkman, before Theodore was born, had written of "green undulations like motionless swells of the ocean"; Theodore writes that "the grassland stretches out in the sunlight like a sea." "The very shadow of civilization lies a hundred leagues behind," wrote Parkman. "Civilization seems as remote as if we were living in an age long past," Theodore says.

"Oh, bury me not on the lone prairie!" was the cowboys' song.

But in some of what he wrote it is as if Theodore has found a way at last to unburden what he could never talk about. The voice of a mourning dove in his own cottonwoods seems ever "far away and expresses more than any other sound in nature the sadness of gentle, hopeless, never-ending grief." And later, having seen winter there, he would write:

When the days have dwindled to their shortest, and the nights seem never-ending, then all the great northern plains are changed into an abode of iron desolation. Sometimes furious gales blow out of the north, driving before them the clouds of blinding snow-dust, wrapping the mantle of death round every unsheltered being that faces their unshackled anger. They roar in a thunderous bass as they sweep across the prairie or whirl

through the naked canyons; they shiver the great brittle cottonwoods, and beneath their rough touch the icy limbs of the
pines that cluster in the gorges sing like the chords of an Aeo-
lian harp. Again, in the coldest midwinter weather, not a
breath of wind may stir; and then the still, merciless, terrible
cold that broods over the earth like the shadow of silent death
seems even more dreadful in its gloomy rigor than is the law-
less madness of the storms. All the land is like granite; the
great rivers stand still in their beds, as if turned to frosted steel.
In the long nights there is no sound to break the lifeless silence. . . .

But as in the summer following his father's death, this in the
West also had its flights of exhilaration, of pure soaring exuberance more than matching the depths of his other moods. Again
he is incapable of holding himself down. Something within refuses to be subdued. In the West, in his gaudy regalia, on his
horse, he can be something entirely different from the man he had
been.

He was on the frontier he had dreamed of and imagined for as
long as he could remember, living a life free of more than just
fences. More even than Harvard or politics it was a world without
women. Background, family, all the conventions of polite society,
counted for nothing. Nobody knew him; nobody knew his family
or cared particularly. "Everybody in New York has always known
everybody," wrote Edith Wharton, describing "the tight little cita-
del" of the New York they both knew so well. Here everybody was
a stranger and liked it that way. It was customary not to ask too
many questions about a man's past. "What was your name in the
States?" another old song began. In Medora alone there were three
men who went by the name Bill Jones. Antecedents counted for
nothing and Theodore felt himself a new man. "You would be
amused to see me . . ." he had written to Lodge, which was another
way of saying, "You would hardly know me." He felt, he wrote, "as
absolutely free as a man could feel."

Life here was elemental, he said. He was constantly in the
midst of birds and animals. The letters and literary efforts alike are
filled with deer, antelope, buffalo, bighorn sheep, pack rats and
mice, the howling of wolves at night, birds on the wing, birds
stalking the mud flats of the river, a great golden eagle, the gaudy
black-and-white magpies that are so common to the Bad Lands,
meadowlarks that sang like no meadowlarks he had ever heard:
"this I could hardly get used to at first, for it looks exactly like the

Eastern meadowlark, which utters nothing but a harsh disagreeable chatter. But the plains air seems to give it a voice . . ."

Most marvelous of all was his horse, Manitou. Manitou was the
"best and most valuable animal on the ranch," "a treasure," "as
fast as any horse on the river," "very enduring and very hardy,"
"perfectly sure-footed," "willing and spirited." There was never
such a horse as "good old Manitou" and there were never such
mornings as those of the "long, swift rides" over the prairie with
his men, when Manitou carried him on and on endlessly in the
"sweet, fresh air," under a crystal sky . . .

> and the rapid motion of the fiery little horse combine to make
> a man's blood thrill and leap with sheer buoyant lighthearted-
> ness and eager, exultant pleasure in the boldness and freedom
> of the life he is leading. As we climb the steep sides of the first
> range of buttes, wisps of wavering mist still cling in the hol-
> lows of the valley; when we come out on the top of the first
> great plateau, the sun flames up over its edge, and in the level,
> red beams the galloping horsemen throw long, fantastic shad-
> ows. Black care rarely sits behind a rider whose pace is fast
> enough . . .

From the Elkhorn to the Maltese Cross Ranch was a distance
of forty miles. And it was all extremely "rough riding." To get from
the Elkhorn to Medora, following the river, meant crossing and
recrossing the river more than twenty times. One day, as he told
Bamie proudly, he covered seventy-two miles between dawn and
darkness.

"I have been fulfilling a boyish ambition of mine," he tells her
at another point. "We are so very rarely able to, actually and in real
life, dwell in our ideal 'hero land,' " he tells Corinne.

> *What with the wild gallops by day, and the wilder tales by the
> night watch-fires, I became intoxicated with the romance of
> my new life* [Captain Mayne Reid had written]. *. . . It grew
> upon me apace. The dreams of home began to die within me;
> and with these, the illusory ideas of many a young and foolish
> ambition. Died away, too—dead out of my heart—the allure-
> ments of the great city—the memory of soft eyes and silken
> tresses . . . all died away, as if they had never been, or I had
> never felt them!*
>
> *My strength increased both physically and intellectually.
> I experienced a buoyancy of spirits and a vigor of body I had
> never known before. I felt a pleasure in action. My blood*

seemed to rush warmer and swifter through my veins; and I
fancied that my eyes reached to a more distant vision. I could
look boldly upon the sun, without quivering in my glance.

With his horse and his Winchester rifle, he felt like a figure
from other days; and the rifle, like the horse, was the finest thing of
its kind and of greatest importance to him. It was a lever-action
45-75 Winchester (Model 1876) that had been custom made to his
specifications—"stocked and sighted to suit myself." It was engraved with deer and buffalo and antelope, but more than that,
"the best weapon I ever had . . . handy to carry, whether on foot or
on horseback . . . comes up to the shoulder as readily as a shotgun
. . . deadly, accurate . . . unapproachable for the rapidity of its fire
and the facility with which it is loaded." Not since his father presented him with his first gun had anything pleased him so much
and not since the winter on the Nile had he known such shooting.

On August 18 he set out on an expedition to the Big Horns in
Wyoming three hundred miles to the southwest. "How long I will
be gone I cannot say," he wrote Bamie. He took Bill Merrifield
with him and a man named Lebo, who did the cooking and drove
the team, and who at one point made the mistake of calling him
Theodore, instead of Mr. Roosevelt, and was told not to do it again.
They traveled by what Theodore described as a light prairie
schooner drawn by two horses.

Days later, seeing a chance rider who agreed to serve as a mail
carrier, Theodore wrote again to Bamie.

I am writing this on an upturned water keg, by our canvas-
covered wagon, while the men are making tea, and the solemn
old ponies are grazing round about me. I am going to trust it to
the tender mercies of a stray cowboy whom we have just met,
and who may or may not post it when he gets to "Powderville,"
a delectable log hamlet some seventy miles north of us.
We left the Little Missouri a week ago, and have been
traveling steadily some twenty or thirty miles a day ever since,
through a desolate, barren-looking and yet picturesque country, part of the time rolling prairie and part of the time broken,
jagged Bad Lands. We have fared sumptuously, as I have shot
a number of prairie chickens, sage hens and ducks, and a couple of fine bucks—besides missing several of the latter that I
ought to have killed.
Every morning we get up at dawn, and start off by six

o'clock or thereabouts, Merrifield and I riding off among the hills or ravines after game, while the battered "prairie schooner," with the two spare ponies led behind, is driven slowly along by old Lebo, who is a perfect character. He is a wizened, wiry old fellow, very garrulous, brought up on the frontier, and a man who is never put out or disconcerted by any possible combination of accidents. Of course we have had the usual incidents of prairie travel happen to us. One day we rode through a driving rainstorm, at one time developing into a regular hurricane of hail and wind, which nearly upset the wagon, drove the ponies almost frantic, and forced us to huddle into a gully for protection. The rain lasted all night and we all slept in the wagon, pretty wet and not very comfortable. Another time a sharp gale of wind or rain struck us in the middle of the night, as we were lying out in the open (we have no tent), and we shivered under our wet blankets till morning. We go into camp a little before sunset, tethering two or three of the horses, and letting the others range. One night we camped in a most beautiful natural park; it was a large, grassy hill, studded thickly with small, pine-crowned chalk buttes, with very steep sides, worn into the most outlandish and fantastic shapes. All that night the wolves kept up a weird concert around our camp—they are most harmless beasts.

As it turned out, they were gone nearly two months. They did not return until October 5. In that time Theodore shot and killed quantities of duck, grouse, prairie chickens, sage hens, doves, rabbits—more than a hundred birds and small game—as well as elk, deer, and bear. On August 29 he killed two blacktail bucks with a single shot and at a distance of more than four hundred yards. ("I went back and paced off the distance. . . . This was the best shot I ever made.") He killed a blacktail doe, several elk, including a yearling calf, because, he later said, the party was in need of meat.

The blacktail buck, he wrote, was one of the most noble-looking of all deer. "Every movement is full of alert, fiery life and grace, and he steps as lightly as though he hardly trod the earth." The bugling of the elk seemed such a beautiful, musical cry, he wrote, it was "almost impossible to believe that it is the call of an animal." Yet he would kill either at any chance, he would drive himself to his physical limits to kill such animals, and to no one who was a hunter need he ever explain why. He was in the Big Horns when he shot his "best" elk of the trip, "killing him very neatly" at a distance of about seventy-five yards.

That was on September 12, somewhere along a branch of Ten Sleep Creek, at about nine thousand feet, the nearest sign of civilization being the army post at Buffalo, Wyoming. They had left their wagon behind twelve days earlier, packed into the mountains with supplies enough for two weeks. He shot the elk in the late afternoon, removed the head, and then, just before dark, crossing a patch of burned-over forest, he saw the "huge, half-human footprints" of a grizzly. The next day, September 13, he confronted "the great bear" and killed it.

"I was very proud over my first bear," he would write in his *Hunting Trips of a Ranchman*. His brother, he said, had killed tigers in India, but never a grizzly, and though it would be "hard to say" which was the more savage, he himself was sure a grizzly, with its size and strength, its teeth as large as a tiger's, its tremendous claws, could "make short work" of any tiger. And his, he stressed, was a "monstrous" bear, nearly nine feet in height, weighing about twelve hundred pounds. Until then neither he nor Merrifield had ever seen a grizzly, dead or alive.

Everything had happened very suddenly. It was all over in a matter of seconds. They had returned to where the elk was shot and found the bear had been feeding on the carcass during the night. From the size of the tracks they knew the bear was enormous. The tracks strayed off and they followed, moving noiselessly over a pine-needle forest floor, on and on in the half-light beneath tremendous pines. Presently, they picked up very distinct prints in the dust of a game trail that led across a hillside, where the terrain was broken by hollows and boulders. Then at a windfall, the trail veered off into a thicket. They could still follow the tracks, by claw marks on the fallen trees and by bent and broken twigs.

They started slowly into the thicket and all at once there was the bear. Merrifield saw it first and Theodore, his rifle cocked, stepped forward. The bear was not more than twenty feet off, in among some young spruces. It turned and reared up on its haunches, then, seeing Theodore, dropped down again on all fours.

"I found myself face to face with the great bear," he was to tell Bamie, ". . . doubtless my face was pretty white, but the blue barrel was as steady as a rock . . . I could see the top of the bead fairly between his two sinister-looking eyes; as I pulled the trigger I jumped aside out of the smoke, to be ready if he charged, but it was needless . . . as you will see when I bring home his skin, the bullet hole in his skull was as exactly between his eyes as if I had measured the distance with a carpenter's rule."

Between them, in the next few days, he and Merrifield killed three more grizzlies, including a cub that Theodore shot, as he noted, "clean through him from end to end." And then, their horses loaded down with elk heads, antlers, bearskins, they started down out of the mountains and by September 19, having reached their wagon and repacked, set off on the three-hundred-mile trek back to the Bad Lands.

Three of his elk heads were magnificent, exactly the thing for the house at Oyster Bay, as he told Bamie.

So I have had good sport; and enough excitement and fatigue to prevent over much thought; and moreover I have at last been able to sleep well at night. But unless I was bear hunting all the time I am afraid I should soon get as restless with this life [as I] was with life at home.

I shall be very, very glad to see you all again. . . .

Long afterward he was to write, "There were all kinds of things of which I was afraid at first, ranging from grizzly bears to 'mean' horses and gunfighters; but by acting as if I was not afraid I gradually ceased to be afraid."

· 3 ·

IN AUTUMN in the Bad Lands the light is luminous, the immeasurable sky something to take the breath away. Cottonwoods along the Little Missouri are a blaze of gold. Then, in no time at all, autumn is over and winter descends, the Bad Lands are the end of the world.

A fierce north wind was blowing the sand so hard one could hardly see, Bill Sewall wrote as early as October 19, 1884. In December the temperature hit 26 below, then one night it got down to 65 below. In February he was writing his brother in Maine, "I never saw cold weather till this winter." He and Dow had the cabin finished and "my grit is good," Sewall said, "but I believe it is a better country to live in at home than here . . ."

Theodore had gone East the first week in October, immediately upon returning from the Big Horns, to see his Baby Lee, as he called her, and to take a part in the Blaine campaign as he had promised Lodge he would. In November he was back again— Blaine had lost, Grover Cleveland had won, and Theodore, convinced his own political career was finished, had decided that it was definitely as a writer that the world would hear from him. This made his fourth trip to the Bad Lands in little more than a year and his first taste of a Dakota winter. But then he departed again before Christmas, not to return until spring.

In describing the ranchman's "very pleasant" life, Theodore would stress that the ranchman, though bound on occasion to experience hard work and hardship, need not "undergo the monotonous drudgery attendant upon the tasks of the cowboy." A ranchman had time for hunting expeditions of a month or more, for reading or writing. But some ranchmen had also—as he did not say —the choice of not being there at all, which is what he chose more often than not. His own Bad Lands years, as they were to be known, lasted from 1883 to 1886, but in that time he was unable to keep away from New York for more than a few months at a stretch. He crossed the continent on the Northern Pacific time after time, Pullman porters came to know him by name. He never "disappeared into the West," as Wister put it. His time in the Bad Lands, taken altogether, added up to little more than a year and most of his best writing about his home on the range was written at home in the East. As Wister was to write *The Virginian* in Charleston, South Carolina, and Remington to do much of his best work in a studio in suburban New Rochelle, New York, so Theodore was to write of raging Dakota blizzards and spring roundups in his "house on the hill" at Oyster Bay. As it was for Wister and Remington, the West for Theodore was a fountain of inspiration, and it was not the length of time he spent there that mattered, but the intensity of the experience.

The most immediate and important benefit of his time in the Bad Lands was what it did to restore him in body and spirit. But he had also found a subject and, with it, found he could write as he had not before—not certainly in his naval history—with life and feeling. Some of his writing on the West was to be repetitious and overly sentimental. Still the scenes and events he pictured were drawn from direct experience, from real people, real places, all closely observed. If he was never really a cowboy, but (as he stressed) a ranchman, and largely an absentee ranchman at that, he did take what he saw greatly to heart, recognizing also that he had arrived at the very last hour, that the "great free ranches," "the pleasantest, healthiest, and most exciting kind of life an American could live," were about to vanish forever.

•   •

Returning in mid-April for a stay of two months, he "put on" another thousand head of cattle (at a cost of another $12,500), lunched with the Marquis at the château (they discussed the rigors of the Meadow Brook hunt), and then in mid-May he started south with his "outfit" to take part in his first spring roundup, as rugged a physical test as he had ever been put through in his life and the best chance he had had thus far to see cowboys in action.

"Invariably he was right on the job holding his own with the best of them . . . with all his natural intensiveness," Lincoln Lang remembered. "Riding circle twice a day, often taking the outer swing, taking his turn on day-herd or night-guard duty, helping with the cutting-out operations, branding calves . . . he was in the saddle all of eighteen hours per day . . . like the rest of us . . ." After a time, as he himself recalled, "all strangeness . . . passed off, the attitude of my fellow cowpunchers being one of friendly forgiveness even toward my spectacles."

The roundup involved the Langs, the Eatons, the Huidekoper outfit, the "Three-Sevens," and the "OX," every ranch big or small in the Little Missouri basin, a hundred men or more, nearly a thousand horses, thousands upon thousands of cattle, taking in a territory of perhaps ten thousand square miles. It was, as A. C. Huidekoper remembered, "a very vivid affair . . . like a reunion . . . There is a great deal of life. . . . The ponies are fresh and some buck hard, the men shout, 'Stay by him,' 'Go to him,' and if a man is thrown they shout with glee." Breakfast was at three in the morning, dinner about ten o'clock in the morning.

By custom, the men drew straws for their horses at the start of the day and the morning Theodore drew a mean, bucking horse he climbed on and, as Lincoln Lang said, "gave us all an exhibition of the stuff he was made of . . . he had his grip and like grim death he hung on. . . . Hat, glasses, six-shooter, everything unanchored about him took the count. But there was no breaking his grip . . . he stuck . . ."

"I rode him all the way from the tip of his ear to the end of his tail," Theodore later remarked.

Thrown by another horse, he landed on a stone and broke a rib. Still another horse pitched over backward on him and broke something in the point of his shoulder, "so that it was some weeks before I could raise the arm freely." Still he kept on, saying nothing of the pain. He appears never to have excused himself for any reason from any part of the work. He was "very thorough in whatever work was assigned to him [and] . . . game to the core," remembered John Goodall, one of the Marquis's men, who was foreman of the roundup. "He would grab a calf or a cow and help drag it right into the fire to be branded," Bill Merrifield recalled. "He could rassle a calf just as good as anybody. He used to be all over dirt from head to foot."

Some days he rode as much as a hundred miles. The dust and heat were terrific. On stifling hot evenings the mosquitoes would rise from the river bottoms in great clouds to make the nights "one long torture" for men and horses. One night in early June, when the roundup had reached a point a little south of the Maltese Cross, a lightning storm stampeded the herd. Theodore was among those on night duty and there was nothing a cowboy dreaded more, nothing so dangerous as a stampede at night.

For a minute or two I could make out nothing except the dark forms of the beasts running on every side of me, and I should have been very sorry if my horse had stumbled, for those behind would have trodden me down. Then the herd split, part going to one side, while the other part seemingly kept straight ahead, and I galloped as hard as ever beside them. I was trying to reach the point—the leading animals—in order to turn them, when suddenly there was a tremendous splashing in front. I could dimly make out that the cattle immediately ahead and to one side of me were disappearing, and the next moment the horse and I went off a cut bank into the Little Missouri. I bent away back in the saddle, and though the horse almost went down he just recovered himself, and, plunging and struggling through water and quicksand, we made the other side. . . . I galloped hard through a bottom covered with big cottonwood trees, and stopped the part of the herd that I was with, but very soon they broke on me again, and repeated this twice. Finally toward morning the few I had left came to a halt.

It had been raining hard for some time. I got off my horse and leaned against a tree, but before long the infernal cattle started on again, and I had to ride after them. Dawn came soon after this, and I was able to make out where I was and head the cattle back, collecting other little bunches as I went. After a while I came on a cowboy on foot carrying his saddle on his head. . . . His horse had gone full speed into a tree and killed itself, the man, however, not being hurt. I could not help him, as I had all I could do to handle the cattle. When I got them to the wagon, most of the other men had already come in and the riders were just starting on the long circle. One of the men changed my horse for me while I ate a hasty breakfast and then we were off for the day's work.

By the time he had finished that "day's work" he had been in the saddle nearly forty hours and worn out five horses. "I can now do cowboy work pretty well," he wrote Lodge a day or so later.

In his next book, *Ranch Life and the Hunting Trail*, most of which appeared first as a series of articles in *Century Magazine*, these illustrated by Remington, he wrote of the cowboy with an appreciation not to be found in the work of previous writers. He was, as Wister said, the pioneer in taking the cowboy seriously. He wrote of their courage, their phenomenal physical endurance. He liked their humor, admired the unwritten code that ruled the cow camp. "Meanness, cowardice, and dishonesty are not tolerated," he observed. "There is a high regard for truthfulness and keeping one's word, intense contempt for any kind of hypocrisy, and a hearty dislike for a man who shirks his work." It was, of course, exactly the code he had been raised on. (Recalling his father years later, he would use very nearly the same words: "He would not tolerate in us children selfishness or cruelty, idleness, cowardice, or untruthfulness.") The cowboy was bold, cared about his work; he was self-reliant and self-confident. Perhaps most important of all, the cowboy seemed to know how to deal with death, death in a dozen different forms being an everyday part of his life.

It was not only to the meadowlark that the plains air gave new voice and spirit. Theodore was looking different, even sounding different from what he had. The change is cited in numerous surviving accounts and appears to have become obvious by the time the roundup ended. He himself was to describe the experience as "superbly health-giving."

The spectacled dude who appeared on the scene the year before had been "a light little feller." "I have seen him when you could have spanned his waist with your two thumbs and fingers," remembered a cowboy named Roberts. From what Bill Sewall wrote, it appears Theodore had suffered from both asthma and stomach trouble that first year, and Bill Merrifield, recalling their hunting trip in the Big Horns, would tell how Theodore "ate heart medicine," whatever that may have been. But after this Bad Lands spring of 1885—the point, by all signs, that marks the final turn in his lifelong battle for health—no such references are to be found again. He is even called "rugged" in an account in a St. Paul paper written in late June as he headed home again. "Rugged, bronzed, and in the prime of health, Theodore Roosevelt passed through St. Paul yesterday, returning from his Dakota ranch to New York and civilization," we read in the *Pioneer Press*. In New York later, in the *Tribune*, another reporter wrote of "his sturdy walk and firm bearing," again attributes not to be found in previous accounts.

Theodore, remembered William Roscoe Thayer, had become "physically a very powerful man. . . . with broad shoulders and stalwart chest, instead of the city-bred, slight young friend I had known earlier."

When Theodore passed through Pittsburgh on the *Chicago Limited* later that summer, on his way back to Medora, another reporter thought he had put on perhaps thirty pounds. "But what a change! . . . The voice which failed to make an echo in the . . . [Albany] capitol when he . . . piped 'Mistah Speakah,' is now hearty and strong enough to drive oxen."

· 4 ·

THE SUMMER OF 1885 the Marquis was indicted again, taken to court still another time on the old Riley Luffsey murder charge, and again, after a travesty of a trial, he got off. But in the meantime, he was kept in jail at Mandan and the story was splashed across the newspapers east and west. Alone, brooding in his cell, the Marquis saw it all as a conspiracy by his business enemies—the Chicago beef trust—to destroy him, and in this he may have been partly correct. But his notion that Theodore, too, had a hand in his troubles was nonsense.

Rumors of bad blood between Theodore and the Marquis had circulated off and on since the time they both arrived in the Bad Lands and these were now picked up by the papers. Sometime that spring, apparently, Theodore and several of his men had delivered a hundred head of cattle to Medora only to find that the Marquis had decided to disregard the agreed-to price. There had been a moment when they stood face-to-face with a number of others looking on. Theodore had asked the Marquis if he had not quoted a higher price the day before and the Marquis said he had, but that there had since been a drop in the Chicago market. Theodore asked the Marquis if he was not going to stick to his original figure, and when the Marquis said no, Theodore said nothing, then turned and ordered that the animals be driven out of the yards and back to the range. Neither man, however, had since expressed any hard feelings over the episode and they had continued to exchange the usual pleasantries.

Numbers of local people claimed later that a showdown between the two had been inevitable all along and were they two figures in a western we would know it had to come. In what actually took place, however, it is the part played by the Marquis that is particularly fascinating, since it is so at odds with the whole violent pattern of his life.

Four days after he was imprisoned at Mandan, the Marquis sent Theodore a letter that Theodore immediately took to be a challenge to a duel. Conceivably the Marquis meant it as just that, but not likely; the whole tone of the letter suggests otherwise. It was dated September 3 and read as follows:

MY DEAR ROOSEVELT,

My principle is to take the bull by the horns. Joe Ferris [Theodore's old hunting guide, now a storekeeper in Medora] is very active against me and has been instrumental in getting me indicted by furnishing money to witnesses and hunting them up. The papers also publish very stupid accounts of our quarrelling—I sent you the paper to N.Y. Is this done by your orders? I thought you my friend. If you are my enemy I want to know it. I am always on hand as you know, and between gentlemen it is easy to settle matters of that sort directly.

Yours very truly,
MORES

I hear the people want to organize the county. I am opposed to it for one year more at least.

Plainly the Marquis wanted Theodore as a friend. Nor would a formal note designed to provoke a duel close with some offhand postscript about another wholly irrelevant subject. In any event, Theodore answered at once that he was emphatically not the Marquis's enemy, but that if the Marquis was threatening him, then he, Theodore, stood "ever ready to hold myself accountable . . ."

But there was no duel because the Marquis kept his head and let the matter drop. Theodore was sure he had called the man's bluff—the Marquis had "backed off," he would later boast. Others, including several who had no use for the Marquis, were equally sure he had done nothing of the kind. "Whatever else is to be said for or against de Mores," wrote Lincoln Lang, "even his worst enemy could not accuse him of cowardice . . ." The Marquis, it was argued, made nothing of Theodore's response because the Marquis had never challenged him in the first place.

Had there been a duel—with rifles, pistols, swords (Theodore wanted Winchester rifles at twelve paces)—almost certainly Theodore would have been killed. So it can be fairly said for the Marquis that his unaccountably cool head in this instance spared Theodore for other things.

Passing through Mandan sometime later, Theodore took time out to go to the jail to see the Marquis and is said to have found him sitting on his bunk calmly smoking a cigarette, but nothing is known of what was said.

Life at the Elkhorn had changed considerably, meantime. Will Dow had gone home to Maine to be married and returned bringing his new bride, as well as Mrs. Sewall and the Sewalls' small daughter, who was the same age as Baby Lee. "We were all a very happy family," Sewall wrote. That was in the summer of 1885. The next year Theodore was at work on another book, this a biography of Senator Thomas Hart Benton, and seemed, Sewall thought, as happy as he had ever known him.

"I miss both you and darling Baby Lee dreadfully . . ." he wrote Bamie. "Yet I enjoy my life at present. I have my time fully occupied . . . so have none of my usual restless, caged wolf feeling. I work two days out of three at my book or papers; and I hunt, ride and lead the wild, half adventurous life of a ranchman all through it. The elements are combined well."

He wished only that Bamie would send on some toys for the Sewall child. He thought a big colored ball, some picture blocks, letter blocks, a little horse and wagon, and a rag doll would be perfect.

But time was running out. The Marquis's empire had already begun to come apart by then, that is, a whole year before the tragic winter of 1886–87. A stagecoach line from Medora to Deadwood proved a failure. The Marquis's sheep turned out to be the wrong breed for the climate, and more than half died. His powerful father-in-law began questioning expenditures, then withdrew his financial support.

Yet none of this seemed to faze the young entrepreneur. Like another celebrated Frenchman of the day, Ferdinand de Lesseps, who was then promoting his doomed attempt at a Panama canal, the Marquis talked only of success and dazzled reporters with still more innovative schemes to come. He would open his own retail stores in New York and sell his Bad Lands beef at three cents a pound below the going price. Good beef at a good price for the workingman was his dream. Stock in his National Consumers Meat Company was listed at $10 a share. His shareholders, he said, were to be the common working people (just as de Lesseps was counting on the common people of France to pay for his canal). The slogan for the bright-red stores, three of which actually opened in New York, was "From Ranch to Table."

But the stock issue failed. Pressures—from the railroad interests, the Chicago packers, the retail butchers—were too strong. Even had the Marquis been a more adroit businessman, it is unlikely he could have survived. It is also true that his range-fed beef simply did not taste as good as beef fattened in the Chicago yards.

The packing plant was shut down in the fall of 1886. It is not known what the venture had cost, and estimates on the Marquis's losses vary from $300,000 to $1.5 million. But it is also possible that he lost nothing at all, such was the eventual market value of his landholdings.

He and Madame de Mores were gone before winter came. The château was left exactly as it was, as though they would return at any time. And Theodore too had departed by then. "Overstocking may cause little or no harm for two or three years," he had written that fall in one of his articles for *Century*, "but sooner or later there comes a winter which means ruin to the ranches that have too many cattle on them; and in our country, which is even now getting crowded, it is merely a question of time as to when a winter will come that will understock the ranges by the summary process of killing off about half of all the cattle throughout the Northwest." There had been little or no rain all summer, the growing time for grass. The range was bone-dry and still more cattle were being driven in from the south; one outfit brought in some six thousand head. Prices fell drastically. Sewall and Dow, shipping off to Chicago what was marketable from Theodore's herd, found the price they received was less than the cattle had cost. So they decided it was time they got out of the cattle business. "Sept. 22, 1886, squared accounts with Theodore Roosevelt," reads the entry in Sewall's diary. By early October the Sewalls and the Dows had departed for Maine.

Storm on top of storm, blinding snows, relentless, savage

winds, the worst winter on record swept the Great Plains. In the
Bad Lands, children were lost and froze to death within a hundred
yards of their own doors. Cattle, desperate for shelter, smashed
their heads through ranch-house windows. The snow drifted so
deep in many places that cattle were buried alive and temperatures
hovered at about 40 below. People locked up in their houses could
only wait and hope that elsewhere conditions were not so bad. A
few who could not wait blew their brains out.

The losses, when they were tallied up in March, were beyond
anyone's worst estimates. Not a rancher along the Little Missouri
had come through with half his herd. The average loss was seventy-
five percent. Theodore, when he finally returned to survey the
damage, called it a perfect "smashup." He rode for three days without seeing a live steer.

He would come back as time went on, every other year or so,
but only for hunting, never again in the same spirit, and he seldom
stayed more than a week or two. All told he had invested $52,500
in cattle, which, added to another $30,000 spent on his cabin, on
wages, travel, equipment, made a total of $82,500. Eventually he
sold off what little he had left in the Bad Lands, added up his losses
and arrived at a figure of $20,292.63. But beyond that, of course, he
had lost the interest on the investment—five percent over a period
of nearly fifteen years—which figured to about $50,000. So the
complete loss was more on the order of $70,000, or in present-day
money, about $700,000.

So the glorious Bad Lands days had lasted all of three years,
and numbers of other ranchers, like Theodore, gave up and went
on to other things. Howard Eaton, for example, resettled in Wyoming, to found one of the best-known dude ranches in the West.

The subsequent career of the Marquis was one most people
who had known him preferred to put out of their minds. Following
a tiger hunt in India, he went home to France to proclaim himself
the victim of a Jewish plot. The Chicago beef trust was now portrayed as the "Jewish beef trust." He turned to politics, launched
a crusade to save France, a blend of socialism and rabid anti-
Semitism, and went parading about Paris at the head of a gang of
toughs, all of them dressed in ten-gallon hats and cowboy shirts.
With the collapse of the French effort at Panama, he joined with
the unsavory Édouard Drumont, a notorious anti-Semite, in an attempt to blame that failure too on the Jews. It was this mania that
led eventually to the Dreyfus Affair, and the Marquis, before he
went storming off to Africa, kept himself in the forefront. His plat

form rantings set off riots, and in a series of duels with important
Jewish army officers he became known as one of the most dangerous duelists in France.

The Marquis was himself murdered in June 1896 by a band of
Tuareg tribesmen in North Africa, where he had set off on a lone,
harebrained scheme to unite the Muslims under the French flag in
an all-out holy war against the Jews and the English. He seems to
have been mourned only by his children and by Madame de
Mores, who remained his stout defender until her dying day.

Once, on the morning of April 11, 1886, the spring before the
disastrous winter, in the little town of Dickinson, forty miles east
of Medora on the Northern Pacific, a young physician, a Vermonter
named Victor Hugo Stickney, had come out of his office about noon
on his way home to lunch when he saw "the most bedraggled
figure I'd ever seen come limping down the street." The man was
covered with mud, his clothes in shreds, and he struck Stickney as
"the queerest specimen of strangeness that had descended on
Dickinson in the three years I had lived there."

> He was all teeth and eyes. . . . He was scratched, bruised and
> hungry, but gritty and determined as a bull dog. He was ac-
> tually a slender young fellow, but I remember that he gave me
> the impression of being heavy and rather large. As I ap-
> proached him he stopped me with a gesture asking me
> whether I could direct him to a doctor's office. I was struck by
> the way he bit off his words and showed his teeth. I told him
> that I was the only practicing physician, not only in Dickinson
> but in the whole surrounding country.
>
> "By George," he said emphatically, "then you're exactly
> the man I want to see. . . . My feet are blistered so badly that I
> can hardly walk. I want you to fix me up."
>
> I took him into my office and while I was bathing and
> bandaging his feet, which were in pretty bad shape, he told
> me the story . . .

The story, one Theodore was to tell many times and one that
was to be told about him for years after he had left the Bad Lands,
was of his last and biggest adventure in the West and may be
summarized briefly as follows. It has the ring of the adventure
stories he had loved so as a boy, but it also happened just as he
said.

Earlier in March, having just returned to the Elkhorn after a

winter in New York, Theodore was informed by Sewall one morning that a boat, a light, flat-bottomed scow that they kept on the
river, had been stolen in the night by someone who had obviously
taken off in it downstream. They suspected the culprit was a man
named Finnegan, who lived upriver, toward Medora, with two cronies of equally bad reputation. So in the next few days Sewall and
Dow put together a makeshift boat, and after waiting for a blizzard
to pass, the three of them took off in pursuit, pushing into the icy
current on March 30, Sewall steering.

It was a matter of principle, Theodore later said. "To submit
tamely and meekly to theft or to any other injury is to invite almost
certain repetition of the offense . . ."

They were three days on the river before catching up with the
thieves, their boat charging along between snow-covered buttes
and weird Bad Lands configurations that looked to Theodore like
"the crouching figures of great goblin beasts." He had brought
along some books to read and his camera, expecting there might be
a magazine article in the adventure. Each man had his rifle. The
second night the temperature dropped below zero.

The next day, at a point about a hundred miles downstream
from where they had started, they spotted the missing boat and
going ashore found Finnegan and his partners, who surrendered
without a fight. ("We simply crept noiselessly up and rising when
only a few yards distant covered them with the cocked rifles.")
From there they spent another six days moving on down the river,
making little headway now because of ice jams, and taking turns at
night guarding the prisoners, who because of the extreme cold
could not be bound hand and foot. Food ran low and the cold and
biting winds continued. But not the least extraordinary part of the
story is that during these same six days after catching the thieves,
Theodore, in odd moments, read the whole of *Anna Karenina*, and
"with very great interest." (Tolstoy was truly a great writer, he
would tell Corinne in a letter written at Dickinson the day after his
encounter with Dr. Stickney. But had Corinne noticed the un-
moral, as opposed to the immoral, tone of the book? "Do you notice
how he never comments on the actions of his personages?" For his
own part Theodore found Anna "curiously contradictory; bad as
she was, however, she was not to me nearly as repulsive as her
brother Stiva; Vronsky had some excellent points. I like poor Dolly
—but she should have been less of a patient Griselda with her
husband.")

At a remote cow camp Theodore was able to borrow a horse

and ride another fifteen miles to the main ranch, at the edge of the Killdeer Mountains, where he got supplies and hired a team, a wagon, and a driver. And then came the roughest part of the escapade. It was agreed that Sewall and Dow would continue downstream with the two boats and that he, Theodore, would go with the three captives overland heading due south some forty-five miles to Dickinson, where he could turn them over to the sheriff. The captives rode in the wagon with the driver; Theodore walked behind, keeping guard with his trusty Winchester. So by the time Dr. Stickney saw him he had walked forty-five miles in something less than two days with no sleep and had at last deposited his prisoners in jail.

When Stickney and others at Dickinson asked why he had not simply shot or hanged the thieves when he first found them and saved himself all that trouble, Theodore answered that the thought had never occurred to him.

"He impressed me and he puzzled me," wrote Stickney years afterward, "and when I went home to lunch, an hour later, I told my wife that I had met the most peculiar and at the same time the most wonderful man I had ever come to know. I could see that he was a man of brilliant ability and I could not understand why he was out there on the frontier."

At Dickinson's Fourth of July celebration that summer, Theodore was asked to be the "orator of the day." It was the first time Dickinson (population: 700) had made an all-out occasion of the Fourth and Dr. Stickney, who in a lifelong career of patching up broken cowboys and delivering babies at remote ranches would become as legendary locally as Theodore or the Marquis, was the presiding officer. The crowd was also the largest ever seen in Stark County and included about half of Medora, its citizens having come over on the same train as Theodore. A parade led by the Dickinson Silver Cornet Band included a wagon drawn by four white horses carrying thirty-eight little girls dressed in white, representing the states of the Union. According to one Medora man, everybody got caught up in the spirit and wanted to be part of the parade, with the result that there was no one left to watch it except two drunks who were beyond watching anything.

Somebody named Western Starr read the Declaration of Independence and the crowd joined in singing "America, the Beautiful." Another speaker, well practiced in oratorical flourishes, spoke in advance of Theodore, his theme the size of the country on its one hundred and tenth birthday; and then it was Theodore's turn.

I am peculiarly glad to have an opportunity of addressing you, my fellow citizens of Dakota, on the Fourth of July, because it always seems to me that those who dwell in a new territory, and whose actions, therefore, are peculiarly fruitful, for good and for bad alike, in shaping the future, have in consequence peculiar responsibilities. . . . Much has been given to us, and so, much will be expected of us; and we must take heed to use aright the gifts entrusted to our care.

The Declaration of Independence derived its peculiar importance, not on account of what America was, but because of what she was to become; she shared with other nations the present, and she yielded to them the past, but it was felt in return that to her, and to her especially, belonged the future. It is the same with us here. We, grangers and cowboys alike, have opened a new land; and we are the pioneers, and as we shape the course of the stream near its head, our efforts have infinitely more effect, in bending it in any given direction . . . In other words, the first comers in a land can, by their individual efforts, do far more to channel out the course in which its history is to run than can those who come after them; and their labors, whether exercised on the side of evil or on the side of good, are far more effective than if they had remained in old settled communities.

So it is peculiarly incumbent on us here today so to act throughout our lives as to leave our children a heritage, for which we will receive their blessing and not their curse. . . . If you fail to work in public life, as well as in private, for honesty and uprightness and virtue, if you condone vice because the vicious man is smart, or if you in any other way cast your weight into the scales in favor of evil, you are just so far corrupting and making less valuable the birthright of your children. . . .

It is not what we have that will make us a great nation; it is the way in which we use it.

I do not undervalue for a moment our material prosperity; like all Americans, I like big things; big prairies, big forests and mountains, big wheat fields, railroads—and herds of cattle, too—big factories, steamboats, and everything else. But we must keep steadily in mind that no people were ever yet benefited by riches if their prosperity corrupted their virtue. It is of more importance that we should show ourselves honest, brave, truthful, and intelligent, than that we should own all the

railways and grain elevators in the world. We have fallen heirs
to the most glorious heritage a people ever received, and each
one must do his part if we wish to show that the nation is
worthy of its good fortune. Here we are not ruled over by
others, as in the case of Europe; we rule ourselves. All American citizens, whether born here or elsewhere, whether of one
creed or another, stand on the same footing; we welcome every
honest immigrant no matter from what country he comes, provided only that he leaves off his former nationality, and remains neither Celt nor Saxon, neither Frenchman nor German,
but becomes an American, desirous of fulfilling in good faith
the duties of American citizenship.

When we thus rule ourselves, we have the responsibilities
of sovereigns, not of subjects. We must never exercise our
rights either wickedly or thoughtlessly; we can continue to
preserve them in but one possible way, by making the proper
use of them. In a new portion of the country, especially here
in the Far West, it is peculiarly important to do so; and on this
day of all others we ought soberly to realize the weight of the
responsibility that rests upon us. I am, myself, at heart as much
a Westerner as an Easterner; I am proud, indeed, to be considered one of yourselves, and I address you in this rather
solemn strain today, only because of my pride in you, and
because your welfare, moral as well as material, is so near my
heart.

On the train back to Medora later in the day, Theodore sat with
Arthur Packard, the editor-proprietor of *The Bad Lands Cow Boy,*
and remarked to Packard that he thought now he could do his best
work "in a public and political way." "Then," responded Packard,
"you will become President of the United States."

What impressed Packard was that Theodore seemed to have
arrived at the same conclusion.

Remembering how it all had ended in the Bad Lands, Bill
Sewall was to write, "We were glad to get back home—gladder, I
guess, than about anything that had ever happened to us, and yet
we were melancholy, for with all the hardships and work it was a
very happy life . . . the happiest time that any of us have known."

Of Theodore's status as things wound up, Sewall said simply:
"When he got back into the world again, he was as husky as almost
any man I have ever seen who wasn't dependent on his arms for a
livelihood. He weighed one hundred and fifty pounds, and was
clear bone, muscle, and grit."

CHAPTER SIXTEEN

Return

· 1 ·

SHE REMAINED "the strong good wise old sister," sole survivor of the original "big people." In January she had turned thirty-one. So she was well established now as a spinster, the role everyone had long since consigned her to. Family and friends spoke of her attributes of character, her poise and wonderful vitality, seldom ever of her looks. "She has no looks," a friend once remarked. "She is very nearly ugly—she is almost a cripple, and yet no one for a moment thinks of those things." She was prized for her wit, her breadth of knowledge, her insights, her strong, logical approach to things. "In many ways hers was the best mind in the family, and her personality one of the most dominant and fascinating," we read in the reminiscences of a Roosevelt of the next generation. There was a subtleness to her not present in her brothers or her sister, she was more of a diplomat, she had more ballast, as it was said. She was stable, capable, a "powerful" figure with a strong sense of duty, and the resources of energy she drew upon, somewhere in her small misshapen frame, seemed greater even than Theodore's. She was constantly busy—"dear busy Bamie"—but more than that her energy and activity stirred others into motion. Anyone around her for long got going, doing things. She liked minding other people's affairs, liked responsibility, and because she was so extremely dependable, she was depended upon time and again.

She was, as another of the next generation would say of her, "intensely on-the-ball." She seemed always to know what was going on, in the world and in the family. She made it her business to know and to keep the others abreast, with letters, clippings, telegrams if necessary. She was the indispensable gatherer and dispenser of vital Roosevelt information, out of thoughtfulness in part, but also because she knew that was what was expected of her and it gave her influence if not exactly control. How would he know anything of importance if it were not for Bamie's correspondence, James Alfred Roosevelt once remarked while traveling abroad, and her letters to Theodore in the Bad Lands had arrived some weeks by the bundle.

She could deal with "situations" better than anyone, the others felt. In time of need or crisis she was the first person they turned to. When Elliott's wife, Anna, gave birth to her first child on October 11, 1884, after months of family worry, because of what had happened to Alice, it was Bamie they wanted on the scene to help.

"Bamie's telegram at 11:30 this morning brought us the joyful news," reads a message from Aunt Anna Gracie. The child had been christened Anna Eleanor—Anna for her mother and for Bamie, Eleanor for her father, Ellie—but she was to be known only as Eleanor and in time would become deeply attached to Bamie, depending on her for the love and understanding she desperately needed and could find nowhere else. Indeed, for the two children born to her two brothers in the year 1884—Theodore's Alice and Elliott's Eleanor, two very individual, very different little girls— Bamie was to be childhood's primary source of kindness, stories, humor, guidance, sympathy, interest, and from what each was to write of her in later years there is no question as to the influence she had on their lives or their utter devotion to "Auntie Bye." (Bye and Bysie were nicknames her father had sometimes used and that Theodore and others used interchangeably with Bamie as time went on.)

In the world of blond, blue-eyed Alice, now approaching age three, there was no more marvelous figure. Except for summers, when she stayed with her grandparents at Chestnut Hill, she was with Bamie constantly, and no one, as she later said, had such importance. "Always Auntie Bye meant more to me than anyone," Auntie Bye was "always the mainstream somehow," it was she who "brought the generations together."

"Auntie Bye provided . . . a great warmth and pooling of the generations. . . . It was *that*."

She used to tell me stories about her, Father's, Uncle Elliott's, and Corinne's childhood, and about Grandfather and Grandmother Roosevelt, what they looked like and the things they did—how Grandfather Roosevelt drove a four-in-hand, how he used to bring them peaches when he came home in the afternoon. . . . She told of the sad, difficult times during the Civil War when Grandmother Roosevelt's brothers were fighting on the southern side, she living in New York with her northern husband. There were stories too about their trips abroad when they were children, of the time when she was in school near Paris during the Franco-Prussian War. I used to make her describe to me over and over the soldiers marching past, singing, on their way to the fighting.

More wonderful still, Auntie Bye would tell the child about her own real mother who was in heaven. "She was the only one who did," Alice remembered years afterward. "You see none of the others ever mentioned her. . . . Oh, she said how pretty she was and how attractive she was and how fond Auntie Bye was of her . . . things of that sort."

"Auntie Bye had a mind that worked as a very able man's mind works," remembered Eleanor. "She was full of animation, was always the center of any group she was with . . . wherever she lived there was an atmosphere of comfort. . . . The talk was always lively . . . and, young or old, you really felt Auntie Bye's interest in you."

To Eleanor she was "one of the most interesting women I have ever known." Alice, in an interview years later, said Auntie Bye would have been President had she been a man—"because she had such determination . . . [and] an *extraordinary* gift with people."

"Her hair was lovely, soft and wavy," remembered Eleanor. "Her eyes were deep set and really beautiful, making you forget the rest of the face, which was not beautiful. . . . To young people . . . she was an inspiration . . ."

If she had a fault it was an instinct for the cutting or caustic remark about those who were perhaps not quite so "on-the-ball" as she, an ability "to stick the knife in" with a word or two, and not without certain pleasure. Yet no one seems to have been damaged as a result. And as Corinne's daughter—her second child, Corinne Douglas Robinson—was to remark, "She was such a tremendous personality that you wanted to be in her favor."

As in childhood, because of her back, Bamie was required still to lie down part of each day. She still wore a piece of ram's wool as a cushion on her back, to ease the discomfort of sitting, and the evidence is that, sitting or standing, she was in pain much of the time, though she never said so.

She read widely, saw a great deal of a few particular friends, visited, entertained constantly, and made one long trip to Mexico and California that spring of 1886, traveling in "the most ideal way," by private railroad car as the guest of Cousin Sally, still among her closest friends, and James Roosevelt, whom she regarded as "the most *absolutely* honorable upright gentleman" she knew. Her best friend was Mrs. Whitelaw Reid—Elizabeth Mills Reid—whose husband owned the *Tribune* and who, somewhat like Bamie herself, would be remembered as a "queer, little dumpy figure, but bursting with vitality and intelligence."

Her joy was in good talk. She was in her element in stimulating company, with friends who traveled, with artists, men of affairs, "people who wrote," Theodore's political friends—"every kind of person," as Eleanor remembered proudly. All the Roosevelts were talkers, but with Bamie conversation was an art form. She was never torrential, as Theodore could be when off on one of his subjects. She often listened more than she spoke. Corinne was more imaginative, mercurial and gregarious like Theodore. Bamie chose her words with care. But she could, by all accounts, draw out the very best in people; even in the dullest guest she could find something and make that person shine under her encouragement. ("I amused myself by drawing the little there was in him out," her father had written Mittie of someone he had met on a train.) But she could also pick up at once on virtually any subject. "She grasped everything immediately," remembered a cousin.

Her letters, it is said, suggest little of the life and originality that characterized her talk. Something happened in conversation that did not on paper. She was somebody people wanted to meet and when they did they opened up to her as they did not to others. Theodore, who was enormously proud of her, kidded her about the "incongruous" circle she attracted, but also saw her as the center of a future salon and hoped, for his own benefit, that she might take that role very seriously.

He called her "the Driving Wheel of Destiny and Superintendent-in-Chief of the Workings of Providence."

Theodore mattered most of all. He gave focus to her life; he was her consuming interest, her favorite subject, her primary means of self-fulfillment. His child, his house, his health, his career, his future, had become uppermost in her life. The house on Madison Avenue was maintained as much for his as for her own use, as his base of operations in New York. "I always insisted that we did not live together," she later explained, "that we only visited one another." That way, she said, a breakup, if it ever came, would be easier for both of them. Her teas and "evenings" were for his benefit often as not; the parties—summer dinner dances, hunt breakfasts—she gave at Sagamore Hill (as he had renamed the Oyster Bay house) were designed to bring him back into society, back to the life he knew.

She wanted him to return to politics. She was certain it was where he belonged and she both encouraged whatever she thought beneficial to his career and discouraged anything she thought potentially detrimental. She strongly encouraged his friendship with Henry Cabot Lodge, for example, and included Lodge now in her correspondence as though he were one of the family. ("Theodore would not be happy out of public affairs," Lodge concurred early in what was to be a lifelong correspondence with Bamie.) When Theodore gave her his account of capturing the thieves, she (with Lodge) strongly advised against his doing it as an article for *Century*, sure that such heroics might strike an eastern audience as a bit extravagant and self-aggrandizing. ("I shall take good care," he promised her, "that the pronoun 'I' does not appear once in the whole piece.")

She felt she was closer to him than anyone. She knew what he was spending on his cattle venture, and like James Alfred, she worried about it; she knew what the Oyster Bay place had cost, having overseen its construction from the start; she knew what was in his checking account, what his bills were, because in his absences she paid them. "Can you send me at once three or four blank checks from my checkbook?" he writes at one point from the West. "I need them immediately. Darling old Bysie, as usual I am bothering you with my affairs."

Politics fascinated her and she had followed every step of his career with intense interest. Moreover, she knew how much that interest meant to him, how few people mattered to him in the way she did and how much he needed her approval of all his exploits. In some letters, such as the one describing his battle on the convention floor at Chicago or the one about the bear hunt, it is as if he carries with him his own proscenium arch and is performing for her alone, his audience of one. "Look how well I am doing," he seems to be saying to her again and again, just as he had done at Harvard when writing to her or to their father.

Possibly more than anyone in the family, she knew how much of himself he withheld from view—the tenderness in him, the overriding attachment to home, to family, how much of the "great little home-boy" he remained at heart.

Women, she knew, did not greatly interest him and this made her role in his life all the more exceptional. He did not enjoy the company of women the way their father had, or as Elliott obviously did. Until that summer, and the mention of a Mrs. Selmes at Mandan, there had been nothing since Alice's death to suggest the slightest interest in any woman beyond the Roosevelt circle. Tilden Selmes was a young lawyer, a Yale man and neophyte rancher; his wife, Martha Flandrau Selmes, was the daughter of a distinguished Minnesota jurist and historian, Charles Eugene Flandrau. Theodore had been a guest at their Mandan home on several occasions in August and September and "the singularly attractive" Mrs. Selmes was somebody he wanted Bamie to know about. "She is, I think, very handsome," he wrote; ". . . she is very well read, has a delicious sense of humor and is extremely fond of poetry—including that of my favorite, Browning, as well as my old one, Swinburne." Other accounts of Mrs. Selmes and several surviving photographs bear him out—she was indeed a vivacious and strikingly beautiful young woman—and unquestionably she impressed him as few women ever had or ever would (he was to refer to her, as time went on, as "the wonderful Mrs. Selmes"), but the fact that there was also a Mr. Selmes would, for Theodore—and doubtless for Bamie also—have precluded any thought of a romantic involvement. The contribution Mrs. Selmes makes to what can be pieced together of the larger story is a recollection, offered years later, of Theodore pacing the floor during one of his visits, muttering audibly that he had no "constancy."

· 2 ·

IN THE LAST DAYS of August 1886 *The New York Times* carried a small social item reporting the engagement of ex-Assemblyman Theodore Roosevelt to Miss Carow of New York and then, on September 5, a retraction, which was doubtless placed in the *Times* by Bamie:

The announcement of the engagement of Mr. Theodore Roosevelt, made last week, and which came from a supposedly
authoritative source, proves to have been erroneous. Nothing
is more common in society than to hear positive assertions
constantly made regarding the engagement of persons who
have been at all in each other's company, and no practice is
more reprehensible.

Theodore was notified as to what had happened and Bamie
waited for his answer. It came by return mail in a letter from Medora dated September 20. What the *Times* had reported was true,
he told her. "I am engaged to Edith and before Christmas I shall
cross the ocean to marry her." How anyone had found out was a
mystery to him. "You are the first person to whom I have breathed
one word on the subject." He had hoped to be able to tell her
before this, but that had been impossible. He would explain everything when he saw her.

I utterly disbelieve in and disapprove of second marriages [his
remarkable letter continued]; I have always considered that
they argued weakness in a man's character. You could not reproach me one-half as bitterly for my inconstancy and unfaith-
fulness as I reproach myself. Were I sure there were a heaven
my one prayer would be I might never go there, lest I should
meet those I loved on earth who are dead. No matter what your
judgment about myself I shall assuredly enter no plea against
it. But I do very earnestly ask you not to visit my sins upon
poor little Edith. It is certainly not her fault; the entire blame
rests on my shoulders.

Bamie could keep Baby Lee, she was told. Nor should she feel
obligated to inform the others; he would take care of that himself
by letter. Meantime, he wanted nothing said to anyone beyond the
immediate family.

Bamie and Corinne were both taken totally unawares by this
news. Nor were they at all pleased.

Edith Carow was, of course, a very known and admired quantity, as close to the family as anyone could be, very like "family,"
no less than ever. She was someone they had both continued to see
on a regular basis, until just that previous spring when Edith's
widowed mother, due to straitened circumstances, sold her house
and departed with Edith and another daughter for an indefinite

stay in Europe. "It makes me quite blue," Corinne had written at the time.

Edith was lovely-looking, with a mind of her own and wide-ranging interests. If somewhat reserved by Roosevelt standards and somewhat disapproving of fashionable society, she had a quiet kind of dignity and a will to match Bamie's, which was the problem. "They didn't want it at all," said Alice years afterward, "because they knew her too well and they knew they were going to have a difficult time with her, that she would come between them and Father."

Doubtless they too wished Theodore had more "constancy." Ideally, by the prevailing, romantic code, he would never remarry —as a testimony of his love for his beautiful dead wife, his first and only great love. Or, at the least, a decent interval of several more years would have been expected, during which the widower brother and the spinster sister could carry on just as they were and quite happily.

He was home by early October. He and Edith, Bamie learned, had been secretly engaged for nearly a year. It had been the previous September in Bamie's front hall that they had met one day by chance, having until then seen little or nothing of each other since Alice's death. Theodore had started calling on her in New York after that—quietly, discreetly, and though he even asked Edith to attend a hunt ball at Sagamore Hill in October, apparently no one imagined there could be anything between them. In November he had asked her to marry him and she had said yes, with the understanding that the engagement would be kept secret until a more propitious moment. He had returned to the Bad Lands in March; in April she sailed for Europe. "What day does Edith go abroad, and for how long does she intend staying?" he had inquired innocently, almost as an afterthought, in a letter to Corinne, the same letter with his observations on *Anna Karenina*, written at Dickinson the day after bringing in the thieves. "Could you not send her, when she goes, some flowers from me? I suppose fruit would be more useful, but I think flowers 'more tenderer' as Mr. Weller would say."

Bamie, whatever misgivings or pain she felt, was ready to stand by him. In the face of his overwhelming good health and high spirits it is hard to imagine her doing anything else. He was ready to embrace life again. He was also being asked by the Republicans to run for mayor of New York, almost from the moment he had his bags unpacked, an offer he at once accepted, to her great delight, even though, as they both appreciated, he had little chance of winning. . . . *Get action! Seize the moment!* It was to be a three-way race. His opponents were the Democrat Abram Hewitt and a Labor candidate, Henry George. Hewitt, distinguished in manner, admired as an "enlightened" businessman, had been a friend of their father's and appeared the likely winner. Henry George was the author of *Progress and Poverty,* famous as the great exponent of the single-tax scheme, and a fiery speaker who drew huge street-corner crowds and gave newspaper editors and propertied people a bad case of the jitters. Theodore set up headquarters at the Fifth Avenue Hotel and Bamie, by all signs, could not have been happier. The office of mayor, since the passage of Theodore's Reform Charter Bill, was one of real consequence.

He was called "the Cowboy Candidate" and the *Times* at one point claimed he was in the lead. "We haven't had campaign headquarters that looked so much like business in this county since ex-President Arthur was chairman of the county committee and carried things with a rush," one party worker was quoted as saying. "It seems like old times and warms the cockles of an old-time Republican's heart. This is just glorious . . ."

So convinced was Theodore that he had no serious chance of being elected that he bought two tickets under false names—Mr. and Miss Merrifield—on the *Etruria,* which was due to sail for England on Saturday, November 6, or four days after the election. Bamie had agreed to go with him to London, where he and Edith were to be married. The only thing she would not agree to was any talk of her keeping the child.

"It almost broke my heart to give her up," Bamie was to recall years later. "Still I felt . . . it was for her good, and that unless she lived with her father she would never see much of him . . ." It was remembering what she had felt as a child for her own father, the knowledge of what his love had meant to her own life, she said, that made her decide as she did.

In a letter to Edith Carow dated October 23, Bamie wrote in a swift, strong, somewhat illegible hand:

MY DEAREST EDITH,
    You will be astonished at another letter so soon, but though of course Theodore writes you of everything, still you wish to hear what I try to write; of the wonderful enthusiasm he certainly inspires; never mind what the results . . . it is astounding the hold that he has on the public. . . . Douglas has

been as always a trump, having organized "the Roosevelt Campaign Club of Businessmen" which brings in many active workers. Theodore breakfasts and sleeps at home where he is very comfortable . . . by half after nine he is in the Headquarters at the Fifth Avenue, never leaving except for lunch and dinner . . . even then he can but spare a short time; he is very bright and well considering the terrific strain which of course will be worse constantly until the second [of November] is past. It is such happiness to see him at his very best once more; ever since he has been out of politics in any active form, it has been a real heart sorrow to me, for while he always made more of his life than any other man I knew, still with his strong nature it was a permanent source of poignant regret that even at his early age he should lose these years without the possibility of doing his best and most telling work; in that there should be the least chance that he might find his hold over the public gone when he once more came before them and this is the first time since . . . [Albany] days that he has enough work to keep him exerting all his powers. Theodore is the only person who had the power, except Father, who possessed it in a different way, of making me almost worship him and now it is such a desperate feeling to realize that in all this excitement I cannot help him in the least except that he knows how interested I am. I would never say or write this except to you, but it is very restful to feel how you care for him and how happy he is in his devotion to you . . . I go back again tomorrow [to Sagamore Hill] to remain over the Hunt Ball. I wish you were to be there this year also as you were last . . . I send you the pieces from this morning's *Times,* they are samples of what appear daily, of course, the favorable side, but those most against him can find nothing but his youth, supposed wealth, and being born a gentleman to say as detrimental. . . .

"Theodore is radiantly happy and we sail on Saturday for England," she wrote on Election Day to Lodge's wife, Nannie.

Edith will be in London and they are to be married there early in December. . . . Edith we have known intimately always. She is very bright and attractive and I believe absolutely devoted to Theodore so I think their future looks most promising. . . . Today is of course politically one of intense excitement to me personally and apparently to New York generally. Theodore, Douglas and a number of men have been in to lunch and tonight I shall simply haunt the streets. . . .

Abram Hewitt was swept into office as expected, and as Bamie later observed, he "made an admirable mayor." Henry George ran second and Theodore, for all the excitement he had generated, finished third. Large numbers of Republicans, fearful that a vote for Theodore might increase George's chances of winning, had voted instead for Hewitt. Historically, it would stand as one of the most interesting campaigns the city had ever seen and at the age of twenty-eight Theodore was the youngest man who had ever been a candidate for mayor. "At least I have a better party standing than ever before," he wrote to Lodge, who had just been elected to Congress.

Friday night, after the horse show, their last night before sailing, Bamie and he worked together until nearly daybreak addressing the last of the engagement announcements.

Afterword

ANNA

In the summer of 1895, to the astonishment of all the Roosevelt tribe, Bamie announced her engagement to Navy Commander (later Admiral) William Sheffield Cowles, a large, dignified, placid man from Connecticut. She was forty, he nearly fifty, and at age forty-three, she gave birth to a son, William Sheffield Cowles, Jr. In the years Theodore was President she established a home on N Street that became known as "the little White House." As Eleanor was to recall, "There was never a serious subject that came up while he was President that he didn't go to her at her home on N Street and discuss it with her before making his decision. He talked things over with her, that was well known by all the family. He may have made his own decision, but talking with her seemed to clarify things for him."

In her middle years Bamie became almost totally deaf, yet few people ever knew since she learned to read lips, and later still, living in Connecticut, she suffered intensely from arthritis, a condition she refused to discuss. Recalling an evening at her Connecticut home, when she sat in a wheelchair talking and laughing with Cousin Sally's son, Franklin, who by then was also in a wheelchair, a family friend remarked, "You felt such *gallantry* in all of them, you know, such humor, such complete elimination of any problem about bodies."

Though devoted to her husband, her own dear "Mr. Bearo," she refused to let him call her Bamie or Bye, only Anna, and her feelings for him were never what they were for her brother Theodore, who remained the center of her universe for as long as he lived.

Bamie died in August 1931, at the age of seventy-six.

THEODORE

With the assassination of William McKinley in 1901, Theodore became at forty-two the youngest President in history and possibly the best prepared. He had by then served six years as a reform Civil Service Commissioner (under Presidents Harrison and Cleveland), two years as Police Commissioner of New York City, as Assistant Secretary of the Navy on the eve of the Spanish-American War, as a colonel in the Rough Riders—and "hero of San Juan Hill"—as Governor of New York, and as Vice President. He was also the first President born and raised in a big city, and the first rich man's son to occupy the White House since William Henry Harrison. He was a well-to-do, aristocratic, big-city, Harvard-educated Republican with ancestral roots in the Deep South and a passionate following in the West, which taken all together made him something quite new under the sun.

As President he was picturesque, noisy, colorful in ways that amused and absorbed the press, worried the elders of his party, and delighted the country. To his admirers he was "the outstanding, incomparable symbol of virility in his time" (Mark Sullivan), "a stream of fresh, pure, bracing air from the mountains, to clear the fetid atmosphere of the national capital" (Harry Thurston Peck), "the most striking figure in American life" (Thomas Edison); while to others, some of whom had once been his friends, he was "that damned cowboy" (Mark Hanna), a man "drunk with himself" (Henry Adams), "an excellent specimen of the genus Americanus egotisticus" (Poultney Bigelow). The cartoonists had a field day. But he was also a President with a phenomenal grasp of history, who spoke German and French (in a style entirely his own) and knew something of the world from having traveled abroad from the time he was a child. More important, he was as able an executive as ever occupied the office. He loved being President, loved the power, for what he could accomplish with it.

He settled the great anthracite coal strike of 1902 by entering the mediation as no President had done before. He initiated the first successful antitrust suit against a corporate monopoly, the giant Northern Securities Company (and when his father's old friend J. P. Morgan came to Washington to demand an explanation, such action served only to harden his resolve). He "took the Isthmus" and built the Panama Canal, and served as peacemaker in the Russo-Japanese War, for which he received the Nobel Peace Prize. And he was openly proud of all his achievements.

As President, the boy who adored hero stories, and who idolized Captain James Bulloch, built a new Navy and sent a fleet of battleships around the world on a good-will mission. As President, the asthmatic child who craved the out of doors—for whom the unspoiled natural world had literally meant life itself—increased the area of the national forests by some forty million acres, established five national parks, sixteen national monuments (including the Grand Canyon), four national game refuges, fifty-one national bird sanctuaries, and made conservation a popular cause. As President, the son of the first Theodore Roosevelt made the White House "a bully pulpit," preached righteousness, courage, love of country, "The Strenuous Life"—which, everything considered, may have been his greatest contribution. Once, when the old family friend Louisa Schuyler asked how he "felt the pulse" of the country, his response was: "I don't know the way the people *do* feel . . . I only know how they *ought* to feel."

Ironically, he who had worried that he might never live up to his father's name loomed so large in his own time that he obliterated his father's name. Only one Theodore Roosevelt was to be remembered, once his father's generation had passed from the scene.

His devotion to the memory of his father, a feeling of his father's presence in his life, remained with him to the end. "My father, Theodore Roosevelt, was the best man I ever knew," he would say. It was to him he felt he must be true. In the study at Sagamore Hill between small portraits of Lincoln and Grant, he hung a large oil portrait of his father. Four duplicate portraits had been done posthumously from a photograph, one for each of the four children, and Theodore placed his so the pale-blue eyes kept steady watch over him at his desk. His first day in the White House following McKinley's death was September 22, his father's birthday. (Had he been alive then, in 1901, the elder Theodore would have been seventy.) "I have realized it as I signed various papers all day long, and I feel that it is a good omen," he remarked to Bamie and Corinne, who with their husbands were his only guests at dinner that evening. "I feel as if my father's hand were on my shoulder."

Among his first acts as President was to have all those Victorian embellishments introduced by Chester A. Arthur, including the fifty-foot Tiffany screen, torn out and the house restored to its original "stately simplicity."

His highest-ranking Cabinet officer, the Secretary of State, inherited from McKinley, was his father's friend John Hay. (In 1905 Theodore named another of his father's friends, Elihu Root, to succeed Hay; when Root resigned in 1909, Theodore filled the position with his Harvard classmate Robert Bacon.)

"It was peculiarly pleasant having you here. How I wish Father could have lived to see it too!" he wrote to Uncle Rob following his inauguration in 1905. "You stood to me for him and all that generation, and so you may imagine how proud I was to have you here." (Uncle Rob was in his seventy-sixth year. Following the death of Aunt Lizzie Ellis, in 1887, he had married Mrs. Minnie O'Shea Fortescue.)

Of his mother Theodore was to say comparatively little. But to some who had known her, he was more a Bulloch than a Roosevelt. The New York *Sun* in 1900 quoted an unnamed New Yorker, a transplanted "old-time southern gentleman" of social prominence: "I have always thought, and others who knew Miss Bulloch in Savannah have quite agreed with me, that it was from his mother that Governor Roosevelt got his splendid dash and energy."

Of Alice Lee, Theodore was to say nothing. Nor, supposedly, was her name ever spoken within the new family he and Edith established. To judge by his *Autobiography* (1913) she never existed; their romance, his first marriage, never happened. Whether this was his doing or Edith's remains an issue of debate among later-day Roosevelts. The one possible explanation to be found in his own writings is a comment in a letter to Corinne concerning a mutual friend whose life had taken a tragic turn.

I hate to think of her suffering; but the only thing for her to do now is to treat the past as past, the event as finished and out of her life; to dwell on it, and above all to keep talking of it with anyone, would be both weak and morbid. She should try not to think of it; this she cannot wholly avoid, but she *can* avoid speaking of it. She should show a brave and cheerful front to

the world, whatever she feels; and henceforth she should
never speak one word of the matter to anyone.

His own brave and cheerful front was what the world knew
him for, what the large proportion of his countrymen most loved
him for. No one seemed to do so much or to enjoy what he did so
thoroughly. Yet his favorite contemporary poet was Edwin Arling-
ton Robinson, whose themes were loneliness and the burden of
personal memory. The robust, quick-stepping, legendary "T.R."
was a great deal more pensive and introspective, he dwelt more on
the isolation and sadness inherent in human life, than most people
ever realized. Black care, for all the phenomenal pace he maintained through life, clung to him more than he let on.

He kept at his writing. In his public career, it is estimated, he
wrote 150,000 letters. He also wrote his own speeches and presidential messages, and more than twenty books dealing with history, literature, politics, and natural history. His *Autobiography* is
particularly interesting if read with a view to all that is left out.
(Not only does he make no mention of Alice Lee or their marriage,
he neglects to mention his sisters by name and devotes all of three
sentences to his mother. He leaves out his race for mayor of New
York—the one resounding political defeat of his early career. He
says nothing of his father's actions at the time of the Civil War, just
as he says nothing about Elliott's tragic life and other lesser family
"failures.")

Judged by almost any criteria, his second marriage was an unequivocal success. Edith, a person of marked intelligence, poise,
and common sense, brought "wonderful balance" to his life. She
was, "in many ways, as formidable a figure as Bamie, or even as
Theodore," said a cousin. "It is curious and notable that few great
men have had closely related to them three women of such exceptional intelligence and gifts as those of Bamie, Corinne and Edith."

The second marriage produced five children—Theodore, Kermit, Ethel, Archibald, and Quentin—to whom their father was
openly, passionately devoted. He read to them at night, told ghost
stories (of which he knew many), joined headlong in their games
(pillow fights, hide-and-seek, running obstacle courses down the
halls of the White House); he bounced with them in the haymow
at Sagamore Hill, led them on long morning excursions on horseback, exactly as his father had done and over the same hills, a half
dozen of their cousins or friends usually joining the cavalcade. "To
be with him was to have fun," remembered one of the cousins, "if

for no other reason than that he so obviously was having a good time himself." "I love all these children and have great fun with them, and am touched by the way in which they feel that I am their special friend, champion, and companion," he wrote Edith's sister. The letters he wrote his children—from Cuba, the White House, Panama, whenever separated from them—were to become famous when published as a best-selling book the year of his death.

Yet there is evidence that being his child could be very difficult. Just before the Spanish-American War, when the family was living in Washington, young Ted, who had asthma, began suffering from severe headaches or "nervous prostration," because, as the family doctor was convinced, his father was driving him too hard. At the doctor's urging, the boy was sent to stay with Bamie in New York, where the headaches and other ailments quickly went away. "Hereafter I shall never press Ted either in body or mind," Theodore wrote Bamie. "The fact is that the little fellow, who is peculiarly dear to me, has bidden fair to be all the things I would like to have been and wasn't, and it has been a great temptation to push him."

Theodore continued to ride, shoot, hike, spar, row, play tennis. He never did kill a tiger, but of the other most fearsome beasts of the wilds he could claim at least one of each—as all the world was made aware. His knowledge of the large animals of North America probably surpassed that of anyone of his day. The last letter he wrote, like the first that we know of, had to do with birds.

A book was about the only thing that could make him sit still and his love of books lasted as long as he lived. He read everything and anything, sometimes two books in an evening, and his favorites —the Irish sagas, Bunyan, Scott, Cooper, the letters of Abraham Lincoln, *Huckleberry Finn*—he read many times over.

The two cousins who had been closest to him in boyhood, Emlen and West, had families of their own close by at Oyster Bay. Emlen was Theodore's financial adviser and West, who was a physician, delivered two of Theodore's children.

His health was not particularly good in later life, appearances to the contrary. He was dogged by all his old ailments, by stomach trouble, insomnia, chest colds, and by asthma from time to time. Poor eyesight was a lifelong handicap. Sailing off to fight in Cuba in 1898, he carried a dozen extra pairs of glasses in his pockets and in the lining of his hat, and a blow suffered during a sparring match in the White House blinded him permanently in his left eye, something about which the public was to be told nothing. He put on weight (he weighed over two hundred pounds when he was President) and as time passed he was bothered with rheumatism or gout, he did not know which. "I am falling behind physically," he told his son Ted as early as 1903.

When he died, in his sleep at Sagamore Hill in the early hours of January 6, 1919, he was sixty years old, yet seemed much older. But by then, since leaving the White House, he had fallen out with his hand-picked successor (Taft); broken up the 1912 Republican National Convention; launched his own Progressive ("Bull Moose") Party; campaigned again for President; been shot in the chest by a fanatic in Milwaukee (his glasses case and a folded copy of a speech in his breast pocket saved his life); lost the 1912 election; he had hunted big game in Africa, flown in a plane, led an exploring expedition in the Amazon jungles (during which he contracted malaria, lost fifty pounds, and again nearly died); campaigned to get the country into the First World War; and suffered the loss of a son, Quentin, the youngest, who was killed in aerial combat behind German lines in 1918.

Theodore was buried with a minimum of ceremony on a bitter cold day in a small cemetery at Oyster Bay, just off the road between Tranquillity and Sagamore Hill. Of the things said in his memory, among the simplest and best is this by a friend since childhood, Edith Wharton:

> . . . he was so alive at all points, and so gifted with the rare faculty of living intensely and entirely in every moment as it passed . . .

ELLIOTT

Elliott's tragic life ended in August 1894, at age thirty-four, after a torturous battle with alcoholism. His marriage had become a shambles, he had been involved in a paternity suit, threatened suicide more than once, and was placed in various institutions in Europe and the Middle West for the "cure," beginning the winter of 1891 when Bamie escorted him to a sanitarium in the Austrian Alps, at Graz. Determined that nothing go amiss, she persuaded the head of the sanitarium to break the rules and let her have a room also, so she could keep watch over him.

In 1892 his wife, Anna, died of diphtheria. In May 1893 his son and namesake, "little Ellie," died of scarlet fever. "Poor Elliott is wandering about New York. Heaven knows where," wrote Edith the following summer. "He rarely spends a night in his rooms . . . drinks a great deal . . . will not come to Sagamore . . . it wears on Theodore dreadfully and if he gets thinking of it he cannot sleep."

Corinne and Douglas Robinson tried to keep track of Elliott, going regularly to his hotel. Theodore eventually gave up on him. "He can't be helped," he told Bamie. Little Eleanor, who was being looked after by her Grandmother Hall, came to visit at Sagamore Hill in the spring of 1894. "Poor little soul," wrote Edith to Bamie, "she is very plain. Her mouth and teeth seem to have no future, but as I wrote to Theodore, the ugly duckling may turn out to be a swan."

In that last year of his life Elliott was living under an assumed name with a mistress on West 102nd Street, "like some stricken, hunted creature," Theodore wrote to Bamie, who was in London. "His house was so neat and well kept," Theodore continued, "with his Bible and religious books, and Anna's pictures everywhere, even in the room of himself and his mistress. Poor woman, she had taken the utmost care of him, and was broken down at his death."

> I only need to have pleasant thoughts of Elliott now [Theodore later wrote to Corinne]. He is just the gallant, generous, manly, loyal young man whom everyone loved. I can think of him when you and I and he used to go round "exploring" the hotels, the time we were first in Europe; do you remember how we used to do it? And then in the days of the dancing class, when he was distinctly the polished man-of-the-world . . . Or when we were off on his little sailing boat for a two or three days' trip on the Sound, or when we first hunted . . .

Eleanor, who had idolized her father, would strive to be as brave and selfless as he had wanted her to be, guided by Bamie and encouraged by Theodore, who, in 1905, while President, gave her away at her wedding to Cousin Franklin, for whom Elliott had once served as a godfather.

CORINNE

The youngest of the four, Corinne lived until February 1933, or long enough to know that another Roosevelt had been elected President. More gregarious even than Theodore, she became a figure and patron in literary circles, and among her own large, loud, spirited family she thrived especially on talk and roars of laughter and huge dinner parties. On an evening when Fanny Smith and her new husband, James Parsons, were going to Corinne's house for dinner, Fanny is said to have advised him, "Now, don't forget! Talk as loudly as you possibly can and answer your own questions!"

While her marriage to Douglas Robinson survived satisfactorily, Corinne never found it in her heart to love him. Like Bamie, her strongest affection was reserved for Theodore, who, she said, "was truly the spirit of my father reincarnate." Together with Bamie after his death, she organized a reconstruction of the 20th Street house as a memorial, complete in every detail, exactly as it was when they were growing up. She lectured on the subject of Theodore Roosevelt, and wrote and published poetry in his honor, as well as *My Brother Theodore Roosevelt*, an adoring book of personal memories.

Like so many others she never ceased to be amazed by her brother or to be inspirited by his power of curiosity, by that delight in so much else other than self, which, with courage, had carried him forward since childhood. Walking beside him on the White House grounds one spring morning she watched him stop, stoop, pick up, and examine a minute feather, which he held between thumb and forefinger. "Very early for a fox sparrow," he said.

Notes

Notes

The following abbreviations have been used throughout these notes:

TR Sr.	Theodore Roosevelt, Senior
MBR	Martha Bulloch Roosevelt
B	Anna Roosevelt Cowles (Bamie)
TR	Theodore Roosevelt
E	Elliott Roosevelt
C	Corinne Roosevelt Robinson
MSB	Martha Stewart Bulloch
ALR	Alice Lee Roosevelt
ARL	Alice Roosevelt Longworth
RBR	Robert Barnwell Roosevelt
(TRC)	Theodore Roosevelt Collection, Harvard University
(TRB)	Theodore Roosevelt Birthplace National Historic Site, New York City
(LC)	Library of Congress
(FDRL)	Franklin Delano Roosevelt Library, Hyde Park, N.Y.
(WSCC)	W. Sheffield Cowles, Jr., Collection (private)
DAB	*Dictionary of American Biography*

All family correspondence cited is from the Theodore Roosevelt Collection unless otherwise indicated.

PART ONE

1. GREATHEART'S CIRCLE

Recollections of life in the house on East 20th Street and heartfelt, often effusive descriptions of Theodore senior are to be found in the later-day writings of all the Roosevelt children but Elliott: Bamie in a series of unpublished reminiscences (TRC); Theodore in his *Autobiography;* and Corinne in *My Brother Theodore Roosevelt* (referred to here as Robinson). Of the many family letters dealing with domestic details perhaps the most revealing are those written by Martha Stewart Bulloch (Grandmamma) to her daughter Susan West (also TRC). Among secondary sources Nathan Miller's *The Roosevelt Chronicles* provides a good general account of family roots and branches.

page

20   "gloomy respectability": TR, *Autobiography,* 8.

20   Goelet garden: B reminiscences.

20   Robert Roosevelt on family origins: It was RBR, in 1903, with his nephew in the White House, who clarified for the public (in a letter to the N.Y. *Sun,* May 25) how the name Roosevelt was to be pronounced. "In English when we try to distinguish the long from the short 'o' we get into trouble. In Dutch they do not. The double 'o' is simply the long 'o'. The word 'Roos' means rose and is pronounced in identically the same way under all circumstances and in all combinations. So the first syllable of the President's name is 'Rose' pure and simple."

21   Aunt Lizzie Ellis and her misadventures: B reminiscences.

22   Robert an Elizabethan: N. Roosevelt, *Front Row Seat,* 15.

22   Robert and the green gloves: interview with Mrs. Philip J. Roosevelt.

22   Robert and Minnie O'Shea: interview with Roosevelt genealogist Timothy Beard.

22   "never put himself forward," "sunshine of his affection": *Theodore Roosevelt* (Sr.). Memorial Meeting, 42, 15.

23   TR Sr. on Robert's attire: TR Sr. to MBR, June 29, 1873.

23   TR Sr. the perfect gentleman: Riis, 11.

23   Mittie passes on the wine: Robinson, 18.

23   "My personal impression": W. Emlen Roosevelt to Hagedorn, Hagedorn files (TRC).

23   TR Sr.'s feelings for his mother: TR Sr. to B, July 22, 1870.

24   Margaret Barnhill Roosevelt and the spirit of *noblesse oblige:* N.Y. *World,* Feb. 11, 1878.

24   Bamie's description of the Union Square house: B reminiscences.

24   "Economy is my doctrine": quoted in Churchill, 104.

24   CVS rules out college: N.Y. *World,* Feb. 11, 1878.

25   "I'm afraid, Theodore": RBR to TR Sr., Aug. 1, 1851 (WSCC).

25   "I have it in mind": RBR to TR Sr., Aug. 30, 1851 (WSCC).

25   "Firstly, Advice": RBR to TR Sr., Feb. 20, 1852 (WSCC).

25   "I scarce know terms": TR Sr. to his mother, Aug. 13, 1851 (WSCC).

26   "He was dressed": TR Sr., Russian journal, Aug. 24, 1851 (WSCC).

26   The gilt Russian and sledge on the square of malachite is one of the numerous original pieces to be seen in the restoration of the 20th Street house. Its value in the eyes of the children is described by TR in his *Autobiography* (page 8).

26   James Alfred's marriage to an Emlen does the family fortune "no harm": P. James Roosevelt to the author.

27   Chemical Bank meets obligations in gold: Cobb, 46. See also, *History of the Chemical Bank*, 111.

27   Broadway Improvement Association: Cobb, 46.

27   Weir Roosevelt responds to *Gallaxy* article: *N.Y. Times*, Apr. 25, 1868.

27   "where such a thing as sentiment": TR Sr. to MBR, Aug. 18, 1853.

27   Bookkeeper's views: TR Sr. to MBR, Aug. 2, 1853.

27   TR Sr. scales the Treasury Building: TR Sr. to MBR, Feb. 2, 1860.

28   "Whatever he had to do": *Theodore Roosevelt* (Sr.). Memorial Meeting, 25.

28   "maniacal benevolence": John Hay to TR Sr., Feb. 4, 1862 (WSCC).

28   "as much as I enjoy loafing": TR Sr. to MBR, June 29, 1873.

28   Twenty thousand homeless children: Brace, 31.

28   Clean bed for five cents: Lynch, 269–70.

28   Brace sees society threatened: *First Report of the Children's Aid Society* (1854), quoted in the *N.Y. Times*, Feb. 21, 1869.

28   Approach taken by the Children's Aid Society: *16th Annual Report of the Children's Aid Society* (1869), quoted in the *N.Y. Times*, Feb. 21, 1869.

29   "troublesome conscience": *Theodore Roosevelt* (Sr.). Memorial Meeting, 26.

29   "He knew them by name": *ibid.*, 24.

29   Friends take out checkbooks: Riis, 447. One foresees saving a thousand dollars: *Nation*, Feb. 14, 1878.

29   TR Sr.'s feelings for New York: TR Sr. to MBR, Sept. 28, 1873.

29   Original charter for the American Museum of Natural History approved in 20th Street parlor: Bickmore, 12.

30   "Professor, New York wants a museum": *ibid.*, 17.

30   TR Sr.'s "rich power of enjoyment": Brace, 325.

30   TR Sr. on horseback: Rev. Henry C. Potter, quoted in the *N.Y. Tribune*, Feb. 18, 1878.

30   "I amused myself": quoted in Putnam, 41.

30   TR Sr.'s fondness for yellow roses: Robinson, 207.

30   "The city is deserted": TR Sr. to MBR, July 10, 1873.

31   "just my ideal": E to TR Sr., Mar. 6, 1875 (FDRL).

31   Morning prayers on the sofa: TR, *Autobiography*, 13–14.

31   Lessons on climbing trees: Robinson, 8.

31   Preachment on accepting the love of others: *ibid.*, 88.

31   "I always believe in showing affection": TR Sr. to B, July 31, 1868.

31   TR Sr. on unselfishness: Robinson, 88.

31   Hatred of idleness: TR, *Autobiography*, 11–12.

31   "never . . . become an oyster": TR Sr. to Mrs. J. A. Roosevelt, Dec. 25, 1851 (WSCC).

32   "I think I did it": quoted in Putnam, 31.

32   "singular compound": *Theodore Roosevelt* (Sr.). Memorial Meeting, 47.

32   Fear of father: TR to Edward Sanford Martin, Nov. 26, 1900, *Letters*, II, 1443.

32   *"Come now, and follow me"*: Bunyan, 269.

32   "never was anyone so wonderful": B reminiscences.

33   "uneasy about her back": MSB to Susan West, Apr. 29, 1858 (?).

33   Care for Bamie: In a letter to Susan West dated Dec. 1858, Grandmamma Bulloch writes: "We get up and have breakfast. At ten, or half past ten, Dr. Davis comes to adjust the apparatus. Then stories must be told or stories read all of the time during the operation to keep her from crying. Under her arms, her back and chest are bathed first with water, and then alum and water to prevent chafing. Then the abscess has to be washed with castile soap and water and greased. . . . Then the Dr. puts on the apparatus again. She then has her lunch and is put to bed to take a little nap. Sometimes she sleeps, sometimes she does not. At one she is taken up and changed, takes her dinner at two, then goes out a little while if the weather is good. When she comes in again it requires constant effort to amuse her and keep her quiet. In the evening about half past seven she goes through the same process with the apparatus as in the morning except Thee fixes her instead of the Dr. Then she is put to bed and I rub her little legs until she goes to sleep."

33   TR Sr. and Bamie: B reminiscences.

33   Charles Fayette Taylor and the "movement cure": article in *The Stethoscope* (published by the Columbia-Presbyterian Medical Center), Dec. 1956; MSB to Susan West, Aug. 22, 1859. See also, DAB.

34   Ram's wool for back: interview with W. Sheffield Cowles, Jr.

34   Bamie's appearance: E. Roosevelt, *This Is My Story*, 57.

34   "Poor little thing": TR Sr. to MBR, May 31 [n.d.].

34   Abraham Lincoln's lap: interview with W. Sheffield Cowles, Jr.

34   TR Sr. and Bamie's photograph: TR Sr. to B, Sept. 10, 1873.

34   "Try to cultivate": TR Sr. to B, undated.

34   Teedie punished: TR, *Autobiography*, 10.

35   "When I put 'We 3' ": TR, *Diaries of Boyhood*, 11.

35   Ellie gives away his coat: E. Roosevelt, *Hunting Big Game*, IX.

35   "ardent" blue eyes: Parsons, 18.

35   "great little home-boy": Robinson, 45.

35   "quiet patrician air": MBR to Anna Gracie, June 14, 1869.

35   "My mouth opened wide": TR to MBR, Apr. 28, 1868, *Letters*, I, 3. This is the earliest known letter by TR.

35   TR's natural history collection: TR, "Record of the Roosevelt Museum" (TRC).

36 TR Sr. walks the floor with TR: TR, *Autobiography*, 15; TR to Edward Sanford Martin, Nov. 26, 1900, *Letters*, II, 1443.

37 Influence of Hilborne West: Robinson, 54.

38 CVS goes to the kitchen: TR Sr. to MBR, Aug. 28, 1853.

38 "careful . . . in chance acquaintances": TR Sr. to E, Jan. 6, 1877 (FDRL).

2. LADY FROM THE SOUTH

With few exceptions almost everything published about Mittie Bulloch Roosevelt has been superficial and misleading. It is mainly in her own unpublished correspondence—letters numbering in the many hundreds to her husband, children, and sister Anna—that she emerges as a person of vivid personality and great interest. Of her children's published recollections the most sympathetic and admiring are those of Corinne in *My Brother Theodore Roosevelt*.

For background details on the Conscription Act and the entire substitute system during the Civil War, the author is indebted to the late Bruce Catton.

page

39 Roosevelts "cling to the fixed": N.Y. *World*, Feb. 11, 1878.

39 CVS sees move uptown as final: *ibid.*

40 James Alfred's fondness for waffles: reminiscences of his son Emlen, private collection of Mrs. Philip J. Roosevelt.

40 Claes Martenszen known as Shorty: Cobb, 9.

40 Rev. Archibald Stobo arrives at Charleston: Pringle, 8; also Wallace, 57.

41 "even a French strain of blood": B reminiscences.

41 Bulloch family history can be found in *The Colonial Records of the State of Georgia*, XV, 1907; J. G. B. Bulloch, *A History and Genealogy of the Families of Bulloch and Stobo and of Irvine of Cults;* B reminiscences; and in the biographical notes provided by Robert Manson Myers in his monumental *The Children of Pride*.

41 Background on Roswell has been drawn from Leckie, *Georgia;* Martin, *Roswell;* and Temple, *First Hundred Years*.

41 Mystery surrounding Archibald Bulloch's grave: Harden, 55.

42 "The relationships in Savannah": Anna Gracie to MBR, Apr. 8, 1858.

43 "Exposure to cold and rain": quoted in Temple, 109.

43 Barrington Hall: Like Bulloch Hall, indeed like most of the old Roswell mansions, Barrington Hall still stands, looks very much as it did in Mittie's day.

44 Corinne Elliott Hutchison lost on the *Pulaski:* Myers, *Children of Pride*, 1559.

44 Story of Bear Bob: TR, *Autobiography*, 7.

44 "It was all so picturesque": B reminiscences.

44 Bulloch slaves: *Seventh Census of U.S., 1850, Georgia Slave Schedule*.

45 Daddy Luke, Mom Charlotte, Toy, and Bess: B reminiscences.

45 Daniel Stuart Elliott kills his "little shadow": *ibid*.

45 Battle between the slave and the cougar: TR, *Hunting Trips*, 22–23.

45 Duel with Tom Daniell: Gamble, 249–56.

46 Gilbert Moxley Sorrel "the best staff officer": quoted in Myers, *Children of Pride*, 1682.

46 "In the roomy old home": Robinson, 10.

46 "none . . . had any particular education": B reminiscences.

47 "more moonlight-white": Robinson, 18.

47 Friends' descriptions of Mittie: condolence letters to B, Feb. 1884 (TRC).

47 Margaret Mitchell's visit to Roswell: Atlanta *Journal*, June 10, 1923.

48 TR Sr.'s first visit to Roswell: B reminiscences.

48 "Does it not seem strange": MBR to TR Sr., June 9, 1853.

48 "I have never interfered": MSB to TR Sr., May 21, 1853.

49 "I promised to tell you": MBR to TR Sr.; also quoted in Robinson, 13–14.

49 "promised to ride back with Henry Stiles": MBR to TR Sr., July 27, 1853; also quoted in Robinson, 14.

50 Dancing past midnight, world "without kisses": MBR to TR Sr., Sept. 22, 1853.

50 "it is a southern young lady": quoted in Putnam, 16.

50 "Capricious": MBR to TR Sr., Sept. 27, 1853.

50 "It may be a southern idea": MBR to TR Sr., Oct. 12, 1853.

50 "how are you going to behave": MBR to TR Sr., Nov. 13, 1853.

50 "how to do *the thing*": MBR to TR Sr., Oct. 12, 1853.

51 Baker recollections: Mitchell interview, Atlanta *Journal*, June 10, 1923.

51 "much else . . . unfortunate": B reminiscences.

51 "I do not think she will get strong": MSB to TR Sr., 1855.

52 "Darling, it would be impossible": MBR to TR Sr., May 1, 1855.

52 "You have proved that you love me": MBR to TR Sr., May 2, 1855.

52 "dreariness reigning everywhere": TR Sr. to MBR, May 1, 1855.

52 "bed does not offer": TR Sr. to MBR, May 6, 1855.

53 Sister Anna laments separation: July 1, 1854; Sept. 1854.

53 Grandmamma's account of TR's birth: MSB to Susan West, Oct. 28, 1858; also partly quoted in Putnam, 22–23.

54 Baby doing splendidly: MSB to Susan West, Nov. 1 and Nov. 3, 1858.

54 "Are me a soldier laddie?": Anna Gracie to MBR, Sept. 9, 1861.

54 Mittie hangs a Confederate flag: TR denied any truth to the story in a letter to Rev. J. L. Underwood. See Underwood, 216.

55 Grandmamma wishes to be buried in a common grave: MSB to Susan West, Nov. 16, 1861.

55 Mittie and Anna send packages: B reminiscences; also MSB to Susan West, Dec. 18, 1862.

56   Letter from Irvine: quoted, MSB to Susan West, Feb. 10, 1863.
56   Mittie breaks with traditional Saturday dinners: Dec. 15, 1861, she writes to TR Sr.: "I went down [to his father's house] yesterday to dinner but, Thee, something occurred there which has made me determine not to dine there again . . . I felt my blood boil . . . I could not touch another mouthful . . . Thee, I wish I could see you tonight."
56   "I should hate to have married into them": Abbott, *Letters of Archie Butt*, 278–79.
56   "You know he does not feel as we do": MSB to Susan West, Nov. 29, 1862.
56   TR Sr. helps with anti-war rally: Churchill, 126.
57   TR Sr. "felt that he had done a very wrong thing": B reminiscences.
57   Corinne sees influence on TR: interview, W. Sheffield Cowles, Jr.
57   War game in Central Park: B reminiscences.
58   Prays for Almighty to "grind . . . troops to powder": Robinson, 17.
58   "poor mechanics" oppose draft: MSB to Susan West, July 14, 1863.
58   "I would never have felt satisfied": TR Sr. to MBR, Jan. 1, 1862.
59   "Teedie was afraid" of a bear: MBR to TR Sr., Nov. 13, 1861.
59   "You must not . . . get sick": TR Sr. to MBR, Dec. 6, 1861.
59   Mittie has "hands full": MSB to Susan West, Nov. 18, 1861.
59   Up "six or seven times": MBR to TR Sr., Dec. 9, 1861.
59   "children deserted by their papa": MBR to TR Sr., Nov. 13, 1861.
59   TR Sr. goes to the White House: TR Sr. to MBR, Nov. 7, 1861.
59   Mistaken for Lincoln at church: TR Sr. to MBR, Nov. 10, 1861.
60   Shops for Mrs. Lincoln's hat: Robinson, 26.
60   TR Sr.'s account of the White House ball is contained in two letters to Mittie, Feb. 5 and Feb. 6, 1862.
60   Gaining political experience: TR Sr. to MBR, Dec. 6, 1861.
60   "utter inability of congressmen": *Theodore Roosevelt* (Sr.). Memorial Meeting, 19.
61   "The delays were so great": TR Sr. to MBR, Jan. 1, 1862; also quoted in Robinson, 22–23.
61   Forty-eight-hour adventure in Virginia: TR Sr. to MBR, Oct. 14, 1862; also quoted in Robinson, 30–31.
61   "hope you will take a good long nap": TR Sr. to MBR, Dec. 19, 1861.
61   TR Sr. arranges for Grandmamma to get through the lines: TR Sr. to MBR, Feb. 14 and Mar. 1, 1862.
62   Wishes he had kept a diary: TR Sr. to MBR, Feb. 27, 1862.
62   "Tell Bamie": TR Sr. to MBR, Nov. 10, 1861.
62   Death of Willie Lincoln: TR Sr. to MBR, Feb. 21, 1862.
62   "I wish we sympathized together": TR Sr. to MBR, Mar. 2, 1862.
63   "Thee is a good young man": MSB to Susan West, Nov. 15, 1862.
63   Mittie risking life or reason: MSB to Susan West, June 23, 1863.
63   Grandmamma on the Russian Ball: MSB to Susan West, Nov. 9, 1863.

64 "too much gaiety"; downstairs, carriages at the door: MSB to Susan West, Dec. 30, 1863.

64 Mrs. Burton Harrison's views on Mittie: Harrison, 278–79.

65 Mittie's exchange with Hay: B reminiscences.

65 "nothing more like a Roosevelt than a Roosevelt wife": interview with Mrs. Philip J. Roosevelt.

66 "If she was only a Christian": MSB to Susan West, Dec. 15, 1863.

66 TR Sr. preferred Mittie in white: letter dated Dec. 27, 1861.

66 Bursts of housekeeping: MSB to Susan West, Jan. 9, 1863.

67 Mittie more economical: TR Sr. to MBR, Jan. 23, 1862.

67 Thinks of her as "one of my little babies": TR Sr. to MBR, June 16, 1873.

67 "loving tyrant": MBR to Anna Gracie, Jan. 12, 1873.

68 "just received your letter": TR to MBR, Apr. 28 1868, *Letters*, I, 3.

68 Mittie amused by prayer: TR, *Autobiography*, 13.

68 Takes Bamie to theater: MSB to Susan West, Feb. 8, 1864.

68 "devotion wrapped us round": Robinson, 18.

3. GRAND TOUR

Unless otherwise indicated this chapter has been drawn from TR's boyhood diaries for the years 1869 and 1870, the originals of which are in the Theodore Roosevelt Collection. Background on James D. Bulloch and the building of the *Alabama* has come from Rush and Woods, *Official Records;* Kell, *Recollections;* Meriwether, *Semmes;* and from Bulloch's own *Secret Service.*

page

69 *Scotia* fastest ship to Europe: *N.Y. Times*, July 25, 1866.

69 Fellow passengers: *ibid.*, May 13, 1869.

69 Sillerton Jackson: Wharton, *Age of Innocence*, 10.

70 "I basked in the happiness": Kaplan, 42.

70 "vulgar, vulgar, vulgar": Edel, 304.

70 Rhyme by CVS: (TRB).

71 Mittie meets Mr. St. John: Robinson, 42.

71 "It was one wild scene of commotion": MBR to Anna Gracie, May 1869.

71 "Strange child!": *ibid.*

72 Irvine's secret return: Robinson, 36–37.

72 "You have no idea of my enthusiasm": MBR to Anna Gracie, undated.

72 Richard Henry Dana's impression of James D. Bulloch: To Dana it seemed a great shame that men of the caliber of Captain Bulloch had to give up careers in the Navy in order to make a better living. "By night, I walk deck for a couple of hours with the young captain," Dana wrote. "After due inquiries about his family in Georgia, and due remembrance of those of his mother's line whom we loved,

and the public honored . . . the fascinating topic of the navy, the frigates and the line-of-battle ships and little sloops, the storms, the wrecks, and the sea fights, fill up the time. He loves the navy still, and has left it with regret; but the navy does not love her sons as they love her. On the quarter-deck at fifteen, the first in rank of his year, favored by his commanders, with service in the best vessels, making the great fleet cruise under Morris, taking part in the actions of the Naval Brigade on shore in California, serving on the Coast Survey, a man of science as well as a sailor—yet what is there before him, or those like him, in our navy?" (*To Cuba and Back,* 13–14.)

73 Bulloch like Thackeray's Colonel Newcome: TR, *Autobiography,* 14.

73 "When civilization . . . fighting a last battle": Donald, 374.

73 Response in British press: London *Times,* May 25, June 11, 14, and 17, 1869.

74 "Father, did Texas . . . annex itself": MBR to Anna Gracie, June 11, 1869.

74 Heroes in books and among southern kinsfolk: TR, *Autobiography,* 30.

74 Talks of Irvine in speech at Roswell: *N.Y. Times,* Oct. 21, 1905.

76 "as valiant . . . a soul as ever lived": TR, *Autobiography,* 14–15.

76 TR's influence on James D. Bulloch: TR to MBR, Sept. 14, 1881, *Letters,* I, 52. "I have persuaded him to publish a work which only he possesses the materials to write," TR reported proudly to his mother.

76 Furness Abbey: background from Lefebure, *English Lake District;* details of the Roosevelt visit from MBR's long letter to Anna Gracie dated June 3, 1869.

78 "on magic ground": MBR to Anna Gracie, June 11, 1869.

78 TR Sr. reads from *Lady of the Lake: ibid.*

78 Excursion on Loch Lomond: *ibid.*

79 "I want to learn about things, too": *ibid.*

79 Sights seen at the British Museum: MBR to Anna Gracie, July 15, 1869.

80 "I wore my pale-green silk": *ibid.*

81 Asthma in London: TR to Edith Carow, July 10, 1869, private collection of Sarah Alden Gannett.

82 TR douses candle in tumbler: MBR to Anna Gracie, July 15, 1869.

82 Teedie "decidedly better": *ibid.*

83 "A course of travel of this sort": Forbes, 12–13.

83 "a token of some future potency": Edel, 296.

84 "lovely times when . . . not obliged to think of sculpture or painting": Robinson, 49.

84 Long-distance hikes: The figures quoted, from TR's diaries, are substantiated by other references. Aug. 16, 1869, TR Sr. writes to Anna Gracie, "Teedie and Ellie have walked today thirteen miles each and are very proud of their performance, although Teedie has been farther several times." (Quoted in Putnam, 63.)

84 Details on the Rigi-Kulm: Baedeker, *Switzerland* (1869).

85   "Rose immediately": MBR diary, Sept. 4, 1869.
85   "He takes a great deal of interest now": MBR to Anna Gracie, June
      11, 1869.
89   "Now, darling, this is one of the greatest works of art": Robinson,
      48.
89   "We are going to commence vigorously": MBR to Anna Gracie,
      [n.d.] 1869.

4. A DISEASE OF THE DIREST SUFFERING

In addition to material from the Roosevelt papers this chapter is based on
extensive interviews with asthmatics, the parents of asthmatics, and physicians specializing in the treatment of asthma. Those technical writings
that have been most helpful include Kemp, *Understanding Bronchitis and
Asthma;* Travis, *Chronic Illness in Children;* Knapp, "The Asthmatic
Child and the Psychosomatic Problem of Asthma"; Knapp, "The Asthmatic
and His Environment"; and Knapp, Mathé, and Vachon, "Psychosomatic
Aspects of Bronchial Asthma."

page
90   Asthma as a family affliction: see essay by Miriam Pachacki in
      Travis, 189–94; Liebman, Minuchin, and Baker, "The Use of Struc-
      tural Family Therapy in the Treatment of Intractable Asthma."
91   "genetic predisposition" already noted: Rosenblatt, "History of
      Bronchial Asthma," in Weiss and Segal, 11.
91   "neurotic character of the complaint": Thorowgood, 35.
92   Work by Laënnec: Rosenblatt, in Weiss and Segal, 9.
92   Findings of Joshua Bicknell Chapin: Chapin, 13–14.
93   Findings of Henry Hyde Salter: Salter, 33–34.
93   "Organs are made for action": *ibid.,* 102.
94   Ways to avert an attack: Chapin, 16; Rosenblatt, in Weiss and Segal,
      10.
94   Salter on the use of tobacco: Salter, 120–21.
94   Agony of an asthmatic attack: interviews with Cort Sutton and Ed-
      ward T. Hall. Of published accounts of the anxieties experienced,
      the finest by far is still that written by Salter more than a century
      ago, *On Asthma,* 61.
95   "If I were drowning": interview with Edward T. Hall.
95   "wretched," "suffered much": TR to Edward Sanford Martin, Nov.
      26, 1900, *Letters,* II, 1443; *Autobiography,* 15.
95   "nobody seemed to think I would live": TR quoted in N.Y. *World,*
      Nov. 16, 1902.
95   Smokes a cigar: this treatment also described in MBR's Oct. 3, 1869,
      letter to Anna Gracie.
95   "Poor little Teedie is sick again": quoted in Putnam, 64.
96   Bronchial tubes in spasm: see Weiss, *Bronchial Asthma.*
96   "everything under . . . turned to lead": interview with Mrs. John
      Curtiss.

98   Interplay of emotions and the asthmatic "habit": see especially Pa-chacki, in Travis, 189–94; Kemp, 28.

98   "It isn't that the emotions . . . are different": Kemp, 33.

99   Experiment with house dust: Knapp, Mathé, and Vachon, in Weiss and Segal.

99   "We tend to use what is available": Pachacki, in Travis, 190.

100   "suppressed cry for the mother": Travis, 168–71; Knapp, in Schneer, 245.

100   TR Sr.'s absence during the Civil War: "the syndrome of the absent father" is described by Pachacki, in Travis, 191.

101   Hurried departure from Berlin: Robinson, 45.

102   Grandmamma's description of the departure for Saratoga and the first known mention of the word "asthma" in the Roosevelt papers are contained in her letter to Susan West, June 22, 1863.

102   "periodicity": Salter, 35.

102   Sunday a day "we children did not enjoy": TR, *Autobiography*, 8.

103   The story of TR and the "zeal" is from Hagedorn, *Boys' Life*, 19–21, and was written in cooperation with TR. Yet, curiously, in one of his own essays, "The Bible and the People" (*Works*, XIII, 647–48), TR tells the story as though it had happened to another little boy.

104   *"let them that are most afraid"*: Bunyan, 294.

106   Asthma lends a kind of power: see Liebman, Minuchin, and Baker, "The Use of Structural Family Therapy in the Treatment of Intract-able Asthma."

106   "A hanging—how long does that take?": interview with Cort Sut-ton.

107   Life as a battle: Travis, 174–75.

107   "We enjoy fine music": quoted in Miller, *Nostalgia*, 189.

107   Proust's case: see especially Knapp, "The Asthmatic and His En-vironment."

108   Salter on the asthmatic's future life: Salter, 18.

108   Making the child "a participant, not a spectator": Travis, 183.

108   Horseback riding as therapy: Thorowgood, 64.

5. METAMORPHOSIS

page

109   Red Cloud on Fifth Avenue, eight-hour day, East River Bridge: *N.Y. Times* for June 1870.

110   "without imminent danger of losing caste": Nevins and Thomas, 246.

110   Heat wave: *N.Y. Times*, July 1870. Thirty-five people died of heat prostration in the city in one day (July 19).

110   French troops singing: Longworth, 20.

110   CVS anxious about Bamie's safety: TR Sr. to B, [n.d.] 1870.

110   TR "peculiarly well": TR Sr. to B, July 20, 1870.

111   "I am away with Teedie again": TR Sr. to B, undated.

111   "Do not let them spoil you": TR Sr. to B, Aug. 15, 1870.

111   "Your mother came back": TR Sr. to B, Sept. 1, 1870.

111   "The spasm yielded": MBR to B, Sept. 5, 1870.

111   "bad news from your mother": TR Sr. to B, Sept. 6, 1870.

112   "You must *make* your body": Robinson, 50.

112   Sessions at Wood's gymnasium: interview with John Wood, N.Y. *World*, Jan. 24, 1904.

112   "widening his chest": Robinson, 50.

112   Impact of "The Flight of the Duchess": Hagedorn, *Boys' Life*, 39–40.

113   Humiliated by boys in Maine: TR, *Autobiography*, 30–31.

113   "he did not think a sugar diet was good for me": TR to Quentin Roosevelt, Nov. 4, 1914, *Letters*, VIII, 829.

113   Bamie's Saturdays with TR Sr.: B reminiscences.

114   "Menu as usual": July 11, 1872.

114   Fox the face of God: Robinson, 23.

115   Incident of the dead seal: TR, *Autobiography*, 16.

115   Favorite reading: *ibid.*, 17–19.

115   "Unroll the world's map": Reid, *Scalp Hunters*, 7.

116   "What with wild gallops": *ibid.*, 19.

116   "Chain of Destruction": Reid, *Boy Hunters*, 105.

116   "About noon": *ibid.*, 333.

116   Uncle Hilborne introduces TR to Darwin: Hagedorn, *Boys' Life*, 38.

116   At the Academy "every spare moment": TR to TR Sr., Sept. 18, 1872, *Letters*, I, 6.

116   Hilborne "talked science": quoted in Putnam, 78–79.

117   Studying English, French, German, and Latin: TR to Anna Gracie, July 7, 1872, *Letters*, I, 6.

117   Summers "the special delight": Robinson, 51.

117   Teedie lives "a life apart": *ibid.*, 36.

117   Newborn squirrels and tree frog: TR, "Notes on Natural History," Aug. 1872 (TRC).

117   "the loss to science": Thayer, *Roosevelt*, 8.

117   Expedition to Paul Smith's: TR, diary, Aug. 1871 (TRC).

118   TR's contributions to the museum: *Third and Fourth Annual Reports of the American Museum of Natural History*.

118   "stuffer" John G. Bell: Herrick, 253; Adams, *Audubon*, 461; TR, "My Life as a Naturalist," *Works*, V, 385–86.

118   First gun: TR, *Autobiography*, 20–21.

118   Spectacles open "an entirely new world": *ibid.*

119   Sees birds on the Nile: TR, diary, Dec. 3, 1872; Jan. 8, 1873 (TRC).

119   Kills first bird, Dec. 13: TR, diary (TRC).

120   TR Sr. rescues yellow jacket: MBR, diary, Aug. 27, 1869 (TRC).

120   "Father and I" shoot eighteen birds: TR, diary, Dec. 31, 1872 (TRC).

120   "eyes sparkling with delight": MBR to Anna Gracie, Feb. 3, 1873.

120   The look of the Great Prairies: TR, diary, Dec. 3, 1872 (TRC).

120   "serious work" the "chief zest": TR, *Autobiography*, 22.

120   Comic figure on a donkey: Robinson, 57; B reminiscences.

121   TR Sr. has trouble keeping up: Robinson, 57.

121   "The sporting is injurious to my trousers": Robinson, 60.

121   Skinning procedure was the same then as now. See Labrie, *Amateur Taxidermist*.

122   "traveler is perfect king": quoted in Bull and Lorimer, 44.

122   TR Sr. reads Egyptian history: Robinson, 58.

122   "back to old Bible times": quoted in Putnam, 91.

122   Circassian lady and TR Sr.: TR, diary, Dec. 7, 1872 (TRC).

123   Mittie relishes weather and privacy: MBR to Anna Gracie, Jan. 12, 1873.

123   "In such a climate": MBR to Anna Gracie, Feb. 3, 1873.

123   Henry Adams on the Nile: Ford, *Letters of Henry Adams*.

123   "The children have gone to bed": MBR to Anna Gracie, Jan. 12, 1873.

123   Aboard the *Aboul Irdan:* copy of the original contract between TR Sr. and Antonio Sapienza, dragoman, Dec. 10, 1872 (WSCC).

123   "nicest, coziest, pleasantest little place": TR, diary, Dec. 12, 1872 (TRC).

123   Harvard men and Clift family: B reminiscences.

123   "Sometimes we sail head foremost": Robinson, 57.

124   "as we go for the entirely different life": quoted in Putnam, 82.

124   "Our life on board": E to Archibald Gracie, Dec. 15, 1872 (FDRL).

124   Moonlight expedition to Philae: TR, diary, Jan. 18, 1873 (TRC).

124   Bamie and Mittie: B reminiscences; interview with W. Sheffield Cowles, Jr.

125   *"There was an old fellow named Teedie":* E to Archibald Gracie, Sept. 5, 1873 (FDRL).

125   Visit with Emerson: Robinson, 63.

125   Ellen Emerson's impression: quoted in Rusk, *Emerson*, 470.

125   New Year's party: *ibid.*, 59; also C to Edith Carow, Feb. 1, 1873.

126   Flying the Stars and Stripes: E to Archibald Gracie, Dec. 15, 1872 (FDRL).

126   CVS Roosevelt estate as high as $7 million: W. Sheffield Cowles, Jr., and Corinne Robinson Alsop to Hermann Hagedorn, Dec. 1954 (TRB); as low as $3 million: P. James Roosevelt to the author.

126   Cost of Nile winter: original contract previously cited (WSCC).

127   Union Square house demolished: Nevins and Thomas, 422.

127   "If one allowed himself to dwell": quoted in Putnam, 91.

128   Total birds killed: TR to Anna Gracie, Feb. 9, 1873.

PART TWO

6. UPTOWN

page

131   Fighting loneliness: TR Sr. to B, Sept. 24, 1873.

131   Business from Chicago: Cobb, 51.

131   Weekend activities: TR Sr. to B, July 17 and Aug. 9, 1873.

132   "Fritz goes beautifully": TR Sr. to B, Oct. 9, 1873.

132   Tears down plaster beams: TR Sr. to MBR, July 20, 1873.

132   "can see all who pass": TR Sr. to B, June 29, 1873.

132   Windows and showcases: Hellman, 27.

132   "I think without egotism": TR Sr. to MBR, July 20, 1873.

132   Annual contributions: *Fifth and Sixth Annual Reports of the American Museum of Natural History.*

133   Letter misdated: TR Sr. to B, July 17, '63 [1873].

133   "so anxious to see you home": TR Sr. to MBR, June 6, 1873.

133   Pleased with "self-denial": TR Sr. to MBR, June 16, 1873.

133   Return of asthma: TR, diary, Feb. 22, 1873 (TRC).

133   TR Sr. pressed into service at Vienna: newspaper clippings, Robert B. Roosevelt Papers, New York Historical Society.

133   TR in the doldrums: Putnam, 101.

133   "hand tremble awfully": TR to TR Sr., June 29, 1873, *Letters*, I, 11.

133   Switzerland works wonders: MBR to TR Sr., Aug. 17, 1873.

134   Panic of 1873: Nevins, *Emergence of Modern America*, 290–304.

134   "poor Mr. Clews": TR Sr. to B, Sept. 24, 1873.

134   Mittie "anxious": MBR to TR Sr., Sept. 21, 1873.

134   Mittie on shopping spree: B reminiscences.

134   New furnace going: TR Sr. to MBR, Sept. 21, 1873.

134   Carpet in port: TR Sr. to B, Sept. 24, 1873.

134   Billiard room: *ibid.*

135   Trouble with staircase: B reminiscences.

135   Return on *Russia*: *N.Y. Times*, Nov. 6, 1873.

135   Mittie and the family fortune: B reminiscences.

135   Interiors at 57th Street: photographs (TRB).

136   Top-floor gymnasium: Hagedorn, *Boys' Life*, 50.

136   "boxing lessons": E to Archibald Gracie, Nov. 16, 1873 (FDRL).

136   Teedie's Nile specimens: Several of these, with their original cards, are at the American Museum of Natural History.

137   "All that gives me most pleasure": TR Sr. to TR, Oct. 6, 1874.

137   The "power of being . . . focused": Robinson, 3.

137   Schuyler on "power of concentration": *Theodore Roosevelt* (Sr.). Memorial Meeting, 10–11.

138   Work with Bureau of Charities, remarks to reporters: miscellaneous clippings, scrapbook (TRC).

138   Incident of the silver trowel: Hellman, 23–24.

138   "no ascetic": *Theodore Roosevelt* (Sr.). Memorial Meeting, 11.

138   "I can see him now": *ibid.*

139   Crippled children on the dining-room table: Robinson, 5.

139   "neither spoiled by good fortune": *Theodore Roosevelt* (Sr.). Memorial Meeting, 52.

139   Interested in "every good thing": *ibid.*, 10.

139   "control the strongest affections": *ibid.*, 33.

139   "wish you were not *so good*": MBR to TR Sr., June 2, 1873.

139   "love you and wish to please": MBR to TR Sr., Oct. 15, 1873.

139   "mingled feelings": B reminiscences.

140   Dancing class for forty: MBR to B, Nov. 11, 1874.

140   Sara Delano friendship: letters to B, 1876, 1877 (FDRL).

140   Mittie's portrait: it now hangs at TRB.

140   Mittie in her finery: B reminiscences.

141   Chemical Bank weathers the panic: According to *History of the Chemical Bank*, the old institution remained "a veritable beacon light of returning confidence" in 1873 when it declared a dividend of 100 percent.

141   Roosevelt venture in Montana mining: an undated clipping from a publication called *Copper* (TRC).

141   TR Sr. and Alexander Graham Bell: Mrs. TR, Jr., *Day Before Yesterday*, 37–38.

141   TR Sr.'s various activities: TR Sr. to B, June 6, 1875.

141   "What business I shall enter": TR to Anna Fisher (Dresden, Germany), Feb. 5, 1876, *Letters*, I, 14.

142   "I had a very delightful visit": quoted in Martin, *Choate*, 329.

142   Times of "every special delight": Robinson, 89.

142   Mornings on horseback, Father in the lead: *ibid.*, 8.

143   "But, Uncle": Parsons, 32.

143   Fanny Smith's recollections: *ibid.*, 18–26.

143   "How I will enjoy": TR Sr. to B, June 6, 1875.

143   "He will be with us now": TR to B, July 25, 1876, *Letters*, I, 15.

144   Ellie at times "very ill": TR to Anna Fisher, Feb. 5, 1876, *Letters*, I, 14.

144   Illness thought to be epilepsy: ARL, interview with Hermann Hagedorn (TRB).

144   "congestion of the brain": TR Sr. to MBR, Nov. 9, 1874.

144   "What will I become": E to TR Sr., Sept. 19, 1873 (FDRL).

145   "The attack . . . decidedly the worst": TR Sr. to MBR, Nov. 9, 1874.

145   "fear . . . alone at night": TR Sr. to MBR, Nov. 14, 1874.

145   "pleasure to receive your letters": TR Sr. to TR, Nov. 23, 1874.

146   "It is so funny, my illness": E to TR, Nov. 22, 1874.

146   "scarce know how": TR Sr. to MBR, Nov. 27, 1874.

146   "not had a respectable suit": quoted in E. Roosevelt, *Hunting Big Game*, 6.

146   "Dear Old Governor": E to TR Sr., Mar. 6, 1875 (FDRL); also quoted in Lash, 31–32.

147   "Yesterday, during my Latin lesson": E to TR Sr., Oct. 1, 1875 (FDRL); also quoted in E. Roosevelt, *Hunting Big Game*, 6.

147   "Poor Ellie Roosevelt": quoted in Lash, 33.

148   "just a sell my being down here": Jan. 14, 1876, quoted in E. Roosevelt, *Hunting Big Game*, 26.

148   "have not taken a drink": *ibid.*

148   Enjoying Texas; dog for a pillow: E to TR Sr., Jan. 9 and 12, 1876 (FDRL); latter also quoted in Lash, 33–34.

7. THE MORAL EFFECT

None of the Roosevelt children, for all they wrote about their father, mentioned a thing about his political activities. Nor have any of TR's biographers touched on this side of the family story; rather, the impression given is of a wholly apolitical patriarch. Only Jacob Riis, in his *Theodore Roosevelt the Citizen*, even mentions, in a sentence, the fact that TR Sr. attended the Cincinnati convention. So it has been primarily from contemporary newspapers and TR Sr.'s own correspondence that this account has been drawn.

For material on Roscoe Conkling, the author has relied on David M. Jordan's *Roscoe Conkling of New York*, Donald Barr Chidsey's *The Gentleman from New York*, and *Gentleman Boss*, the superb biography of Chester A. Arthur by Thomas C. Reeves.

page

149   Robert Roosevelt's activities: miscellaneous clippings, letters, notebooks in the Robert B. Roosevelt Papers, New York Historical Society; also DAB.

149   "Let us try some plan": N.Y. *Tribune*, Aug. 28, 1877.

150   "Absolutely the only protection": *ibid.*

150   TR Sr.'s fondness for *The Potiphar Papers:* letter to MBR, May 31, 1853.

151   "While good men sit at home": Norton, *Orations*, 269.

151   "the image and figure": *Theodore Roosevelt* (Sr.). Memorial Meeting, 51–53.

151   Grant scandals: White, *Republican Era*, 365–74.

151   Charles Francis Adams warns: *ibid.*, 366.

151   Fifth Avenue Conference: N.Y. *Times*, May 16, 1876. See also, Garraty, *Lodge*, 44–47.

151   "weighty and reliable of our friends": Ford, 273.

151   "Oh, they reenacted the moral law": Garraty, *Lodge*, 47.

152   The "saving element": N.Y. *Tribune*, May 17, 1876.

152   "Men whose names ring": Boston *Evening Transcript*, May 16, 1876.

152   "fight Conkling at all events": quoted in Jordan, 239.

152   Ideal candidate according to Adams: Ford, 279.

153   "When Dr. Johnson defined patriotism": quoted in Jordan, 279.

153   "grandiloquent swell": quoted in Muzzey, 61.

153   Conkling's appearance: from a reporter's account, N.Y. *Commercial Gazette*, June 18, 1883, quoted in Reeves, 42–43.

154   Too good-looking to be pure: Chidsey, 116–17.

154   A mind approaching genius: see Depew, 77–79.

154   Conkling thought his hour had arrived: Chidsey, 203.

155   "bail for all those fellows": quoted in Reeves, 93.

155   Convention excitement, activities: N.Y. *Sun*, N.Y. *Times*, N.Y. *Tribune*, N.Y. *Herald*, Cincinnati *Daily Gazette*.

155 "You would never recognize your father": TR Sr. to B, June 13, 1876.

156 "Carl, you won't *oppose* me": Fuess, 220.

156 TR Sr.'s attack on Conkling: Cincinnati *Daily Gazette*, June 13, 1876. See also, Shores, 247–48.

157 Headlines: Cincinnati *Daily Gazette*, June 14, 1876.

157 Curtis on Conkling: quoted in Muzzey, 104.

157 "How is New York?": quoted in Reeves, 96.

8. FATHER AND SON

page

160 An "ungreased squeak": quoted in Putnam, 78.

160 "At times he could hardly get them out": Thayer, *Roosevelt*, 20.

161 Likes his ears: Fraser, "Sculpting TR."

161 Richard Welling's first impression: Welling, "My Classmate Theodore Roosevelt."

161 "Sporting Calendar" entries: Aug. 21, 1875 (TRC).

161 Time lost "through sickness": TR to MBR, Mar. 4, 1876, *Letters*, I, 15.

161 Bamie picks his rooms: "Theodore would prefer you decide upon and take his rooms," TR Sr. writes B, May 22, 1876.

162 "As I saw the last of the train": TR Sr. to TR, Sept. 28, 1876.

162 Never knew "what idleness was": Cutler, unpublished memoir dated Sept. 18, 1901 (TRC).

162 "rather smelly room": TR to B, June 20, 1875, *Letters*, I, 13.

162 TR's description of the shrew: quoted in Cutright, 36–37.

163 Theatrically superior: Parsons, 28.

163 "If I were writing to Theodore": quoted in Robinson, 96.

163 *King Olaf, Song of Roland, Nibelungenlied:* TR, *Autobiography*, 19, 326, 23.

163 "somewhat supercilious": McDougall, 129–30.

163 "such fun, the most original": Parsons, 34.

164 "and don't frizzle her hair": TR to C, Feb. 5, 1877, *Letters*, I, 23.

164 Dancing class "very orderly": quoted in Putnam, 121.

164 "Little Pet Pussie": Mar. 27, 1877, quoted in Robinson, 98.

164 First letter to Mittie: TR to MBR, Sept. 29, 1876, *Letters*, I, 16.

164 "opponents played very foul": TR to MBR, Nov. 19, 1876, *ibid.*, 20.

165 The "gentleman sort": TR to B, Oct. 15, 1876, *ibid.*, 17.

165 "antecedents": TR to C, Nov. 26, 1876.

165 Lamson there only to enjoy himself: TR to B, Nov. 12, 1876.

165 "Take care of your morals": quoted by TR in a letter to MBR, Mar. 24, 1878, *Letters*, I, 33.

165 "Sundays I have all to myself": TR to B, Oct. 15, 1876, *Letters*, I, 17.

165 "never spent an unhappy day": TR to MBR, Oct. 29, 1876, *ibid.*, 19.

165 "not . . . a fellow in college": TR to TR Sr., Oct. 22, 1876, *ibid.*, 18.

166 "in beautiful health": TR to MBR, Nov. 19, 1876, *ibid.*, 20.

166   "rug, which *will* curl": TR to B, Nov. 26, 1876.

167   In touch with Dr. Wyman: TR to MBR, Jan. 18, 1877, *Letters*, I, 22.

167   "a little asthma in November": TR to TR Sr. and MBR, Feb. 11, 1877, *ibid.*, 26.

167   Asthmatic children removed from home lives: see Purcell, "The Effect on Asthma in Children of Experimental Separation from the Family."

167   "We all like his friends": Anna Gracie to E, Jan. 5, 1877 (FDRL).

167   "He went off most cheerfully": TR Sr. to E, Jan. 6, 1877 (FDRL).

167   Sleighing party: TR to C, Feb. 5, 1877, *Letters*, I, 23.

168   Cost of a year at Harvard: King, 18; also, Grant, "Harvard College in the Seventies."

168   "send on my gun": TR to TR Sr. and MBR, Feb. 11, 1877, *Letters*, I, 26.

168   TR in Hayes parade: Hagedorn, *Boys' Life*, 51–52.

169   "He talked very pleasantly": TR Sr. to TR, Oct. 27, 1876.

169   Hayes shot at: Russell, 99.

170   Evarts proposes TR Sr. for Customhouse: Barrows, 327.

170   Evarts' past work with TR Sr.: *ibid.*, 469.

171   Above crass temptations: *Nation*, Nov. 1, 1877.

171   Collectorship and the Customhouse: see Reeves, 62–63, 67–68.

172   Melville a customs inspector at $4 a day: Howard, 284.

172   Phelps, Dodge case: see Reeves, 82–83; also Lowitt, 276–81.

173   "We look back . . . we were fools": quoted in Reeves, 82.

173   Delmonico's banquet: *N.Y. Times*, May 15, 1877.

174   TR Sr. escorts Hayes on museum tour: *ibid.*, May 16, 1877.

174   TR Sr. rides with Hayes entourage: *ibid.*, May 17, 1877.

175   Conkling at Rochester convention: Jordan, 278–79.

175   "all excited here about politics": quoted in Martin, *Choate*, 329.

175   TR Sr.'s interest in Cleopatra's Needle: interview with W. Sheffield Cowles, Jr.

175   TR Sr. leads group for Harvard visit: TR to C, June 3, 1877, *Letters*, I, 28.

175   Butterfly reduced to a grub: TR Sr. to B, Aug. 15, 1877.

175   Saratoga charities meeting: *N.Y. Times*, Sept. 8, 1877.

176   "I am clear": Williams, *Hayes, Diary*.

176   "even up there they lift their skirts": N.Y. *Herald*, Nov. 9, 1877.

176   "TERRIBLE CHARGES": N.Y. *Herald*, Oct. 31, 1877.

176   Denounces management of city's asylums: *N.Y. Times*, Oct. 31, 1877.

177   "he seemed to me another man": *Theodore Roosevelt* (Sr.). Memorial Meeting, 34.

177   "in the prime of vigorous manhood": N.Y. *Tribune*, Oct. 30, 1877.

177   "Tell Father I am watching": TR to B, Oct. 14, 1877, *Letters*, I, 29.

177   Republicans caucus in secrecy: *N.Y. Times*, Nov. 11, 1877.

178   Compromise reported: *ibid.*, Dec. 5, 1877.

178   Nominees called "good men": *ibid.*, Dec. 7, 1877.

178   Afraid Conkling has "won the day": TR to TR Sr., Dec. 8, 1877, *Letters*, I, 30.

178   Conkling's speech of Dec. 12: *N.Y. Times,* N.Y. *Tribune,* N.Y. *Evening Post,* Dec. 13, 1877.

179   Calls TR Sr. his "bitter personal enemy": N.Y. *Tribune,* Dec. 13, 1877.

179   "the end is not yet": Williams, *Hayes, Diary.*

180   "uneasy about Father": TR to B, Dec. 16, 1877, *Letters,* I, 31.

180   "brilliant daylight assemblages": *N.Y. Times,* Dec. 23, 1877.

181   "couldn't have your appendix out then": Wister, 17.

181   Entries from Anna Gracie's diary: (TRC).

181   Schuyler note: Dec. 22, 1877 (TRC).

181   New "Private Diary": Dec. 25, 1877 (LC).

182   Sleigh upsets: TR to B, Jan. 19, 1878.

182   "sat with him some seven hours": quoted in Putnam, 147.

182   "I was with your dear father": Anna Gracie to TR, Feb. 8 [1878].

182   Crowd gathered: Robinson, 105.

183   "young strength . . . poured out": *ibid.,* 104.

183   Elliott's account of his father's death: (TRC).

185   Newspaper tributes: scrapbook (TRC).

185   "What a glorious example!": condolence note (TRC).

186   "something . . . inspiring": Robinson, 105.

186   "hard to have parted": MBR to TR, Mar. 8, 1878.

186   "work out our own salvation": B reminiscences.

186   "best . . . sufferings should end": TR to Henry Minot, Feb. 20, 1878, *Letters,* I, 31.

186   Private anguish: Private Diary (LC).

187   Marks 69th Psalm: TR's personal Bible (WSCC).

187   "easier for me": TR to B, Mar. 17, 1878, *Letters,* I, 32.

187   "My own sweet sister": TR to B, Mar. 3, 1878.

187   "working away pretty hard": May 7, 1878, Private Diary (LC).

187   "as if he were present": TR to MBR, Feb. 28, 1878, *Letters,* I, 32.

188   Private feelings of remorse and inadequacy: all drawn from June entries, Private Diary (LC).

188   Swinburne on Cooper's Bluff: Robinson, 100–101.

189   Not so sad as expected: TR to C, Mar. 3, 1878, *Letters,* I, 32.

189   "Theodore craved": Robinson, 102.

189   *"For ye shall go out with joy":* Isaiah 55:12.

190   "we both of us had . . . tempers": TR to B, Sept. 20, 1886 (TRB); also quoted in Morris, *Edith Kermit Roosevelt,* 58.

190   "Look out for Theodore": Sewall, "Bill Sewall Remembers TR," clipping (TRC).

190   TR Sr. strained himself: B reminiscences; Robinson, 104.

190   "talismans against evil": Robinson, 106.

191   " 'A rare and radiant maiden' ": TR was especially fond of Poe, so this undoubtedly refers to "The Raven" (*"For the rare and radiant maiden whom the angels name Lenore—"*).

PART THREE

9. HARVARD

Among the greatest of all pleasures in the research for this book has been
the chance to work with material in the Harvard University Archives—
photographs, scrapbooks, class records, class biographies, memorabilia of
all kinds dating from the years when TR was an undergraduate. Of published works the most valuable has been the two-volume biography
Charles W. Eliot, by Henry James.

page

195   "You belonged to Harvard": Thayer, 15.
195   "*crescent* institution": *ibid.*, 16.
195   Science "the firm foundation": quoted in *N.Y. Times,* Dec. 23,
       1877.
196   Petty rules: see Morison, *Three Centuries,* 357–58.
196   Rule book reduced: Hawkins, 110.
196   "a deal of drudgery": James, *Eliot,* II, 44.
196   "Do you think it is a wise parent": *ibid.*, 45.
196   Eliot and Hale motto: *ibid.*, I, 317.
196   Looking neither left nor right: Harry Rand, Hagedorn interview
       (TRC).
196   Eliot was disliked: James, *Eliot,* I, 311.
196   "flagstaff in motion": Wister, 20.
196   "that *scoundrel* King David": Eliot, "Eliot of Harvard."
197   Mental condition has physical origin: James, *Eliot,* II, 38.
197   Disapproves of baseball: *ibid.*, 69.
197   Memorial Hall: The great building still stands, though in some-
       what neglected condition. See also Whitehill, 12–14.
197   "The effect of the place": James, *The Bostonians,* 208–09.
198   "Its occupant . . . is its master": Martin, "Undergraduate Life."
198   "to look at the new bookcase": TR to B, Nov. 9, 1877, *Letters,* I, 30.
198   One in five thousand went to college: Putnam, 134.
198   Harvard said to offer diversity of student views and backgrounds:
       Thayer, *Roosevelt,* 15.
199   Records for the Class of 1880: Harvard Archives.
199   Three Roman Catholics: *Class of 1880, Secretary's Report, Number
       1, Commencement 1880,* Harvard Archives.
199   Humor anti-Irish, anti-Semitic, and mocking Negro aspirations:
       see *Lampoon,* Mar. 7, Oct. 24, and Dec. 19, 1879.
199   Scott on Harvard "temper": Hagedorn interview (TRC).
200   Asthmatics excused from chapel: William Hooper, Hagedorn inter-
       view (TRC).
200   Younger faculty recruited by Eliot: James, *Eliot,* I, 254–55.
201   Students and professors a different species: Santayana, "The Aca-
       demic Environment at Harvard."

201 "Don't take it upon yourself": *Crimson,* Oct. 6, 1876.

201 *"We ask but time to drift":* quoted in Pringle, 32.

201 "My system was simple": Garraty, *Lodge,* 51–52.

201 "A boy could go completely to pieces": Harold Fowler, Hagedorn interview (TRC).

202 "Students got drunk": John Woodbury, Hagedorn interview (TRC).

202 Eliot on "intemperance": Hagedorn interview (TRC).

202 "unwholesome experiment": Martin, "Undergraduate Life."

203 Rand's recollections: Hagedorn interview (TRC).

203 "pleasant doors": Wister, 19–20.

203 *Crimson* on "digs": Sept. 28, 1876.

204 Class of 1880 known as Bacon's class: John Woodbury, Hagedorn interview (TRC).

204 Thayer's recollections: Hagedorn interview (TRC).

204 "Funnily enough": TR to MBR, Oct. 8, 1878, *Letters,* I, 34.

204 "delighted" to be in the Porcellian: TR to B, Nov. 10, 1878, *Letters,* I, 35.

205 "send my silk hat": TR to MBR, Jan. 11, 1880, *Letters,* I, 42.

205 Jackson on splendor at 57th Street: Hagedorn interview (TRC).

205 Few could afford a horse: Grant, "Harvard College in the Seventies."

205 TR's financial position and expenses for 1877, 1878, 1879, and 1880 are all to be found in his private diaries (LC).

205 Eliot's salary: Eliot, "Eliot of Harvard."

206 "keep the fraction constant": TR, *Autobiography,* 26.

206 "ready to join anything": Richard Saltonstall, Hagedorn interview (TRC).

207 Academic achievement: for a complete account of TR's grades at Harvard, see *Letters,* I, 25–26.

207 "sort of spluttered": George H. Palmer, Hagedorn interview (TRC).

207 "See here, Roosevelt": Wilhelm, 35.

208 Saltonstall remembered no caged animals, nothing unusual: Hagedorn interview (TRC).

208 TR chiefly "a joke": Thayer, Hagedorn interview (TRC).

208 " 'whether he is the real thing' ": Thayer, *Roosevelt,* 21.

208 Foresees future professor of history: John Woodbury, Hagedorn interview (TRC).

208 Martha Cowdin (Bacon) recollections: Hagedorn interview (TRC).

208 Rose Lee on TR dancing: *ibid.*

209 "Old Dick . . . on par with the Roosevelts": Diary, Oct. 1, 1879 (LC).

209 Welling's account of the skating expedition: "My Classmate."

210 Rage at drunken classmate's imitation: William Hooper, Hagedorn interview (TRC).

210 Wister's version of the boxing match: Wister, 4–5.

210 *N.Y. Times* account: Mar. 23, 1879.

211 Spalding's denunciation of the story: letter to the editor in *Time,* Dec. 14, 1931 (TRC).

211   "As athletes we are about equal": Diary, July 30, 1879 (LC).
211   "always thought that he could do things better": quoted in Putnam, 100.
211   "Only one gentleman stands ahead of me": TR to B, Oct. 13, 1879, *Letters*, I, 41–42.
212   Words under the ink blot: A laboratory examination of the diary page was made at the author's request by the Manuscript Division of the Library of Congress, working with the Library's Preservation Office.
212   "He is a disgrace": Diary, Oct. 23, 1878.
212   "I told the clergyman": TR to MBR, Jan. 11, 1880, *Letters*, I, 43.
212   "The first two or three days": TR to MBR, Mar. 16, 1879, *ibid.*, 37.
213   Prefers political economy to natural history: TR to MBR, Oct. 8, 1878, *ibid.*, 33–34.
213   Blames Harvard for killing interest in natural history: TR, *Autobiography*, 26–27.
214   Shaler: Shaler's inspirational powers are attested to again and again. "Students whose unimaginative lives had never carried them beyond home and prep school and Harvard Square sat in Shaler's presence and saw the face of the earth becoming an endless wonderland," writes Rollo Walter Brown in *Harvard Yard*, 106. See also William Roscoe Thayer's memorial essay on Shaler in the *Harvard Graduates' Magazine*.
214   TR's dislike for A. S. Hill: John Woodbury, Hagedorn interview (TRC).
214   Saltonstall recollection: Hagedorn interview (TRC).
214   Eliot recollection: *ibid.;* also Pringle interview notes (TRC).
215   Claims to have held lightweight crown: biographical sketch prepared for an Albany newspaper editor, May 1, 1884, *Letters*, I, 67.
215   Claims to have been in top ten percent: TR, *Autobiography*, 25.
215   Note to the Kaiser: Morison, *Three Centuries*, 427.
215   Hagedorn observations: Hagedorn interviews (TRC).
215   "the golden years": TR, Diary, Dec. 21 1878 (LC).
215   "can't conceive . . . possibly enjoying himself": TR, Diary, May 8, 1879 (LC).
215   "ever enjoy myself so much again": TR, Diary, June 28, 1879 (LC).
216   Letter of Oct. 20, 1879: *Letters*, I, 42.
216   "I have had just as much money": Diary, May 5, 1880 (LC).

10. ESPECIALLY PRETTY ALICE

page
218   Lee and Saltonstall homesteads: Though greatly altered in appearance, the two houses still stand and amid surroundings that are very little different.
219   Leverett Saltonstall and George Cabot Lee: biographical sketches in (Harvard) *Class of 1848* and *Class of 1850*, as well as miscellaneous clippings, Harvard Archives.

219   "safe as Lee's vaults": Amory, 66.
220   Atmosphere "so homelike": TR, Diary, Oct. 18, 1878 (LC).
220   "Call me by my first name": *ibid.*, Nov. 28, 1878.
221   "Remember me": TR to C, Nov. 10, 1878, *Letters*, I, 36.
221   "especially pretty Alice": TR, Diary, Jan. 26, 1879 (LC).
221   "All the family . . . just lovely": TR to B, Apr. 20, 1879, *Letters*, I, 38.
221   "I want you particularly": TR to C, May 20, 1879, *Letters*, I, 40.
221   Summer activities at Oyster Bay: TR, Diary, entries for July 1879 (LC).
222   Class Day evening with Alice: *ibid.*, June 20, 1879.
222   "made everything subordinate": TR to Henry Minot, Feb. 13, 1880, *Letters*, I, 43.
222   "one all-absorbing object": July 5, 1880, quoted in Putnam, 194.
222   "See that girl?" Mrs. Bacon quoted in Pringle notes (TRC).
223   Dueling pistols: Pringle interview with Mrs. Thomas Lee (a cousin of Alice's), Pringle notes (TRC).
223   Cousin West sent for: C to Pringle, letter dated Sept. 22, 1930, Pringle notes (TRC).
224   "you mustn't feel melancholy": TR to MBR, Feb. 8, 1880, *Letters*, I, 43.
224   "Alice . . . did not want to marry him": Mrs. Bacon quoted in Pringle notes (TRC).
224   "it will be my aim . . . to endear myself": ALR to MBR, Feb. 1880.
224   "wish I had you here": TR to B, Mar. 1, 1880, *Letters*, I, 44.
224   "don't think Mr. Lee": TR to C, Mar. 8, 1880, *ibid.*
224   "invitations to *all* my friends": TR to MBR, Mar. 11, 1880, *ibid.*
225   "brilliant prowess": N.Y. *Sun*, Feb. 17, 1884.
226   Mittie's activities: miscellaneous family correspondence; Anna Gracie's diary for 1880 (TRC).
226   "He talked to her the whole time": Kleeman, 101.
226   "If I had not come then": Davis, 37.
227   "genuine intellectual power": Parsons, 29.
227   "readiness to meet all situations": Robinson, 18.
228   "As soon as we got here": TR to C, Sept. 12, 1880, *Letters*, I, 46.
228   "Last Sunday night": quoted in Putnam, 203.
228   "I am so glad": E to B, Aug. 29 [1880] (FDRL).
229   Warning of heart trouble: Hagedorn, *Boys' Life*, 63–64.
229   Asthma and colic: Putnam, 207.
229   "brown and well": E to B, Aug. 29 [1880] (FDRL).
230   "Thee is well able": *ibid.*
230   Wants no best man if not Elliott: TR to B, May 11, 1880.
230   Fanny Smith's diary entry: Parsons, 43.
230   "Theodorelike tones": *ibid.*
230   "cannot take my eyes off her": quoted in Putnam, 209.
231   Law school urged by Uncle Rob: Hagedorn, *Boys' Life*, 69.
231   "perfect dream of delight": TR to MBR, Oct. 31, 1880, *Letters*, I, 47.
232   TR turning purple: C to Douglas Robinson, Feb. 10, 1881.
232   "going to Republican meetings": *ibid.*

232   Law work "very interesting": TR, Diary, Nov. 24, 1880 (LC).
232   Likes law school "very much": *ibid.*, Dec. 4, 1880.
232   Loves to take Alice sleighing: *ibid.*, Dec. 22, 1880.
233   "She enjoyed it like a child": TR Sr. to B, Feb. 18, 1871.
233   "the little inner group of people": Wharton, *Age of Innocence*, 48.
234   Alice "greatly admired": TR, Diary, Dec. 11, 1880 (LC).
234   Douglas Robinson on being married to a Roosevelt: quoted in Butt, I, 175.
235   Alice's playing heard through the wall: Emlen Roosevelt to B, Feb. 21, 1881.
235   Mittie finds Alice "so companionable": MBR to E, Dec. 25 [1880] (FDRL).
235   Wister vignette: Wister, 24.
235   "Oh, Energy, thy name is Bamie!": TR to B, Apr. 1, 1877.
235   "Do you always have to run": C to E, Dec. 6, 1880 (FDRL).
235   "Sometimes we succeed": *ibid.*
236   "Such a lovely long talk": C to Douglas Robinson, Mar. 17, 1881.
236   Alice's feelings about Bamie: ALR to B, Sept. 8, 1881.
236   Talk in Mittie's room: C to Douglas Robinson, Mar. 19, 1881.
236   Alice shares TR: C to Pringle (TRC); also Pringle, 49–50.

11. Home Is the Hunter

Unless shown, the details of Elliott's adventures in India and Ceylon, as well as quotations from his letters home, are from *Hunting Big Game in the Eighties,* a collection of his letters and journal entries from this period that was compiled and edited by his daughter, Eleanor. The observations of John S. Wise are from his *Recollections of Thirteen Presidents.*

page
238   "Is Bamie showing any signs": E to TR, Mar. 23, 1881.
238   "have tried to make Corinne understand": MBR to E, Aug. 7, 1881 (FDRL).
238   "Teddy brought out from London": MBR to E, Dec. 4, 1881 (FDRL).
238   Edith Carow's party: *ibid.*
238   "Has not our dear Thee": quoted in Lash, 37.
239   Letter from Evarts: original (FDRL).
240   "Three hours after the blood had been running": E to TR, Mar. 6, 1881.
240   "brave, old Heart of Oak Brother": E to TR, Apr. 24, 1881.
240   "It is the life": *ibid.*
240   Alice worried: B to E, Dec. 7, 1880 (FDRL).
240   "Poor dear Teddy": MBR to E, Dec. 7, 1880 (FDRL).
241   "This is your last hunt": TR to E, Dec. 6, 1880 (FDRL).
241   Servants pleased to be remembered: MBR to E, Aug. 7, 1881 (FDRL).
241   Upset by wretchedness: quoted in Lash, 38.

241   Speculates on Age of Chivalry: TR to B, Aug. 21, 1881, *Letters*, I, 50.

241   "We will *all* live there happily": E to TR, Mar. 23, 1881.

241   "It delights me beyond bounds": *ibid.*

241   "How proud of you": E to TR, Aug. 8, 1881.

241   "Do take care of yourself": E to TR, Apr. 24, 1881.

242   Not " 'our way' ": quoted in Lash, 39.

242   Letter from Aunt Ella Bulloch: Jan. 8, 1882 (FDRL).

243   Anna Gracie worries over Elliott: Anna Gracie diary, Mar. 30, Apr. 5, 1882 (TRC).

243   "dear mother . . . persuaded": quoted in Davis, 54.

243   "My little heart": E to C, Nov. 29, 1881 (FDRL).

243   "Why if you don't take him": E to C, June [n.d.] 1881 (FDRL).

243   "such a loving, tender brother": C to Douglas Robinson, Mar. 19, 1881.

244   "If you were my brother": C to Douglas Robinson, Mar. 31, 1881.

244   "The respectable . . . young men": N.Y. *Tribune*, Oct. 13, 1882.

244   "comfort child": MBR to E, undated note (FDRL).

244   Mittie's "slight unevenness": E to Douglas Robinson, May 9, 1881 (FDRL).

245   Remarks about Mittie by Mrs. Alsop and W. Sheffield Cowles, Jr.: interview transcript, Oral History Collection, Columbia University.

245   "I was very proud": Kleeman, 129–30.

246   "I am very jealous": MBR to E, Dec. 4, 1881 (FDRL).

246   "My darling son": MBR to E, undated (FDRL).

246   "they mistook me for you": TR to E, Nov. 21, 1880 (FDRL).

247   Hunt's impression: Harvard Club Transcript (TRC).

247   "If he noticed me at all": Parsons, 29.

247   "drank like a fish": from notes made by Mrs. Philip J. Roosevelt after a conversation with Edith Carow Roosevelt, Jan. 1941, courtesy of P. James Roosevelt.

247   "can't get it into words": TR to B, Aug. 21, 1881, *Letters*, I, 50.

248   Indebtedness to Uncle Jimmie Bulloch: see Introduction, *Naval War* (*Works*, VI).

248   "that foolish grit": quoted in Lash, 37.

248   Elliott's unpublished short story: typescript (FDRL).

249   Anna Hall admired by Browning: Lash, 50.

249   "I am honestly delighted": TR to C, July 1, 1883, *Letters*, I, 61.

249   "to marry and settle down": TR to MBR, July 8, 1883, *Letters*, I, 62.

249   "You must be very pure": Anna Gracie to E, July 1, 1883 (FDRL).

249   "old Indian trouble": quoted in Lash, 46.

249   "I known I am blue": *ibid.*

250    $10,000 in Wyoming ranch: Putnam, 334.

250    $20,000 in G. P. Putnam's Sons: Pringle, 54.

250   "one of the most brilliant social events": quoted in Lash, 47.

12. POLITICS

The remembrances and observations of George Spinney and Isaac Hunt quoted in this chapter are from an interview conducted by Hermann Hagedorn at the Harvard Club, New York City, in 1923, and are referred to below as Harvard Club Transcripts (TRC). For background on Jay Gould and his conquests, Matthew Josephson's *The Robber Barons* has been especially useful.

page

252   "capable of conduct and utterances": DAB.
252   "intended to be one of the governing class": TR, *Autobiography*, 59.
252   "full of purpose to live": James, *Bostonians*, 137.
252   "could join only the Republican Party": TR, *Autobiography*, 58.
252   "one thing I like particularly": C to Douglas Robinson, Mar. 14, 1881.
252   "saloon keepers, horsecar conductors": TR, *Autobiography*, 59.
252   "I feel that I owe": TR to Joseph Choate, Nov. 10, 1881, *Letters*, I, 55.
253   Depew at Delmonico's: Depew, 158–60.
253   Uncle Rob and Michael Murphy: Pringle, 69–70.
253   "We hailed him as the dawn": Bigelow, 276.
253   "All my friends": TR, Diary, Oct. 22, 1881 (LC).
253   Emlen Roosevelt to Hagedorn (TRC); also quoted in Pringle, 57.
253   "It is very plain": Emlen Roosevelt to B, July 13, 1876.
253   "did not relish the personnel": Emlen Roosevelt to Hagedorn (TRC); also Pringle, 57.
253   Jake Hess, Joe Murray, the decor at Morton Hall: see TR, *Autobiography*, 59–60.
254   "Not to insist on the spoils": TR quoted in Shannon, 15.
254   "They rather liked the idea": *ibid.*
254   TR's views of other assemblymen: from TR's Legislative Diary, Appendix I, *Letters*, II.
255   Views on Curtis, Kruse, Kelly, Hunt, O'Neil: TR, *Autobiography*, 67–69.
255   "What on earth": Nevins, *Cleveland*, 139.
256   "came in as if he had been ejected by a catapult": Harvard Club Transcripts (TRC).
256   N.Y. *Sun* on TR: Jan. 25, 1882.
256   N.Y. *World* on TR: Apr. 15, 1883.
257   "he got right in with people": Sewall, 6.
257   "He threw each paper": Hudson, 144–45.
259   "As a matter of fact": TR, *Autobiography*, 82–83.
259   Gompers: DAB; Putnam, 301.
260   "I have always remembered": TR, *Autobiography*, 83.
260   "aggressiveness": quoted in Harbaugh, 40.

261   Gould and the Manhattan Elevated: Josephson, 209–12; Putnam, 261–72.

261   Gould spreads his stocks on the desk: Myers, *Great American Fortunes*, 491.

261   Gould unacceptable socially: Josephson, 205.

261   James Alfred Roosevelt and Gould: Cobb, 55.

261   Hunt puts TR on to Westbrook: Harvard Club Transcripts (TRC).

262   TR sees Loewenthal: *ibid.*

262   "willing to go to the very verge": TR, *Autobiography*, 79.

262   N.Y. *World* view: Oct. 18, 1881.

263   Advice from family friend: TR, *Autobiography*, 80.

264   "I am aware": *N.Y. Times*, Apr. 7, 1882; also, *Works*, XIV, 7–11.

264   Clerk's tally: Putnam, 266.

265   Bribes: Harvard Club Transcripts (TRC).

265   "He may have been": TR, *Autobiography*, 79.

265   Gould and Cyrus Field: Josephson, 211.

266   "The Governor would sit large": Hudson, 146–47.

267   "like wild geese without a gander": Hunt, Harvard Club Transcripts (TRC).

268   "a pulpit concealed on his person": unidentified clipping, Scrapbook (TRC).

268   "I have to say with shame": N.Y. *World*, Mar. 3, 1883; also quoted in Putnam, 285.

269   "Never indulge yourself": quoted in Wister, 21.

270   Reactions of N.Y. *Evening Post* and *World:* Scrapbook (TRC).

270   "The difference between our party and yours": quoted in Putnam, 287–88; also, full speech in *Works*, XIV, 16–21.

270   N.Y. *Observer:* Mar. 10, 1883.

271   "Now, Theodore": quoted in Pringle, 70.

271   Erastus Brooks incident: recalled by Assemblyman F. S. Decker (TRC).

271   Court ruling on the Cigar Bill: TR, *Autobiography*, 84–85; also Harbaugh, 40–42.

272   Admirers skeptical of O'Brien support: *N.Y. Times*, Dec. 27, 1883.

273   Reporter notes "friends of the Administration" in Delavan lobby: N.Y. *Evening Post*, Jan. 2, 1884.

273   "I am a Republican": TR to Jonas S. Van Duzer, Nov. 20, 1883, *Letters*, I, 63.

273   "That young fellow": *N.Y. Times*, Dec. 29, 1883.

273   "most ambitious man": Emlen Roosevelt to Hagedorn (TRC).

274   Larger employer than Carnegie: Reeves, 46.

274   Seth Low on city government: Low in Bryce, I, 650–66.

275   TR on Hubert O. Thompson: TR, Legislative Diary, Appendix I, *Letters*, II.

275   "we stood shoulder to shoulder": TR, *Autobiography*, 67.

276   "blamelessness and the fighting edge": *ibid.*, 88.

276   Mark Sullivan observation: Sullivan, II, fn. 221.

276   Unwillingness to "face the rather intimate association": TR to Henry Cabot Lodge, Jan. 28, 1909, *Letters*, VI, 1490.

276   *"The wicked flee":* Proverbs 28:1.
276   Eliot on a man in a fight: Brown, *Harvard Yard*, 25.

13. Strange and Terrible Fate

page
277   "I have a bad headache": TR to C, July 1, 1883, *Letters*, I, 61.
277   "I felt much better for it": TR to ALR, Jan. 22, 1884, *Letters*, I, 64.
278   James Alfred worried: TR to E, Nov. 28, 1880 (FDRL).
278   Income and sources: TR, Diary, 1883 (LC).
278    $20,000 to Putnam: Pringle, 54.
278   "before a bright fire": TR, Diary, Jan. 3, 1883 (LC).
278   Anna Gracie's instructions: Parsons, 44–45.
279   Friends to see Alice: *ibid.*
279   "All of the men": TR to ALR, Jan. 28, 1884, *Letters*, I, 64.
279   End to social life: The social doings of Elliott and his wife, mean-
         time, were a pet topic in the papers. When Mrs. Astor's ball was
         front-page news that January, Mrs. Elliott Roosevelt's importance
         in *The New York Times* account was second only to that of Mrs.
         Astor. "Mrs. Elliott Roosevelt wore white tulle and green velvet
         and silver. It was made with a long train and a low neck, fastened
         with a diamond. Pearls and diamonds were the ornaments," re-
         ported the *Times*, Jan. 22, 1884.
279   "I tried faithfully": Riis, 36–37.
279   Disillusioned by the law: TR, *Autobiography*, 57.
281   "I hardly knew what to do": TR to B, Sept. 15, 1882, *Letters*, I, 57.
281   Remarks to *Country Life:* Hagedorn, *Roosevelt Family of Saga-
         more Hill*, 7.
281   Final cost $17,000: *ibid.*, 9.
283   Hunt's recollections: Harvard Club Transcripts (TRC).
283   Corinne's account of return to 57th Street: C to Pringle, Sept. 1930,
         Pringle notes (TRC).
283   Mittie's death at three o'clock: TR, memorial to MBR (TRC).
284   Double funeral service: *N.Y. Times, Sun,* and *Tribune*, Feb. 17,
         1884.
284   Chester A. Arthur and Bright's disease: Reeves, 317–18.
285   Talk of criminal negligence: Mrs. Robert Bacon, Pringle interview,
         Pringle notes (TRC). Since Mrs. Bacon's husband was then em-
         ployed at Lee, Higginson, it is possible that the Lee family too had
         similar thoughts concerning Alice's death.
285   "He does not know what he does": quoted in Sewall, 11.
285   "bravely in the darkness": quoted in Putnam, 389.
286   Hunt's account of all-night work: Hagedorn files (TRC).
286   "I have taken up my work": TR to Carl Schurz, Feb. 21, 1884,
         Letters, I, 66.
286   Schurz and the death of his wife: Fuess, 219.
286   "as sweet and gentle as ever": C to E, Mar. 4, 1884 (FDRL).
286   Sale of 6 West 57th Street: B reminiscences.

286   "That year seems a perfect nightmare": *ibid.*
287   Condolence letters; J. Bulloch cable: (TRC).
287   Alice entrusted to Bamie: B reminiscences.
287   "so few that one really cared for": C to E, Mar. 4, 1884 (FDRL).
288   Memorial to Alice: (TRC).

14. CHICAGO

Newspapers of the late nineteenth century, in a day when it was still not possible technically to publish photographs, reported events in a vivid, pictorial style seldom found in present-day journalism; and since newspapers then were also intensely competitive and openly partisan politically, the coverage of a national convention to be found in the files of almost any great paper of the era is especially alive and colorful, filled with detail. The papers referred to for this account of the Republican National Convention of 1884 include *The N.Y. Times, N.Y. Sun, N.Y. Tribune, N.Y. Herald, N.Y. Evening Post, N.Y. World,* Chicago *Tribune,* Boston *Transcript,* and the Washington *Post.* Excerpts from various speeches have all been taken from *Proceedings of the Eighth Republican National Convention Held at Chicago, Illinois, June 3, 4, 5, and 6, 1884.*

page
289   "Fast and thick the delegates": *N.Y. Times,* June 1, 1884.
289   California delegates in the Palmer House barbershop: a composite of several newspaper accounts, but especially Chicago *Tribune,* May 31, 1884.
290   "All were filled": N.Y. *Sun,* June 1, 1884.
290   TR to Bamie: June 8, 1884, *Letters,* I, 71–72.
291   "Tattooed Man": cartoon by Bernard Gillam, *Puck,* Apr. 16, 1884.
291   TR to Lodge: May 26, 1884, *Letters,* I, 70.
291   "He isn't 'Chet' Arthur any more": quoted in Reeves, 260.
292   Failure of Grant and Ward: Rhodes, 205.
292   Arthur transforms the White House: Reeves, 268–71.
292   Beecher endorsement: *ibid.,* 368.
292   Orders return of $100,000: *ibid.,* 374.
293   *Harper's Weekly* on Edmunds: Feb. 2, Mar. 1, 1884.
293   State convention at Utica: for a thorough account see Putnam, 413–24.
293   Washington trip with Lodge: Lodge journal, Mar. 20, 1885, Massachusetts Historical Society.
294   "We are breaking up house": TR to Henry Cabot Lodge, May 5, 1884, *Letters,* I, 69.
294   To Chicago in a private car: N.Y. *World,* June 6, 1884.
294   *Evening Post* appraisal of TR: May 31, 1884.
294   Nast cartoon of TR and Cleveland: *Harper's Weekly,* Apr. 19, 1884.
294   "mouth full of regular white teeth": N.Y *Tribune,* June 6, 1884.
294   Statement to the Chicago *Tribune:* Chicago *Tribune,* June 1, 1884.
294   "as if the fate of the nation": N.Y. *Herald,* June 1, 1884.

294   Lodge doubts Blaine can be stopped: Lodge journal, Mar. 20, 1885, Massachusetts Historical Society.
295   "Bits of good news": N.Y. *Tribune,* June 1, 1884.
295   McKinley a sign: *ibid.,* June 3, 1884.
295   "Not for forty nominations": Stone, *Fifty Years,* 150.
296   "pulled together": TR to B, June 8, 1884, *Letters,* I, 72.
296   "Many of our men": *ibid.*
296   "Chicagoe" a "marvelous city": TR to B, Sept. 2, 1880.
297   Badges cast in gold: Sullivan, II, 215.
297   "What I liked about him": Platt, 185.
298   "The leader was Mr. George William Curtis": Chicago *Tribune,* June 4, 1884.
298   Platt stroking his beard: N.Y. *Times,* June 4, 1884.
299   "rather dudish-looking" TR: unidentified newspaper account quoted in Foraker, 167–68.
300   "Up from the midst of the Empire State": N.Y.*Times,* June 4, 1884.
300   "It was the first time": TR to B, June 8, 1884, *Letters,* I, 72.
300   TR's speech: *Proceedings,* 10; also, *Works* XIV, 37–38.
301   N.Y. *Times* praise: June 4, 1884.
301   "quick, watchful, rather enjoying": N.Y. *Tribune,* June 6, 1884.
302   Andrew White's scorn of the convention: White, *Autobiography,* 204.
302   "his voice rang like a trumpet": TR to B, June 8, 1884, *Letters,* I, 72.
304   "It is eager, bitter, and peculiar": Chicago *Herald,* quoted in Bryce, II. (Bryce thought so highly of the *Herald's* coverage of the convention, thought it such a classic bit of political Americana, that he included it in the Appendix of his own classic work.)
304   "It was a tumultuous crowd": *ibid.*
305   TR tries to get on stage: N.Y. *Times,* June 7, 1884.
305   McKinley calms the storm: Chicago *Herald,* quoted in Bryce, II.
305   "This is the hour": quoted in Fuess, 286.
306   "I decline to say anything": N.Y. *World,* June 7, 1884.
306   "A grave would be garrulous": Boston *Transcript,* June 7, 1884.
307   Arthur pledges support, confides he does not have long to live: Reeves, 381.
307   TR's encounter with Horace White: White, letter to *N.Y. Times,* Oct. 20, 1884. TR, in answer to the *Times* (Oct. 21), expressed surprise that any gentleman would so divulge a private conversation. He had been "savagely indignant at our defeat," TR said, as explanation of his own behavior.
307   *Pioneer Press* interview and newspaper response: clippings in B's scrapbook (TRC).
308   "The gallant young man": N.Y. *World,* June 27, 1884.
308   Reaction in Boston: Nevins, *Cleveland,* 157.
309   Letters to the *Times: N.Y. Times,* June 8, 1884.
309   Putnam response: Nevins, *Cleveland,* 157.
309   "Mr. Lodge maintains": William Everett quoted in Garraty, *Lodge,* 80.

309   Schurz advice: quoted, *ibid.*, 81.

309   Lodge answer: July 14, 1884, Lodge Papers, Massachusetts Historical Society.

310   Lodge on pre-Chicago pact with TR: Lodge journal, Mar. 20, 1885, Massachusetts Historical Society.

310   "I am absolutely ignorant": TR to Henry Cabot Lodge, June 17, 1884, *Letters*, I, 73.

310   "precisely the proper course": TR to Henry Cabot Lodge, June 18, 1884, *ibid.*, 75.

311   Chicago *Tribune* tribute: June 7, 1884.

311   Chicago *Times* tribute: quoted in the N.Y. *Evening Post*, June 6, 1884.

311   "first revelation of that immense pluck": White, *Autobiography*, 205.

311   "You'll know more, sir, later": quoted in Riis, 69.

312   "I can't help writing you": TR to Henry Cabot Lodge, Oct. 11, 1895, *Letters*, I, 484.

312   "never been able to work so well": TR to Henry Cabot Lodge, Aug. 12, 1884, *ibid.*, 77.

313   "It may be that 'the voice of the people' ": TR to B, June 8, 1884, *ibid.*, 71.

313   "the most serious crisis": Bishop, 35–36.

313   View of Nicholas Roosevelt: N. Roosevelt, *Roosevelt*, 97.

314   Letter to Josephine Shaw Lowell: Feb. 24, 1882, *Letters*, VIII, 1425.

314   TR's statement to the Boston *Herald:* see also, N.Y. *World*, July 21, 1884.

315   "We thought of him as a lost leader": Thayer, *Roosevelt*, 55.

315   "As for Cabot Lodge": Wister, 26.

315   "Young men like Mr. Roosevelt": N.Y. *Evening Post*, July 21, 1884.

315   "Most of my friends": TR to Henry Cabot Lodge, July 28, 1884, *Letters*, I, 75.

315   "You would be amused": TR to Henry Cabot Lodge, Aug. 12, 1884, *Letters*, I, 77.

15. GLORY DAYS

The standard work on TR's time in the West is Hermann Hagedorn's *Roosevelt in the Bad Lands* (here referred to as Hagedorn, *RBL*), which was based on interviews with a number of the principals in the story and appeared in 1921. And though it is plainly flawed by Hagedorn's almost blind adulation of TR and by the use of fictitious names for any characters presented in a bad light, it remains the single most valuable source for what was one of the most important periods in TR's life. Hagedorn's Bad Lands notes for the book are also part of the great Theodore Roosevelt Collection at Harvard.

Material in this chapter concerning the influence of Remington, Wister, and TR on the overall aura of the cowboy West has been drawn chiefly from G. Edward White's *The Eastern Establishment and the Western Ex-*

perience (1968); background for eastern investment in the cattle empire comes from Gene M. Gressley's excellent *Bankers and Cattlemen* (1966). Of the several articles from *North Dakota History* relied upon, the most useful have been "Ranching in the Dakota Badlands," by Ray H. Mattison, referred to here as Mattison, and "The Career of the Marquis de Mores in the Badlands of North Dakota," by Arnold O. Goplen, referred to as Goplen.

Of TR's own voluminous published accounts, the best is *Ranch Life and the Hunting Trail*, which is included with *Hunting Trips of a Ranchman* in Volume I of the collected *Works* (page numbers below refer to that edition).

page

316   Clarence Day on cowboys: Day, 12.

317   TR's recommended reading: TR, *Hunting Trips*, 11.

317   Warns of financial disaster: *ibid.*, 17; also TR, *Ranch Life*, 290.

317   Gorringe interests: Hagedorn, *RBL*, 8–10.

318   Teschemacher and the Paris paper: Clay, 76.

318   Trimble and his poodle: Forbis, 216.

318   Bacon, Agassiz, the Seligmans, et al.: Gressley, *Bankers*.

318   "little in common with the humdrum": TR, *Ranch Life*, 274.

319   "nor are the mechanics": *ibid.*, 278.

319   "Of course every ranchman carries": TR, *Hunting Trips*, 27–28.

319   "In the hot noontide hours": TR, *Ranch Life*, 309.

320   "perfect picture": Wister, "The Young Roosevelt," in *Works*, I, 260.

320   "This life has a psychological effect": quoted in White, *Eastern Establishment*, 123.

320   "wonder if there is such a place as Philadelphia": *ibid.*

320   "a queer episode": *ibid.*, 132.

320   TR's costly regalia: see Wilson, 44.

320   "having a glorious time": TR to B, June 17, 1884, *Letters*, I, 73.

320   Sewall's observations: Mattison, "Life at Roosevelt's Elkhorn Ranch."

321   Bad Lands terrain: TR's own descriptions in both *Hunting Trips* and *Ranch Life;* also, Winser, *The Great Northwest*, the Northern Pacific Railroad's 1883 guidebook, and Clark, *The Badlands*.

321   Hell with the fires out: remark attributed to General Alfred Sully, 1864.

321   "a place for stratagem": quoted in White, *Eastern Establishment*, 104.

322   "What a wondrous country": Clay, 90.

322   Large and small ranchers: Mattison.

323   "All the security he had": quoted in Hagedorn, *RBL*, 43.

323   "By Godfrey": *ibid.*, 36.

323   Ferris recollection: Ferris, "When Roosevelt Came to Dakota."

323   Champagne over a tent peg: *N.Y. Times*, Sept. 21, 1884.

323   "It takes me only a few seconds": Hagedorn, *RBL*, 61.

324   Marquis had already killed two men: Dresden, 20.

324 Wife's income $90,000: Goplen.
324 Twenty-one thousand acres, twelve thousand sheep, salmon ship-
     ments: *ibid.*
325 "I like this country": Hagedorn, *RBL*, 335.
325 "Why, shoot": Dresden, 60.
325 Pleasure and vice synonymous: TR, *Hunting Trips*, 7.
325 "preach King Cattle": *Bad Lands Cow Boy*, Feb. 7, 1884.
325 "Again and again is the fitness": *ibid.*, Feb. 21, 1884.
326 "There are now in the Bad Lands": *ibid.*, Mar. 13, 1884.
326 *N.Y. Times* reports on Medora and the Marquis: Sept. 21, 1884.
326 Marquis quoted in N.Y. *World:* Dresden, 90.
326 The château: Except for a big box elder beside the back door, the
     house looks today no different from what it does in old photographs
     and is furnished throughout just as it was. The Marquis and Ma-
     dame de Mores left everything behind—trunks, children's clothes,
     his books, rifles, the lead-filled walking stick, her china and water-
     colors. The property now belongs to the State Historical Society of
     North Dakota.
327 "most dignified, stately, and aristocratic": C. O. Armstrong quoted
     in Goplen.
327 Madame kills bears: Bismarck *Weekly Tribune*, Sept. 4, 1885.
327 Langs bury Luffsey: Lang, 75.
327 TR and Marquis turned down as vigilantes: Putnam, 461.
327 "Theodore did not care for the Marquis": quoted in Hagedorn,
     RBL, 338.
328 "lost about 25 head from wolves": TR to B, June 17, 1884, *Letters*,
     I, 73.
328 TR's share of Mittie's trust fund: Putnam, 337.
328 Additional $26,000 in cattle: Hagedorn, *RBL*, 94.
328 "I designed the house myself": Sewall, 19. (The house is gone,
     but the site today looks as it did in TR's time. One can sit among
     the cottonwoods and look over the river to the distant plateaus and
     understand perfectly why he so adored the place.)
329 "Hasten forward": Hagedorn, *RBL*, 101.
329 Fight in the Mingusville bar: TR, *Autobiography*, 125–26.
329 "gained him some reputation": Sewall, 43.
329 "He worked like the rest of us": *ibid.*, 39.
329 "A man who will steal *for* me": Hagedorn, *RBL*, 256.
329 Exchange between TR and Sewall: Sewall, 47–48.
329 "must have a depraved idea": Mattison, "Life at Roosevelt's Elk-
     horn Ranch."
330 "The country is growing on me": quoted in Hagedorn, *RBL*, 105.
330 Bad Lands looked the way Poe sounds: TR, *Hunting Trips*, 11.
330 "Nowhere . . . does a man feel more lonely": *ibid.*, 151–52.
330 Parkman and TR on sea of grass and being far afield from civiliza-
     tion: Parkman, 34; TR, *Ranch Life*, 274, 307.
330 Sound of the mourning dove: TR, *ibid.*, 309–10.
330 "When the days have dwindled": *ibid.*, 341.
331 Edith Wharton on New York: *Age of Innocence*, 30–31.

331   Voice of the meadowlark: TR, *Hunting Trips,* 12.

332   Praise for Manitou: *ibid.,* 28–29.

332   "and the rapid motion": TR, *Ranch Life,* 329.

332   "fulfilling a boyish ambition": quoted in Hagedorn, *RBL,* 105.

332   "in our ideal 'hero land' ": quoted in Robinson, 138.

332   *"What with the wild gallops":* Reid, *Scalp Hunters,* 19.

333   "the best weapon I ever had": TR, *Hunting Trips,* 27.

333   Lebo and TR: Hagedorn BL notes, Merrifield interview (TRC).

333   Letter to Bamie: quoted in Hagedorn, *RBL,* 179–80.

334   "I went back and paced off the distance": TR, Diary, 1884 (LC).

334   Describes blacktail buck: TR, *Hunting Trips,* 116–17.

335   Bear hunt and kill: TR, Diary, 1884 (LC).

335   Remarks on Elliott's tiger: *ibid.,* 231.

335   "I found myself face to face with the great bear": TR to B, Sept. 20, 1884, *Letters,* I, 82.

336   "So I have had good sport": *ibid.*

336   "all kinds of things of which I was afraid": TR, *Autobiography,* 55–56.

336   Sewall on Bad Lands winter: Mattison, "Life at Roosevelt's Elkhorn Ranch."

338   An additional $12,500: Hagedorn, *RBL,* 255.

338   TR lunches at the château: TR to Lodge, May 15, 1885, *Letters,* I, 90.

338   Two fine accounts of a Bad Lands roundup, besides what TR wrote, are to be found in Huidekoper, 29–36, and Lang, 176–200.

338   "Invariably he was right on the job": Lang, 185.

338   "all strangeness . . . passed off": TR, *Autobiography,* 105.

338   "a very vivid affair": Huidekoper, 29.

338   "he gave us all an exhibition": Lang, 183–84.

338   "I rode him all the way": quoted in Hagedorn, *RBL,* fn. 289.

338   Broke something in his shoulder: TR, *Ranch Life,* 320.

338   "very thorough in whatever work": Burdick, 12.

339   "He could rassle": Hagedorn BL notes, Merrifield interview (TRC); also quoted in Putnam, 524–25.

339   TR's account of the night stampede: TR, *Autobiography,* 107–08.

340   "can now do cowboy work": TR to Lodge, June 5, 1885, quoted in Hagedorn, *RBL,* 299.

340   "Meanness, cowardice, and dishonesty": TR, *Ranch Life,* 325.

340   "He would not tolerate": TR, *Autobiography,* 9–10.

340   "I have seen him when": unidentified clipping, Hagedorn BL notes (TRC); also quoted in Putnam, 527.

340   Asthma and stomach trouble: Sewall, 41.

340   "ate heart medicine": Hagedorn BL notes, Merrifield interview (TRC).

341   "Rugged, bronzed"; quoted in Hagedorn, *RBL,* 308.

341   "a very powerful man": Thayer, *Roosevelt,* 57.

341   "But what a change!": Pittsburgh *Dispatch,* Aug. 23, 1885, quoted in Putnam, 530.

341   TR sees Marquis in jail: Hagedorn, *RBL,* 344.

342   Marquis's Sept. 3 letter to TR: (TRC); also quoted in full (postscript included) in Putnam, 537–38.

342   Marquis "backed off": TR to Bill Sewall, Dec. 28, 1893, quoted in Sewall, 102.

343   Lang on the Marquis: Lang, 75. Huidekoper, too, took the same view as Lang, except that Huidekoper also greatly admired the Marquis as a person: "The Marquis was a fine man and game as a pebble; when they tell the story of Roosevelt backing him down, they are sure guessing wrong." (Huidekoper, 27.)

343   TR wanted Winchester rifles at twelve paces: Sewall, 27.

343   "all a very happy family": *ibid.*, 38–39.

343   TR to Bamie: May 15, 1886, *Letters*, I, 101.

344   Marquis launches retail stores: Goplen.

344   Marquis done in by the beef trust: Dresden, 140–46.

344   Loss estimates: Goplen.

344   TR on "overstocking": TR, *Ranch Life*, 290.

344   Sewall's diary entry: Mattison, "Life at Roosevelt's Elkhorn Ranch."

345   Seventy-five percent losses: Mattison.

345   TR's losses: Hagedorn, *RBL*, Appendix, 482.

346   Stickney recollection: undated article by Stickney, Hagedorn BL notes (TRC); see also Hagedorn, *RBL*, 382–83; Putnam, 568–69.

347   Chase after the thieves: TR's own account is in *Ranch Life*, 383–98; see also, Sewall, 58–83.

347   "To submit tamely": TR, *Ranch Life*, 384–85.

347   TR to Corinne on Tolstoy: Apr. 12, 1886, *Letters*, I, 96.

348   "He impressed me": undated article by Stickney, Hagedorn BL notes (TRC); also quoted in Hagedorn, *RBL*, 383.

349   TR's July 4 speech: quoted in Hagedorn, *RBL*, 407–10.

350   Packard predicts presidency: *ibid.*, 411.

350   "We were glad to get back": Sewall, 94–95.

350   "When he got back": *ibid.*, 41.

16. RETURN

page

351   "She has no looks": quoted in Longworth, 19.

351   "hers was the best mind": N. Roosevelt, *Front Row Seat*, 33.

351   "intensely on-the-ball": Mrs. W. Sheffield Cowles, Jr., to the author.

352   "Bamie's telegram at 11:30": quoted in Lash, 52.

352   "Always Auntie Bye meant more": ARL, Hagedorn interview (TRB).

353   "She used to tell me stories": Longworth, 20.

353   "She was the only one": ARL, Hagedorn interview (TRB).

353   Eleanor on Bamie: E. Roosevelt, *This Is My Story*, 57–58.

353   Auntie Bye would have been President: ARL, Hagedorn interview (TRB).

353 "to stick the knife in": W. Sheffield Cowles, Jr., to the author.

353 "She was such a tremendous personality": Mrs. J. Alsop, Oral History Collection, Columbia University.

354 Trip to Mexico with the James Roosevelts: B reminiscences.

354 "queer, little dumpy figure": Mrs. J. Alsop, Oral History Collection, Columbia University.

354 "She grasped everything": Helen Roosevelt quoted in N. Roosevelt, *Theodore Roosevelt*, 32.

354 TR wants Bamie to organize a salon: TR to B, Apr. 22, 1886, *Letters*, I, 98.

355 "insisted that we did not live together": B reminiscences.

355 "Theodore would not be happy": quoted in Rixey, 56.

355 TR promises to forgo the pronoun "I": TR to B, June 28, 1886, *Letters*, I, 104.

355 "Can you send me at once": Nov. 3, 1884, *Letters from Theodore Roosevelt to Anna Roosevelt Cowles*, 70.

356 Remarks on the "singularly attractive" Mrs. Selmes: Aug. 11, 1886, *ibid.*, 88–89.

356 TR laments he has no "constancy": Putnam, 557 (Putnam heard the story from Mrs. Selmes's daughter, the Arizona congresswoman Isabella Greenway).

357 TR's letter to Bamie of Sept. 20, 1886: (TRB); also quoted in Morris, *Edith Kermit Roosevelt*, 90–91.

357 Bamie could keep Baby Lee: *ibid.*

358 "makes me quite blue": C to B, Mar. 29, 1886.

358 "They didn't want it": ARL, Hagedorn interview (TRB).

358 Chance meeting in Bamie's front hall: Fanny Smith (Parsons) to Putnam; see Putnam, 556–57.

358 TR and Edith: see Morris, *Edith Kermit Roosevelt*, 79–83.

358 "What day does Edith go abroad": TR to C, Apr. 12, 1886, *Letters*, I, 96.

359 "We haven't had campaign headquarters": undated *N.Y. Times* clipping, scrapbook (TRC).

359 "It almost broke my heart": B reminiscences.

359 Bamie's letter to Edith, Oct. 23: Sarah Alden Gannett collection (private).

360 Bamie's letter to Nannie Lodge: quoted in Rixey, 62.

361 "At least I have a better party standing": *ibid.*

361 Addressing the engagement announcements: B reminiscences.

AFTERWORD

page

362 "There was never a serious subject": quoted in Rixey, 230.

362 "You felt such *gallantry*": Mrs. Emory Gardiner, Oral History Collection, Columbia University.

364 TR's response to Louisa Schuyler: N. Roosevelt, *Theodore Roosevelt*, 100.

364   "My father, Theodore Roosevelt": TR, *Autobiography*, 9.

364   "I have realized . . . all day": quoted in Robinson, 206–07.

365   "peculiarly pleasant having you here": TR to RBR, Mar. 6, 1905, *Letters*, IV, 1131.

365   Recollection of Mittie in the N.Y. *Sun:* Oct. 21, 1900.

365   "I hate to think of her suffering": quoted in Robinson, 240–41.

366   "wonderful balance"; "in many ways, as formidable": Nicholas Roosevelt to Lilian Rixey, Jan. 15, 1964 (courtesy of P. James Roosevelt).

366   "To be with him was to have fun": N. Roosevelt, *Theodore Roosevelt*, 11.

367   "I love all these children": TR to Emily Carow, Aug. 16, 1903, *Theodore Roosevelt's Letters to His Children (Works*, XIX), 441.

367   "Hereafter I shall never press Ted": TR to B, Mar. 1898, *Letters*, II, 804.

368   "I am falling behind physically": TR to Theodore, Jr., Oct. 24, 1903, *Theodore Roosevelt's Letters to His Children (Works*, XIX), 449.

368   The life of ex-President TR: see Gardner, *Departing Glory*.

368   Lines from Edith Wharton: quoted in Wagenknecht, 109.

368   Bamie at Austrian sanitarium with Elliott: B reminiscences.

368   "Poor Elliott": Edith Roosevelt to B, July 19, 1893.

369   "He can't be helped": quoted in Lash, 89.

369   "the ugly duckling may turn out to be a swan": Edith Roosevelt to B, Apr. 18, 1894.

369   "like some stricken, hunted creature": TR to B, Aug. 18, 1894 (TRB); also quoted in Morris, *Edith Kermit Roosevelt*, 143–44.

369   "I only need to have pleasant thoughts of Elliott now": quoted in Lash, 96.

370   "Talk as loudly": N. Roosevelt, *Theodore Roosevelt*, 34.

370   "Very early for a fox sparrow": quoted in Robinson, 232.

Bibliography

Bibliography

I. MANUSCRIPT COLLECTIONS

American Museum of Natural History, New York: early records and correspondence.

Cowles, W. Sheffield, Jr., Farmington, Connecticut: private collection of Roosevelt family papers, photographs, scrapbooks.

Derby, Ethel Roosevelt, Collection: Roosevelt family correspondence, privately held, Sarah Alden Gannett, Brattleboro, Vermont.

Hagedorn, Hermann, notes and interview transcripts: Theodore Roosevelt Collection, Houghton Library, Harvard.

Lodge, Henry Cabot, Papers: Massachusetts Historical Society, Boston.

Oral History Collection, Columbia University: transcripts of conversations and recollections of various Roosevelt family members and friends of Theodore Roosevelt.

Pringle, Henry F., notes for his *Theodore Roosevelt:* Theodore Roosevelt Collection, Houghton Library, Harvard.

Roosevelt, Elliott, Papers: Franklin D. Roosevelt Library, Hyde Park.

Roosevelt, Robert B., Papers (fragmentary): New York Historical Society, New York City.

State Historical Society of North Dakota, Bismarck: correspondence, photographs, memorabilia, and taped interviews dealing with the early days of Medora.

Theodore Roosevelt Birthplace, New York City: a large collection of Roosevelt family memorabilia, photographs, some correspondence (unsorted), interview transcripts.

Theodore Roosevelt Collection, Houghton Library, Harvard: *the* great assembly of Theodore Roosevelt correspondence, family correspondence, diaries, journals, family scrapbooks, mementos, and photographs.

Theodore Roosevelt Papers: mainly the official correspondence of Theodore Roosevelt's presidential years, and mementos.

II. NEWSPAPERS, MAGAZINES, AND JOURNALS

American Heritage
American Journal of the Medical Sciences
American Journal of Psychiatry
American Legion
The Bad Lands Cow Boy
Bismarck *Weekly Tribune*
Boston *Advertiser*
Boston *Evening Transcript*
Brooklyn *Eagle*
Chicago *Times*
Chicago *Tribune*
Cincinnati *Daily Gazette*
The Crimson (Harvard)
Frank Leslie's Illustrated Newspaper
Harper's New Monthly Magazine
Harper's Weekly
Harvard Advocate
Harvard Graduates' Magazine
Harvard Lampoon
Journal of Nervous and Mental Disease
London *Times*
The Nation
New York *Evening Post*
New York *Herald*
New York *Observer*
New York *Sun*
The New York Times
New York *Tribune*
New York *World*
North Dakota History
The Outlook
Psychosomatic Medicine
Puck
St. Paul *Pioneer Press*
San Francisco *Chronicle*
Springfield *Daily Republican*
The Stethoscope
Time
Washington *Post*
Wide World

III. PUBLISHED WORKS ON THE BULLOCHS AND THE ROOSEVELTS

Bulloch, J. G. B., *A History and Genealogy of the Families of Bulloch and Stobo and of Irvine of Cults*. Washington, 1911.

Bulloch, Joseph Gaston, *History and Genealogy of the Stewart, Elliott and Dunwody Families*. Savannah, 1895.

Churchill, Allen, *The Roosevelts: American Aristocrats*. Harper & Row, New York, 1965.

Cobb, William T., *The Strenuous Life: The "Oyster Bay" Roosevelts in Business and Finance*. William E. Rudge's Sons, New York, 1946.

Davis, Kenneth S., *FDR: The Beckoning of Destiny*. G. P. Putnam's Sons, New York, 1971.

Hagedorn, Hermann, *The Roosevelt Family of Sagamore Hill*. The Macmillan Co., New York, 1954.

Kleeman, Rita Halle, *Gracious Lady*. D. Appleton-Century Co., New York, 1935.

Lash, Joseph P., *Eleanor and Franklin*. New American Library, New York, 1971.

Longworth, Alice Roosevelt, *Crowded Hours*. Charles Scribner's Sons, New York, 1933.

Miller, Nathan, *The Roosevelt Chronicles*. Doubleday & Co., Garden City, New York, 1979.

Morris, Sylvia Jukes, *Edith Kermit Roosevelt*. Coward, McCann and Geoghegan, New York, 1980.

Parsons, Frances Theodora (Smith), *Perchance Some Day*. Privately printed, 1951.

Rixey, Lilian, *Bamie: Theodore Roosevelt's Remarkable Sister*. David McKay Co., New York, 1963.

Roosevelt, Eleanor, ed., *Hunting Big Game in the Eighties: The Letters of Elliott Roosevelt, Sportsman*. Charles Scribner's Sons, New York, 1933.

Roosevelt, Eleanor, *This Is My Story*. Harper and Bros., New York, 1937.

Roosevelt, Nicholas, *A Front Row Seat*. University of Oklahoma Press, Norman, 1953.

Roosevelt, Theodore, II, *All in the Family*. G. P. Putnam's Sons, New York, 1929.

Roosevelt, Mrs. Theodore, Jr., *Day Before Yesterday*. Doubleday & Co., Garden City, New York, 1959.

Theodore Roosevelt (Sr.). Memorial Meeting of the State Charities Aid Association, New York, 1878.

Theodore Roosevelt [Sr.]: *A Tribute*. The Proceedings at a Meeting of the Union League Club, New York City, February 14, 1878. New York, 1902.

IV. ON AND BY THEODORE ROOSEVELT

Abbott, Lawrence F., *Impressions of Theodore Roosevelt.* Doubleday, Page & Co., New York, 1919.

Beale, Howard K., *Theodore Roosevelt and the Rise of America to World Power.* Collier Books, New York, 1970.

Bishop, Joseph Bucklin, *Theodore Roosevelt and His Time,* Vol. I. Charles Scribner's Sons, New York, 1920.

Blum, John Morton, *The Republican Roosevelt.* Harvard University Press, Cambridge, 1977.

Butt, Archie, *Taft and Roosevelt: The Intimate Letters of Archie Butt.* 2 vols. Doubleday, Doran & Co., Garden City, New York, 1930.

Chessman, G. Wallace, *Theodore Roosevelt and the Politics of Power.* Little, Brown & Co., Boston, 1969.

Cutright, Paul Russell, *Theodore Roosevelt the Naturalist.* Harper and Bros., New York, 1956.

Douglas, George William, *The Many-Sided Roosevelt.* Dodd, Mead & Co., New York, 1907.

Ferris, Joseph A., "When Roosevelt Came to Dakota." *Wide World,* 1921.

Fraser, James Earle, "Sculpting T. R." *American Heritage,* Apr. 1972.

Gardner, Joseph L., *Departing Glory: Theodore Roosevelt as ex-President.* Charles Scribner's Sons, New York, 1973.

Guild, Curtis, Jr., "Theodore Roosevelt at Harvard." *Harvard Graduates' Magazine,* Dec. 1901.

Hagedorn, Hermann, *The Boys' Life of Theodore Roosevelt.* Harper and Bros., New York, 1918.

——, *Roosevelt in the Bad Lands.* Houghton Mifflin Co., Boston, 1921.

Harbaugh, William H., *The Life and Times of Theodore Roosevelt.* Oxford University Press, New York, 1975.

Hart, Albert Bushnell, and Herbert Ronald Ferleger, eds., *Theodore Roosevelt Cyclopedia.* Roosevelt Memorial Association, New York, 1941.

Iglehart, Ferdinand C., *Theodore Roosevelt: The Man as I Knew Him.* Christian Herald, New York, 1919.

Lang, Lincoln A., *Ranching with Roosevelt.* J. B. Lippincott Co., Philadelphia, 1926.

Leupp, Francis E., *The Man Roosevelt.* D. Appleton and Co., New York, 1915.

Lorant, Stefan, *The Life and Times of Theodore Roosevelt.* Doubleday & Co., Garden City, New York, 1959.

Mattison, Ray H., "Life at Roosevelt's Elkhorn Ranch, The Letters of William W. and Mary Sewall." *North Dakota History,* Vol. 27, Nos. 3 and 4, Summer and Fall 1960.

——, "Roosevelt's Elkhorn Ranch." *North Dakota History,* Vol. 27, No. 2, Spring 1960.

Morison, Elting E., ed., *The Letters of Theodore Roosevelt.* 8 vols. Harvard University Press, Cambridge, 1951–54.

Morris, Edmund, *The Rise of Theodore Roosevelt.* Coward, McCann and Geoghegan, New York, 1979.

Pringle, Henry F., *Theodore Roosevelt: A Biography*. Harcourt, Brace & Co., New York, 1931.

Putnam, Carleton, *Theodore Roosevelt: The Formative Years, 1858–1886*. Charles Scribner's Sons, New York, 1958.

Riis, Jacob A., *Theodore Roosevelt the Citizen*. Johnson, Wynne Co., Washington, D.C., 1904.

Robinson, Corinne Roosevelt, *My Brother Theodore Roosevelt*. Charles Scribner's Sons, New York, 1921.

Roosevelt, Nicholas, *Theodore Roosevelt: The Man as I Knew Him*. Dodd, Mead & Co., New York, 1967.

Roosevelt, Theodore, *An Autobiography*. (*Works,* Vol. XX.) Charles Scribner's Sons, New York, 1926.

———, *Hunting Trips of a Ranchman* and *Ranch Life and the Hunting Trail*. (*Works,* Vol. I.) Charles Scribner's Sons, New York, 1926.

———, *Letters from Theodore Roosevelt to Anna Roosevelt Cowles, 1870–1918*. Charles Scribner's Sons, New York and London, 1924.

———, *The Naval War of 1812*. (*Works,* Vol. VI.) Charles Scribner's Sons, New York, 1926.

———, *Theodore Roosevelt's Diaries of Boyhood and Youth*. Charles Scribner's Sons, New York, 1928.

———, *Theodore Roosevelt's Letters to His Children*. (*Works,* Vol. XIX.) Charles Scribner's Sons, New York, 1926.

———, *The Works of Theodore Roosevelt*, ed. Hermann Hagedorn. National Edition, 20 vols. Charles Scribner's Sons, New York, 1926.

Selections from the Correspondence of Theodore Roosevelt and Henry Cabot Lodge, 1884–1918, Vol. I. Charles Scribner's Sons, New York, 1925.

Sewall, William Wingate, *Bill Sewall's Story of T.R.* Harper and Bros., New York and London, 1919.

Thayer, William Roscoe, *Theodore Roosevelt: An Intimate Biography*. Houghton Mifflin Co., Boston, 1919.

Wagenknecht, Edward, *The Seven Worlds of Theodore Roosevelt*. Longmans, Green & Co., New York, 1958.

Welling, Richard, "My Classmate Theodore Roosevelt." *American Legion*, Jan. 1929.

———, "Theodore Roosevelt at Harvard." *The Outlook*, Oct. 27, 1920.

Wilhelm, Donald, *Theodore Roosevelt as an Undergraduate*. John W. Luce, Boston, 1910.

Wilson, R. L., *Theodore Roosevelt, Outdoorsman*. Winchester Press, New York, 1971.

Wister, Owen, *Roosevelt: The Story of a Friendship*. The Macmillan Co., New York, 1930.

Wood, Frederick S., *Roosevelt as We Knew Him: The Personal Recollections of One Hundred and Fifty of His Friends and Associates*. John C. Winston Co., Philadelphia, 1927.

V. ON ASTHMA

Chapin, Joshua Bicknell, *Asthma, Its Causes and Treatment.* Thomas H. Webb and Co., Boston, 1843.

Cohen, Samuel I., "Psychological Factors," in T. J. H. Clark and S. Godfrey, eds., *Asthma.* W. B. Saunders Co., Philadelphia, 1977.

Derbes, Vincent J., and Hugo Tristram Engelhardt, eds., *The Treatment of Bronchial Asthma.* J. B. Lippincott Co., Philadelphia, 1946.

Kemp, Robert, *Understanding Bronchitis and Asthma.* Tavistock Publications, London, 1963.

Kendig, Edwin L., ed., *Disorders of the Respiratory Tract in Children.* W. B. Saunders Co., Philadelphia, 1967.

Kiell, Norman, "Effects of Asthma on the Character of Theodore Roosevelt," in Henry Irving Schneer, ed., *The Asthmatic Child.* Harper & Row, New York, 1963.

Knapp, Peter H., "The Asthmatic Child and the Psychosomatic Problem of Asthma," in Henry Irving Schneer, ed., *The Asthmatic Child.* Harper & Row, New York, 1963.

————, "The Asthmatic and His Environment." *Journal of Nervous and Mental Disease,* Vol. 149, 1969.

Knapp, Peter H., Aleksander A. Mathé, and Louis Vachon, "Psychosomatic Aspects of Bronchial Asthma," in E. B. Weiss and M. S. Segal, eds., *Bronchial Asthma: Mechanisms and Therapeutics.* Little, Brown & Co., Boston, 1976.

Liebman, Ronald, Salvador Minuchin, and Lester Baker, "The Use of Structural Family Therapy in the Treatment of Intractable Asthma." *American Journal of Psychiatry,* May 1974.

Mackenzie, John Noland, "The Production of the So-called 'Rose Cold' by Means of an Artificial Rose." *The American Journal of the Medical Sciences,* 1886.

McDermott, Neil T., and Stanley Cobb, "A Psychiatric Survey of Fifty Cases of Bronchial Asthma." *Psychosomatic Medicine,* Apr. 1939.

Miller, Milton L., *Nostalgia: A Psychoanalytic Study of Marcel Proust.* Houghton Mifflin Co., Boston, 1956.

Purcell, Kenneth, "The Effect on Asthma in Children of Experimental Separation from the Family." *Psychosomatic Medicine,* Vol. XXXI, 1969.

Salter, Henry Hyde, *On Asthma.* Philadelphia, 1864.

Thorowgood, John C., *Notes on Asthma.* Philadelphia, 1873.

Travis, Georgia, *Chronic Illness in Children.* Stanford University Press, Stanford, 1976.

Weiss, Earle, *Bronchial Asthma.* CIBA Pharmaceutical Co., Summit, N.J., 1975.

Weiss, Earle B., and Maurice S. Segal, *Bronchial Asthma: Mechanisms and Therapeutics.* Little, Brown & Co., Boston, 1976.

VI. OTHER

Abbott, Lawrence F., ed., *The Letters of Archie Butt*. Doubleday, Page & Co., New York, 1924.

Adams, Alexander B., *John James Audubon*. G. P. Putnam's Sons, New York, 1966.

Adams, Henry, *The Education of Henry Adams*. Sentry Edition. Houghton Mifflin Co., Boston, 1961.

Amory, Cleveland, *The Proper Bostonians*. E. P. Dutton & Co., New York, 1947.

Barrows, Chester L., *William M. Evarts*. University of North Carolina Press, Chapel Hill, 1941.

Bickmore, Albert S., *An Autobiography*. Unpublished, 1908.

Bigelow, Poultney, *Seventy Summers*, Vol. I. Edward Arnold & Co., London, 1925.

Boorstin, Daniel J., *The Americans: The Democratic Experience*. Random House, New York, 1973.

Brace, Charles Loring, *The Dangerous Classes of New York and Twenty Years' Work Among Them*. 1880.

Brown, Henry Collins, *New York in the Elegant Eighties*. New York, 1926.

Brown, Rollo Walter, *Harvard Yard in the Golden Age*. Current Books, New York, 1948.

Bryce, James, *The American Commonwealth*, 2nd ed. 2 vols. Macmillan and Co., New York, 1891.

Bull, Deborah, and Donald Lorimer, *Up the Nile*. Clarkson N. Potter, New York, 1979.

Bulloch, James D., *The Secret Service of the Confederate States in Europe*. 2 vols. London, 1883.

Bunyan, John, *The Pilgrim's Progress*. Penguin Books, Middlesex, 1965.

Burdick, Usher L., "Life and Exploits of John Goodall." *McKenzie County Farmer*, Watford City, N.D., 1931.

"Cambridge on the Charles." *Harper's New Monthly Magazine*, Jan. 1876.

Cary, Edward, *George William Curtis*. Houghton Mifflin Co., Cambridge, 1894.

Chidsey, Donald Barr, *The Gentleman from New York: A Life of Roscoe Conkling*. Yale University Press, New Haven, 1935.

Clark, Champ, *The Badlands*. Time-Life Books, New York, 1974.

Class of 1848. Harvard University Press, Cambridge, 1896.

Class of 1850. Harvard University Press, Cambridge, 1900.

Class of 1880, Secretary's Report, Number 1, Commencement 1880. Cambridge.

Clay, John, *My Life on the Range*. University of Oklahoma Press, Norman, 1962.

Coleman, Kenneth, ed., *A History of Georgia*. University of Georgia Press, Athens, 1977.

Croly, Herbert, *Marcus Alonzo Hanna*. The Macmillan Co., New York, 1912.

Curtis, George William, *The Potiphar Papers*. New York, 1853.

Dana, Richard Henry, *To Cuba and Back*. Ticknor and Fields, Boston, 1859.

Day, Clarence, *Life with Father*. Alfred A. Knopf, New York, 1935.

Depew, Chauncey M., *My Memories of Eighty Years*. Charles Scribner's Sons, New York, 1924.

Donald, David, *Charles Sumner and the Rights of Man*. Alfred A. Knopf, New York, 1970.

Dresden, Donald, *The Marquis de Mores, Emperor of the Bad Lands*. University of Oklahoma Press, Norman, 1970.

Edel, Leon, *Henry James, 1843–1870, the Untried Years*. J. B. Lippincott Co., Philadelphia and New York, 1953.

Eliot, Alexander, "Eliot of Harvard." *American Heritage*, Aug. 1974.

Eliot, Charles W., *Harvard Memories*. Harvard University Press, Cambridge, 1923.

Fancher, Betsy, *Savannah: A Renaissance of the Heart*. Doubleday & Co., Garden City, New York, 1976.

Fifth and Sixth Annual Reports of the American Museum of Natural History. New York, 1874.

Foraker, Joseph Benson, *Notes of a Busy Life*, Vol. 1. Stewart & Kidd Co., Cincinnati, 1917.

Forbes, John, *The Physician's Holiday, or a Month in Switzerland in the Summer of 1848*. London, 1853.

Forbis, William H., *The Cowboys*. Time-Life Books, Alexandria, Va., 1973.

Ford, Worthington Chauncey, ed., *Letters of Henry Adams*. Houghton Mifflin Co., Boston, 1930.

Fuess, Claude Moore, *Carl Schurz, Reformer*. Dodd, Mead & Co., New York, 1932.

Gamble, Thomas, *Savannah, Duels and Duellists, 1733–1877*. The Reprint Co., Spartanburg, S.C., 1974.

Garraty, John A., *Henry Cabot Lodge*. Alfred A. Knopf, New York, 1953.

———, *The New Commonwealth*. Harper & Row, New York, 1968.

George William Curtis, Proceedings at the Memorial Meeting of the Unitarian Club of New York. Nov. 14, 1892.

Goplen, Arnold O., "The Career of the Marquis de Mores in the Badlands of North Dakota." *North Dakota History*, Vol. 13, Nos. 1 and 2, Jan. and Apr. 1946.

Grant, Robert, "Harvard College in the Seventies." *Scribner's Magazine*, May 1897.

Gressley, Gene M., *Bankers and Cattlemen*. Alfred A. Knopf, New York, 1966.

Harden, William, *Recollections of a Long and Satisfactory Life*. Negro Universities Press, New York, 1968.

Harriman, Mrs. J. Borden, *From Pinafores to Politics*. Henry Holt & Co., New York, 1923.

Harrison, Mrs. Burton, *Recollections Grave and Gay*. Charles Scribner's Sons, New York, 1911.

Harvard Class of 1880, Secretary's Report. Cambridge, 1905.

Hawkins, Hugh, *Between Harvard and America*. Oxford University Press, New York, 1972.

Hellman, Geoffrey, *Bankers, Bones and Beetles*. National History Press, Garden City, New York, 1969.

Herrick, Francis Hobart, *Audubon the Naturalist*. 2 vols. D. Appleton and Co., New York, 1917.

Historical Collections of the Joseph Habersham Collection, Daughters of the American Revolution, Vol. II. Genealogical Publishing Co., Baltimore, 1968.

History of the Chemical Bank, 1823–1913. Privately published, 1913.

Howard, Leon, *Herman Melville: A Biography*. University of California Press, Berkeley, 1951.

Howe, George Frederick, *Chester A. Arthur: A Quarter-Century of Machine Politics*. Dodd, Mead & Co., New York, 1934.

Hudson, William C., *Random Recollections of an Old Political Reporter*. Cupples & Leon Co., New York, 1911.

Huidekoper, A. C., *My Experience and Investment in The Bad Lands of Dakota and Some of the Men I Met There*. Wirth Bros., Baltimore, 1947.

James, Henry, *The Bostonians*. Penguin Books, Middlesex, 1966.

——, *Charles W. Eliot*. 2 vols. Houghton Mifflin Co., Boston, 1930.

Jordan, David M., *Roscoe Conkling of New York*. Cornell University Press, Ithaca, 1971.

Josephson, Matthew, *The Robber Barons*. Harcourt, Brace & World, New York, 1934.

Kaplan, Justin, *Mr. Clemens and Mark Twain*. Simon and Schuster, New York, 1966.

Kell, John McIntosh, *Recollections of a Naval Life*. The Neal Co., Washington, D.C., 1900.

King, Moses, *Harvard and Its Surroundings*. Cambridge, 1882.

Labrie, Jean, *The Amateur Taxidermist*. Hart Publishing Co., New York, 1972.

Leckie, George G., ed., *Georgia: A Guide to Its Towns and Countryside*. American Guide Series. Tupper and Love, Atlanta, 1954.

Lefebure, Molly, *The English Lake District*. Hastings House, New York, 1964.

Lowitt, Richard, *A Merchant Prince of the Nineteenth Century, William E. Dodge*. Columbia University Press, New York, 1954.

Lynch, Denis Tilden, *The Wild Seventies*. 2 vols. (Reprint) Kennikat Press, Port Washington, N.Y., 1971.

"Many Years of Benevolence Lead to Outstanding Advances Against Various Kinds of Crippling." *The Stethoscope*, Vol. II, No. 10, Dec. 1956.

Marcus, Robert D., *Grand Old Party*. Oxford University Press, New York, 1971.

Martin, Clarece, *Roswell, Historic Homes and Landmarks*. Roswell Historical Society, Roswell, Ga., 1974.

Martin, Edward Sanford, *The Life of Joseph Hodges Choate*, Vol. I. Charles Scribner's Sons, New York, 1921.

——, "Undergraduate Life at Harvard." *Scribner's Magazine*, May 1897.

Mattison, Ray H., "Ranching in the Dakota Badlands." *North Dakota History*, Vol. 19, Nos. 2 and 3, Apr. and July 1952.

McDougall, Walt, *This Is the Life!* Alfred A. Knopf, New York, 1926.

Meriwether, Colyer, *Raphael Semmes*. George W. Jacobs & Co., Philadelphia, 1913.

Mitchell, Margaret, *Gone With the Wind*. Macmillan Publishing Co., New York, 1936.

Morgan, H. Wayne, *From Hayes to McKinley: National Party Politics, 1877–1896*. Syracuse University Press, Syracuse, 1969.

Morison, Samuel Eliot, *Three Centuries of Harvard*. Harvard University Press, Cambridge, 1946.

Muzzey, David Saville, *James G. Blaine, a Political Idol of Other Days*. Dodd, Mead & Co., New York, 1934.

Myers, Gustavus, *History of the Great American Fortunes*. Modern Library, Random House, New York, 1937.

Myers, Robert Manson, ed., *The Children of Pride*. Yale University Press, New Haven, 1972.

Nevins, Allan, *The Emergence of Modern America, 1865–1878*. Quadrangle Books, Chicago, 1971.

———, *Grover Cleveland: A Study in Courage*. Dodd, Mead & Co., New York, 1933.

Nevins, Allan, and Milton Halsey Thomas, eds., *The Diary of George Templeton Strong*, Vol. 4. The Macmillan Co., New York, 1952.

North Dakota, A Guide to the Northern Prairie State. Oxford University Press, New York, 1950.

Norton, Charles Eliot, ed., *Letters of James Russell Lowell*, Vol. II. Harper and Bros., New York, 1894.

———, *Orations and Addresses of George William Curtis*, Vol. 1. Harper and Bros., New York, 1894.

Osborn, Henry Fairfield, *The American Museum of Natural History*. The Irving Press, New York, 1911.

Parkman, Francis, *The Oregon Trail*. New American Library, New York, 1950.

Platt, Thomas Collier, *The Autobiography of Thomas Collier Platt*. B. W. Dodge and Co., New York, 1910.

Proceedings of the Eighth Republican National Convention Held at Chicago, Illinois, June 3, 4, 5, and 6, 1884.

Rasenel, Mrs. St. Julien, *Charleston*. The Macmillan Co., New York, 1925.

Reeves, Thomas C., *Gentleman Boss: The Life of Chester Alan Arthur*. Alfred A. Knopf, New York, 1975.

Reid, Captain Mayne, *The Boy Hunters; or Adventures in Search of a White Buffalo*. (Reprint) Gregg Press, Ridgewood, N.J., 1968. (Originally published in New York in 1852.)

———, *The Scalp Hunters*. New York, 1863.

Rhodes, James Ford, *History of the United States from Hayes to McKinley*. The Macmillan Co., New York, 1919.

Robinson, Elwyn B., *History of North Dakota*. University of Nebraska Press, Lincoln, 1966.

Rush, Richard, and Robert H. Woods, *Official Records of the Union and Confederate Navies in the War of the Rebellion*. Series I, Vol. I. Government Printing Office, Washington, D.C., 1894.

Rusk, Ralph L., *The Life of Ralph Waldo Emerson*, Charles Scribner's Sons, New York, 1949.

Russell, Francis, *The American Heritage History of the Confident Years*. American Heritage Publishing Co., New York, 1969.

Santayana, George, "The Academic Environment at Harvard in the 80's and 90's." *Harvard Alumni Bulletin*, undated, Theodore Roosevelt Collection.

Saum, Lewis O., "The Marquis de Mores: Instrument of American Progress." *North Dakota History*, Vol. 36, No. 2, Spring 1969.

Scott, James Brown, *Robert Bacon*. Doubleday, Page & Co., Garden City, N.Y., 1923.

Shannon, David A., ed., *Beatrice Webb's American Diary*. University of Wisconsin Press, Madison, 1963.

Sherman, John, *Recollections of Forty Years*, Vol. II. Werner Co., Chicago, 1895.

Shores, Venila Lovina, "The Hayes-Conkling Controversy." *Smith College Studies in History*, Vol. IV. Department of History of Smith College, Northampton, Mass., 1919.

Steele, Joan, *Captain Mayne Reid*. Thayne Publishers, Boston, 1978.

Stone, Candace, *Dana and The Sun*. Dodd, Mead & Co., New York, 1938.

Stone, Melville E., *Fifty Years a Journalist*. Doubleday, Page & Co., Garden City, N.Y.,1921.

Sullivan, Mark, *Our Times*, Vol. 2. Charles Scribner's Sons, New York, 1927.

Taylor, Bayard, *By-Ways of Europe*. G. P. Putnam and Son, New York, 1869.

Temple, Sarah Blackwell Gover, *The First Hundred Years*. Walter W. Brown Publishing Co., Atlanta, 1935.

Thayer, William Roscoe, "Nathaniel Southgate Shaler." *Harvard Graduates' Magazine*, Sept. 1906.

Third and Fourth Annual Reports of the American Museum of Natural History. New York, 1872.

Thomas, Harrison Cook, *The Return of the Democratic Party to Power in 1884*. Columbia University Press, New York, 1919.

Underwood, Rev. J. L., *The Women of the Confederacy*. Neale Publishing Co., New York, 1906.

Wagner, Charles A., *Harvard, Four Centuries and Freedoms*. E. P. Dutton & Co., New York, 1950.

Wallace, David Duncan, *South Carolina*. University of North Carolina Press, Chapel Hill, 1951.

Weinstein, Gregory, *The Ardent Eighties*. International Press, New York, 1928.

Wharton, Edith, *The Age of Innocence*. Charles Scribner's Sons, New York, 1920.

———, *A Backward Glance*. D. Appleton-Century Co., New York, 1934.

White, Andrew D., *Autobiography of Andrew Dickson White*. Century Co., New York, 1905.

White, G. Edward, *The Eastern Establishment and the Western Experience*. Yale University Press, New Haven and London, 1968.

White, Leonard D., *The Republican Era, 1869–1901*. The Macmillan Co., New York, 1958.

Whitehill, Walter Muir, *Boston and the Civil War*. Boston Athenaeum, Boston, 1963.

Wilkins, Robert P., and Wynona Huchette, *North Dakota, a Bicentennial History*. W. W. Norton & Co., New York, 1977.

Williams, T. Harry, ed., *Hayes: The Diary of a President, 1875–1881*. David McKay Co., New York, 1964.

Winser, Henry J., *The Great Northwest, A Guidebook and Itinerary for the Use of Tourists and Travellers over the Lines of the Northern Pacific Railroad*. G. P. Putnam's Sons, New York, 1883.

Wise, John S., *Recollections of Thirteen Presidents*. (Reprint) 1968. (Originally published 1906.)

VII. REFERENCE

The American Heritage Dictionary of the English Language. Houghton Mifflin Co., Boston, 1969.

The American Heritage Pictorial History of the Presidents of the United States. American Heritage Publishing Co., New York, 1968.

The Annals of America. Encyclopaedia Britannica, Chicago, 1968.

Baedeker, K., *Switzerland, and the Adjacent Portions of Italy, Savoy, and the Tyrol, Handbook for Travellers*. London, 1869.

Berkow, Robert, M.D., ed., *The Merck Manual of Diagnosis and Therapy*. Merck Sharp & Dohme Research Laboratories, Rahway, N.J., 1977.

The Colonial Records of the State of Georgia, Vol. XV. Franklin-Turner Co., Atlanta, 1907.

Dictionary of American Biography. Charles Scribner's Sons, New York, 1936.

Dunglison, Robley, *A Dictionary of Medical Science*. Philadelphia, 1866.

1840 Census for the Cobb County, Georgia.

Kouwenhoven, John A., *The Columbia Historical Portrait of New York*. Doubleday & Co., Garden City, New York, 1953.

The New Encyclopaedia Britannica, 15th ed. Encyclopaedia Britannica, Chicago, 1974.

Seventh Census of U.S., 1850, Georgia Slave Schedule.

White, Norval, and Elliot Willensky, eds., *AIA Guide to New York City*. The Macmillan Co., New York, 1968.

Index

Index

About the Author

DAVID MCCULLOUGH is the author of *The Johnstown Flood* (1968), *The Great Bridge* (1972), and *The Path Between the Seas* (1977), all of which received wide critical and popular acclaim, and the last (a book about the Panama Canal) not only won a number of literary prizes, including the National Book Award, but also was a major factor in the consideration of this nation's policy with respect to the Canal.

Also available by
DAVID MCCULLOUGH

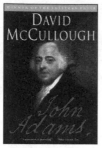
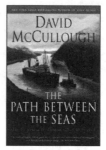
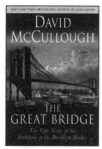
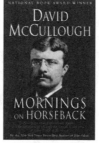
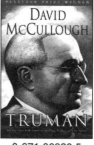
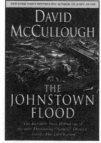
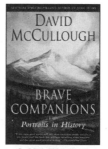